The Nature of
Human Values

The Nature of Human Values

MILTON ROKEACH

THE FREE PRESS
New York
Collier Macmillan Publishers
London

The Free Press
A Division of Macmillan Publishing Co., Inc.
866 Third Avenue
New York, N.Y. 10022

Collier–Macmillan Canada Ltd.

Library of Congress Catalog Card Number: 72–92870

Printed in the United States of America

printing number
1   2   3   4   5   6   7   8   9   10

Contents

PART THREE · Values and Politics

PART FOUR · Long- and Short-term Change in Values, Attitudes, and Behavior

PART FIVE · Summary

Preface

This book is a continuation but, it is hoped, not the culmination of my life-long interest in the nature of belief systems. What men believe, why they believe, and what difference it makes are the main recurrent themes that have preoccupied me for the past quarter of a century, and have led me to the problem of values, which is what this book is all about.

The findings reported in this book serve to reinforce the view I have taken previously in *Beliefs, Attitudes and Values* that the concept of values, more than any other, is the core concept across all the social sciences. It is the main dependent variable in the study of culture. society, and personality, and the main independent variable in the study of social attitudes and behavior. It is difficult for me to conceive of any problem social scientists might be interested in that would not deeply implicate human values.

In philosophical and theoretical orientation, the present formulations have been heavily influenced by my reading of what many others have written about the nature of human values. I have probably been influenced most by the work of A. O. Lovejoy in philosophy, Robin Williams in sociology, Clyde Kluckhohn in anthropology, and M. Brewster Smith in psychology. Dr. Fred Strodtbeck influenced my thinking by goading me to face up to the theoretical question: When and why are the more centrally located values easier to change than less centrally located attitudes? The present formulations are, however, most different in orientation from Skinner's recent statement denying that human beings possess values. The findings reported in this book, especially those concerning the long-term cognitive and behavioral consequences of value change, cannot, in my opinion, be explained by a radical behaviorist "scientific analysis of behavior."

In writing this book I have kept two audiences in mind. First, it is intended for colleagues in all the social science disciplines and in philosophy and religion as well. Second, it is intended as a textbook in courses on human values which, paradoxically, do not yet exist in most colleges and universities, despite the increasing clamor for social relevance in the social sciences.

Several organizations and individuals have aided me immeasurably in various ways to bring this work to completion. Once again, I am grateful to the National Science Foundation for providing me with the funds necessary to carry out the extensive research that is reported in this book. A return stay at The Center for Advanced Study in the Behavioral Sciences gave me an uninterrupted three months to write the early chapters. A two-year visiting professorship at the University of Western Ontario provided me with a warm and stimulating atmosphere, a peaceful academic haven and, to boot, excellent facilities, thus enabling me to complete this book even sooner than I had expected. I owe special debts to Dr.

William McClelland and Dr. Mary Wright who made my stay at the University of Western Ontario possible and so very pleasant.

I am grateful to many students at Michigan State University who have worked with me over the past seven or eight years on one or another facet of the research project described here. I relied most heavily on D. Daniel McLellan, who has since gone on to attend law school at the University of Michigan, and on Mr. Ted Greenstein. Others who have substantially contributed their ideas and energies to this project include Dr. Ray Cochrane, Dr. Charles Hollen, Dr. Robert Homant, Dr. Louis Penner, Dr. Robert Beech, and Emanuel Berman. I would also like to single out for special mention Dr. James C. Morrison and Theda Skocpol who both made substantial contributions to the work reported in Chapters 6 and 7.

I would like to thank Mr. Alvin H. Perlmutter, Executive Producer of National Educational Television; Dr. Lois K. Cohen, Chief of the Behavioral Studies Section of the Division of Dental Health of the U.S. Public Health Service; and Dr. Burton W. Marvin of the Office of Communication of the National Council of Churches for granting free access to their portions of the Amalgam Survey conducted by the National Opinion Research Center.

I would also like to thank Dr. Emanuel Hackel. chairman of the Natural Science Department at Michigan State University, and many other members of his department for their extensive cooperation in carrying out Experiment 1 described in this book. Many persons in Madison and Briggs Colleges at Michigan State deserve special thanks for their help in carrying out Experiments 2 and 3. I would especially like to thank Dean Herbert Garfinkel and Assistant Dean Gary Frost, of Madison College, and Dean Frederick B. Dutton and Assistant Dean Donald Harden, of Lyman Briggs College.

I owe a special debt of gratitude to Lynne Mitchell and to Sandy Brown for their painstaking care in typing what must have seemed to them never-ending revisions of the manuscript, and especially for their careful proofreading of the many tables in this book. Responsibility for any errors that may still remain is, however, mine rather than theirs.

Another person to whom I am especially indebted is Professor Thomas M. Ostrom, who reviewed the manuscript for Free Press and made many incisive suggestions for improving the manuscript. I gladly followed many of them when revising the manuscript for the last time.

Finally, my wife, Sandra J. Ball-Rokeach, read the various chapters and gave me the benefit of many thoughtful and constructive suggestions, resulting in a book that it far more comprehensive and readable than it would have been otherwise.

PART ONE
Human Values

I
The Nature of Human Values and Value Systems

Any conception of the nature of human values, if it is to be scientifically fruitful, should satisfy at least certain criteria. It should be intuitively appealing yet capable of operational definition. It should clearly distinguish the value concept from other concepts with which it might be confused—such concepts as attitude, social norm, and need—and yet it should be systematically related to such concepts. It should avoid circular terms that are themselves undefined, such terms as "ought," "should," or "conceptions of the desirable." It should, moreover, represent a value-free approach to the study of human values; that is, an approach that would enable independent investigators to replicate reliably one another's empirical findings and conclusions despite differences in values.

In this introductory chapter a conception of human values will be formulated with criteria such as these in mind. These formulations were guided by five assumptions about the nature of human values: (1) the total number of values that a person possesses is relatively small; (2) all men everywhere possess the same values to different degrees; (3) values are organized into value systems; (4) the antecedents of human values can be traced to culture, society and its institutions, and personality; (5) the consequences of human values will be manifested in virtually all phenomena that social scientists might consider worth investigating and understanding. These assumptions also represent a set of reasons for arguing that the value concept, more than any other, should occupy a central position across all the social sciences—sociology, anthropology, psychology, psychiatry, political science, education, economics, and history. More than any other concept, it is an intervening variable that shows promise of being able to unify the apparently diverse interests of all the sciences concerned with human behavior. "Problems of values,"

3

Robin Williams writes, "appear in all fields of the social sciences, and value elements are potentially important as variables to be analyzed in all major areas of investigation" (1968, p. 286).

The value concept has been employed in two distinctively different ways in human discourse. We will often say that a person "has a value" but also that an object "has value." These two usages, which have been explicitly recognized by writers from various disciplines—writers such as Charles Morris in philosophy (1956), Brewster Smith in psychology (1969), and Robin Williams in sociology (1968)—require from us at the outset a decision whether a systematic study of values will turn out to be more fruitful if it focuses on the values that people are said to have or on the values that objects are said to have.

Such a decision is not easy to make because a reading of the literature reveals important writings issuing forth from both camps (Handy, 1970). Perry (1954), Lewis (1962), Hilliard (1950), Thomas and Znaniecki (1918–20), Katz and Stotland (1959), Jones and Gerard (1967), and Campbell (1963), for example, have approached the problem of values from the object side. These writers merely conceive of all objects as having a one-dimensional property of value (or valence) ranging from positive to negative, and the value concept thus has no additional properties or surplus meaning. Even more recently, behaviorist B. F. Skinner has vigorously denied that men possess values and has instead argued that "the reinforcing effects of things are the province of behavioral science, which, to the extent that it is concerned with operant reinforcement, is a science of values" (1971, p. 104). On the person side are such approaches as those of Allport, Vernon, and Lindzey (1960), Kluckhohn (1951), Kluckhohn and Strodtbeck (1961), Maslow (1959, 1964), Charles Morris (1956), Brewster Smith (1969), Robin Williams (1968), and Woodruff and DiVesta (1948). Are there theoretical grounds for deciding which approach is likely to be the more fruitful?

Robin Williams, who has explicitly raised the same question, has remarked that a person's values serve as "the *criteria*, or standards in terms of which evaluations are made. . . . Value-as-criterion is usually the more important usage for purposes of social scientific analysis" (1968, p. 283). One implication that follows from Williams' observation is that the number of values-as-criteria that a person possesses is likely to be reasonably small, surely much smaller than the many thousands of things that have reinforcing effects as a result of prior learning. If this number of values-as-criteria turns out to be small enough, the tasks of identifying them one-by-one and measuring them become considerably easier, and it also becomes easier to grapple with theoretical problems and problems of measurement concerning the organization of values into systems of values. And if the total number of human values is relatively small, and if all men everywhere possess them, comparative cross-cultural investigations of values would then become considerably easier also.

It seems, therefore, that there are compelling theoretical reasons for assuming that the study of a person's values is likely to be much more useful for social analysis than a study of the values that objects are said to have. Williams' argument makes sense on grounds of theoretical economy and social relevance and for other reasons as well. I have suggested elsewhere (Rokeach, 1968b), when comparing the relative power of the value concept as against other concepts, that by focusing upon a person's values "we would be dealing with a concept that is more central, more dynamic, more economical, a concept that would invite a more enthusiastic interdisciplinary collaboration, and that would broaden the range of the social psychologist's traditional concern to include problems of education and reeducation as well as problems of persuasion" (p. 159).

With the preceding considerations in mind, we may now offer the following definitions of what it means to say that a person has a *value* and a *value system.*

A *value* is an enduring belief that a specific mode of conduct or end-state of existence is personally or socially preferable to an opposite or converse mode of conduct or end-state of existence. A *value system* is an enduring organization of beliefs concerning preferable modes of conduct or end-states of existence along a continuum of relative importance.

These definitions, from which such terms as "ought," "should," and "conceptions of the desirable" have been deliberately excluded, are central to the present work. It should be noticed that the term "preferable" that is still present in the definition is not employed as a noun (i.e., a conception of the preferable) but as a predicate adjective, specifying that something is preferable to something else, that a particular mode of conduct or end-state of existence is preferable to an opposite mode or end-state. These definitions, and the elaborations of them that follow here, have affected for better or worse all the work to be reported in this book—on the measurement of values and value systems, their distribution in various segments of American society, their conceived antecedents and consequences, their relation to attitudes and behavior, the conditions under which values will undergo long-term change, and the cognitive and behavioral consequences that may be expected to follow from value change.

The two sections of this chapter which follow explain more fully what is intended by the above definitions of value and value system. In the course of doing so, related formulations that may be found in the literature will be reviewed and, moreover, compared with the present ones.

THE NATURE OF VALUES

A Value Is Enduring

If values were completely stable, individual and social change would be impossible. If values were completely unstable, continuity of human personality and society would be impossible. Any conception of human values, if it is to be fruitful, must be able to account for the enduring character of values as well as for their changing character.

It may be suggested that the enduring quality of values arises mainly from the fact that they are initially taught and learned in isolation from other values in an absolute, all-or-none manner. Such-and-such a mode of behavior or end-state, we are taught, is always desirable. We are not taught that it is desirable, for example, to be just a little bit honest or logical, or to strive for just a little bit of salvation or peace. Nor are we taught that such modes or end-states are sometimes desirable and sometimes not. It is the isolated and thus the absolute learning of values that more or less guarantees their endurance and stability.

Paradoxically, however, there is also a relative quality of values that must be made explicit if we are to come to grips with the problem of value change. As a child matures and becomes more complex, he is increasingly likely to encounter social situations in which several values rather than one value may come into competition with one another, requiring a weighing of one value against another—a decision as to which value is the more important. In this particular situation, is it better, for instance, to seek success or to remain honest, to act obediently or independently, to seek self-respect or social recognition? Gradually, through experience and a process of maturation, we all learn to integrate the isolated, absolute values we have been taught in this or that context into a hierarchically organized system, wherein each value is ordered in priority or importance relative to other values.

A simple analogy may be helpful here. Most parents tend to think they love each of their children in an absolute, unqualified manner. Yet, in a particular circumstance, a parent may nevertheless be forced to show a preference for one child over the others—for the one who is perhaps the most ill, or the most needful or frustrated, or the least able in school. Our values are like the children we love so dearly. When we think about, talk about, or try to teach one of our values to others, we typically do so without remembering the other values, thus regarding them as absolutes. But when one value is actually activated along with others in a given situation, the behavioral outcome will be a result of the relative importance of all the competing values that the situation has activated.

It is this relative conception of values that differentiates the present approach most distinctively from other approaches to the study of values. It is crucial for the theory and experimental work on long-term value change to be reported in later chapters, and it is also crucial for the strategy to be proposed in the next chapter for measuring values.

A Value Is a Belief

Three types of beliefs have previously been distinguished (Rokeach, 1968b): descriptive or existential beliefs, those capable of being true or false;

evaluative beliefs, wherein the object of belief is judged to be good or bad; and prescriptive or proscriptive beliefs, wherein some means or end of action is judged to be desirable or undesirable. A value is a belief of the third kind—a prescriptive or proscriptive belief. "A value is a belief upon which a man acts by preference" (Allport, 1961, p. 454).

Values, like all beliefs, have cognitive, affective, and behavioral components: (1) A value is a cognition about the desirable, equivalent to what Charles Morris (1956) has called a "conceived" value and to what Kluckhohn (1951) has called a "conception of the desirable." To say that a person has a value is to say that cognitively he knows the correct way to behave or the correct end-state to strive for. (2) A value is affective in the sense that he can feel emotional about it, be affectively for or against it, approve of those who exhibit positive instances and disapprove of those who exhibit negative instances of it. (3) A value has a behavioral component in the sense that it is an intervening variable that leads to action when activated.

A Value Refers to a Mode of Conduct or End-state of Existence

When we say that a person has a value, we may have in mind either his beliefs concerning desirable *modes of conduct* or desirable *end-states of existence*. We will refer to these two kinds of values as *instrumental* and *terminal* values. This distinction between means- and ends-values has been recognized by some philosophers (Lovejoy, 1950; Hilliard, 1950), anthropologists (Kluckhohn, 1951; Kluckhohn and Strodtbeck, 1961), and psychologists (English and English, 1958). But others have concentrated their attention more or less exclusively on one or the other kind of value. Thus, French and Kahn (1962), Kohlberg (1963), Piaget (1965), and Scott (1965) have for the most part concerned themselves with certain values representing idealized modes of conduct; Allport, Vernon and Lindzey (1960), Maslow (1959), Morris (1956), Rosenberg (1960), Smith (1969), and Woodruff (1942) have concerned themselves for the most part with certain values representing end-states.

This distinction between the two kinds of values—instrumental and terminal—is an important one that we cannot afford to ignore either in our theoretical thinking or in our attempts to measure values. For one thing, the total number of terminal values is not necessarily the same as the total number of instrumental values. For another, there is a functional relationship between instrumental and terminal values that cannot be ignored. These points will be developed more fully later on in this chapter.

Two Kinds of Terminal Values: Personal and Social. While there are no doubt many ways of classifying terminal values, one a priori classification that deserves to be singled out for special mention is that the terminal values may be self-centered or society-centered, intrapersonal or inter-personal in focus. Such end-states as salvation and peace of mind, for instance, are intrapersonal while world peace and brotherhood are inter-personal. It seems reasonable to anticipate that persons may vary reliably from one another in the priorities they place on such social and personal values; that their attitudes and behavior will differ from one another depending on whether their personal or their social values have priority; that an increase in one social value will lead to increases in other social values and decreases in personal values; and, conversely, that an increase in a personal value will lead to increases in other personal values and to decreases in social values.

Two Kinds of Instrumental Values: Moral Values and Competence Values. The concept of moral values is considerably narrower than the general concept of values. For one thing, moral values refer mainly to modes of behavior and do not necessarily include values that concern end-states of existence. For another, moral values refer only to certain kinds of instrumental values, to those that have an interpersonal focus which, when violated, arouse pangs of conscience or feelings of guilt for wrongdoing. Other instrumental values, those that may be called compe-tence or self-actualization values, have a personal rather than interpersonal focus and do not seem to be especially concerned with morality. Their violation leads to feelings of shame about personal inadequacy rather than to feelings of guilt about wrongdoing. Thus, behaving honestly and respon-sibly leads one to feel that he is behaving morally, whereas behaving logically, intelligently or imaginatively leads one to feel that he is behaving competently. A person may experience conflict between two moral values (e.g., behaving honestly and lovingly), between two competence values (e.g., imaginatively and logically), or between a moral and a competence value (e.g., to act politely and to offer intellectual criticism).

One may raise the question whether there is a close connection between the two kinds of instrumental values, concerning morality and competence, and the two kinds of terminal values, concerning social and personal end-states. Will persons who place a higher priority on social end-states also place a higher priority on moral values? It might appear at first glance that the answer to this question is "yes," that the common thread running across the two kinds of terminal and instrumental values is an intraper-sonal or interpersonal orientation. But further reflection suggests that such a simple one-to-one relationship cannot be expected. A person who is more oriented toward personal end-states may, for example, defensively place a higher priority on moral behavior. A person who is more oriented toward the social may also have a strong drive for personal competence (White, 1959), reflected in a greater priority placed on competence values. There is thus reason to doubt that there is any simple one-to-one connec-tion between the two kinds of terminal and instrumental values.

On the "Oughtness" of Terminal and Instrumental Values.   Virtually all writers have pointed to the "ought" character of values. "Ought," according to Heider (1958), is impersonal, relatively invariant, and interpersonally valid, deriving from what Kohler (1938) has called "objective requiredness." A person phenomenologically experiences "oughtness" to be objectively required by society in somewhat the same way that he perceives an incomplete circle as objectively requiring closure. The experience of "ought" can be "represented as a cognized wish or requirement of a suprapersonal objective order which has an invariant reality, and whose validity therefore transcends the point of view of any one person" (Heider, 1958, p. 222).

Can all terminal and instrumental values be claimed to have an "ought" character? It can be suggested that "oughtness" is more an attribute of instrumental than terminal values and more an attribute of instrumental values that concern morality than of those concerning competence. A person may feel more pressure upon him from the suprapersonal objective order to behave honestly and responsibly than to behave competently and logically; he may feel a greater pressure emanating from society to behave morally toward others than to seek such personal end-states as happiness and wisdom. It would thus appear that "oughtness" is not necessarily an attribute of all values. The more widely shared a value, the greater the societal demands placed upon us and therefore the greater the "oughtness" we experience. The "oughtness" of certain values is seen to originate within society, which demands that all of us behave in certain ways that benefit and do not harm others. It is an objective demand that we perceive society to place upon others no less than upon ourselves in order to ensure that all people live out their lives in a social milieu within which people can trust and depend upon one another. There seems to be little point in one person's behaving morally unless others also behave morally. In contrast, society seems somewhat less insistent in its demands concerning competent modes of behavior or concerning terminal end-states. Such values do not seem to be characterized by the same amount of "oughtness" that characterizes moral values. At most, there is a more subdued experience of "oughtness."

A Value Is a Preference as Well as a "Conception of the Preferable"

A good deal has been made of the distinction between the "desirable" and the "merely desired." Brewster Smith writes: "The more serious problem, which has yet to be solved in systematic research, is to distinguish dependably between values and preferences, between the desirable and the merely desired" (1969, p. 116). A value, as Kluckhohn defines it, is a "conception of the desirable," and not something "merely desired." This view of the nature of values suffers from the fact that it is extremely difficult to define "desirable." We are no better off and no further along talking about "conceptions of the desirable" than talking about values. More important, however, is that a conception of the "desirable which influences the selection from available modes, means, and ends of action" (Kluckhohn, 1951, p. 395) turns out, upon closer analysis, to represent a definable preference for something to something else. The something is a specific mode of behavior or end-state of existence; the something else is an opposite, converse, or contrary mode or end-state. Two mutually exclusive modes of behavior or end-states are compared with one another—for example, responsible and irresponsible behavior, or states of peace and war; one of the two is distinctly preferable to the other. Moreover, the person who prefers one believes that same one to be consensually preferred. A "conception of the desirable" thus seems to be nothing more than a special kind of preference—a preference for one mode of behavior over an opposite mode, or a preference for one end-state over an opposite end-state. Other kinds of preferences that do not implicate modes of behavior or end-states of existence, for instance, preferences for certain kinds of foods, would not qualify as "conceptions of the desirable."

There is also another sense in which a value represents a specific preference. A person prefers a particular mode or end-state not only when he compares it with its opposite but also when he compares it with other values within his value system. He prefers a particular mode or end-state to other modes or end-states that are lower down in his value hierarchy.

A Value Is a Conception of Something
That Is Personally or Socially Preferable

If a person's values represent his "conceptions of the desirable" the question arises: desirable for whom? for himself? for others? When a person tells us about his values, it cannot be assumed that he necessarily intends them to apply equally to himself and to others. Consider, for example, the meaning of that familiar expression: "Children should be seen and not heard." Translated into the language of values, this statement apparently means to the person asserting it: "I believe it is desirable for children but not for adults to behave in certain ways." A person who informs us about his values may (or may not) intend to apply them differentially to young and old, men and women, blacks and whites, rich and poor, and so on.

Indeed, one of the most interesting properties that values seem to have is that they can be employed with such extraordinary versatility in everyday life. They may be shared or not shared and thus employed as single or double (or even triple) standards. They may be intended to apply equally to oneself and to others, to oneself but not to others, to others but not to oneself, to oneself more than to others, or to others more than to oneself. We know very little indeed about the conditions under which values might be so diversely employed. We may speculate, for example, that competitive conditions will encourage the employment of values as double standards, whereas cooperation will encourage their employment as single standards. A more systematic attack on this problem of single and double standards presents a major challenge to further theory and research on human values.

THE NATURE OF VALUE SYSTEMS

"It is the rare and limiting case," Robin Williams writes (1968, p. 287), "if and when a person's behavior is guided over a considerable period of time by one and only one value. . . . More often particular acts or sequences of acts are steered by multiple and changing clusters of values." After a value is learned it becomes integrated somehow into an organized system of values wherein each value is ordered in priority with respect to other values. Such a relative conception of values enables us to define change as a reordering of priorities and, at the same time, to see the total value system as relatively stable over time. It is stable enough to reflect the fact of sameness and continuity of a unique personality socialized within a given culture and society, yet unstable enough to permit rearrangements of value priorities as a result of changes in culture, society, and personal experience.

Variations in personal, societal, and cultural experience will not only generate individual differences in value systems but also individual differences in their stability. Both kinds of individual differences can reasonably be expected as a result of differences in such variables as intellectual development, degree of internalization of cultural and institutional values, identification with sex roles, political identification, and religious upbringing. A more detailed discussion of such individual differences will be presented in Chapter 2.

Number of Terminal and
Instrumental Values

As already stated, the number of values human beings possess is assumed to be relatively small and, if small enough, it should be possible to identify and measure them. But how small? On various grounds—intuitive, theoretical, and empirical—we estimate that the total number of terminal values that a grown person possesses is about a dozen and a half and that the total number of instrumental values is several times this number, perhaps five or six dozen. On intuitive grounds, it seems evident that there are just so many end-states to strive for and just so many modes of behavior that are instrumental to their attainment. This number could not possibly run into the thousands or even into the hundreds, and, whatever the actual number may eventually turn out to be, it moreover seems evident that man possesses fewer terminal than instrumental values.

Certain theoretical considerations help bring us somewhat closer to an approximation of the total number of values. It can be argued that the total number of values is roughly equal to or limited by man's biological and social makeup and most particularly by his needs. How many needs do theorists say man possesses? Freud (1922) has proposed two, Maslow (1954) five, and Murray (1938) twenty-eight. These estimates suggest that the total number of terminal values may range somewhere between Freud's two and Murray's twenty-eight and that the total number of instrumental values may be several times this number.

Finally, the estimates arrived at here are based upon certain empirical procedures which will be described more fully in the next chapter.

Relation between Instrumental and Terminal Values

What can be said about the relation between instrumental and terminal values? At this stage of theoretical thinking, it is safest to assume that they represent two separate yet functionally interconnected systems, wherein all the values concerning modes of behavior are instrumental to the attainment of all the values concerning end-states. This instrumentality is not necessarily a consciously perceived instrumentality, and there is not necessarily a one-to-one correspondence between any one instrumental value and any one terminal value. One mode of behavior may be instrumental to the attainment of several terminal values; several modes may be instrumental to the attainment of one terminal value.

Gorsuch (1970) has correctly pointed out that the "terminal-instrumental distinction may not go quite far enough" since "any value which is not the *ultimate* value could be considered an instrumental value." There is nevertheless a conceptual advantage to defining all terminal values as referring only to idealized end-states of existence and to defining all instrumental values as referring only to idealized modes of behavior. It may well be that one terminal value, so defined, is instrumental to another terminal value or that one instrumental value is instrumental to another instrumental value. Without ruling out such possibilities, it can nevertheless be suggested that the best strategy at an early stage of conceptualization is to conceive all instrumental values as modes of behavior that are instrumental to the attainment of all values concerning end-states of existence. In the final analysis, the fruitfulness of such a conceptualization will have to be tested empirically. Several kinds of evidence bearing on this issue will be presented later on in this work.

FUNCTIONS OF VALUES AND VALUE SYSTEMS

One way to approach the question: what functions do values serve? is to think of values as standards that guide ongoing activities, and of value systems as general plans employed to resolve conflicts and to make decisions. Another way is to think of values as giving expression to human needs.

Values as Standards

Values are multifaceted standards that guide conduct in a variety of ways. They (1) lead us to take particular positions on social issues, and (2) predispose us to favor one particular political or religious ideology over another. They are standards employed (3) to guide presentations of the self to others (Goffman, 1959), and (4) to evaluate and judge, to heap praise and fix blame on ourselves and others. (5) Values are central to the study of comparison processes (Festinger, 1954; Latane, 1966); we employ them as standards to ascertain whether we are as moral and as competent as others. (6) They are, moreover, standards employed to persuade and influence others, to tell us which beliefs, attitudes, values, and actions of others are worth challenging, protesting, and arguing about, or worth trying to influence or to change.

Finally, (7) values are standards that tell us how to rationalize in the psychoanalytic sense, beliefs, attitudes, and actions that would otherwise be personally and socially unacceptable so that we will end up with personal feelings of morality and competence, both indispensable ingredients for the maintenance and enhancement of self-esteem. An unkind remark made to a friend, for example, may be rationalized as an honest communication; an inhibited sex life may be rationalized as a life guided by self-control; an act of aggression by a nation may be justified on the basis of one human value or another such as national security or the preservation of liberty. The process of rationalization, so crucial a component in virtually all the defense mechanisms, would be impossible if man did not possess values to rationalize with.

Indeed, the employment of values as standards is a distinctively human invention that is not shared with other species and is therefore one way of defining the difference between being human and nonhuman. It is an Aesopian language of self-justification on the one hand and of self-deception on the other (Frenkel-Brunswik, 1939) that enables us to maintain and enhance our self-esteem no matter how socially desirable or undesirable our motives, feelings, or actions may be. Values provide a basis for rational self-justification insofar as possible but also a basis for rationalized self-justification insofar as necessary. Either way, values serve to maintain and enhance self-esteem.

The proposition that values are standards that can be employed in so many different ways raises many difficult questions requiring further analysis and empirical investigation. Under what conditions will a value be employed as one kind of standard rather than another? Are there reliable individual differences in the way values are employed? Do some people typically employ certain values as standards of action, others as standards of judgment or evaluation, and yet others as standards to rationalize with?

Value Systems as General Plans for Conflict Resolution and Decision Making

Since a given situation will typically activate several values within a person's value system rather than just a single one, it is unlikely that he will be able to behave in a manner that is equally compatible with all of them. A given situation may, for example, activate a conflict between behaving independently and obediently or between behaving politely and sincerely; another situation may activate a conflict between strivings for salvation and hedonic pleasure or between self-respect and respect from others. A value system is a learned organization of principles and rules to help one choose between alternatives, resolve conflicts, and make decisions.

This is not to suggest, however, that a person's total value system is ever fully activated in any given situation. It is a mental structure that is more comprehensive than that portion of it that a given situation may activate. It is a generalized plan that can perhaps best be likened to a map or architect's blueprint. Only that part of the map or blueprint that is immediately relevant is consulted, and the rest is ignored for the moment. Different subsets of the map or blueprint are activated in different social situations.

Motivational Functions

If the immediate functions of values and value systems are to guide human action in daily situations, their more long-range functions are to give expression to basic human needs. Values have a strong motivational component as well as cognitive, affective, and behavioral components. Instrumental values are motivating because the idealized modes of behavior they are concerned with are perceived to be instrumental to the attainment of desired end-goals. If we behave in all the ways prescribed by our instrumental values, we will be rewarded with all the end-states specified by our terminal values. Terminal values are motivating because they represent the supergoals beyond immediate, biologically urgent goals. Unlike the more immediate goals, these supergoals do not seem to be periodic in nature; neither do they seem to satiate—we seem to be forever doomed to strive for these ultimate goals without quite ever reaching them.

But there is another reason why values can be said to be motivating. They are in the final analysis the conceptual tools and weapons that we all employ in order to maintain and enhance self-esteem. They are in the service of what McDougall (1926) has called the master sentiment—the sentiment of self-regard. A more detailed description of the ways in which values serve this sentiment of self-regard may profitably begin with certain formulations previously presented by Smith, Bruner, and White (1956) and by Katz (1960)—formulations that were primarily concerned with the functions of attitudes rather than values. According to these writers, attitudes serve value-expressive, adjustment, ego-defense, and knowledge functions. Any given attitude need not, however, serve all these functions and it may serve various combinations of these functions.

The present formulation differs somewhat from the preceding formulation about the four functions of attitudes. The value-expressive function is conceived here to be superordinate to the adjustment, ego defense, and knowledge functions because the content of values must concern itself with the relative desirability or importance of adjustment, ego defense, and knowledge. Put another way, the latter three functions represent nothing more than expressions or manifestations of different values that all people possess and hold dear to varying degrees. Thus, all of a person's attitudes can be conceived as being value-expressive, and all of a person's values are conceived to maintain and enhance the master sentiment of self-regard —by helping a person adjust to his society, defend his ego against threat, and test reality.

The Adjustive Function of Values. The *content* of certain values directly concerns modes of behavior and end-states that are adjustment- or utilitarian-oriented. For example, certain instrumental values concern the desirability of obedience, getting along well with others, politeness and self-control; certain terminal values concern the desirability of material comfort, success, prestige, and "law and order." Other values that may point somewhat less explicitly to the adjustment function are those stressing the importance of responsible and achievement-oriented behavior, and those emphasizing such terminal end-states as peace of mind and the security of self, family, and nation. Although we can all be assumed to possess such adjustment-oriented values, we differ in the importance we place on them relative to other values.

McLaughlin has suggested that adjustment-oriented values are really "pseudo-values" because they are "espoused by an individual as a way of adapting to group pressures" (1965, pp. 273–274). But the desirability of compliance (Kelman, 1961) to group pressures may be a genuine value in its own right, no less internalized than other values. We cannot expect, of course, that a person who values compliance will come right out and admit to possessing a value so baldly put, either to himself or to others. He would first have to transform it cognitively into values that are more socially and personally defensible—such values as success and getting along well with others.

The Ego-defensive Function of Values. Psychoanalytic theory suggests that values no less than attitudes may serve ego-defensive needs. Needs, feelings, and actions that are personally and socially unacceptable may be readily recast by processes of rationalization and reaction formation into more acceptable terms; values represent ready-made concepts provided by our culture to ensure that such justifications can proceed smoothly and effortlessly. All instrumental and terminal values may be employed to serve ego-defensive functions, but we can nevertheless single out certain values which especially lend themselves to such purposes. Research on the authoritarian personality (Adorno, *et al*, 1950) suggests that an overemphasis on such modes of behavior as cleanliness and politeness and on such end-states as family and national security may be especially helpful to ego defense. Research by many investigators (Allen and Spilka, 1967; Allport, 1954; Allport and Ross, 1967; Glock and Stark, 1965, 1966; Kirkpatrick, 1949; Lenski, 1961; Rokeach, 1969a, 1969b) also suggests that religious values more often than not serve ego-defensive functions.

The Knowledge or Self-actualization Function of Values. Katz defines the knowledge function as involving "the search for meaning, the need to understand, the trend toward better organization of perception and belief to provide clarity and consistency" (1960, p. 170). Certain instrumental and terminal values explicitly or implicitly implicate this knowledge and, somewhat more broadly, the self-actualization function. Thus, people value such end-states as wisdom and a sense of accomplishment and such modes of behavior as behaving independently, consistently, and competently. We all possess such values, as we do adjustment and ego-defensive values, but again we differ in the priority we place on them. One person may, for example, attach greater importance to adjustment-oriented than knowledge-oriented values whereas another may reverse these priorities.

Higher- and Lower-order Values

Thus far in this discussion we have deliberately avoided labeling certain values as better or of a higher order than others. We have done so in the hope of demonstrating that it is possible to describe the values that people hold in a value-free manner. But it is now perhaps appropriate to suggest that values serving adjustive, ego-defensive, knowledge, and self-actualization functions may well be ordered along a continuum ranging from lower- to higher-order, as is suggested by Maslow's well-known hierarchical theory of motivation (1954). Different subsets of values may differentially serve Maslow's safety, security, love, self-esteem, and self-actualization needs. Maslow also (1959) speaks of B(being)-values and D(deficiency)-values, and in doing so he is again proposing that certain values are better, higher, more desirable for psychological fulfillment than others:

> For one thing, it looks as if *there were* a single ultimate value for mankind, a far goal toward which all men strive. This is called variously by different authors self-actualization, self-realization, integration, psychological health, individuation, autonomy, creativity, productivity, but they all agree that this amounts to realizing the potentialities of the person, that is to say, becoming fully human, everything that the person *can* become (p. 123).

The value concept employed by Maslow differs, however, in certain respects from the one presented here. He employs it in a manner that is more or less synonymous with the concept of need, drawing no distinction between instrumental and terminal values and dealing more with what has been identified here as end-states than with modes of behavior. These differences notwithstanding, Maslow's conception of higher- and lower-order values can be fruitfully employed. To the extent that a person's value system reflects a differential preoccupation with values that are adjustive, ego-defensive, and self-actualizing, we may say that he is operating at lower or higher levels. It remains to be seen to what extent various segments of American society can be thus described.

VALUES DISTINGUISHED FROM OTHER CONCEPTS

Brewster Smith (1969) is one of a small band of social scientists who has forcefully drawn our attention to the conceptual disarray of the value concept in the social sciences:

> But the increased currency of explicit value concepts among psychologists and social scientists has unfortunately not been accompanied by corresponding gains in conceptual clarity or consensus. We talk about altogether too many probably different things under one rubric when we stretch the same terminology to include the utilities of mathematical decision theory..., fundamental assumptions about the nature of the world and man's place in it..., ultimate preferences among life styles..., and core attitudes or sentiments that set priorities among one's preferences and thus give structure to a life.... And, at the same time, we are embarassed with a proliferation of concepts akin to values: attitudes and sentiments, but also interests, preferences, motives, cathexes, valences. The handful of major attempts to study values empirically have started from different preconceptions and have altogether failed to link together to yield a domain of cumulative knowledge (pp. 97–98).

To reduce this conceptual disarray, we will attempt to distinguish the value concept employed here from various other concepts—attitude, social norm, need, trait, interest, and value orientation.

Values and Attitudes

Over the past fifty years empirically oriented social psychologists have paid considerably more attention to the theory and measurement of attitudes than to the theory and measurement of values. Despite the fact that many hundreds of value studies have accumulated over these years (Albert and Kluckhohn, 1958; Duffy, 1940; Dukes, 1955; Pittel and Mendelsohn, 1966) the ratio of attitude studies to value studies cited in *Psychological Abstracts* between 1961 and 1965 was roughly five or six attitude studies for every value study. There is little reason to think that this ratio would be markedly different for other years. This generally greater emphasis on attitudes has not arisen from any deep conviction that man's attitudes are more important determinants of social behavior than his values. Rather, it seems to have been forced upon us or to have evolved out of the more rapid development of methods for measuring attitudes, combined perhaps with a lack of clarity about the conceptual differences between values and attitudes and about their functional interconnections. Newcomb, Turner, and Converse, for instance, see values as but "special cases of the attitude concept" (1965, p. 45) and use the value concept only "informally"; Campbell regards the value and attitude concepts to be fundamentally similar (1963).

An attitude differs from a value in that an attitude refers to an organization of several beliefs around a specific object or situation (Rokeach, 1968a, 1968b). A value, on the other hand, refers to a single belief of a very specific kind. It concerns a desirable mode of behavior or end-state that has a transcendental quality to it, guiding actions, attitudes, judgments, and comparisons across specific objects and situations and beyond immediate goals to more ultimate goals. So defined, values and attitudes differ in a number of important respects. First, whereas a value is a single belief, an attitude refers to an organization of several beliefs that are all focused on a given object or situation. A Likert scale, for example, consists of a representative sample of beliefs all of which concern the same object or situation. When summed, it provides a single index of a person's favorable or unfavorable attitude toward an object or situation. Second, a value transcends objects and situations whereas an attitude is focused on some specified object or situation. Third, a value is a standard but an attitude is not a standard. Favorable or unfavorable evaluations of numerous attitude objects and situations may be based upon a relatively small number of values serving as standards. Fourth, a person has as many values as he has learned beliefs concerning desirable modes of conduct and end-states of existence, and as many attitudes as direct or indirect encounters he has had with specific objects and situations. It is thus estimated that values number only in the dozens, whereas attitudes number in the thousands.

Fifth, values occupy a more central position than attitudes within one's personality makeup and cognitive system, and they are therefore determinants of attitudes as well as of behavior. This greater centrality of values has occasionally been noted by others: "attitudes themselves depend on pre-existing social values" (Allport, 1961, pp. 802–803); "attitudes express values" (Watson, 1966, p. 215); "attitudes are functions of values" (Woodruff, 1942, p. 33). Closely related is the notion of perceived instrumentality (Peak, 1955; Carlson, 1956; Rosenberg, 1960; Homant, 1970; Hollen, 1972). A particular attitude object is perceived to be instrumental to the attainment of one or more values; a change in an attitude object's perceived instrumentality for one or more values should lead to a change in attitude; linking a particular attitude to more important values should make it more resistant to change than linking it to less important values (Ostrom and Brock, 1969; Edwards and Ostrom, 1969). Sixth, value is a more dynamic concept than attitude, having a more immediate link to motivation. "The now massive literature on attitudes serves to demonstrate nothing more clearly than that attitudes are not basic directive factors in behavior but that they are secondary to more personal characteristics. . ." (Woodruff, 1942, p. 33). If an attitude also has a motivational component, this is so only because the valenced (valued) attitude object or situation is perceived to be positively or negatively instrumental to value attainment. And, seventh, the substantive content of a value may directly concern adjustive, ego defense, knowledge or self-actualizing functions while the content of an attitude is related to such functions only inferentially.

Values and Social Norms

There are three ways in which values differ from social norms. First, a value may refer to a mode of behavior or end-state of existence whereas a social norm refers only to a mode of behavior. Second, a value transcends specific situations; in contrast, a social norm is a prescription or proscription to behave in a specific way in a specific situation. Navaho Indians, for example, should refrain from having ceremonials at the time of an eclipse of the moon (Kluckhohn, 1951, p. 413); Americans should stand respectfully at attention when the "Star Spangled Banner" is played at a public gathering but not when it is played in one's home. Third, a value is more personal and internal, whereas a norm is consensual and external to the person. Williams has aptly captured this difference between values and norms in the following passage:

> Values are standards of desirability that are more nearly independent of specific situations. The same value may be a point of reference for a great many specific norms; a particular norm may represent the simultaneous application of several separate values. . . . Values, as standards (criteria) for establishing what should be regarded as desirable, provide the grounds for accepting or rejecting particular norms (1968, p. 284).

Values and Needs

If some writers regard values and attitudes as more or less equivalent, others regard values and needs as equivalent. Maslow, for instance, refers to self-actualization both as a need and as a higher-order value (1959, 1964). Murray's list of needs (1938) is transformed into White's list of values (1951). French and Kahn (1962) point out that in some respects the properties of a value and of a need are similar. A person may want to do something but also feel that he ought to do it, since a value is not only a belief about what he ought to do but also a desire to do it.

> In other cases, perhaps especially in approach motivation, a single motivation system seems to have the properties of a need and also the properties of a value. In many people, for example, the achievement motive represents both something a person wants to do and something he feels he ought to do. For such

social motives we assume that they have developed through a process of reinforcement similar to the development of moral values, and therefore, will have some of the same conceptual properties. Thus we shall try to define the conceptual properties of motives, including both needs and values, in such a way that they are not separated into a sharp dichotomy but instead have many conceptual properties in common (p. 11).

If values are indeed equivalent to needs, as Maslow and many others have suggested, then the lowly rat, to the extent that it can be said to possess needs, should to the same extent also be said to possess values. If such a view were adopted, it would be difficult to account for the fact that values are so much at the center of attention among those concerned with the understanding of human behavior and so little at the center of attention among those concerned with the understanding of animal behavior. That values are regarded to be so much more central in the one case than in the other suggests that values cannot altogether be identical to needs and perhaps that values possess some attributes that needs do not.

Man is the only animal that can be meaningfully described as having values. Indeed, it is the presence of values and systems of values that is a major characteristic distinguishing humans from infrahumans. Values are the cognitive representations and transformations of needs, and man is the only animal capable of such representations and transformations.

This proposition is not the whole story, however: Values are the cognitive representation not only of individual needs but also of societal and institutional demands. They are the joint results of sociological as well as psychological forces acting upon the individual—sociological because society and its institutions socialize the individual for the common good to internalize shared conceptions of the desirable; psychological because individual motivations require cognitive expression, justification, and indeed exhortation in socially desirable terms. The cognitive representation of needs as values serves societal demands no less than individual needs. Once such demands and needs become cognitively transformed into values, they are capable of being defended, justified, advocated, and exhorted as personally and socially desirable. For example, the need for sex which is so often repressed in modern society may be cognitively transformed as a value for love, spiritual union, or intimacy; needs for dependence, conformity, or abasement may be cognitively transformed into values concerning obedience, loyalty, or respect for elders; aggressive needs may be transformed into values concerning ambition, honor, family or national security. Needs may or may not be denied, depending on whether they can stand conscious personal and social scrutiny, but values need never be denied. Thus, when a person tells us about his values he is surely also telling us about his needs. But we must be cautious in how we infer needs from values because values are not isomorphic with needs. Needs are cognitively transformed into values so that a person can end up smelling himself, and being smelled by others, like a rose. Because infrahumans are incapable of such cognitive representations and transformations of needs, they cannot have values; consequently, a study of the laws governing animal behavior can lead to the discovery neither that men possess values nor that men use values as tools or weapons to preserve and enhance self-esteem.

Values and Traits

The concept of trait has had a long tradition in theory and research in personality (Allport, 1961; Rotter, 1954). It carries with it a connotation of human characteristics that are highly fixed and not amenable to modification by experimental or situational variation. It is difficult to locate experimental studies that are concerned with changes in traits, probably because the trait concept does not readily lend itself to alteration by experimental manipulation. About the only operations that one can easily perform on traits are to correlate them with other traits and to factor-analyze them. Nor are they amenable to change as a result of education or psychotherapy. Although psychotherapists often talk about the effects of therapy on habits, needs, attitudes, values, personality, and behavior, they rarely talk about the effects of therapy on traits.

A person's character, which is seen from a personality psychologist's standpoint as a cluster of fixed traits, can be reformulated from an internal, phenomenological standpoint as a system of values. Thus, a person identified from the "outside" as an authoritarian on the basis of his F-scale score can also be identified from the "inside" as one who places relatively high values on being obedient, clean, and polite and relatively low values on being broad-minded, intellectual and imaginative. A person identified as an introvert on the basis of a score of an introversion-extroversion scale might identify himself as a person who cares more for wisdom and a life of the intellect and less for friendship, prestige, and being cheerful. A person we might identify as aggressive might see himself as merely ambitious, as one who cares about being a good provider for his family, and as one who cares about accomplishing something important in life.

A major advantage gained in thinking about a person as a system of values rather than as a cluster of traits is that it becomes possible to conceive of his undergoing change as a result of changes in social conditions. In contrast, the trait concept has built into it a characterological bias that forecloses such possibilities for change in advance. This very fixedness that has been built into the trait concept probably accounts for the fact that it has received so little attention from social psychologists and sociologists on the one hand and from students of behavior modification on the other.

Values and Interests

To Ralph Barton Perry (1954), a value is any object of interest, and the two are therefore identical concepts. Some writers have criticized the classical Study of Values (Allport, Vernon, and Lindzey, 1960) on the ground that it is primarily or solely a test of occupational interest (Duffy, 1940; McLaughlin, 1965).

An interest is but one of the many manifestations of a value, and therefore it has some of the attributes that a value has. An interest may be the cognitive representation of needs; it may guide action, evaluations of self and others, and comparisons of self with others. It may serve adjustive, ego-defense, knowledge, and self-actualization functions. But interest is obviously a narrower concept than value. It cannot be classified as an idealized mode of behavior or end-state of existence. It would be difficult to argue that an interest is a standard or that it has an "ought" character. It would, moreover, be difficult to defend the proposition that the interests that men have are relatively small in number and universally held or that they are organized into interest systems that serve as generalized plans for conflict resolution or decison making. Interests seem to resemble attitudes more than values, representing a favorable or unfavorable attitude toward certain objects (e.g., art, people, money) or activities (e.g., occupations).

Value Systems and Value Orientations

These two concepts seem at first glance to be more or less synonymous. But as employed by Kluckhohn and Strodtbeck, value orientation does not appear to be altogether interchangeable with the present notion of value system. Clyde Kluckhohn has defined a value orientation as "a set of linked propositions embracing both value and existential elements" (1951, p. 409). Florence Kluckhohn and Fred Strodtbeck (1961) measure value orientations operationally by asking respondents to rank-order alternative responses to each of five separate dimensions. Their value orientation refers to a pattern of rank-ordered results obtained within each of five separate dimensions and is not a rank ordering of the five dimensions with respect to one another. The notion of value system, in contrast, implies a rank ordering of terminal or instrumental values along a single continuum.

There is another reason this notion of value orientation is not considered to be equivalent to the notion of value system. The five separate dimensions formulated by Kluckhohn and by Kluckhohn and Strodtbeck—human nature is good or evil; subjugation to, harmony with, or mastery over nature; past, present, or future time perspective; being, being-in-becoming, or doing; linearity, collaterality, or individualism—seem to be somewhat far removed from what we ordinarily mean by a "conception of the desirable." A person may indeed believe that man is subjugated to nature but this circumstance does not necessarily imply that he has a value for "subjugation to nature," that he believes such a state of affairs to be desirable, or that man "ought" to be subjugated to nature. It appears that Kluckhohn and Strodtbeck's five dimensions can be more aptly described as basic philosophical orientations than as value orientations.

ANTECEDENTS AND CONSEQUENCES
OF VALUES AND VALUE SYSTEMS

A major conceptual advantage of an approach wherein values are central is that we can with equal facility think of values as dependent or as independent variables. On the dependent side, they are a result of all the cultural, institutional, and personal forces that act upon a person throughout his lifetime. On the independent side, they have far-reaching effects on virtually all areas of human endeavor that scientists across all the social sciences may be interested in.

Antecedents of Values

Even if it were true that man possesses but a relatively small number of values, the number of theoretically possible variations in value systems is truly enormous, far more than needed to account for the rich differences that may exist among cultures, societies, institutional arrangements, and even among all individual personalities existing on planet Earth. A mere dozen and a half terminal values, for instance, can be arranged in order of importance in 18 factorial ways, which comes to over 640 trillion different ways. But it is extremely unlikely that all such theoretically possible permutations will actually be observed. We may expect that similarities in culture will sharply reduce the total number of possible variations to a much smaller number, shaping the value systems of large numbers of people in more or less similar ways. Further reductions in possible variations can moreover be expected within a given culture as a result of socialization by similar social institutions; similarities of sex, age, class, and race (Rokeach and Parker, 1970; Kohn, 1969); religious upbringing (Rokeach, 1969a, 1969b); political identification (Rokeach, 1968–1969); and the like. Data pointing to the effects of such variables on values will be presented in Chapter 3.

We may also expect that similarities in personal experience and in the expression of individual needs will further reduce the total number of possible variations by shaping the value systems of many people in similar ways. Kluckhohn and Strodtbeck (1961) express a similar view concerning the limited number of variations in value orientations that are likely to be found within cultures:

First, it is assumed that *there is a limited number of common human problems for which all peoples at all times must find some solution.* This is the universal aspect of value orientations because the common human problems to be treated arise inevitably out of the human situation. The second assumption is that *while there is variability in solutions of all the problems, it is neither limitless nor random but is definitely variable within a range of possible solutions.* The third assumption, the one which provides the main key to the later analysis of variation in value orientations, is that *all alternatives of all solutions are present in all societies at all times but are differentially preferred.* Every society has, in addition to its dominant profile of value orientations, numerous *variant* or *substitute profiles*. Moreover, it is postulated that in both the dominant and the variant profiles there is almost always a *rank ordering* of the preferences of the value-orientation alternatives (p. 10).

Consequences of Values

The values that are internalized as a result of cultural, societal, and personal experience are psychological structures that, in turn, have consequences of their own. These consequences have already been discussed in an earlier section on values as standards and therefore need be only briefly reiterated here. Values are determinants of virtually all kinds of behavior that could be called social behavior—of social action, attitudes and ideology, evaluations, moral judgments and justifications of self and others, comparisons of self with others, presentations of self to others, and attempts to influence others. Boiling all these down to a more succinct theoretical statement, it can perhaps be stated that values are guides and determinants of social attitudes and ideologies on the one hand and of social behavior on the other. Empirical evidence bearing on this proposition is presented in Chapters 4 and 5.

TOWARD A CLASSIFICATION
OF HUMAN VALUES

"Much of the confusion in discussion about values," Kluckhohn writes,

undoubtedly arises from the fact that one speaker has the general category in mind, another a particular limited type of value, still another a different specific type. We have not discovered any comprehensive classification of values. Golightly has distinguished essential and operational values; C. I. Lewis instrinsic, extrinsic, inherent, and instrumental values. The Cornell group speaks of asserted and operating values. Perry has discriminated values according to modalities of interest: Positive-negative, progressive-recurrent, potential-actual, and so on. There are various content classifications such as: hedonic, aesthetic, religious, economic, ethical, and logical. The best known of the content groupings is Spranger's (used in the Allport-Vernon test of values): theoretical, economic, aesthetic, social, political, and religious. The object to these content classifications is that they are culturebound. Ralph White has distinguished one hundred "general values" and twenty-five "political values" all with special references to Western culture (1951, p. 412).

Rather than burden the reader with yet another classification of values, I prefer to ask instead whether there might be some compelling theoretical basis for suggesting a systematic classification of values. A reasonable point of departure for such an attempt at classification is the observation that it is just as meaningful to speak of institutional values as of individual values. Every human value, as English and English have noted (1958), is a "social product" that has been transmitted and preserved in successive generations through one or more of society's institutions. We may define an institution as a social organization that has evolved in society and has been "assigned" the task of specializing in the maintenance and enhancement of selected subsets of values and in their transmission from generation to generation. Thus, religious institutions are institutions that specialize in furthering a certain subset of values that we call religious values; the family is an institution that specializes in furthering another subset of values; educational, political, economic, and legal institutions specialize in yet other subsets. The values that one institution specializes in are not necessarily completely different from those in which other institutions specialize. They may overlap and share certain values in common and thus reinforce each other's values, as in the case of the family and religious institutions. To the extent they do not overlap, however, they will compete with one another, as in the case of religious and secular institutions within a society that insists on separation of church and state.

If it is indeed the case that the maintenance, enhancement, and transmission of values within a culture typically become institutionalized, then an identification of the major institutions of a society should provide us with a reasonable point of departure for a comprehensive compilation and classification of human values. The approach to the measurement of values described in the next chapter is based, in part, upon an informal attempt to identify the main values that the various institutions of society appear to have specialized in.

SUMMARY

The following more extended definitions of a *value* and a *value system* are offered. To say that a person has a value is to say that he has an enduring prescriptive or proscriptive belief that a specific mode of behavior or end-state of existence is preferred to an oppositive mode of behavior or end-state. This belief transcends attitudes toward objects and toward situations; it is a standard that guides and determines action, attitudes toward objects and situations, ideology, presentations of self to others, evaluations, judgments, justifications, comparisons of self with others, and attempts to influence others. Values serve adjustive, ego-defensive, knowledge, and self-actualizing functions. Instrumental and terminal values are related yet are separately organized into relatively enduring hierarchical organizations along a continuum of importance.

2
The Measurement of Values
and Value Systems

It is difficult to conceive of a human problem that would not be better illuminated if reliable value data concerning it were available. Differences between cultures, social classes, occupations, religions, or political orientations are all translatable into questions concerning differences in underlying values and value systems. Differences between the generations, black and white Americans, and the rich and poor are all amenable to analysis in terms of value differences. Studies of change as a result of maturation, education, persuasion, therapy, and cultural, institutional, and technological change are all similarly capable of being formulated as questions concerning development and change in values and value systems.

To pose and answer a wide variety of questions such as these, considerable attention has been devoted over the past few years to the development and standardization of a simple method for measuring values and value systems. It was also hoped that such a method would prove useful as a social indicator (Gross, 1966; Bauer, 1966; U.S. Department of HEW, 1969; Gross and Springer, 1970) and have a wide variety of applications to psychology and psychiatry, sociology and anthropology, political science and education.

Before deciding on the particular approach to be described in this chapter, two others were considered. One concerns the drawing of inferences about a person's values from his behavior in structured situations. This approach was rejected because it had too many drawbacks: It is time-consuming and expensive; it cannot be employed with large numbers of people; it is difficult to interpret and to quantify; and it may be biased by the observer's own values. A second approach is to ask a person to tell us in his own words about his values—a simple phenomenological approach. This was also rejected because it has drawbacks: A person might not be willing or able to tell us about them, or he might be highly selective in what he chooses to tell us.

To get around such limitations, we presented the respondent at the outset with previously constructed lists of terminal and instrumental values, wherein the only burden placed upon him is to rank them for importance. The two lists were designed to be reasonably comprehensive and were at the same time worded in a manner that would, it was hoped, yield phenomenologically valid data. That is, the measuring instrument was designed to elicit information about values that the respondent would be willing or even eager to admit he had, which meant that it could neither be couched in negative terms (e.g., cowardly, irresponsible) nor in terms so positive as to give the impression of immodesty or boastfulness (e.g., brilliant, clever).

THE VALUE SURVEY

Table 2.1 shows two lists of 18 alphabetically arranged instrumental and terminal values that we ended up with after several years of research. Each value is presented along with a brief definition in parentheses. The instruction to the respondent is to "arrange them in order of importance to YOU, as guiding principles in YOUR life." The ranking method assumes that it is not the absolute presence or absence of a value that is of interest but their relative ordering. Form E, one of the two final versions now being employed, presents the respondent with two mimeographed lists of 18 terminal and 18 instrumental values. The respondent ranks each list in order of importance by writing in numbers from 1 to 18. Form D of the Value Survey (Rokeach, 1967), the alternate form now being more widely used, presents each value printed on a removable gummed label, as shown in Appendix A. The respondent is instructed to "Study the list carefully and pick out the one value which is the most important for you. Peel it off and paste it in Box 1 on the left. Then pick out the value which is second most important for you. Peel it off and paste it in Box 2. Then do the same for each of the remaining values. The value which is least important goes in Box 18. Work slowly and think carefully. If you change your mind, feel free to change your answers. The labels peel off easily and can be moved from place to place. The end result should truly show how you really feel." No attempt is made to disguise the test. It is represented as a "Value Survey" and the opening sentence of the instructions states: "On the next page are 18 values listed in alphabetical order."

The respondent has only his own internalized system of values to tell him how to rank the 18 terminal and the 18 instrumental values. Responses to the test are not suggested by the stimulus material. Thus, the ranking task is highly projective in nature, somewhat like the Rorschach or the Thematic Apperception Test. The stimulus material is nonetheless far more structured than the ambiguous material ordinarily employed in

TABLE 2.1   TEST-RETEST RELIABILITIES OF 18 TERMINAL AND 18 INSTRUMENTAL VALUES, FORM D (N = 250)

Terminal Value	r	Instrumental Value	r
A comfortable life (a prosperous life)	.70	Ambitious (hard-working, aspiring)	.70
An exciting life (a stimulating, active life)	.73	Broadminded (open-minded)	.57
A sense of accomplishment (lasting contribution)	.51	Capable (competent, effective)	.51
A world at peace (free of war and conflict)	.67	Cheerful (lighthearted, joyful)	.65
A world of beauty (beauty of nature and the arts)	.66	Clean (neat, tidy)	.66
Equality (brotherhood, equal opportunity for all)	.71	Courageous (standing up for your beliefs)	.52
Family security (taking care of loved ones)	.64	Forgiving (willing to pardon others)	.62
Freedom (independence, free choice)	.61	Helpful (working for the welfare of others)	.66
Happiness (contentedness)	.62	Honest (sincere, truthful)	.62
Inner harmony (freedom from inner conflict)	.65	Imaginative (daring, creative)	.69
Mature love (sexual and spiritual intimacy)	.68	Independent (self-reliant, self-sufficient)	.60
National security (protection from attack)	.67	Intellectual (intelligent, reflective)	.67
Pleasure (an enjoyable, leisurely life)	.57	Logical (consistent, rational)	.57
Salvation (saved, eternal life)	.88	Loving (affectionate, tender)	.65
Self-respect (self-esteem)	.58	Obedient (dutiful, respectful)	.53
Social recognition (respect, admiration)	.65	Polite (courteous, well-mannered)	.53
True friendship (close companionship)	.59	Responsible (dependable, reliable)	.45
Wisdom (a mature understanding of life)	.60	Self-controlled (restrained, self-disciplined)	.52

projective tests, its most distinctive feature being that the stimuli are words and the only responses elicited from the respondent are numbers from 1 to 18.

In view of the projective nature of the Value Survey and the fact that the values it contains are virtually all socially desirable ones, it is hardly surprising that many respondents report the ranking task to be a very difficult one—one they have little confidence in having completed in a reliable manner and one they are often sure they had completed more or less randomly. The extent to which this is indeed the case will be discussed shortly.

A few words are in order about how the particular values shown in Table 2.1 were selected. They had evolved first of all from earlier versions containing 12 terminal and 12 instrumental values. These sets of 12 were later increased to 18 when it became evident that too many important values had been omitted. A ceiling of 18 was imposed because it was felt to be too burdensome for respondents to rank-order more than 18 values and, moreover, because the two lists of 18 terminal and 18 instrumental values were felt to be reasonably comprehensive.

The 18 terminal values are distilled from a much larger list obtained from various sources: a review of the literature mentioning various values found in American society and in other societies, the writers own terminal values, those obtained from about 30 graduate students in psychology, and those obtained by interviewing a representative sample of about 100 adults in metropolitan Lansing who had been asked to tell us what terminal values they possessed (after the notion of terminal values had been explained to them). The number of values thus compiled—several hundred—was then reduced on the basis of one or another consideration: We eliminated those values judged to be more or less synonymous with one another (e.g., freedom and liberty, brotherhood of man and equality, peace of mind and inner harmony), those which were empirically known to be more or less synonymous (e.g., the correlation between rankings of *salvation* and *unity with God* was over .80), those which overlapped (e.g., religion and salvation), those which were too specific (e.g., spousehood is more specific than family security), or those which simply did not represent end-states of existence (e.g., wisdom is an end-state but education is not).

A very different procedure was followed in selecting the 18 instrumental values. This time the point of departure was Anderson's (1968) list of 555 personality-trait words for which he has reported positive and negative evaluative ratings. Anderson derived his list from a larger one of about 18,000 trait-names originally compiled by Allport and Odbert (1936), retaining only those trait-names that "were likely to be useful," and eliminating extreme words, words denoting temporary states, physical characteristics, sex-linked words, and relatively unfamiliar words. Since we were interested not in negative but in positive values that would be suitable for self-attribution, Anderson's list of 555 trait-names could be quickly reduced to about 200. The 18 instrumental values were selected from this list according to several criteria: by retaining only one from a group of synonyms or near-synonyms (e.g., helpful, kind, kindhearted, thoughtful, considerate, friendly, unselfish); by retaining those judged to be maximally different from or minimally intercorrelated with one another; by retaining those judged to represent the most important values in American society; by retaining those deemed to be maximally discriminating across social status, sex, race, age, religion, politics, etc.; by retaining those judged to be meaningful values in all cultures; and by retaining those one could readily admit to having without appearing to be immodest, vain, or boastful (thus eliminating such values as being brilliant, clever, ingenious, and charming).

As can be seen, the overall procedure employed in selecting the two lists is admittedly an intuitive one, and there is no reason to think that others working independently would have come up with precisely the same list of 18 terminal and 18 instrumental values. It would be interesting to see which values others might produce working independently and using the same criteria that have been described here.

Ranking such lists of 18 values, however, stretches the limits of human attention. George Miller informs us (1956) that the number of "chunks" of information that most people can keep in the immediate span of their attention is the magical number of seven, plus or minus two. Form D was invented to make the ranking of 18 terminal and 18 instrumental values easier than traditional rankings normally made with pen or pencil. Each of the values—along with defining phrases—is printed on a pressure-sensitive gummed label, $\frac{3}{8}$ of an inch wide and $2\frac{3}{4}$ inches long (Appendix A), thus bringing them all into one's visual field simultaneously. Each set of 18 gummed labels is alphabetically arranged down the right-hand side of the page. The respondent's task is to rearrange each set by pasting them in Boxes 1 to 18 printed down the left-hand side of the page. This technique, which is perhaps a cross between ranking and sorting methods, has several advantages over the traditional ranking method. First, it has a game-like quality; the respondent is doing something with his hands and does not require pen or pencil. The typical respondent finds it enjoyable to paste, remove, and repaste labels without having to become anxious about one's hands and fingers becoming "messy." This technique is especially advantageous when testing those who would find the traditional method of rank ordering difficult or burdensome—for example: children, the aged, and people with little education. The vast majority of respondents are able to complete the Value Survey within 10 to 20 minutes, typically ranking them sequentially from 1 to 18, and, somewhat less often, selecting the most important values first for ranking, then the least important values, and then those in the middle.

More important from a measurement standpoint, the respondent's task becomes progressively easier with every gummed label that he ranks. As he proceeds with the rankings, he does not have to hunt through or "stumble over" those already ranked in order to find the next most important one. After the respondent has moved twelve values over to the left-hand side of the page, for instance, he has only six more on the right-hand side to compare with one another. Thus, it is not altogether accurate to say that the ranking task is a test 18 items long. This is so only when all 18 values are still in place. After one value has been ranked, it becomes a 17-item ranking task, etc. Thus, the average length of the scale demanding the respondent's attention turns out to be 9.5—a figure not far off from Miller's magical number of seven—plus or minus two.

VALUE MEASURES

A variety of measures may be obtained with the rank-ordering procedure described here. Some of these are parameters of value systems considered as a whole; others are parameters of values taken one at a time. These measures along with pertinent results that are presently available are discussed below.

1. Value System Stability

An index of value system stability is obtained for each respondent by correlating his rankings on one occasion with those made on a later occasion. Table 2.2 shows the median reliabilities (rho) found for various groups tested with various versions of the Value Survey. The initial Form A, consisting of 12 values without defining phrases, was presented to college students seven weeks apart. A median test-retest reliability of .65 was obtained for both terminal and instrumental values. Since these reliabilities were judged to be too low to be satisfactory for general use, Form A was revised by adding defining phrases for each value, on the assumption that the semantic meaning of the values might thus become clearer. The resulting increase in Form B's reliability was negligible: the median terminal value stability increased from .65 to .69, while the median instrumental value stability decreased from .65 to .62. It would thus appear that adding the defining phrases had no effect. Other results obtained with Forms A and B, concerning the relation between values and attitudes and between values and behavior, led to a similar conclusion. With or without the defining phrases highly similar reliabilities and validities were obtained.

Form C consisted of two sets of 18 values with defining phrases added. The lists were increased from 12 to 18 for two reasons—in the hope that the increase would result in a substantially improved reliability, and to end up with more comprehensive lists of terminal and instrumental values. Too many important values had been left out of the 12-value versions. But 18 values, it was anticipated, would present a more formidable ranking task to the respondent unless special steps were taken to overcome it. Accordingly, the respondent was first instructed to identify the six most important values, then the six least important values. He then ranked the high, middle, and low thirds from 1 to 6, from most to least important. One unfortunate consequence of this procedure, we were soon to discover, was that about 10 percent of the college students serving as respondents failed to complete the rankings. The remaining 90 percent of the respondents showed a median test-retest reliability (seven weeks apart) of .71 for terminal values and .66 for instrumental values. These reliabilities were an improvement over those obtained with Forms A and B, but not much of an

TABLE 2.2   MEDIAN TEST-RETEST RELIABILITIES FOR VARIOUS FORMS OF THE VALUE SURVEY

Form	Description	N	Sample	Time between Test-Retest	Terminal Reliability	Instrumental Reliability
A	12 values without definitions	210	College	7 weeks	.65	.65
B	12 values with definitions	218	College	7 weeks	.69	.62
C	18 values with definitions; first sorted high, middle, and low thirds; then ranked within each third	95	College	7 weeks	.71	.66
D	18 values, defining phrases added, gummed labels	26*	7th grade	3 weeks	.62	.53
		26*	9th grade	3 weeks	.63	.61
		26*	11th grade	3 weeks	.74	.71
		117	College	3 weeks	.78	.72
		36	College	4.5 weeks	.80	.70
		100	College	7 weeks	.78	.71
		216	College	2–4 months	.76	.65
		204	College	14–16 months	.69	.61
E	18 values, defining phrases added, mimeographed version	189	College	3 weeks	.74	.65
		32†	Lansing Adults	12 weeks	.74	—
		77‡	S. Australia College	5 weeks	.74	.70
Paired comparison method	18 values, defining phrases added	30	College	5 weeks	.87	.60

* From McLellan, D. D. (1970).
† From Homant, R. (1970).
‡ From Feather (1972).

improvement. It was, therefore, necessary to experiment with other techniques in the hope that they might improve reliability more markedly without increasing the attrition rate.

Form D is identical to Form C except for the fact that each value, along with defining phrase, is printed on a gummed label, as previously described. Attrition due to failure to complete the rankings is extremely low among college students and school children—about one or two percent. As Table 2.2 shows, the best reliability results have been obtained with Form D. Median test-retest reliabilities of terminal values increase steadily from .62 for seventh graders in the Lansing area to .78–.80 for college students at Michigan State University; for instrumental values, median test-retest reliabilities increase from .53 for seventh graders to .70–.72 for college students. The time intervals between test and retest vary from 3 to 7 weeks. For longer test-retest time intervals the reliabilities for college students are only slightly lower. For the terminal values the median reliability is .76 after a 2 to 4 month interval and .69 after a 14 to 16 month interval; for the instrumental values, the comparable median reliabilities are .65 and .61. The findings obtained with the 14 to 16 month test-retest interval are especially noteworthy because they suggest an impressive degree of value system stability among college students over relatively long periods of time.

Form E presents the identical 18 values more conventionally, the respondent merely ranking the values by writing in numbers from 1 to 18 in the blank spaces provided. Test-retest reliabilities are usually somewhat lower than those obtained for Form D: .74 for terminal values and .65 for instrumental values for American samples and .74 for terminal values and .70 for instrumental values for a sample of South Australian college students tested by Feather (1972b), suggesting a high degree of cross-cultural consistency in value system stability. Thus, mimeographed Form E is a slight improvement over Forms A and B, about as good as Form C, but—on the whole—somewhat inferior to Form D, the gummed label version. Attrition rate is, moreover, somewhat higher for Form E than for Form D among college students—anywhere from about 5 to 19 percent.

Finally, Table 2.2 shows test-retest results obtained by Penner, Homant, and Rokeach (1968) with the method of paired comparison. Each of the 18 terminal values and each of the 18 instrumental values was systematically paired with every other value in the list, the respondent in each case indicating which of the two is the more important. This was a rather time-consuming procedure involving 153 paired comparisons for terminal values and another 153 paired comparisons for instrumental values. Test-retest after 5 weeks showed median reliabilities of .87 for the terminal values, but, surprisingly, only .60 for the instrumental values. Comparing these reliabilities with those previously obtained leads to the conclusion that a simple ranking of the 18 values gives results that are on balance about as reliable as those obtained with the more cumbersome and time-consuming method of paired comparison.

Further inspection of Table 2.2 reveals that the terminal value reliabilities are consistently higher than the instrumental value reliabilities. One possible reason for this finding is that terminal values are learned earlier and thus become stabilized earlier in the development of the individual than do instrumental values. Another possible reason is that the terminal list is a more complete list of values and the respondent is thus more certain of his rankings than in the case of instrumental values. A third possibility is that terminal values represent ideas that are more distinctively different from one another than is the case with instrumental values. There are perhaps other interpretations. It is not possible at this time to specify more definitively the determinants of this consistent finding. The reasons for the consistently greater stability of terminal values merits further investigation.

Most of the data shown in Table 2.2 were obtained with college students for the simple reason that college students are more easily available for testing and retesting. But attention must be drawn to the fact that Form D data are also reported for seventh, ninth, and eleventh graders, and that Form E data are also reported for a random sample of adults in the city of Lansing. The former were obtained by McLellan (1970) and the latter by Homant (1970). The median terminal value reliability for Lansing adults is .74, using a 12 week test-retest interval, a result identical to that obtained with American and South Australian college students who had been retested after a 3- to 5-week interval.

In summary, several considerations indicate that Form D of the Value Survey is the best version developed thus far. First, Form D reliabilities are consistently higher than those obtained with the other forms. Second, Form D is intrinsically more interesting than the more traditional rating methods. Third, we have obtained a surprisingly high completion rate with Form D. Virtually all the school children tested to date have been able to complete Form D. And of a national area probability sample of 1,489 adult Americans tested by the National Opinion Research Center only about 5 percent were unable to complete the Value Survey, mainly because of illiteracy and secondarily because of a lack of interest or perseverance in completing the rankings. In no instance have we encountered a respondent who objected to the Value Survey as an invasion of privacy.

Individual Differences in Value System Stability. The frequency distribution of the individually obtained reliabilities reported in Table 2.2 are typically highly skewed, as shown in Table 2.3. Individual reliabilities obtained for college students tested with Form D range from the − .30's to the high .90's for terminal value systems and from the .10's to the high .90's for the instrumental value systems. For Form E, reliabilities range

TABLE 2.3   FREQUENCY DISTRIBUTIONS OF VALUE SYSTEM
RELIABILITIES FOR FORMS D AND E

	Terminal Value Scale		*Instrumental Value Scale*	
Reliability	*Form D*	*Form E*	*Form D*	*Form E*
.90 to .99	21	11	15	5
.80 to .89	84	54	46	26
.70 to .79	77	45	73	49
.60 to .69	29	35	43	31
.50 to .59	23	27	32	28
.40 to .49	8	9	20	20
.30 to .39	5	3	16	10
.20 to .29	—	2	4	7
.10 to .19	—	3	1	6
.00 to .09	2			2
−.10 to −.01	—			4
−.20 to −.11	—			1
−.30 to −.21	—			
−.40 to −.31	1			
N=	250	189	250	189

from about .10 to the high .90's for the terminal values, and from about
−.20 to the high .90's for the instrumental values. Feather (1971d) has
reported similar distributions for his South Australian sample. The
median of these reliabilities are as shown in Table 2.2.

Some Factors Affecting Individual Differences in Value System Stability.
The fact that individuals differ so widely in value system stability raises a
question about the correlates or determinants of such individual differences.
Empirical investigation of this problem has led us to discover some of
these correlates. We consistently found small, significant relationships in
the .20's to .30's between terminal value system stability and instrumental
value system stability: the more stable one's terminal value system, the
more stable also one's instrumental value system. Women have significantly
(or near-significantly) more stable terminal and instrumental value systems
than men. More stable terminal and instrumental value systems were also
found in younger compared with older college students, among those with
favorable attitudes toward civil rights compared with those having less
favorable attitudes, and among those preferring intellectual to social
activities.

Political party identification shows a significant relationship with
terminal value system stability but not with instrumental value system
stability. Those who identify themselves as conservative Democrats have

the least stable terminal value systems; those who report themselves as independent have the most stable systems.

We found quite a few variables to be significantly related to instrumental (but not to terminal) value system stability. More stable instrumental value systems were found among honors students as compared with non-honors students, among those planning to go on for higher degrees as compared with those not planning to do so, and among social science and communication majors as compared with home economics majors. College freshmen were found to have the most stable instrumental value systems and sophomores and juniors the least stable, suggesting that a college experience leads to significant reorganizations of instrumental value systems. More stable instrumental value systems were also found among self-styled liberals rather than self-styled conservatives, and among those favoring rather than opposing China's admission to the United Nations. Finally, college students who aspire to moderate future incomes have significantly more stable instrumental value systems than those who aspire to relatively high or low future incomes.

Hollen (1967) found no relationship between value system stability and dogmatism (Rokeach, 1960) or between value system stability and respondent ratings concerning degree of value commitment, importance, vagueness, difficulty, or uncertainty felt about one's value rankings. Other variables that are not significantly related to either terminal or instrumental value system stability are attitude toward public welfare, membership in fraternities or sororities, hours spent studying, degree of aspiration to surpass parents' income, authoritarian versus equalitarian relationship with parents, attitude toward the American presence in Vietnam, frequency of church attendance, rural versus urban background, and religious preference.

These findings with college students are supplemented by McLellan's (1970) findings with 13-, 15-, and 17-year old subjects. He found that age had a significant effect on both terminal and instrumental value system stability. But socioeconomic level and stages of moral development (Kohlberg, 1969) do not effect either terminal or instrumental value system stability.

It is not altogether clear at this stage of research what the major determinants of individual differences in value system stability really are. All that can now be said with some confidence is that sex, age, intellectual ability, and liberalism seem to be implicated as determinants of both terminal and instrumental value system stability. Other variables seem to be determinants only of terminal value system stability or only of instrumental value system stability; yet other variables seem to be unrelated to either kind of stability. The problem of the determinants of individual differences in value system stability continues to be a puzzling one which deserves continued attention.

2. Value System Change

The correlation (rho) between the rank orders obtained on two separate occasions is useful not only as a measure of value stability but also of value system change. A person's total value system may undergo change as a result of socialization, therapy, cultural upheaval, or as a result of experimental procedures designed to change values, as described briefly in earlier publications (Rokeach, 1968a, 1968b, 1971) and as will be described in more detail in later chapters. The smaller the correlation between rankings from test to retest, the greater the value system change. This measure will be employed later on in considering the effects of certain experimental procedures on change in value systems.

3. Value System Similarity between
Two Persons

The correlation (rho) between the rank orderings obtained from any two persons is an index of the similarity between their value systems. Beech (1966) employed this measure in his study of the effects of value system similarity on interpersonal attraction. Sikula (1970) used it in his study of value compatibility between college roommates in conflict and non-conflict with one another. Such a measure would be useful in studies of the acquaintance process (Newcomb, 1961), in studies of similarity in value systems between spouses, peers, parents, and children, etc.

4. Value System Similarity in More Than
Two Persons

The coefficient of concordance can be employed as an index of value system similarity in more than two persons. Thus, in the American sample obtained through the National Opinion Research Center, the terminal value system concordance coefficient obtained for Jews, Catholics, Protestants, and the nonreligious are .37, .28, .28, and .24, respectively, suggesting that Jews are the most and nonreligious the least culturally homogeneous. The concordance coefficients for the same four groups are much lower for instrumental value systems, .21, .16, .21, and .20, respectively, which are obviously not substantially different from one another. But a difficulty with concordance coefficients, is that methods for measuring significance of difference between them are not readily available.

McQuitty's pattern-analysis techniques are probably more useful for the investigation of value system similarities and differences among groups. Given any number of individuals or subgroups of individuals, one correlation matrix can be obtained to represent a matrix of terminal value similarities among subgroups and another to represent a matrix of instrumental value similarities. Pattern analytic techniques applied to such matrices can be usefully employed to serve a variety of purposes: to develop typologies, to ascertain the extent of value pattern similarity and difference within and between various subgroups of persons, and as a diagnostic tool to identify the value patterns of "disturbed" and "normal" individuals (McQuitty, Banks, and Frary, 1970).

5. Perceived Value Systems of Reference Persons and Groups

It is possible to obtain data concerning not only a person's own values but also those that a person might attribute to others. A person's perception of another's value system represents his image or stereotype of the other. The other may be another individual but it may also be a group, a social organization, a total society, or even an ideal society. Graham has pointed out "that people have rather definite impressions of what organizations are like. People tend to ascribe traits and personality attributes to organizations, and the ability to do this appears to be unrelated to the degree of personal involvement or direct contact with the organizations" (1970, p. 1).

We attribute values no less than "traits and personality attributes" to reference persons and groups. Ascribed values can readily be ascertained with such slightly modified instructions as: "Now rank the same values the way you think your spouse (or General Motors, or white or black Americans, or American society) would rank them."

The correlation (rho) between own values and the perceived values of other persons or groups is a measure of perceived similarity, or of positive or negative identification with (or alienation from) others.

6. Reliability of Single Values

The rank-ordering method permits us to obtain stability measures not only for value systems considered as a whole but also for each value separately. Results for Form D test-retest reliabilities that were obtained for time intervals ranging from three to seven weeks are shown for each of the 36 values in Table 2.1. For terminal values the product-moment reliabilities range from .51 for *a sense of accomplishment* to .88 for *salvation*. Three of the 18 values have reliabilities in the .70's, ten have reliabilities in the .60's, and four are in the .50's. Their average reliability is around .65. The reliabilities of the 18 instrumental values are somewhat lower, averaging around .60. They range from .45 for *responsible* to .70 for *ambitious*. Nine of them are in the .60's and seven are in the .50's.

Feather (1973) has reported the reliabilities obtained for each value separately using Form E of the Value Survey. His subjects were South Australian college students and his test-retest interval was five weeks. For the terminal values, the reliabilities ranged from .40 for *wisdom* to .87 for *salvation*, the median reliability being .63. For the instrumental values, the reliabilities ranged from .37 for *capable* and *responsible* to .76 for *imaginative*, the median reliability being .56. Comparing Feather's data with those reported in Table 2.1 it is obvious that they are remarkably similar despite the fact that one set was obtained with college students in the United States and the other in South Australia. It is also apparent that the individual reliabilities obtained for Form D (gummed label) are on the whole somewhat higher than those obtained for Form E (mimeographed version), about two-thirds of the Form D reliabilities being higher than those obtained with Form E.

Considering both sets of data, those obtained in the United States and those obtained in South Australia by Feather, it can be concluded that they are on the whole rather respectable in size, considering the fact that they were all obtained with single-item tests that are one word or at most one phrase long. Likert scales for each of the 36 values composed of, say, 10 items each (making a total of 360 items) would probably be no more reliable than the present single-item scales.

7. Change in Single Values

The measurement of change in single values is useful in a variety of research contexts—in experimental studies of value change to be reported later in this book, in studies of change as a function of development (Beech and Schoeppe, 1970), education (Feather, 1972d), therapy, or other intervening experiences.

To round out our reliability studies, we have measured the extent to which the test-retest change in any given value is a function of its initial ranking position. Are values that are ranked high in importance more stable than those ranked middle or low in importance? Figure 2.1 shows the results obtained for Form D, which are typical of results also obtained with earlier versions of the Value Survey (Hollen, 1967). It is obvious from Figure 2.1 that although terminal values are generally more stable than instrumental values from test to retest, those initially ranked as most and least important change the least from test to retest; those ranked in the middle change the most. The relationship is clearly U-shaped, suggesting that the respondents rank values at the high and low ends of the scale with considerably more confidence than those they rank in the middle. There is no reason to suspect, however, that this U-shaped relationship is peculiar to the present research. It is probably inherent in all ranking procedures.

ORDER EFFECTS

Since the terminal and instrumental values are presented to the respondent in alphabetical order, there is the possibility that he will rank those higher up in the alphabetical order as more important than those lower down. Such an order effect is, of course, methodologically undesirable and, if empirically found, would require elimination or correction. Cochrane and Rokeach (1970) investigated the possible presence of such order effects in several samples. Analysis of Form D data from a national sample of adult Americans (N = 1,409) showed no order effect for the 18 terminal

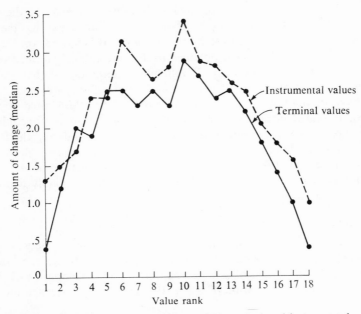

Figure 2.1 Median amount of change for terminal and instrumental
values ranked first to last (N = 115).

values, the rho correlation between alphabetical order and median value
rankings being .07. But Table 2.4 shows that the correlation between
alphabetical order and the median value rankings of instrumental values
was .43 which is significant beyond the .05 level. Moreover, the median
rankings of the first nine values in the alphabetical order was almost four
scale units higher than the median rankings of the second nine values—
7.62 against 11.46. Various subgroups of the national sample—black and
white, male and female, high and low education—showed similar order
effects for instrumental values, the correlations ranging from .33 to .46.

To determine whether this order effect was inherent in the test, data
from two other samples were examined. Male prison inmates (N = 363)
showed the same order effect for instrumental values but a sample of
university students (N = 298) did not.

Now requiring some explanation was the presence of an order effect
on the 18 instrumental values but not on the 18 terminal values, its presence
in the national and prison samples but not in the college sample. The most
obvious explanation is that the order effect represents a response set
(Cronbach, 1946, 1950) which spuriously elevates the ranking of values
appearing toward the top of the alphabetical list and spuriously lowers
those appearing toward the bottom. Possibly the effect is evident on the
instrumental values because these values are always ranked after the
terminal values are ranked, when the subject is more fatigued. Its absence

TABLE 2.4 RHO CORRELATIONS BETWEEN ALPHABETICAL
ORDER AND RANK ORDER OF INSTRUMENTAL VALUES

	Values		
	1–18	*1–9*	*10–18*
National sample			
All subjects	+0.43*	−0.20	−0.66*
White	+0.38	−0.20	−0.71*
Black	+0.33	−0.36	−0.71*
Male	+0.46*	−0.06	−0.71*
Female	+0.37	−0.31	−0.73*
High education	+0.34	−0.15	+0.32
Low education	+0.36	−0.25	−0.76*
Prison sample	+0.27	+0.34	−0.53
College sample	+0.08	+0.07	−0.15

* = $p < .05$.

from the college group, however, would argue against such an interpretation.

We reasoned that if the results found for the national and prison samples were indeed the results of an order effect, it should also be evident within sections of the instrumental value scale as well as across the whole scale. Rho correlations were computed for the first and second nine value rankings separately for various groups and subgroups shown in Table 2.4. The correlations between alphabetical order and median rankings were usually found to be negative rather than positive within each half of the instrumental scale. This is especially evident in the second half of the list where six of the nine rho coefficients are negative and significant. This finding clearly rules out the possibility that the subjects had been influenced by alphabetical order when ranking the instrumental values.

We are left with the possibility that the top half of the instrumental value scale (but not the terminal value scale) happens, by chance, to contain some values that are generally regarded as more important than those contained in the second half. Inspection reveals that such values as *honest*, *ambitious*, and *courageous* appear near the top of the list. In the lower half of the alphabetical list there appear such values as *intellectual*, *obedient*, and *polite*, which are perhaps less valued regardless of their alphabetical position. College students have been consistently found to differ from the national sample and also from the prison sample in assigning considerably higher rankings to such values as *intellectual*, *logical*, and *imaginative*, values appearing in the lower half of the alphabetical list, which college students can reasonably be expected to rank more highly. This would explain why there is no correlation between alphabetical order and value rankings for the college sample and it would also explain why there is a positive correlation between alphabetical order and value rankings in the national and prison samples.

In the light of these findings it can be concluded that what initially appeared to be a possible methodological defect in the Value Survey has a more plausible alternative explanation, and does not necessitate revision of the Value Survey.

SOCIAL DESIRABILITY

Kelly, Silverman, and Cochrane (1972) have studied the effects of social desirability in responding to the 18 terminal values. Experimental subjects filled out the terminal values first under standard instructions and also sometime afterward under "social desirability" instructions; that is, the subject was asked to arrange the values "in the order that you think would make you appear most favorably in the eyes of the experimenter. . . . The final ranking should portray you in a fashion you deem to be the most socially desirable." A rho correlation was computed for each subject, between his rankings of the terminal values administered under the two sets of instructions. Presumably, the higher the correlation the greater the likelihood that the subject had responded in a socially desirable manner to *both* administrations and, therefore, the more this index should be correlated with an independent measure of social desirability. The independent measure that the subjects also filled out—between the first and second administrations of the ranking task—was the Marlowe-Crowne Social Desirability Scale. The resulting correlation between the two sets of scores was only $-.09$, suggesting that there was no significant relationship between the tendency to respond in a socially desirable manner and rankings of the Value Survey under standard instructions.

These results suggest, then, that the ranking of the terminal values cannot be explained as arising from a social desirability response set. Unfortunately, however, Kelly, Silverman, and Cochrane did not investigate this issue with respect to the instrumental values, and it therefore still remains an open question whether social desirability is a factor that influences the instrumental value rankings.

THE STRUCTURE OF VALUES

Any rank-order procedure is, of course, an ipsative procedure (one that generates nonindependent data within individuals), and thus fails to satisfy the assumption of complete independence when statistical comparisons are made across individuals. Guilford (1954) cautions us against analyzing ipsative scores over a sample of subjects by "R-technique." Cattell (1944) is, however, of the opinion that ipsative measures can also be employed normatively across individuals. The Value Survey can be employed to yield what Cattell calls normative ipsative data. It is true, of course, that statistical tests performed on such data across individuals violate the assumption of independence. "Specifically, attribute scores experimentally dependent on one another, and the number of attributes measured is the primary determinant of the degree of the artifactual interdependency" (Hicks, 1970, p. 181). With 18 values, the extent to which this independence assumption is violated is relatively small, the average intercorrelation being only −.06. That is, once a person has ranked 17 values, the ranking of the eighteenth value is completely determined. This amount of ipsativity can be tolerated, but it should nevertheless be taken into account when interpreting statistical findings.

With the ipsative nature of the value data in mind, we may now ask: To what extent are the rankings of the 36 terminal and instrumental values intercorrelated with one another, and—more important—to what extent they can be accounted for by a smaller number of factors? Table 2.5 shows the correlation matrix obtained for the 36 values from the national NORC area probability sample of 1,409 adult Americans over twenty-one. Although a large proportion of the 630 correlations shown are statistically significant (given the large number of cases on which they are based), it is nevertheless obvious that they are on the whole surprisingly small in magnitude. The highest correlation is +.35 (between *a comfortable life* and *pleasure*) and the lowest is −.32 (between *a comfortable life* and *wisdom*). As would be expected with ipsative data, about 58 percent of the correlations are negative, and 42 percent are positive. The average intercorrelation among terminal values (variables 1 to 18) is −.06, and the average correlation is also −.06 among the instrumental values (variables 19 to 36). These findings are precisely what would be expected by chance from ipsative measures. The average correlation between terminal and instrumental values, which is not dependent on ipsative measures, is only .01. These low correlations can be interpreted as being a function, in part, of how the values had been selected in the first place, namely, to maximize diversity and to minimize overlap *within* each of the two sets of terminal and instrumental values. But the correlations *between* terminal and instrumental values are also surprisingly low, even though we made no special effort to minimize overlap of meaning between terminal and instrumental values. It can be anticipated on logical grounds that at least some of these correlations would turn out to be substantial, but this was not found to be the case. Thus, the correlations between the terminal value *salvation* and the instrumental value *forgiving* is only .28; the correlation between the terminal value *mature love* and the instrumental value *loving* is only .31; the correlation between the terminal value *a sense of accomplishment* and the instrumental value *capable* is only .14. These findings suggest that the 36 values of the Value Survey are for the most part negligibly correlated with one another in the adult American population, despite the fact that 306 of the 630 correlations are not altogether independent of one another because they are ipsative in nature.

TABLE 2.5   CORRELATION MATRIX OF 36 VALUES OBTAINED FOR NATIONAL SAMPLE OF AMERICANS

		1	2	3	4	5	6	7	8	9	10	11	12	13	14	15	16
A comfortable life	1																
An exciting life	2	19															
A sense of accomp.	3	−10	11														
A world at peace	4	−08	−18	−20													
A world of beauty	5	−04	10	−01	06												
Equality	6	−21	−13	−04	18	05											
Family security	7	03	−09	−01	−10	−14	−16										
Freedom	8	−16	−08	−05	06	−07	14	−11									
Happiness	9	17	02	−14	−14	−11	−23	08	−12								
Inner harmony	10	−27	−13	07	−10	−01	00	−10	−04	−03							
Mature love	11	−08	09	−07	−23	−04	−14	03	−10	05	03						
National security	12	−08	−21	−10	28	−16	01	01	09	−22	−10	−16					
Pleasure	13	35	23	−14	−15	−02	−23	−03	−10	21	−21	−03	−15				
Salvation	14	−23	−32	−23	06	−13	−03	−06	−06	−13	−02	−07	04	−23			
Self-respect	15	−15	−15	08	−21	−17	−15	02	−09	−09	02	−06	−12	−08	−02		
Social recognition	16	06	−02	−02	−10	−12	−08	−06	−07	−05	−14	−15	02	05	−15	07	
True friendship	17	−07	−11	−15	−10	−05	−15	−05	−11	07	−08	−07	−15	01	00	09	−0
Wisdom	18	−32	−17	06	−16	−08	−01	−09	−08	−17	08	−01	−11	−25	09	12	−0
Ambitious	19	19	07	10	02	−13	−05	04	−02	02	−13	−09	09	03	−05	−02	1
Broadminded	20	−00	05	06	04	04	10	−08	−05	−05	02	01	03	−03	−11	−02	−0
Capable	21	10	08	14	−08	−04	−08	06	−02	−01	−01	−05	04	03	−11	03	0
Cheerful	22	15	09	−14	03	12	−07	01	−11	19	−09	00	−12	23	−06	−06	−0
Clean	23	27	−04	−19	05	00	−09	08	−08	16	−14	−06	−00	18	05	−02	0
Courageous	24	−07	07	01	−02	01	03	−05	05	−09	04	−04	00	−02	04	−03	0
Forgiving	25	−13	−18	−13	15	−01	06	−03	−05	−01	07	−02	01	−09	28	−06	−1
Helpful	26	−07	−10	−09	10	10	18	−06	−02	01	00	−08	−02	−03	13	−09	−0
Honest	27	−12	−14	−06	04	−08	03	07	03	02	01	02	01	−10	16	04	−0
Imaginative	28	−10	25	18	−08	18	05	−13	05	−12	09	11	−08	01	−22	−05	−0
Independent	29	05	09	12	−08	−02	−06	−03	11	−05	−03	−04	02	06	−14	08	0
Intellectual	30	−08	04	11	02	05	07	−09	07	−10	04	−04	05	−12	−10	00	0
Logical	31	−15	02	18	−12	02	03	−03	08	−10	17	05	04	−10	−14	07	−0
Loving	32	−08	03	−15	−04	04	−07	06	−06	15	03	31	−19	03	08	−08	−1
Obedient	33	10	−09	−13	06	−08	00	01	03	−01	−06	−04	03	02	11	−02	0
Polite	34	12	−12	−16	04	−05	−07	05	−04	11	−12	−04	03	06	04	05	0
Responsible	35	−11	−06	10	−08	−14	−01	11	03	−06	05	−02	06	−12	02	11	0
Self-controlled	36	−14	−11	05	−03	−02	−02	03	02	−11	08	02	01	−10	08	10	−0

Note: Decimals have been omitted.

Comparable analyses carried out on subgroups of the total sample of adult Americans—white and black, male and female—confirm the findings obtained for adult Americans considered as a whole. Table 2.6 shows the range of correlations obtained separately for white and black Americans and for American males and females as well as for the total sample. The highest positive correlation found in these five matrices ($630 \times 5 = 3,150$ correlations) is .41, and the highest negative correlation is −.38. The conclusion that seems inescapable from all these data is that the ranking of any one of the 36 values is for all practical purposes unrelated to the ranking of any other value, and it is therefore unlikely that the 36 values can be effectively reduced to some smaller number of factors.

Nevertheless, factor analyses of these matrices suggest that the 36 values are not altogether independent of one another. Certain values do tend to cluster together to form factors, although no factor accounts for more than eight percent of the variance. For the total sample of adult Americans we have been able to identify seven bipolar factors by varimax

(N = 1,409)

17	18	19	20	21	22	23	24	25	26	27	28	29	30	31	32	33	34	35	36
04																			
−09	−14																		
−06	06	01																	
−06	−00	18	06																
12	−17	−09	00	03															
03	−20	06	−12	−08	26														
−03	06	00	−01	−01	−11	−14													
12	00	−23	03	−26	07	00	−02												
08	−05	−15	−06	−14	03	−00	−04	24											
05	05	−16	−16	−19	−10	−01	−12	06	06										
−08	03	−01	06	06	−09	−23	07	−22	−07	−22									
−09	−00	01	−05	02	−20	−16	03	−26	−19	−11	10								
−11	16	−01	01	02	−22	−30	−01	−22	−12	−09	17	13							
−10	14	−13	05	07	−23	−32	−06	−21	−17	−08	21	10	25						
11	−03	−27	−17	−25	15	02	−15	18	02	09	−10	−20	−19	−17					
01	−06	−03	−21	−20	−08	08	−16	08	−01	07	−25	−12	−21	−23	06				
13	−09	−15	−20	−20	06	19	−16	01	−04	12	−29	−19	−22	−20	09	29			
−03	15	−05	−21	02	−29	−19	−12	−19	−15	09	−07	03	01	08	−09	00	00		
01	14	−16	−14	−16	−25	−15	−04	−04	−13	02	−10	−01	−02	08	−04	−03	−00	21	

rotation, as shown in Table 2.7, which all together account for only 41 percent of the variance.

A study of the factorial structure of the Value Survey is informative despite the fact that a majority of the variance is not accounted for by the seven factors. Recall the distinctions made earlier in Chapter 1 between terminal values that are social versus personal in orientation, and between instrumental values that concern competence on the one hand and morality on the other. Factors 2 and 4 provide reasonably strong empirical support for these distinctions. Factor 2 consists primarily of instrumental values, those loading at one pole reflecting a concern with competence (*logical, imaginative, intellectual,* and *independent*) and at the other pole a concern with a religious kind of morality (*forgiving, salvation, helpful, clean*). Factor 4 includes only terminal values, those having high positive loadings being social in nature (*a world at peace, national security, equality* and *freedom*), while those having high negative loadings being personal in nature (*true friendship, self-respect*).

TABLE 2.6 HIGHEST AND LOWEST CORRELATIONS FOUND WITHIN 36-VALUE MATRIX FOR TOTAL
NATIONAL SAMPLE, AMERICAN WHITES AND BLACKS, AND AMERICAN MALES AND FEMALES

Group	N	Highest Correlation (between)		Lowest Correlation (between)
Total NORC sample	1,409	.35	(a comfortable life–pleasure)	-.32	(a comfortable life–wisdom)
Whites	1,195	.38	(a comfortable life–pleasure)	-.32	(an exciting life–salvation)
Blacks	202	.31	(obedient–polite)	-.35	(a comfortable life–wisdom)
Males	665	.30	(cheerful–clean)	-.38	(an exciting life–salvation)
Females	744	.41	(a comfortable life–pleasure)	-.32	(a comfortable life–wisdom)

TABLE 2.7 FACTOR ANALYTIC STRUCTURE OF AMERICAN VALUES (N = 1,409)

Factor	Highest Positive Loadings		Highest Negative Loadings		Percent of Variance
1. Immediate vs. delayed gratification	A comfortable life	(.69)	Wisdom	(−.56)	8.2
	Pleasure	(.62)	Inner harmony	(−.41)	
	Clean	(.47)	Logical	(−.34)	
	An exciting life	(.41)	Self-controlled	(−.33)	
2. Competence vs. religious morality	Logical	(.53)	Forgiving	(−.64)	7.8
	Imaginative	(.45)	Salvation	(−.56)	
	Intellectual	(.44)	Helpful	(−.39)	
	Independent	(.43)	Clean	(−.34)	
3. Self-constriction vs. self-expansion	Obedient	(.52)	Broadminded	(−.56)	5.5
	Polite	(.50)	Capable	(−.51)	
	Self-controlled	(.37)			
	Honest	(.34)			
4. Social vs. personal orientation	A world at peace	(.61)	True friendship	(−.49)	5.4
	National security	(.58)	Self-respect	(−.48)	
	Equality	(.43)			
	Freedom	(.40)			
5. Societal vs. family security	A world of beauty	(.58)	Family security	(−.50)	5.0
	Equality	(.39)	Ambitious	(−.43)	
	Helpful	(.36)	Responsible	(−.33)	
	Imaginative	(.30)	Capable	(−.32)	
6. Respect vs. love	Social recognition	(.49)	Mature love	(−.68)	4.9
	Self-respect	(.32)	Loving	(−.60)	
7. Inner- vs. other-directed	Polite	(.34)	Courageous	(−.70)	4.0
			Independent	(−.33)	

Table 2.7 displays two additional factors that are made up entirely of instrumental values. Factor 3 suggests an instrumental value orientation of self-constriction at one pole (*obedient, polite, self-controlled,* and *honest*) and self-expansion at the other pole (*broadminded, capable*). Factor 7 suggests a different type of instrumental value orientation: other-directedness (*polite*) versus inner-directedness (*courageous, independent*). The remaining three of the seven factors—factors 1, 5, and 6—implicate terminal as well as instrumental values. Factor 1, immediate versus delayed gratification, seems to represent a social status factor—a lower class versus a middle class value orientation (Rokeach and Parker, 1970). Factor 5 identifies a value orientation wherein the family is the focus of concern at one pole, and a broader value orientation that embraces one's nation and the world beyond is the focus at the other. Finally, factor 6 points to a value orientation that can be identified simply as a concern with love, at one pole, and with respect, at the other.

The preceding is a summary of the factorial structure of values found in the national sample considered as a whole. Comparable analyses carried out with subgroups of white and black Americans and with subgroups of male and female Americans yield results that are highly similar and therefore will not be repeated here. The total amount of variance accounted for by seven factors—in whites and blacks, in males and females—is also around 40 percent. When the data for the national sample and for the subgroups of black and white and male and female Americans are considered all together, it must again be concluded that the 36 terminal and instrumental values are not readily reducible to some smaller number. Smallest space analyses (Guttman, 1966; Lingoes, 1966) lead to similar conclusions. We found essentially similar clusterings with Guttman's nonmetric technique as with factor analytic techniques. Smallest space analysis, moreover, revealed that the values form a circular structure, what Guttman calls a "circumplex," suggesting that the 36 values are at the same level of generality.

VALUES AS INDICATORS OF NEEDS

If values are indeed the cognitive representations of needs, as has been suggested in Chapter 1, then variations in value rankings should be systematically related to variations in needs. The standard way of measuring needs is by the projective TAT method employed by McClelland (1953), Atkinson (1958), and their associates. Rokeach and Berman (1971) studied the value correlates of n Achievement, n Affiliation, and n Power in a college sample of 74 subjects. They found that values and needs were indeed significantly related to one another but not quite in ways that might have been anticipated in advance. Need for achievement was the most positively correlated with (higher rankings of) the instrumental values *independent* ($r = .35$) and *intellectual* ($r = .25$) and the most negatively correlated with the instrumental values *honest* ($r = -.35$) and *obedient* ($r = -.25$). Other values that might have been expected on a priori grounds to be positively related to n Achievement—*a sense of accomplishment, ambitious,* and *capable*—were not significantly related. These findings suggest that persons who have a high need for achievement do not necessarily consciously think of themselves as having achievement-related values any more than do those having a low need for achievement. Instead, it would seem that persons high in n Achievement tend to transform this need into values for independence and intellectualism and tend to think of themselves as caring less for the values of honesty and conformity.

The values that showed the largest positive correlation with n Affiliation were *true friendship* ($r = .32$) and *a world at peace* ($r = .23$), and the value showing the largest negative correlation with n Affiliation was *mature love* ($r = -.24$). As for n Power, *freedom* was found to be the value that was the most positively associated with it ($r = -.25$), and *obedient* was the one that was the most negatively associated with it ($r = -.30$).

These findings suggest that our value measures can indeed be taken as measures of needs, but they also suggest that the relation between them is by no means a simple one. The question whether values, as measured by the Value Survey, or needs, as measured by TAT stories, is a more valid measure can perhaps best be assessed by determining their external or predictive validity. Rokeach and Berman (1971) have found that certain values are better predictors of academic performance than n Achievement. But more extensive evidence than this will be needed before concluding that the present approach to the measurement of values is as good a predictor of need-related behavior or a better one than the more traditional method of measuring needs.

THE MEANING OF VALUES

A major question that can be raised is whether the values under consideration mean the same thing to all respondents. Several answers to this question are possible.

First, there is a strictly behavioristic answer: Regardless of the meaning of a given value, it represents a specific stimulus and all that matters is whether or not this stimulus leads to predictable and replicable responses. Such a behavioristic position is altogether indifferent to the question of meaning and concerns itself only with S-R connections.

Second, if by "the meaning" of values we mean connotative meaning, it is possible to measure it with Osgood's semantic differential technique (Osgood, Suci, and Tannenbaum, 1957). Homant (1969) measured the semantic meaning of each of the 18 terminal and 18 instrumental values and correlated semantic differential indices with the rank ordering of values. The median correlations he obtained between the evaluative factor of the semantic differential and the rank ordering of the terminal and instrumental values were .68 and .62, respectively. For the potency factor the correlations were .36 and .46, respectively, and for the activity factor the correlations were .45 and .32, respectively. When we take the far-from-perfect reliabilities of the terminal and instrumental scales into account it is obvious that the correlations between value rankings and Osgood's evaluative factor (which is of greatest interest here) are very high indeed. Homant's findings clearly indicate that simple value rankings from 1 to 18 give us essentially the same information about a person as that obtained with the more complex semantic differential. These findings also suggest that the value rankings measure essentially the same kind of meaning as that measured by Osgood's evaluative factor and that they do so notwithstanding its simplicity.

A third kind of answer emerges when we consider the results obtained with the defining phrases present and absent. Recall that Forms A and B differed from one another primarily in that the former presented the values without definitions while the latter presented them with definitions added in parentheses. The reliability of Forms A and B are nevertheless virtually identical. More important, however, are the data concerning validity. Many findings to be reported in later chapters show systematic relations between values and attitudes and between values and behavior. The magnitude of these relations is essentially the same for all forms, regardless of whether the values are defined. If the values employed in the Value Survey were semantically tyrannical, meaning different things to different people, significant results of a systematic kind would not be possible.

Finally, far more important than semantic meaning is the *psychological significance* that a particular value has for a particular person. The psychological significance of a particular value ranking can best be grasped by noting the manner in which the respondent ranks it in relation to other relevant values. Even if the semantic meaning of a value were identical to two persons, their psychological significance might be very different. *Salvation*, for example, may have identical semantic meaning for two Christian ministers who both rank it first. But suppose the first also ranks the instrumental value *forgiving* first and the second ranks it last. It would then be reasonable to infer that even if *salvation* has the same semantic meaning to both ministers, its psychological significance must nevertheless be very different to them.

Similarly, consider some findings concerning *freedom* and *equality* already reported elsewhere (Rokeach, 1968a, 1968b) and to be reported in more detail in later chapters. Both Hitler and Lenin ranked *freedom* low on their scale of values. Does *freedom* mean the same thing to Hitler and to Lenin? The psychological significance of this fact becomes apparent only when it is noted that Hitler also ranks *equality* low, whereas Lenin ranks *equality* high on his scale of values. These findings suggest that in Hitler's case the denial of *freedom* by the state is a weapon to coerce inequality; in Lenin's case the denial of *freedom* is also a weapon, but a weapon to coerce equality. Thus, the psychological significance of *freedom*, or its denial, is obviously different for Hitler and for Lenin, even though both rank it equally low and even though it may be semantically identical to both. Similarly, both Goldwater and the socialists place a high value on *freedom*. In Goldwater's case, high regard for *freedom* can best be understood by noting also his low regard for *equality*; in the socialists' case, it can best be understood by noting their high regard for *equality*.

Thus, the psychological significance that a particular value has for a particular person must be inferred from observations about the way he relates it to other values within his value system rather than from procedures designed to measure semantic meanings of particular words symbolizing values. In the final analysis, it is probably scientifically more fruitful to be concerned with the question of psychological significance than with the question of the semantic meaning of values.

CONCLUDING COMMENTS ON
THE MEASUREMENT OF VALUES

A major reason psychologists have paid more attention to the attitude than to the value concept is that more sophisticated methods have been available for measuring attitudes because of the efforts of such men as Bogardus, Thurstone, Likert, and Guttman. This greater availability of methods for measuring attitudes brings to mind Abraham Kaplan's *law of the instrument*: "Give a small boy a hammer, and he will find that everything he encounters needs pounding" (1964, p. 28). All such sophisticated research tools notwithstanding, theoretical considerations suggest that values are nevertheless more central than attitudes as determinants of human behavior.

The Value Survey was designed to serve as an all-purpose instrument for research on human values. Even though it is ordinal and ipsative, it is in many other respects an ideal instrument. It is simple in design and economical to administer to individuals and groups. In a matter of 10 to 20 minutes the Value Survey provides us with reasonably reliable and (as will be reported later) reasonably valid measures of variables that are of central importance to the individual and to his society. Research to date suggests that the Value Survey's instructions are easily grasped by people between the ages of 11 and 90, providing that they can read, and that comparative data can be obtained for people within this age range. Respondents tell us that they find the Value Survey, especially the gummed label version, interesting, thought-provoking, and ego-involving. Responses to the Value Survey are directly expressed in quantitative terms, thus eliminating the need to score it. Nonetheless, the Value Survey is in every sense a projective test because it elicits responses—rankings—that come from internal demands rather than from external stimulus characteristics. Unlike other projective tests, however, it does not have to be disguised, does not allow free responses, and does not require trained personnel to administer it. As far as is presently known, it is free of such methodological defects as order effects and social desirability response sets. It yields separate quantitative measures of values and systems of values. As will be reported in a later chapter, it seems to be sensitive to differences between cultures, institutions, group membership, and personal experience. It can be employed to test theoretically derived hypotheses but it can also be used in a purely empirical manner to describe similarities in and differences between any two groups one may happen to be interested in. Finally, the Value Survey can be meaningfully employed across all the social science disciplines to provide data that are substantively relevant to each discipline.

The danger of such an instrument is that it will not only exhibit the properties of Kaplan's hammer but also those of an all-purpose patent medicine. Not only will "everything need pounding" but the Value Survey might also be seen as "good for everything." Ironically, though, it can be suggested that the measurement of values *is* relevant to virtually any human problem one might be able to think of.

PART TWO
Values in American Society

3
Values as Social Indicators of the Quality of Life in America

From de Tocqueville's classic account about America, written a century and a half ago, to the present, a great deal has been written from an impressionistic or journalistic perspective about the values of American society. Supplementing such accounts there are numerous other studies which attempt to inform us in quantitative terms about the values that are distinctive in American society. But an examination of the social science literature quickly reveals that virtually all studies of American values, and of cross-cultural studies as well, suffer from two major methodological defects: The samples employed are typically drawn from the most educated and affluent strata of society, mainly from college students; the psychometric tests employed are typically complex and lengthy, requiring educated respondents with perseverance and the ability to understand instructions and test content.

The simplicity and brevity of the Value Survey freed us from such limitations and enabled us to measure quantitatively the values of a national sample drawn from all strata of American society. As previously stated, the Value Survey was administered in the latter part of April 1968, by the National Opinion Research Center to a sample of adult Americans over twenty-one. Other data obtained from this national sample included the usual demographic information, reactions to the assassination of Dr. Martin Luther King that had occurred a few weeks before, responses to questions concerning many aspects of civil rights, attitudes toward the poor, the American presence in Vietnam, student protest, church involvement in the political and social affairs of society, and preference for the various presidential candidate prior to the national conventions of 1968.

The purpose of this chapter is to report on the values found in various segments of American society—men and women, the poor and the rich, the educated and the uneducated, white and black Americans, the young and the old, the religious and the nonreligious, and the politically conservative and the less conservative. These findings provide us with perhaps the first descriptive data of a systematic nature on the distribution of values in a cross section of adult American society, and they may be regarded as one important social indicator of the "quality of life" in America (Gross, 1966; Bauer, 1966; U.S. Department of HEW, 1969; Gross and Springer, 1970). Moreover, this chapter contains cross-cultural value comparisons among selected samples obtained in the United States, Australia, Canada, and Israel.

Frequency distributions of rankings obtained for each of the 18 terminal and 18 instrumental values are presented in Appendix B, separately for American men and women and separately for subgroups varying in income, education, race, age, and religion. These distributions, although of some interest to the general reader, will be especially useful to research workers who might wish to compare their own frequency distributions with those obtained for the national sample.

A few comments are in order about the frequency distributions shown in Appendix B. It is difficult to find a single one of the 36 values about which it can be said that it is normally distributed. Each value seems to have its own distinctive nonparametric distribution, and many of them show frequency distributions that are highly skewed in one direction or the other. The frequency distributions for *a world at peace* and *family security*, for instance, are heavily skewed toward the higher ranks. *Pleasure* and *an exciting life*, on the other hand, show distributions that are heavily skewed in the other direction, with most of the rankings piling up at the low end.

Because these frequency distributions deviate so markedly from normality and from one another, a circumstance to be expected with ranked data, the measure of central tendency that was considered to be the most appropriate is the median rather than mean, and the nonparametric Median test (Siegel, 1956) was selected as the main test of statistical significance. The Median test is a chi-square test of the significance of difference between the number of persons in two or more subgroups who score above and below the group median. Tabular displays of the data to be presented throughout this work will show the median rankings for each value as well as the rank order of these medians, to be called the *composite rank order*. The composite rank order will be useful not only as a general index of the relative positon of a particular value in the total hierarchy of values but also when comparing the position of a particular value across groups.

It is necessary to draw the reader's attention to the fact that sometimes the magnitude of medians and composite rank orders will not correspond or be consistent with one another. These two measures will be employed only for convenience of description; they do not enter into calculations or statements of statistical significance. As already stated, the main technique we employed to ascertain statistical significance was the Median test.

It should also be mentioned that other tests of significance had been employed in the early stages of the research: t test, one-way analysis of variance, and the Kruskal-Wallis test (Siegel, 1956). Results obtained with all these tests were typically highly consistent with one another. But with small numbers of cases, the t test seemed to be generally more sensitive than the Median test.

VALUES OF AMERICAN MEN AND WOMEN

Tables 3.1 and 3.2 show the terminal and instrumental value rankings for all the men and women in the national sample. We may reasonably expect to find many differences associated with sex, since there is a great deal of evidence to suggest that society socializes men and women to play their sex-roles very differently. Men, for example, are conditioned to place a higher value on achievement and intellectual pursuits; women are conditioned to place a higher value on love, affiliation, and the family.

TABLE 3.1 TERMINAL VALUE MEDIANS AND COMPOSITE RANK ORDERS FOR AMERICAN MEN AND WOMEN

	Male	Female	
N =	665	744	p
A comfortable life	7.8 (4)	10.0 (13)	.001
An exciting life	14.6 (18)	15.8 (18)	.001
A sense of accomplishment	8.3 (7)	9.4 (10)	.01
A world at peace	3.8 (1)	3.0 (1)	.001
A world of beauty	13.6 (15)	13.5 (15)	—
Equality	8.9 (9)	8.3 (8)	—
Family security	3.8 (2)	3.8 (2)	—
Freedom	4.9 (3)	6.1 (3)	.01
Happiness	7.9 (5)	7.4 (5)	.05
Inner harmony	11.1 (13)	9.8 (12)	.001
Mature love	12.6 (14)	12.3 (14)	—
National security	9.2 (10)	9.8 (11)	—
Pleasure	14.1 (17)	15.0 (16)	.01
Salvation	9.9 (12)	7.3 (4)	.001
Self-respect	8.2 (6)	7.4 (6)	.01
Social recognition	13.8 (16)	15.0 (17)	.001
True friendship	9.6 (11)	9.1 (9)	—
Wisdom	8.5 (8)	7.7 (7)	.05

Figures shown are median rankings and, in parentheses, composite rank orders.

TABLE 3.2 INSTRUMENTAL VALUE MEDIANS AND COMPOSITE RANK
ORDERS FOR AMERICAN MEN AND WOMEN

		Male	Female	
N =		665	744	p
Ambitious		5.6 (2)	7.4 (4)	.001
Broadminded		7.2 (4)	7.7 (5)	—
Capable		8.9 (8)	10.1 (12)	.001
Cheerful		10.4 (12)	9.4 (10)	.05
Clean		9.4 (9)	8.1 (8)	.01
Courageous		7.5 (5)	8.1 (6)	—
Forgiving		8.2 (6)	6.4 (2)	.001
Helpful		8.3 (7)	8.1 (7)	—
Honest		3.4 (1)	3.2 (1)	—
Imaginative		14.3 (18)	16.1 (18)	.001
Independent		10.2 (11)	10.7 (14)	—
Intellectual		12.8 (15)	13.2 (16)	—
Logical		13.5 (16)	14.7 (17)	.001
Loving		10.9 (14)	8.6 (9)	.001
Obedient		13.5 (17)	13.1 (15)	—
Polite		10.9 (13)	10.7 (13)	—
Responsible		6.6 (3)	6.8 (3)	—
Self-controlled		9.7 (10)	9.5 (11)	—

Figures shown are median rankings and, in parentheses, composite
rank orders.

Before looking at the value differences between the sexes, however, it
is instructive to note the values that are uniformly considered to be the
most and least important by Americans of both sexes. At the top of the
terminal hierarchy for both sexes are *a world at peace, family security*, and
freedom, and at the bottom is *an exciting life*, and then *pleasure, social
recognition*, and *a world of beauty*. At the top of the instrumental value
hierarchy for both sexes are *honest, ambitious* and *responsible*, and at the
bottom are *imaginative, obedient, intellectual*, and *logical*. These value
patterns that are held in common by men and women thus seem to be
characteristic of Americans in general and might be different from, say,
Russian, or French or Israeli value patterns. Further consideration of
cross-cultural differences will be reserved for the end of this chapter.

Concerning sex differences, 12 of 18 terminal values as shown in Table
3.1, and 8 of 18 instrumental values, as shown in Table 3.2, discriminate
significantly between American men and women. The largest terminal
value difference is found for *a comfortable life*, which men rank fourth on
the average (composite rank order) and which women rank thirteenth.
The medians are 7.8 and 10.0, respectively. The largest instrumental value
difference is found for *imaginative*, which although ranked last on the

average by both sexes is nonetheless significantly more important for men. The median for men is 14.3 and for women, 16.1.

Men also place a significantly higher value than do women on *an exciting life, a sense of accomplishment, freedom, pleasure, social recognition, ambitious, capable, imaginative,* and *logical.* Conversely, women value significantly more than do men *a world at peace, happiness, inner harmony, salvation, self-respect, wisdom, cheerful, clean, forgiving,* and *loving.* These differences seem to be consistent with much that is intuitively known about differences in the ways men and women are socialized in Western industrial societies. Men, the traditional breadwinners, are more materialistic, achievement- and intellectually oriented. They are at the same time more pleasure-seeking than women, reflecting a double standard of hedonism that is probably not unique to American society. Women, on the other hand, seem more oriented toward religious values, personal happiness, love, self-respect, a personal life free of inner conflict, and a world free of intergroup conflict.

Not to be overlooked, however, are the 16 of the 36 values that show similarities rather than differences between the sexes. When comparing the values of men and women and, more generally, of any group with any other group, we are interested in value similarities no less than in value differences. Adult American women are no more romantic than men, no more affiliative, no more egalitarian, no more concerned with the security of the nation, and no more concerned with beauty than men. And contrary perhaps to popular conception, men are as concerned as women are with the security of the family and with being responsible. The men and women of America uniformly place a relatively high value on being honest and helpful, on being tolerant, and on standing up for one's ideas. By contrast, neither American men nor women care all that much for either independence or obedience, nor do they care much for politeness, intellectual pursuits, or self-control.

There are, of course, individual differences among American men and women in the extent to which they reflect the typical male and female value patterns that have been described. It is reasonable to expect that variations in traditional notions of masculinity-femininity will be reflected in variations of male and female value patterns. It is also reasonable to expect that women identifying themselves with the women's liberation movement will manifest a value pattern that is different from the typical female's and also from the typical male's. This expectation has recently received strong support in the work of Ball-Rokeach (1972).

SOCIAL CLASS VALUES: INCOME AND EDUCATION

Income and education are of special interest as indicators of status differences, and one may raise the question whether values are, in turn,

TABLE 3.3　TERMINAL VALUE MEDIANS AND COMPOSITE RANK ORDERS FOR GROUPS VARYING IN INCOME (N = 1,325)

Value	N =	Under $2,000 139	$2,000 –3,999 239	$4,000 –5,999 217	$6,000 –7,999 249	$8,000 –9,999 178	$10,000 –14,999 208	$15,000 and Over 95	p
A comfortable life		7.2 (6)	8.5 (7)	8.4 (7)	8.1 (6)	10.0 (11)	11.0 (13)	13.4 (15)	.001
An exciting life		15.3 (18)	15.4 (18)	15.6 (18)	15.4 (18)	15.4 (18)	15.2 (18)	14.3 (16)	—
A sense of accomplishment		10.4 (12)	10.3 (12)	9.1 (9)	9.4 (10)	8.4 (8)	7.6 (6)	6.1 (5)	.001
A world at peace		2.7 (1)	3.1 (1)	3.2 (1)	3.4 (2)	3.9 (2)	3.8 (2)	3.5 (1)	—
A world of beauty		13.6 (14)	12.7 (14)	13.5 (15)	14.0 (15)	13.8 (15)	13.7 (15)	12.6 (13)	—
Equality		7.0 (5)	8.5 (8)	8.3 (6)	9.0 (9)	7.8 (5)	9.7 (9)	7.5 (6)	.01
Family security		5.6 (2)	4.6 (2)	3.6 (2)	3.2 (1)	3.2 (1)	3.6 (1)	4.1 (2)	.001
Freedom		6.8 (4)	5.2 (3)	5.2 (3)	5.4 (3)	5.9 (3)	5.9 (3)	5.0 (3)	—
Happiness		7.7 (7)	8.0 (6)	7.1 (4)	6.9 (4)	7.6 (4)	8.1 (7)	9.2 (8)	.01
Inner harmony		11.6 (13)	10.9 (13)	10.8 (13)	10.5 (13)	10.2 (13)	9.9 (11)	9.2 (9)	.001
Mature love		14.4 (17)	14.0 (16)	12.3 (14)	12.2 (14)	10.8 (14)	11.5 (14)	11.8 (12)	—
National security		8.9 (11)	9.5 (11)	9.7 (12)	9.5 (11)	9.3 (10)	9.4 (8)	11.3 (11)	—
Pleasure		13.6 (16)	14.5 (17)	14.7 (16)	14.7 (17)	15.1 (17)	15.0 (16)	15.2 (18)	.001
Salvation		6.6 (3)	7.3 (5)	9.4 (11)	8.4 (8)	8.6 (9)	10.1 (12)	13.3 (14)	—
Self-respect		7.9 (8)	7.2 (4)	7.6 (5)	8.4 (7)	7.9 (6)	7.2 (4)	7.8 (7)	—
Social recognition		13.6 (15)	13.9 (15)	14.8 (17)	14.6 (16)	14.2 (16)	15.1 (17)	14.6 (17)	.001
True friendship		7.9 (9)	8.5 (10)	9.2 (10)	9.9 (12)	10.1 (12)	9.7 (10)	9.4 (10)	—
Wisdom		8.7 (10)	8.5 (9)	8.8 (8)	7.0 (5)	8.1 (7)	7.4 (5)	5.6 (4)	.01

Figures shown are median rankings and, in parentheses, composite rank orders.

TABLE 3.4 INSTRUMENTAL VALUE MEDIANS AND COMPOSITE RANK ORDERS FOR GROUPS VARYING IN INCOME (N = 1,325)

Value	Under $2,000	$2,000 -3,999	$4,000 -5,999	$6,000 -7,999	$8,000 -9,999	$10,000 -14,999	$15,000 and Over	p
N =	139	239	217	249	178	208	95	
Ambitious	8.0 (6)	6.9 (3)	6.1 (2)	6.8 (3)	6.6 (3)	5.8 (2)	6.4 (3)	—
Broadminded	8.6 (8)	7.2 (4)	8.1 (8)	8.1 (6)	7.1 (4)	6.4 (4)	7.0 (4)	—
Capable	9.5 (10)	10.5 (14)	9.8 (11)	9.3 (11)	9.8 (11)	8.4 (7)	8.8 (8)	.05
Cheerful	9.0 (9)	8.6 (9)	10.6 (14)	10.3 (12)	10.7 (12)	10.2 (11)	11.3 (14)	.01
Clean	6.4 (2)	7.3 (5)	8.0 (7)	8.6 (8)	9.3 (10)	10.4 (12)	14.4 (17)	.001
Courageous	7.5 (5)	8.1 (8)	8.0 (5)	7.5 (5)	7.4 (6)	8.0 (5)	7.2 (5)	—
Forgiving	6.4 (3)	6.5 (2)	7.3 (4)	6.8 (4)	7.4 (5)	8.1 (6)	10.7 (12)	.01
Helpful	7.1 (4)	7.4 (6)	8.0 (6)	8.2 (7)	8.9 (8)	9.3 (8)	9.1 (9)	.01
Honest	3.3 (1)	3.7 (1)	3.4 (1)	3.0 (1)	3.0 (1)	3.4 (1)	3.0 (1)	—
Imaginative	15.2 (18)	15.8 (18)	15.6 (18)	15.9 (18)	15.0 (18)	14.6 (18)	11.4 (15)	.001
Independent	10.5 (14)	10.3 (12)	10.0 (12)	10.7 (14)	11.4 (13)	11.0 (13)	8.3 (6)	—
Intellectual	13.9 (16)	13.4 (16)	13.3 (16)	13.6 (16)	13.1 (15)	12.1 (15)	8.6 (7)	.001
Logical	15.2 (17)	14.8 (17)	14.7 (17)	14.1 (17)	14.0 (16)	12.8 (16)	10.9 (13)	.001
Loving	10.0 (11)	10.3 (13)	9.5 (10)	9.1 (10)	8.8 (7)	10.2 (10)	9.8 (10)	.001
Obedient	12.0 (15)	12.4 (15)	13.3 (15)	13.2 (15)	14.2 (17)	14.3 (17)	15.3 (18)	.001
Polite	10.4 (13)	10.2 (11)	10.2 (13)	10.4 (13)	11.4 (14)	11.2 (14)	13.2 (16)	.001
Responsible	8.2 (7)	7.8 (7)	7.1 (3)	5.8 (2)	6.0 (2)	6.0 (3)	5.9 (2)	.001
Self-controlled	10.2 (12)	9.9 (10)	9.2 (9)	9.0 (9)	9.0 (9)	9.7 (9)	9.9 (11)	—

Figures shown are median rankings and, in parentheses, composite rank orders.

social indicators of income and educational differences. Tables 3.3 and 3.4 show the terminal and instrumental value rankings for adult Americans differing in income, and Tables 3.5 and 3.6 show the comparable findings for education. Considering the income differences first, 9 of the 18 terminal values and 11 of the 18 instrumental values show significant differences associated with being poor or rich. Of all 36 values, the instrumental value *clean* best distinguishes the poor from the rich. *Clean* decreases linearly as income increases, its composite ranking being second for those in the lowest income bracket and seventeenth for those in the highest income bracket. The low ranking of *clean* by the rich may be interpreted to mean that the affluent take cleanliness for granted, rather than that they do not care about it. Its high ranking by the poor suggests that they are far from indifferent to it, that those who must live under squalid conditions regard cleanliness as a very salient issue indeed.

The value that next best distinguishes the poor from the rich is *a comfortable life*, its composite rank being sixth for the poorest and fifteenth for the richest. As with *clean*, the poor may value *a comfortable life* highly because they lack it and the affluent considerably less because they already possess it.

[This interpretation cannot, however, be generalized to mean that values ranked low always indicate values already possessed and therefore taken for granted or, conversely, that values ranked high always indicate values people strive for because they are unavailable. There are several reasons why a given value may be ranked high or low. A person may, for instance, rank a value high because he wants something he does not have (e.g., poor people rank *clean* high) or because he already has it and wants more of it (e.g., artists rank *a world of beauty* high and professors rank *a sense of accomplishment* high). A person may rank a value low because he is not mature enough to know about it or to appreciate it (e.g., young children rank *a sense of accomplishment* low), because he already has it and therefore takes it for granted (e.g., affluent people rank *clean* low), or because he has neither had it nor wants it (e.g., most Americans rank *imaginative* and *intellectual* low). Thus, there are alternative reasons why a given value may receive a high or low ranking].

Other terminal and instrumental values that are noted to be more characteristic of the poor than of the rich are *salvation*, *true friendship*, being *cheerful*, *forgiving*, *helpful*, *obedient*, and *polite*. In contrast, values more characteristic of the affluent are *a sense of accomplishment*, *family security*, *inner harmony*, *mature love*, *wisdom*, being *capable*, *imaginative*, *intellectual* and *logical*.

The many value differences found between the very poor and rich almost suggest that they come from different cultures. The poor are more religious than the rich, more other-directed and conforming to traditional values, less concerned with taking responsibility and with the security of the family, and more motivated by a desire for affiliation with members of one's own sex than a desire for love with members of the opposite sex. Finally, the poor differ from the rich by placing a lower value on competence, intellectual, and self-actualization values. These findings suggest that the lower and middle class can indeed be characterized, as Kohn (1969) has found, as conformity-oriented on the one hand and self-directed on the other. But the present data also suggest that the culture of poverty (Lewis, 1966) and the culture of affluence differ far more extensively than Kohn's data indicate.

Present findings, however, provide no support for the widely held belief that the culture of poverty is hedonistic and present-oriented. Poor and rich alike rank *an exciting life* and *pleasure* well toward the bottom of the terminal value scale. The findings moreover provide no support for the hypothesis that the poor value immediate gratification more than do the rich; *self-control* has median rankings ranging between 9.0 and 10.2 for all income groups, and the differences in rankings are not significant.

By way of qualification, it should perhaps be stated that the value similarities and differences described here are not to be thought of in a dichotomous manner. It is not altogether correct to speak of a "culture of poverty" and a "culture of affluence." It is obvious from Tables 3.3 and 3.4 (and also from 3.5 and 3.6) that values vary as income varies. But it is also obvious that the value differences usually become more pronounced as the two extremes of poverty and affluence are being compared.

Considering next the relation between values and education, Tables 3.5 and 3.6 contain the value rankings obtained for seven groups of adult Americans who vary in educational level. But where 20 of the 36 values had distinguished significantly among respondents of varying income, now 25 of the 36 values are statistically significant. Here too we find that *clean* and *a comfortable life* best distinguish between the low- and the high-educated, the former ranking both of these values much higher. Two other values that also distinguish sharply, but this time in the opposite direction, are *a sense of accomplishment* and *logical*.

To conserve space, I will not discuss all the value differences associated with differences in education except to say that the pattern of results found for Americans differing in education is essentially the same as that found for Americans differing in income. Whichever measure of socioeconomic status is employed, income or education, pervasive value differences are found between those of lower and higher status. But between the two, education is a somewhat better indicator than income of social status, a finding that supports a good deal of sociological research. There is a somewhat larger value gap between the educated and the less-educated than between the rich and the poor, but either way the value gap is great.

The greater value gap between the less-educated and the educated as compared with the poor and the rich also becomes apparent from an analysis of the simple and multiple correlations between the 36 values on the one hand and education and income on the other. In the national

TABLE 3.5 TERMINAL VALUE MEDIANS AND COMPOSITE RANK ORDERS FOR GROUPS VARYING IN EDUCATION (N = 1,404)

Value		0–4 Yr.	5–8 Yr.	Some High Sch.	Comp. High Sch.	Some Coll.	Comp Coll.	Grad. Sch.	p
N =		64	263	320	426	180	90	61	
A comfortable life		5.5 (3)	7.3 (6)	8.0 (7)	9.5 (12)	11.2 (13)	12.3 (13)	13.8 (15)	.001
An exciting life		14.6 (18)	15.6 (18)	15.5 (18)	15.5 (18)	15.3 (18)	14.5 (16)	13.4 (14)	—
A sense of accomplishment		12.5 (13)	11.1 (12)	9.1 (11)	9.1 (9)	7.6 (6)	6.3 (5)	5.4 (4)	.001
A world at peace		3.1 (1)	2.8 (1)	2.9 (1)	3.7 (2)	4.2 (2)	4.4 (2)	3.5 (1)	.001
A world of beauty		13.6 (16)	13.2 (14)	13.5 (15)	14.0 (15)	13.6 (15)	13.3 (15)	11.3 (12)	—
Equality		10.8 (12)	8.6 (9)	8.5 (9)	8.3 (7)	8.4 (8)	9.2 (8)	8.0 (7)	—
Family security		4.5 (2)	4.6 (2)	3.7 (2)	3.3 (1)	3.5 (1)	3.6 (1)	6.6 (5)	.001
Freedom		6.0 (4)	6.1 (3)	5.7 (3)	5.2 (3)	5.4 (3)	4.7 (3)	5.1 (3)	—
Happiness		7.0 (5)	7.2 (5)	7.4 (4)	7.2 (4)	7.8 (7)	10.3 (10)	9.7 (10)	.001
Inner harmony		10.2 (9)	11.2 (13)	11.2 (13)	10.3 (13)	9.4 (9)	9.3 (9)	9.3 (9)	.001
Mature love		13.9 (17)	13.4 (15)	13.1 (14)	12.1 (14)	12.2 (14)	10.5 (11)	10.1 (11)	.001
National security		10.5 (10)	9.0 (10)	8.9 (10)	9.3 (10)	10.1 (10)	11.0 (12)	13.0 (13)	.01
Pleasure		12.8 (14)	13.7 (16)	14.6 (17)	14.8 (17)	14.8 (16)	15.4 (18)	16.0 (18)	.001
Salvation		9.5 (8)	6.7 (4)	7.9 (6)	8.6 (8)	10.3 (11)	12.5 (14)	15.1 (17)	.001
Self-respect		8.9 (7)	8.3 (8)	7.7 (5)	7.8 (5)	6.9 (5)	6.8 (6)	6.8 (6)	.01
Social recognition		13.5 (15)	13.8 (17)	14.1 (16)	14.8 (16)	15.1 (17)	15.2 (17)	14.3 (16)	.05
True friendship		7.6 (6)	8.2 (7)	9.7 (12)	9.4 (11)	10.4 (12)	8.7 (7)	8.6 (8)	.01
Wisdom		10.8 (11)	9.6 (11)	8.4 (8)	8.1 (6)	6.1 (4)	5.5 (4)	4.6 (2)	.001

Figures shown are median rankings and, in parentheses, composite rank orders.

TABLE 3.6 INSTRUMENTAL VALUE MEDIANS AND COMPOSITE RANK ORDERS FOR GROUPS VARYING IN EDUCATION (N = 1,404)

Value	0–4 Yr.	5–8 Yr.	Some High Sch.	Comp. High Sch.	Some Coll.	Comp. Coll.	Grad. Sch.	p
N =	64	263	320	426	180	90	61	
Ambitious	5.5 (3)	6.1 (3)	6.1 (2)	6.6 (3)	7.7 (5)	7.7 (4)	8.0 (5)	—
Broadminded	9.2 (10)	8.0 (7)	8.1 (8)	6.9 (4)	7.4 (4)	6.2 (3)	5.9 (3)	—
Capable	9.5 (11)	10.3 (13)	10.0 (11)	9.0 (9)	9.1 (7)	9.7 (10)	8.7 (9)	—
Cheerful	7.7 (5)	8.1 (8)	9.4 (9)	10.3 (13)	11.3 (14)	11.8 (14)	11.8 (15)	.001
Clean	5.1 (2)	6.6 (4)	7.8 (7)	8.6 (6)	10.6 (13)	13.2 (17)	14.4 (16)	.001
Courageous	10.8 (13)	7.8 (6)	7.2 (6)	8.6 (7)	6.7 (3)	7.9 (5)	8.0 (4)	.01
Forgiving	6.8 (4)	5.8 (2)	7.0 (4)	7.3 (5)	8.8 (6)	10.7 (12)	8.3 (6)	.001
Helpful	8.5 (7)	7.7 (5)	7.2 (5)	9.0 (8)	9.5 (9)	8.8 (7)	8.6 (8)	.001
Honest	3.3 (1)	3.6 (1)	3.3 (1)	3.1 (1)	3.4 (1)	2.4 (1)	3.8 (1)	—
Imaginative	15.5 (18)	15.9 (18)	15.8 (18)	15.7 (18)	14.0 (17)	11.8 (15)	9.0 (10)	.001
Independent	11.5 (15)	10.7 (14)	10.8 (14)	10.2 (12)	10.2 (11)	9.5 (9)	8.4 (7)	—
Intellectual	15.0 (16)	14.3 (16)	13.7 (16)	13.1 (15)	10.3 (12)	9.4 (8)	9.4 (11)	.001
Logical	15.2 (17)	15.7 (17)	15.5 (17)	13.8 (17)	12.1 (16)	10.6 (11)	11.3 (14)	.001
Loving	8.0 (6)	10.1 (10)	10.0 (10)	9.3 (11)	9.6 (10)	10.8 (13)	9.7 (12)	—
Obedient	11.1 (14)	11.7 (15)	12.8 (15)	13.4 (16)	14.7 (18)	15.5 (18)	16.6 (18)	.001
Polite	10.2 (12)	10.1 (11)	10.4 (13)	10.5 (14)	11.6 (15)	12.4 (16)	14.7 (17)	.001
Responsible	8.8 (9)	8.6 (9)	6.9 (3)	6.1 (2)	5.9 (2)	5.4 (2)	5.7 (2)	.001
Self-controlled	8.8 (8)	10.2 (12)	10.1 (12)	9.2 (10)	9.2 (8)	7.9 (6)	10.4 (13)	—

Figures shown are median rankings and, in parentheses, composite rank orders.

sample, rankings on *clean* correlate $-.32$ with education and $-.24$ with income, those with less education and income ranking *clean* more important. Rankings on *a sense of accomplishment* correlate $+.27$ with education and $+.18$ with income. The multiple correlation between all 36 values and education is .579, and the multiple correlation between all 36 values and income is .445. These multiple correlations would probably be much higher if the 36 values and the two status measures were corrected for unreliability.

VALUES AND RACE

This section summarizes a more extended discussion previously reported by Rokeach and Parker (1970).

To set the stage for a discussion of values as social indicators of whatever it may mean to be racially different in the United States, it is appropriate to review the nature of the controversy provoked by the "Moynihan Report," published by the U.S. Department of Labor in 1965. In this and in other publications, Moynihan (1966, 1967) set forth the proposition that "disorganization" in the black American's family, and its resultant disastrous effects on personality, must be explained not only as a direct response to everyday experiences of discrimination, unemployment, poor housing, and the like, but also as a consequence of a self-perpetuating black subculture of poverty. He further argued that these subculturally distinct attributes are transmitted through the socialization of the young within the context of unstable families.

If Moynihan is right, then merely changing the social condition of the American black, by means of income-redistribution, employment, and the like, would be a necessary but not a sufficient condition for dealing with the problem. If the source of disorganization is rooted in "self-perpetuating" personality and cultural factors, then any long-lasting solution would have to incorporate measures of a re-educative and social-psychiatric nature. Unless this were done, direct situational changes would be ameliorative in merely a temporary way. Needless to say, Moynihan's analysis of the distinctive subculture of black Americans and, more generally, of the poor, provoked a lively controversy because it was so closely linked to social policy formation.

A number of social scientists have raised objections to such a view of the culture of poverty. Gans (1968), Rainwater (1968), and Parker and Kleiner (1970) have all agreed that the social behavior of a deprived people must be conceptualized as composed of two separate components, one describing their adaptations to ongoing day-to-day situations and the other describing their normative aspirations or conceptions of the desirable, in short, their values. Too great an emphasis on the overt adaptational differences between the poor and the rich and between blacks and whites has led some observers mistakenly to interpret such behavioral differences as evidence for a distinctive and self-perpetuating subculture of poverty. But when the focus shifts toward an attempt to understand the more covert and evaluative aspect of culture, as in the participant-observation studies of Rainwater (1968) and Liebow (1967), the distinctiveness of the culture of poverty becomes rather less apparent. These authors maintain that despite the many differences in the observable behavior of the poor and the rich, the standards that they employ to evaluate their own and others' behavior are not all that different. Although these ideas are provocative, the data presently available do not firmly support either view of the culture of poverty. What is needed, if we are to decide between the two views, are data about what people want and aspire to rather than about behavioral accommodations made to a seriously disadvantaged situation. Data on black and white values are, therefore, directly pertinent to the Moynihan controversy.

We have already seen that the values of the more affluent and educated differ in many ways from those of the less affluent and educated. Since American blacks are doubtlessly less affluent and educated on the whole than white Americans, it can be expected that blacks will differ from whites in the same way that the poor differ from the rich and the less-educated differ from the better-educated. But if Moynihan's proposal that blacks

TABLE 3.7   TERMINAL VALUE MEDIANS AND COMPOSITE RANK
ORDERS FOR WHITE AND BLACK AMERICANS (N = 1,397)

Value	N =	White 1,195	Black 202	p
A comfortable life		9.6 (12)	6.6 (5)	.001
An exciting life		15.4 (18)	15.3 (18)	—
A sense of accomplishment		8.8 (8)	10.2 (11)	.01
A world at peace		3.3 (1)	3.5 (1)	—
A world of beauty		13.5 (15)	14.1 (16)	—
Equality		9.6 (11)	4.6 (2)	.001
Family security		3.6 (2)	5.1 (4)	.001
Freedom		5.6 (3)	5.0 (3)	—
Happiness		7.6 (4)	7.6 (7)	—
Inner harmony		10.4 (13)	10.9 (12)	—
Mature love		12.1 (14)	13.7 (14)	.001
National security		9.1 (9)	11.4 (13)	.001
Pleasure		14.7 (17)	14.3 (17)	—
Salvation		8.5 (7)	9.4 (9)	—
Self-respect		7.7 (5)	7.5 (6)	—
Social recognition		14.6 (16)	13.7 (15)	.05
True friendship		9.3 (10)	9.8 (10)	—
Wisdom		7.9 (6)	8.5 (8)	—

Figures shown are median rankings and, in parentheses, composite rank orders.

are characterized by a self-perpetuating culture is valid, then we should also expect to find the values of a "culture of poverty" even among black Americans who are not poor or uneducated.

In considering Tables 3.7 and 3.8, let us first note that, contrary to popular belief, certain value rankings do not distinguish black from white Americans. Blacks and whites do not differ on religious values (*salvation, forgiving*) or on values that suggest hedonism or desire for immediate gratification. *An exciting life* and *pleasure* are ranked seventeenth and eighteenth down the terminal list by both white and black Americans. *Self-controlled* is ranked in the middle of the instrumental value scale by both groups. There is no evidence here that black Americans even have the values that are supposed to be the main "stigmata" of the culture of poverty.

TABLE 3.8   INSTRUMENTAL VALUE MEDIANS AND COMPOSITE RANK ORDERS FOR WHITE AND BLACK AMERICANS (N = 1,397)

Value	N =	White 1,195	Black 202	p
Ambitious		6.7 (3)	5.2 (2)	.01
Broadminded		7.4 (5)	8.0 (8)	—
Capable		9.4 (10)	10.4 (13)	—
Cheerful		9.9 (12)	10.3 (12)	—
Clean		9.3 (8)	5.3 (3)	.001
Courageous		7.8 (6)	7.8 (7)	—
Forgiving		7.0 (4)	7.6 (5)	—
Helpful		8.3 (7)	7.8 (6)	—
Honest		3.2 (1)	3.8 (1)	—
Imaginative		15.3 (18)	15.8 (18)	—
Independent		10.6 (13)	10.2 (10)	—
Intellectual		13.1 (15)	12.6 (16)	—
Logical		13.9 (17)	15.1 (17)	.01
Loving		9.4 (9)	11.9 (15)	.001
Obedient		13.5 (16)	11.5 (14)	.01
Polite		10.9 (14)	10.2 (11)	—
Responsible		6.6 (2)	7.6 (4)	.05
Self-controlled		9.5 (11)	10.1 (9)	—

Figures shown are median rankings and, in parentheses, composite rank orders.

But thirteen terminal or instrumental values do show statistically significant differences between black and white Americans. There are thus many value differences between them, but not as many as have been found between the poor and the rich (20 out of 36) or between uneducated and educated Americans (25 out of 36). Let us nevertheless examine these black-white differences somewhat more closely.

Of all 36 values, *equality* shows the greatest difference between black and white Americans: Its composite rank order is second for blacks and eleventh for whites. Other values that blacks rank higher than whites are *a comfortable life, social recognition*, and being *ambitious, clean*, and *obedient*. On the other hand, certain values are ranked significantly lower by blacks: *a sense of accomplishment, family security, mature love, national security*, and being *logical, loving*, and *responsible*. These findings suggest a portrait of the average black American as a person who, more than the average white American, yearns for a higher standard of living and a more equal status in society and at the same time places a higher value on conformity. Contrary to a widespread stereotype of the black American as lazy, the average black American ranks himself as more *ambitious* than the average white American.

This last difference notwithstanding, the average black American places a lesser emphasis on competence and self-actualization, strivings for love, and identification with and responsibility for family and nation.

All these differences might be taken at first glance as strong evidence for a distinctive black culture. But since large socioeconomic differences are known to exist between them, it is necessary before accepting this conclusion to examine the differences between them after socioeconomic status is held constant.

Tables 3.9 and 3.10 show the terminal and instrumental value rankings of white and black Americans after controlling for income and education. This control was achieved by matching the income and education of 198 whites with that of 198 blacks in the national sample. The 13 significant differences found between them before they had been thus equated (Tables 3.9 and 3.10) were then reduced to seven; moreover, 11 of the original 13 significant differences were then of smaller magnitude. These findings suggest that most of the differences previously observed between them were attributable to socioeconomic differences rather than to race differences. It is these seven value differences that we must now scrutinize more closely if we are to understand better the essence of whatever is meant by black versus white culture.

The only value that continues to show a rather large, undiminished difference between black and white Americans is *equality*. The former rank it second, and the latter, who are matched for income and education with the former, rank it twelfth in importance. Black Americans, moreover, still place a greater value on *a comfortable life* and on being *clean* and *obedient* and a lower value on *a world of beauty, family security*, and being *loving*. But these differences are now, by and large, considerably smaller than those previously obtained, before the two groups had been matched for income and education. It is not difficult to explain the value differences that still remain on grounds other than the existence of a distinctive black culture of poverty. They can be attributed to the fact that black Americans, even those matched on income and education with whites, must still live

TABLE 3.9 TERMINAL VALUE MEDIANS AND COMPOSITE RANK
ORDERS FOR WHITE AND BLACK AMERICANS MATCHED FOR INCOME
AND EDUCATION (N = 396)

Value	N =	White 198	Black 198	p
A comfortable life		8.6 (7)	6.7 (5)	.05
An exciting life		15.5 (18)	15.2 (18)	—
A sense of accomplishment		9.5 (11)	10.1 (11)	—
A world at peace		2.8 (1)	3.5 (1)	—
A world of beauty		13.3 (15)	14.0 (16)	.05
Equality		9.8 (12)	4.6 (2)	.001
Family security		3.7 (2)	5.0 (4)	.01
Freedom		5.5 (3)	4.9 (3)	—
Happiness		6.9 (4)	7.5 (6)	—
Inner harmony		10.7 (13)	11.0 (12)	—
Mature love		12.2 (14)	13.5 (14)	—
National security		9.2 (9)	11.4 (13)	—
Pleasure		14.4 (17)	14.2 (17)	—
Salvation		7.0 (5)	9.3 (9)	—
Self-respect		8.1 (6)	7.5 (7)	—
Social recognition		14.3 (16)	13.6 (15)	—
True friendship		8.6 (8)	9.6 (10)	—
Wisdom		9.5 (10)	8.5 (8)	—

Figures shown are median rankings and, in parentheses, composite rank orders.

for the most part under segregated conditions of relative deprivation in black ghettos. This would explain the findings that black Americans still place a higher value on *a comfortable life* and on being *clean*. The difference between blacks and whites on *a world of beauty*, although statistically significant, is small in magnitude and is ranked low down the value continuum by both groups. Concerning the findings that black Americans rank *family security* fourth in comparison with whites who rank it second, it is instructive to note which values black Americans rank higher than fourth— *a world at peace*, *equality*, and *freedom*. These rankings can readily be interpreted as reflecting a growing emphasis and realization by black Americans that a necessary prerequisite for the security of the disadvantaged family is social reform. That their lower ranking of *family security* does not necessarily reflect a devaluing of the family is further evidenced by the absence of differences between the two matched groups on *responsibility*, on hedonistic values (*an exciting life*, *pleasure*), or on impulsiveness (*self-controlled*). Moreover, none of the values that can be subsumed under the category of competence or self-actualization show any significant differences between the two races matched for income and education.

A note of caution must, however, be introduced about reaching conclusions concerning the existence or nonexistence of cultural differences between the two races. The matching procedure included individuals from all socioeconomic strata whereas the actual black population in our society is concentrated mainly in the lower income and educational categories. It is to this status group, rather than to the relatively assimilated middle class, that Moynihan (1965) attributes a distinctive black culture of poverty. But an examination of the values of white and black Americans within the lowest third of the socioeconomic range shows findings that with only a few minor exceptions are highly similar to those reported in Tables 3.9 and 3.10.

TABLE 3.10 INSTRUMENTAL VALUE MEDIANS AND COMPOSITE RANK ORDERS FOR WHITE AND BLACK AMERICANS MATCHED FOR INCOME AND EDUCATION (N = 396)

Value	N =	White 198	Black 198	p
Ambitious		6.5 (2)	5.2 (2)	—
Broadminded		8.7 (7)	8.0 (8)	—
Capable		9.0 (9)	10.3 (12)	—
Cheerful		8.9 (8)	10.3 (13)	—
Clean		9.0 (10)	5.3 (3)	.001
Courageous		7.8 (5)	7.8 (7)	—
Forgiving		7.0 (4)	7.6 (5)	—
Helpful		8.0 (6)	7.6 (6)	—
Honest		3.4 (1)	3.7 (1)	—
Imaginative		15.1 (18)	15.8 (18)	—
Independent		10.1 (13)	10.0 (9)	—
Intellectual		13.5 (16)	12.5 (16)	—
Logical		14.2 (17)	15.0 (17)	—
Loving		9.0 (11)	11.9 (15)	.001
Obedient		13.3 (15)	11.5 (14)	.05
Polite		10.8 (14)	10.2 (11)	—
Responsible		6.8 (3)	7.5 (4)	—
Self-controlled		9.2 (12)	10.0 (10)	—

Figures shown are median rankings and, in parentheses, composite rank orders.

It is perhaps appropriate at this point to summarize the major substantive findings concerning the effects of social status and race on values. There are many value differences between the poor and the rich, the uneducated and the educated, and blacks and whites in American society. Persons of low socioeconomic status, compared with persons of high status, are more religious, more conformist, less concerned with responsibility, more concerned with friendship than with love, and less concerned with competence and self-actualization. When we analyze differences between white and black Americans, however, we find far fewer value differences that can be attributed solely to race. The major value gap between black and white Americans concerns *equality*. Other differences, such as those involving competence and self actualization, parallel those found between the affluent and the nonaffluent or between the educated and the uneducated. When socioeconomic status is held constant, most of the value differences previously found either disappear or become minimal—with the exception of the difference concerning *equality*.

Returning now to the issue of the Moynihan controversy raised earlier, do the findings support the presence among black Americans of a culture of poverty in the sense that Oscar Lewis (1966) has used the term? The findings do indeed provide extensive support for the hypothesis that the values of the poor differ considerably from those of the more affluent segments of our society. Many of these differences do indeed point to characteristics attributed by various writers to the culture of poverty. With regard to black-white differences, however, the relatively few differences that remain after status is held constant provide virtually no support for a distinctive black culture of poverty.

Based on these findings, can one categorically reject Moynihan's position that social policy for alleviating poverty among black Americans should be predicated on the idea that they are culturally different from whites? In order to answer this, we must refer to our initial discussion of the nature of culture. With regard to values, or to what Gans has called "aspirational culture," the differences are negligible. But at another level, more closely linked to the constraints provided by persisting situations of deprivation to which black Americans have been exposed (Gans, 1968; Rainwater, 1968), it is probable that many differences do indeed exist (Parker and Kleiner, 1970). The extent and nature of such differences to adaptation are not well known and bear further investigation. Given what is known at this point, however, it would be unfortunate if social policy were to be based on the assumption that there are substantial cultural differences between black and white Americans. The data described here show only one big and pervasive value difference between the black and the white races. Black Americans give *equality* high priority; white Americans place a far lower priority on *equality*. This one difference best summarizes the cultural difference observed in our national sample of black and white Americans, and this one cultural difference will undoubtedly decrease if equal opportunity genuinely increases.

AGE DIFFERENCES IN VALUES

The results to be reported here are for several samples of Americans ranging in age from 11 at one extreme to 70 and over at the other. The category "70 and over" consists of 169 respondents in the national sample of whom 37 were between 80 and 90, and 3 were over 90. The findings shown in Tables 3.11 through 3.14 are from three samples. The national NORC sample, already described, provided the data for adult Americans over twenty-one. The college sample was obtained from introductory psychology classes at Michigan State University; most of the students, about evenly divided in sex, ranged in age from eighteen to twenty-one. Needless to say, this sample can hardly be considered to be representative of American youth of the same age. It is essentially a middle-class sample of college students recruited mainly from the Midwest. [Additional data on junior college freshmen in California have recently been reported by Brawer (1971).] The eleven-, thirteen-, fifteen-, and seventeen-year-old groups were obtained by Drs. Robert Beech and Aileen Schoeppe (1970), from the public schools of New York City, and are presented here with their permission. Each age group consists of approximately equal numbers of boys and girls tested in middle-class and lower-class areas. The reader is therefore strongly cautioned to take the nature of these three samples into account when interpreting the findings shown in Tables 3.11 through 3.14. Because of the voluminousness of these findings, the terminal and instrumental value medians are shown separately in Tables 3.11 and 3.12, and the composite rank orders are shown in 3.13 and 3.14. It should, moreover, be noted that significance of differences is shown separately for the national sample (Median test) and for the four adolescent groups (one-way analysis of variance). No attempt was made to test for significance of differences across the total age range because the three samples do not come from the same population.

At least 30 of the 36 values show significant age differences, either in the adolescent or national sample or in both samples. The general impression gained from an inspection of the data is one of continuous value change from early adolescence through old age with the presence of several generation gaps rather than just one. To aid in the interpretation of these findings, the composite rankings were plotted against age for each of the 36 values separately, and an attempt was made to identify those values that showed similar patterns of development. By this process, the developmental patterns observed for each of the 36 values were reduced to 14, and these 14 developmental patterns are described below.

Developmental Pattern 1: A Sense of Accomplishment, Wisdom, Responsible

All values of this subset seem to concern self-realization and show an inverted U-shaped pattern. All three are ranked relatively low or in the middle of the value scale in early adolescence, then increase gradually in importance through the adolescent and college years, and then gradually become less important in the decades beyond. They end up about as unimportant in old age as they were to begin with in early adolescence. The results for *wisdom* are especially noteworthy since they contradict the widely held belief that *wisdom* is especially valued in old age.

TABLE 3.11 TERMINAL VALUE MEDIANS FOR ELEVEN AGE GROUPS

Terminal Values	N = 11	13	15	17	p	College	20's	30's	40's	50's	60's	70's	p
	190	183	186	193		298	267	298	280	236	159	169	
A comfortable life	8.5	9.2	9.2	10.2	—	12.1	9.5	10.1	8.7	9.1	8.0	7.7	.05
An exciting life	10.6	10.8	12.0	11.9	—	11.6	15.3	14.6	15.5	15.4	15.4	16.2	.01
A sense of accomplishment	13.2	11.5	11.8	9.4	.001	7.7	9.0	8.9	8.9	8.7	9.3	10.2	—
A world at peace	3.2	3.2	2.6	3.4	—	8.4	3.8	4.2	3.1	3.0	2.9	2.8	.01
A world of beauty	8.2	11.5	12.2	12.7	.001	13.8	13.9	13.7	13.7	13.3	13.6	12.9	—
Equality	6.9	6.4	5.4	5.4	—	10.6	8.0	8.2	9.0	9.3	10.4	7.7	—
Family security	5.2	3.5	5.3	7.5	.001	8.4	4.0	3.2	3.3	3.7	4.5	5.6	.01
Freedom	4.6	5.1	4.1	5.4	.05	5.1	4.3	5.4	5.9	6.2	5.7	6.6	.01
Happiness	6.8	7.2	8.6	7.4	—	6.2	7.0	7.5	7.3	8.1	8.1	8.0	—
Inner harmony	11.3	13.7	12.4	9.3	.001	8.3	11.0	9.9	10.0	10.7	10.1	11.0	.01
Mature love	9.4	10.9	10.1	10.0	—	7.3	10.0	10.8	12.9	13.1	14.4	15.5	.01
National security	12.6	12.2	9.6	14.2	.001	13.6	9.9	11.4	9.7	8.9	7.4	8.2	.01
Pleasure	11.4	10.9	13.2	12.6	.01	14.0	14.5	15.3	14.8	14.5	14.4	13.4	.01
Salvation	14.6	13.9	13.8	15.9	.01	13.1	9.7	10.0	8.6	6.8	9.0	6.4	.05
Self-respect	12.2	11.6	9.7	8.4	.001	6.7	8.4	7.0	7.9	8.0	7.6	7.6	—
Social recognition	13.8	12.7	12.9	12.2	.05	13.6	14.5	14.7	14.4	14.2	13.6	14.5	—
True friendship	6.5	7.0	8.4	8.5	.01	7.8	10.0	9.9	9.7	8.6	8.7	7.8	.01
Wisdom	9.9	9.1	8.0	7.3	.01	6.4	7.9	7.1	7.9	8.2	8.7	9.0	.05

TABLE 3.12 INSTRUMENTAL VALUE MEDIANS FOR ELEVEN AGE GROUPS

Instrumental Values	11	13	15	17	p	College	20's	30's	40's	50's	60's	70's	p
N =	190	183	186	193		298	267	298	280	236	159	169	
Ambitious	10.0	7.3	7.1	6.2	.001	7.0	7.6	6.4	5.9	6.4	6.1	6.3	—
Broadminded	11.7	13.2	11.6	8.4	.001	6.7	8.2	8.2	7.5	6.3	7.1	6.6	—
Capable	10.2	9.3	9.5	8.8	—	9.4	10.5	9.4	9.1	9.7	9.0	9.7	.05
Cheerful	6.5	9.8	11.2	11.1	.001	11.4	10.9	10.6	10.3	9.3	8.5	8.9	.01
Clean	8.1	8.9	9.6	9.9	—	14.2	8.3	10.1	8.7	8.8	7.5	8.1	.05
Courageous	9.3	9.3	8.8	7.9	—	8.4	8.7	7.4	7.5	7.6	8.6	7.6	—
Forgiving	7.6	8.6	7.9	9.5	.01	9.7	7.6	8.1	6.9	7.4	7.1	6.0	.01
Helpful	6.5	6.5	8.1	9.1	.001	10.6	9.3	8.8	8.0	8.1	8.1	7.2	.01
Honest	4.6	4.5	4.5	5.9	.05	4.2	3.4	2.7	3.4	3.4	3.4	3.5	—
Imaginative	12.5	14.3	14.3	12.9	.01	11.4	15.0	15.1	15.3	15.6	16.0	15.4	—
Independent	10.5	11.8	9.8	8.8	.05	8.1	10.4	9.7	10.8	11.2	10.5	9.9	—
Intellectual	12.5	12.1	11.8	10.9	—	9.2	12.3	13.1	12.8	13.1	13.6	13.6	—
Logical	13.1	15.2	14.0	12.7	.001	10.1	13.9	13.6	14.0	14.6	15.2	14.3	—
Loving	4.8	5.7	5.6	7.2	.05	7.7	8.2	9.1	9.9	9.8	11.2	11.1	.01
Obedient	11.3	10.1	11.9	12.7	.05	15.3	13.0	13.8	13.0	13.7	13.0	13.2	—
Polite	9.1	8.8	10.0	10.9	—	12.9	10.3	10.8	12.2	10.5	10.1	10.7	.01
Responsible	9.3	7.8	7.5	7.4	.01	6.0	6.0	6.3	6.1	6.9	7.7	8.1	.01
Self-controlled	10.5	9.7	10.2	10.7	—	8.8	9.6	8.8	10.0	9.9	9.9	10.0	—

TABLE 3.13   COMPOSITE RANK ORDERS OF TERMINAL VALUES FOR ELEVEN AGE GROUPS.

Terminal Values	11	13	15	17	p	College	20's	30's	40's	50's	60's	70's	p
N=	190	183	186	193		298	267	298	280	236	159	169	
A comfortable life	8	8	8	12	—	13	9	12	8	11	6	6	.05
An exciting life	11	9	13	13	—	12	18	16	18	18	18	18	.01
A sense of accomplishment	16	13	12	10	.001	6	8	8	9	9	11	12	—
A world at peace	1	1	1	1	—	10	1	2	1	1	1	1	.01
A world of beauty	7	12	14	16	.001	17	15	15	15	15	15	14	—
Equality	6	4	4	2	—	11	6	7	10	12	13	7	.01
Family security	3	2	3	6	.001	9	2	1	2	2	2	2	.01
Freedom	2	3	2	3	.05	1	3	3	3	3	3	4	—
Happiness	5	6	7	5	—	2	4	6	4	6	7	9	.01
Inner harmony	12	17	15	9	.001	8	14	9	13	13	12	13	.01
Mature love	9	11	11	11	—	5	13	13	14	14	16	17	.01
National security	15	15	9	17	.001	16	11	14	11	10	4	10	.05
Pleasure	13	10	17	15	.01	18	16	18	17	17	17	15	—
Salvation	18	18	18	18	.01	14	10	11	7	4	10	3	.01
Self-respect	14	14	10	7	.001	4	7	4	5	5	5	5	.05
Social recognition	17	16	16	14	.05	15	17	17	16	16	14	16	—
True friendship	4	5	6	8	.01	7	12	10	12	8	9	8	.01
Wisdom	10	7	5	4	.01	3	5	5	6	7	8	11	.05

TABLE 3.14 COMPOSITE RANK ORDERS OF INSTRUMENTAL VALUES FOR ELEVEN AGE GROUPS

Instrumental Values N =	11 190	13 183	15 186	17 193	p	College 298	20's 267	30's 298	40's 280	50's 236	60's 159	70's 169	p
Ambitious	10	4	3	2	.001	4	4	3	2	3	2	3	—
Broadminded	15	16	14	6	.001	3	6	6	5	2	4	4	—
Capable	11	9	8	7	—	10	13	10	9	10	10	10	.05
Cheerful	3	12	13	15	.001	15	14	13	12	9	8	9	.01
Clean	6	8	9	11	—	17	7	12	8	8	5	7	.05
Courageous	8	10	7	5	—	7	8	4	6	6	9	6	—
Forgiving	5	6	5	10	.01	11	3	5	4	5	3	2	.01
Helpful	4	3	6	9	.001	13	9	7	7	7	7	5	.01
Honest	1	1	1	1	.05	1	1	1	1	1	1	1	—
Imaginative	16	17	18	18	.01	14	18	18	18	18	18	18	—
Independent	12	14	10	8	.05	6	12	11	13	14	13	11	—
Intellectual	17	15	15	14	—	9	15	15	15	15	16	16	—
Logical	18	18	17	16	.001	12	17	16	17	17	17	17	—
Loving	2	2	2	3	.05	5	5	9	11	11	14	14	.01
Obedient	14	13	16	17	.05	18	16	17	16	16	15	15	—
Polite	7	7	11	13	—	16	11	14	14	13	12	13	.01
Responsible	9	5	4	4	.01	2	2	2	3	4	6	8	.01
Self-controlled	13	11	12	12	—	8	10	8	10	12	11	12	—

Developmental Pattern 2: Imaginative, Intellectual, Logical, Inner Harmony

This developmental pattern seems to be closely related to Pattern 1. All four of these personal values are ranked uniformly low to begin with by adolescent groups, then increase suddenly to become moderately important during the college years, and then drop quickly again to a position of relatively low priority for all age groups beyond. The results for *logical* are of special relevance to social-psychological theories concerned with cognitive consistency. *Logical* is ranked sixteenth to eighteenth down the list by adolescents, rises to twelfth among college students, and then drops once again toward the bottom among adult Americans (Table 3.14). College professors, who typically place a high value on being *logical* (ranking it anywhere from 5th to 8th in importance, as Table 5.15 shows), seem in their formulation of consistency and balance theories to have projected their own values for being *logical* onto others, perhaps on the simple assumption that others value what academicians value. But this is obviously not so. The average adolescent and adult American care little indeed about being *logical*, and college students care only a bit more about it. Generalizations about human behavior based upon experiments with college students therefore seem to be unwarranted when the experimental task presupposes logical inconsistency among cognitive components as a major motivating force for attitude or behavioral change.

Developmental Pattern 3: A World of Beauty, True Friendship, Polite

Although it is difficult to discern the common element in these three values, they nonetheless show a similar developmental pattern. They all start out as relatively important in early adolescence but become increasingly less important in the college years and the twenties, at which point they more or less level off to remain relatively unimportant in the following decades. The results for *a world of beauty* deserve special mention in an era of increasing apprehension about quality of life, pollution, and ecology. It is ranked seventh in importance by eleven-year-olds, then declines steadily during the adolescent years to a position of seventeenth down the list by students in college, and there it remains toward the bottom of the terminal value hierarchy—for all age groups beyond. It would seem as if the socialization process had somehow destroyed the young adolescent's initial appreciation of beauty by replacing it with other values that are deemed more important. Perhaps our present concern with ecology will reverse *a world of beauty*'s generally low position in the American value hierarchy in the years to come.

Developmental Pattern 4: Obedience

Somewhat similar to Pattern 3 is the one shown by *obedient*, except for the fact that it starts out lower down the list of instrumental values for eleven-year-olds—fourteenth. It then declines gradually to eighteenth for college students and then gradually rises decade after decade to a position of fifteenth in importance.

Developmental Pattern 5: An Exciting Life, Pleasure

These two hedonistic values are moderately important during early adolescence and then become less and less important. They are virtually at the bottom of the value hierarchy for college students or for people in their twenties, and they are ranked at or near the bottom of the value hierarchy in the decades that follow.

Developmental Pattern 6: Self-respect, Ambitious, Broadminded

These three values, which seem to concern self-realization, are all relatively unimportant, perhaps because they are still meaningless to young adolescents. All three increase steadily during the adolescent years to assume a position of major importance in late adolescence and the college years. They then level off and continue to remain important.

Developmental Pattern 7: Loving

Of all the 36 values *loving* shows the most clearcut linear relation to age. It starts out second in importance for eleven-year-olds and then declines more or less linearly to fourteenth for people beyond seventy. It would thus seem that love is important for young people but, surprisingly, becomes less and less important as people grow older.

Developmental Pattern 8: Mature Love

This value shows a developmental pattern somewhat similar to that found for *loving*, except for the fact that it starts out ninth in importance for young adolescents and declines steadily to seventeenth for people in their seventies and beyond. The only exception is its sudden rise to fifth place in the college years and its sudden decline thereafter. It would seem that *mature love* is an important value mainly for young middle-class college students.

Developmental Pattern 9: A World at Peace, Family Security, Capable

All three of these rather diverse values are more or less equally valued across all age groups except that they all show a sharp decrease in importance in late adolescence and during the college years and then an equally sharp increase. This pattern is most evident for *a world at peace* which is at the top of the terminal value hierarchy for all groups, except that it declines to tenth position for those in college. This devaluation is possibly due to the draft status of college students compared with other groups. Perhaps it is an attempt to rationalize one's continuing in college and avoiding the draft. Similar patterns are noted for *family security* and *capable.* The devaluing of *family security* by those in late adolescence probably reflects the fact that love and marriage are more focal at this age than raising a family. The developmental pattern for *capable*, however, is more surprising. From seventeen through the twenties the importance of being competent declines. From then on until the forties it becomes more important, and then it levels off.

Developmental Pattern 10: A Comfortable
Life, Cheerful, Clean, Forgiving, Helpful

All these are rather conventional values and they all show a gradual decrease in importance during the adolescent years followed, in later decades, by a gradual, though somewhat uneven, increase in importance. Since all these values are significant indicators of socioeconomic status (See Tables 3.3 to 3.6), their developmental pattern can be interpreted as reflecting a lesser concern with socioeconomic status in late adolescence and an increasing concern with it later on, after reaching the age of marriage. All these class-related values, with the exception of *helpful*, seem to become increasingly important in the later years of life, as issues of economic security and religion become more salient.

Developmental Pattern 11: Equality,
Independent

Both of these values show a rather similar complex, undulating pattern of development. They both increase gradually in importance during adolescence, then show a sudden decrease during the college years or the twenties, then another increase, then a gradual decrease, and culminate in yet another increase in importance from the sixties to the seventies.

Developmental Pattern 12: Salvation

This value is evidently one of extremely low priority throughout adolescence, as evidenced by the fact that it is uniformly ranked at the bottom of the terminal value hierarchy during the adolescent years. It then increases in importance to fourteenth during the college years and continues to become more important in succeeding decades, ranking third among those beyond seventy. This smooth developmental trend is, however, interrupted in the sixties when *salvation* drops inexplicably to tenth in importance. It is difficult to say without further research whether this particular finding is due to chance. Whether or not this will turn out to be the case, the overall developmental trend is unmistakable: *Salvation* becomes increasingly important with advancing age.

Developmental Pattern 13: National
Security

This value is a relatively unimportant one for eleven- and thirteen-year-olds, ranking fifteenth among the terminal values. It increases to ninth in importance for fifteen-year-olds and then plummets sharply to sixteenth or seventeenth for seventeen-year-olds and for those in college. It then increases steadily in importance with each decade from the twenties to the sixties at which time it is ranked fourth from the top. It then drops back to tenth in the years beyond the seventies. It seems especially ironic in this era of student protest that *national security* is near the bottom of the terminal value hierarchy for those who are most eligible for military service and edges close to the top of the value hierarchy for those in their later years, prior to retirement, when they are at the height of their identification with and participation in the Establishment. Differences in the perceived importance of *national security* were surely a major component of the generation gap in the late 1960's.

Developmental Pattern 14: Freedom, Happiness, Social Recognition, Courageous, Honest, Self-controlled

Finally, these six values show relatively little fluctuation with age. *Honest* seems to be the most stable of all the 36 values, its composite ranking being first for all age groups without exception. Next most stable as an American value is *freedom*, which is ranked among the top four values for all age groups. The remaining four values—*happiness, social recognition, courageous*, and *self-controlled*—show somewhat more fluctuation with age but the differences are not statistically significant, at least when the adolescent groups are compared or when the age groups in the national adult sample are compared.

Before leaving the issue of value development it should perhaps be stated that the 14 value patterns discussed here are purely descriptive in nature; they are based upon a visual inspection of data obtained from adolescents in New York City, college students in Michigan, and adult Americans from a national sample. Further research is obviously needed to determine whether the value patterns described here are replicable with more representative sampling procedures across the total age range, whether the number of value patterns can be reduced to a still smaller number, and further research is needed in order to account for the developmental patterns observed. Most particularly, further research must determine to what extent the generational differences observed are a function of maturation and to what extent they are a function of changes in generational norms concerning socialization. Even though it is not possible (without longitudinal data) to assess their relative contributions, it is safe to assume that both factors have influenced the observed results.

Perhaps most illuminating from a theoretical standpoint is the finding that value changes take place not only during adolescence but throughout life. Although the data do not permit us to generalize below age eleven, value development is, at least in large part, a continuing maturational process of change from birth to death and does not stop arbitrarily with the end of the period of psychosexual development that Freud speaks of.

The results are therefore more in line with Erikson's view of development (1950) rather than with Freud's more classical view.

In the context of the present discussion of age-related values, it is perhaps appropriate to comment also on the relation between values, as conceived and measured here, and moral development, as conceived and measured by Kohlberg (1964). This relation has been investigated by McLellan (1970) with 78 male subjects from the seventh, ninth, and eleventh grades. These subjects were tested with Kohlberg's Moral Judgment instrument and the Rokeach Value Survey. McLellan found that two values especially, *freedom* and *obedient*, discriminated among Kohlberg's moral stages when age was held constant. As would be predicted from Kohlberg's theory, *freedom* rankings were found to be highest at stage 2 (the instrumentalist relationist orientation) and at stage 5 (the social contract legalistic orientation), and that *obedient* rankings were highest at stage 1 (the punishment and obedience orientation) and at stage 4 (the rigid rule orientation). McLellan's findings suggest that a more extensive study of the relation between stages of moral development and the organization of values would be rewarding.

RELIGIOUS VALUES

Detailed reports of value similarities and differences among the religious, the less religious, and the nonreligious have been reported elsewhere (Rokeach, 1969a, 1969b, 1970a, 1970b) and will therefore only be summarized here. All religious groups are similar in considering *a world at peace, family security*, and *freedom* the most important terminal values, and *an exciting life, pleasure, social recognition*, and *a world of beauty* the least important. Moreover, the religious, less religious, and nonreligious all agree in ranking the instrumental values *honest, ambitious*, and *responsible* highest, and *imaginative, intellectual, logical*, and *obedient* lowest in importance.

At the same time, the several groups varying in religion also differ significantly in many ways. Americans identifying themselves as Jews generally place a higher value than do Christians on *equality, pleasure, family security, inner harmony*, and *wisdom*, and on instrumental values emphasizing personal competence—being *capable, independent, intellectual*, and *logical*. The average nonbeliever's value profile is similar in many respects to that obtained for Jews. Both nonbeliever and Jew put relatively less emphasis than Christians do on such conventional values as being *clean, obedient*, and *polite*.

Two values—*salvation* and *forgiving*—stand out above all the others as the most distinctively Christian values. Whereas Jews and nonbelievers rank *salvation* last, Christians generally rank it considerably higher—third on the average for Baptists and anywhere from ninth to fourteenth for the remaining Christian groups.

This picture of the Christian value system holds up when other definitions of religiousness are employed, such as frequency of church attendance and self-reports about the perceived importance of religion in one's daily life. In the national sample, *salvation* ranks third on the average for those who attend church every week and drops linearly to eighteenth for those never attending; *forgiving* ranks second for those attending every week and decreases linearly to eleventh for nonchurchgoers. With perceived importance of religion as the criterion of religiousness, the composite ranking of *salvation* is first for those reporting religion as very important, and it is last for those reporting religion as unimportant. The comparable finding for *forgiving* is sixth for those regarding religion as important and thirteenth for those regarding it as unimportant.

Sociologists might argue that these differences are not so much a result of differences in religiousness as of social class. But when the various religious groups are matched for income and race, the value differences remain generally about the same as those reported here.

Finally, despite the fact that Christianity teaches love and charity, data from the national survey do not support the proposition that Christians place a greater value than non-Christians on being *loving* or *helpful*. There is no evidence from the national sample that being *loving* and *helpful* are distinctively Christian values.

POLITICAL VALUES

Table 3.15 shows that 10 of the 36 values differentiate significantly among adult Americans identifying themselves as Democrats, Republicans, and Independents. Differences in the rankings of these 10 values seem to be mainly a function of social class differences in party identification, and these differences are small on the whole. The three groups do not differ on *equality*—a value that time and again has been found to differentiate between ideological positions, as will be shown later. The overall impression gained from the findings is that Americans who identify themselves as Democrats, Republicans, and Independents have highly similar value patterns, which may reflect either the fact that there is really very little difference between them or, more likely, that there are just too many different kinds of Democrats, Republicans, and Independents in the United States.

Fortunately, data are also available for respondent preferences for the various presidential candidates in the 1968 election. "As it stands now," they were asked in April 1968, "which one of these possible candidates would you personally like to see elected president next November?" Their selections were limited to Lyndon Johnson, Robert Kennedy, Eugene McCarthy, Richard Nixon, Ronald Reagan, Nelson Rockefeller, and George Wallace. At the time of testing, Kennedy was still alive; Humphrey had not yet announced his candidacy; and, although Johnson had already

TABLE 3.15 SIGNIFICANT VALUE DIFFERENCES AMONG
DEMOCRATS, REPUBLICANS, AND INDEPENDENTS
(NORC SAMPLE)

	Democrats	Republicans	Independents	
N =	768	359	226	p*
Terminal Values				
A comfortable life	8.7 (9)	9.7 (11)	10.2 (11)	.05
An exciting life	15.6 (18)	14.8 (17)	15.0 (17)	.05
A world at peace	3.0 (1)	3.9 (2)	3.6 (1)	.001
Social recognition	14.0 (16)	14.6 (16)	15.3 (18)	.01
Instrumental Values				
Cheerful	9.5 (9)	10.2 (12)	10.9 (13)	.05
Clean	8.0 (7)	9.4 (8)	10.7 (12)	.001
Imaginative	15.6 (18)	15.4 (18)	14.2 (18)	.05
Intellectual	13.5 (16)	12.7 (15)	12.0 (15)	.05
Logical	14.8 (17)	13.9 (17)	12.7 (16)	.001
Self-controlled	10.0 (12)	9.4 (10)	8.8 (7)	.05

Figures shown are median rankings and, in parentheses, composite rank orders.
*Median test.

removed himself from the presidential race, it was too late to remove his
name from the printed NORC survey forms. The results are shown in
Tables 3.16 and 3.17. Eight terminal values and six instrumental values
show significant differences among the seven groups.

Foreign Policy Differences

It is possible to identify two terminal values that seem to underlie differences in foreign policy among the seven groups. Rankings on *a world at
peace* seem to differentiate Democrats on the one hand from Republican
and Wallace supporters on the other; its composite ranking was first for
Johnson, Kennedy, and McCarthy supporters, but second for Republican
and Wallace supporters. These differences in rankings of *a world at peace*
are, however, rather subtle ones and do not throw light on the bitter
differences that had developed by spring 1968 over the American presence
in Vietnam, particularly between Johnson supporters on the one hand and
McCarthy and Kennedy supporters on the other.

The key value that helps account for such differences is *national security*.
Even though the overall Median test turned out to be insignificant,
Johnson supporters valued *national security* more highly than any of the
other groups, ranking it eighth. McCarthy supporters diverged most
sharply from Johnson supporters in this respect, ranking *national security*
thirteenth, and close behind them were the Kennedy supporters who ranked
it twelfth. Rankings by the McCarthy supporters are significantly different

TABLE 3.16 TERMINAL VALUE MEDIANS AND COMPOSITE RANK ORDERS FOR SUPPORTERS OF SEVEN PRESIDENTIAL CANDIDATES IN 1968 (N = 1,233)

	Kennedy	Johnson	McCarthy	Rockefeller	Nixon	Reagan	Wallace	p
N =	273	221	149	129	291	52	118	
A comfortable life	8.1 (7)	8.5 (9)	10.6 (11)	10.5 (12)	9.5 (11)	11.1 (13)	7.0 (5)	.001
An exciting life	15.3 (18)	15.7 (18)	15.0 (17)	14.6 (16)	15.2 (18)	14.7 (17)	14.4 (17)	—
A sense of accomplishment	9.5 (10)	9.3 (10)	8.4 (8)	7.8 (6)	8.6 (8)	8.2 (8)	8.9 (10)	.05
A world at peace	3.4 (1)	2.7 (1)	3.3 (1)	4.1 (2)	3.7 (2)	3.8 (2)	3.6 (2)	.05
A world of beauty	14.2 (16)	13.6 (15)	13.2 (15)	12.6 (14)	13.5 (15)	13.0 (15)	14.0 (15)	.001
Equality	6.2 (4)	7.0 (4)	7.3 (6)	8.6 (9)	9.8 (12)	10.3 (10)	13.0 (14)	—
Family security	4.0 (2)	3.8 (2)	3.9 (2)	4.0 (1)	3.6 (1)	3.3 (1)	3.4 (1)	—
Freedom	5.5 (3)	5.3 (3)	5.1 (3)	5.4 (3)	6.4 (3)	4.8 (3)	5.8 (3)	—
Happiness	7.6 (5)	7.3 (5)	8.0 (7)	8.4 (8)	7.7 (6)	7.3 (5)	8.3 (8)	—
Inner harmony	10.9 (13)	10.9 (13)	10.0 (10)	10.1 (11)	10.4 (13)	9.5 (9)	11.3 (13)	.01
Mature love	13.1 (14)	13.2 (14)	11.9 (14)	12.7 (15)	12.0 (14)	10.5 (12)	10.6 (12)	—
National security	9.9 (12)	8.4 (8)	11.1 (13)	9.0 (10)	8.9 (10)	10.3 (11)	9.3 (11)	—
Pleasure	14.6 (17)	14.2 (16)	15.1 (18)	14.8 (18)	15.0 (17)	13.4 (16)	14.3 (16)	.01
Salvation	9.3 (9)	8.1 (7)	10.7 (12)	11.3 (13)	7.6 (5)	7.3 (6)	6.5 (4)	—
Self-respect	7.7 (6)	7.8 (6)	7.2 (5)	7.7 (5)	7.9 (7)	6.5 (4)	8.1 (6)	.01
Social recognition	13.6 (15)	14.3 (17)	15.0 (16)	14.8 (17)	14.7 (16)	15.5 (18)	14.6 (18)	—
True friendship	9.9 (11)	9.8 (12)	9.4 (9)	8.2 (7)	8.8 (9)	11.7 (14)	8.1 (7)	.01
Wisdom	8.8 (8)	9.6 (11)	6.9 (4)	7.2 (4)	7.2 (4)	7.8 (7)	8.5 (9)	.001

Figures shown are median rankings and, in parentheses, composite rank orders.

camps—between the Rockefeller supporters on the one hand and the Nixon and Reagan supporters on the other. These findings suggest that Rockefeller's appeal among Republicans would have been considerably greater had he been able to project a more "reverent" image. That Rockefeller did not appeal more to those who valued *salvation* highly is probably due to the fact that many Republicans had not altogether forgotten his divorce several years previously.

Among the three Democratic groups, Johnson supporters valued *salvation* most and McCarthy supporters valued it least. It would thus appear that it is the Rockefeller supporters among the Republicans and the McCarthy supporters among the Democrats who were the least religious-minded of the seven groups.

Other Value Differences

A number of other terminal and instrumental values differentiate significantly among the seven groups. These include *a world of beauty, true friendship, wisdom, capable, clean, obedient, polite, responsible,* and *self-controlled.* To conserve space these will not be discussed in detail here. The interested reader can readily ascertain the nature and direction of these differences by inspecting Tables 3.16 and 3.17. Although it would have been difficult to predict all these differences in advance, they nevertheless seem to be consistent with what is generally known about the various groups of presidential supporters. We may note, for instance, that it is the generally young, middle-class McCarthy supporters who ranked *clean, obedient,* and *polite* lowest among the instrumental values, findings that can be attributed to social class and age differences. Wallace supporters, worried as they usually are about racial integration and the law-and-order issue, ranked *self-controlled* higher but, paradoxically, they also ranked *responsible* lower than any of the remaining groups. These findings concerning Wallace supporters are consistent with those reported by Wrightsman (1969); they espoused law-and-order but were delinquent when it came to paying their taxes on time.

Two of the instrumental values that differentiate most reliably among the seven political groups are *clean* and *obedient.* Kennedy, Johnson, and Wallace supporters ranked them both higher, the Republican groups ranked them lower, and the McCarthy supporters ranked them lowest. To a large extent these findings again seem to reflect social class differences among the seven groups, as shown in Table 3.4.

Despite the differences observed for the seven groups, they are on the whole rather alike in their value patterns. Sharper differences would probably have been obtained had we compared French or Italian rather than American political groups. The major differences observed among the seven American groups seem primarily to be differences in the judged importance of a relatively few values, above all, differences in the terminal value, *equality.* For a fuller discussion of political values, however, see Chapters 6 and 7.

SOME CROSS-CULTURAL
COMPARISONS

A major criterion employed in the selection of the 36 values to be included in the Value Survey was that they be reasonably comprehensive and universally applicable. Although no claim can yet be made that this is indeed the case, the question nevertheless arises whether the Value Survey is sensitive enough to identify specific cross-cultural value differences. Ideally, cross-cultural comparisons would be most useful if reliable data employing the same value instrument were available for representative national samples from various countries. It would then be a rather simple matter to compare any one country's values with those of any other, or with those reported in this chapter for adult Americans.

Even though a systematic cross-cultural approach is still some years away, mainly because of the cost and effort that such an undertaking would involve, data are nevertheless available for comparable samples of college men tested in four countries: I have obtained data for a Michigan State University sample in the United States and for a University of Western Ontario sample in Canada; Feather (1970a) has obtained data

TABLE 3.18 TERMINAL VALUE AVERAGES AND COMPOSITE RANK ORDERS FOR AMERICAN, AUSTRALIAN, ISRAELI, AND CANADIAN SAMPLES OF COLLEGE MEN

	United States	Australia	Israel	Canada
N =	169	279	71	125
A comfortable life	10.3 (11)	12.6 (13)	12.8 (15)	11.6 (13)
An exciting life	10.8 (12)	9.2 (11)	8.7 (9)	9.8 (11)
A sense of accomplishment	7.1 (5)	6.3 (4)	7.5 (7)	9.2 (9)
A world at peace	9.3 (10)	8.2 (9)	4.7 (1)	10.0 (12)
A world of beauty	14.4 (18)	13.0 (15)	14.5 (17)	12.3 (15)
Equality	12.3 (13)	9.0 (10)	9.3 (10)	9.7 (10)
Family security	8.1 (7)	9.5 (12)	7.9 (8)	7.5 (7)
Freedom	4.7 (1)	4.9 (3)	6.5 (4)	4.5 (1)
Happiness	6.2 (2)	7.5 (7)	6.0 (3)	4.7 (2)
Inner harmony	8.8 (9)	7.7 (8)	10.9 (13)	7.4 (6)
Mature love	7.4 (6)	6.6 (5)	6.5 (5)	5.6 (3)
National security	13.8 (17)	13.9 (17)	5.6 (2)	16.6 (17)
Pleasure	13.1 (15)	12.7 (14)	11.2 (14)	12.3 (14)
Salvation	13.4 (16)	15.9 (18)	15.9 (18)	17.6 (18)
Self-respect	7.0 (4)	7.5 (6)	9.7 (11)	6.9 (4)
Social recognition	12.9 (14)	13.7 (16)	13.5 (16)	13.9 (16)
True friendship	8.7 (8)	4.9 (2)	10.1 (12)	7.3 (5)
Wisdom	6.8 (3)	4.7 (1)	7.3 (6)	8.3 (8)

Figures shown are median rankings for U.S., Australian, and Canadian samples, mean rankings for Israeli sample, and, in parentheses, composite rank orders.

from a Flinders University sample in South Australia, and Rim (1970) has obtained them from a sample tested at the Israel Institute of Technology in Haifa.

The results (Tables 3.18 and 3.19) are illuminating not only because they illustrate the kinds of cultural differences that can be detected by the Value Survey but also because they are pertinent to the validity of certain hypotheses put forward by Lipset (1963) concerning cultural differences between the United States, Canada, and Australia.

Since these data were obtained by independent investigators who had other purposes, direct statistical tests of significance of differences among the national groups are not available. But visual inspection reveals many sizeable value differences. The largest terminal value differences among the four groups are found for *a world at peace* and *national security*: Although American, Canadian, and Australian male college students rank *a world at peace* ninth to twelfth down the list, Israeli college students rank it first; Americans, Canadians, and Australians place a very low value on *national security*, seventeenth, but Israelis rank it second from the top. The reasons for these value differences are self-evident: They arise from objective conditions that Israelis face daily in a volatile and unstable

TABLE 3.19   INSTRUMENTAL VALUE AVERAGES AND COMPOSITE RANK
ORDERS FOR AMERICAN, AUSTRALIAN, ISRAELI, AND CANADIAN
SAMPLES OF COLLEGE MEN

	United States	Australia	Israel	Canada
N =	169	279	71	125
Ambitious	6.4 (3)	7.8 (6)	8.7 (7)	9.4 (11)
Broadminded	6.7 (4)	4.6 (2)	9.2 (9)	6.4 (4)
Capable	7.5 (5)	8.2 (8)	6.5 (4)	9.9 (12)
Cheerful	12.0 (15)	8.5 (9)	12.2 (14)	8.8 (6)
Clean	14.1 (17)	13.9 (17)	12.6 (15)	15.4 (17)
Courageous	8.4 (8)	8.7 (10)	9.8 (12)	9.1 (8)
Forgiving	10.5 (12)	9.3 (11)	14.3 (18)	9.1 (10)
Helpful	11.9 (14)	10.2 (13)	9.3 (10)	9.1 (9)
Honest	5.2 (1)	4.0 (1)	5.1 (1)	3.0 (1)
Imaginative	10.8 (13)	11.5 (15)	13.1 (16)	10.6 (15)
Independent	7.7 (6)	7.9 (7)	9.9 (13)	6.9 (5)
Intellectual	8.5 (9)	10.6 (14)	7.7 (6)	8.9 (7)
Logical	8.3 (7)	9.9 (12)	5.9 (3)	10.5 (14)
Loving	9.1 (11)	7.5 (4)	9.1 (8)	6.4 (3)
Obedient	15.0 (18)	15.3 (18)	13.6 (17)	16.6 (18)
Polite	13.2 (16)	12.1 (16)	9.7 (11)	14.6 (16)
Responsible	5.9 (2)	5.2 (3)	5.2 (2)	5.6 (2)
Self-controlled	8.6 (10)	7.7 (5)	7.6 (5)	10.2 (13)

Figures shown are median rankings for U.S., Australian, and Canadian samples, mean rankings for Israeli sample, and, in parentheses, composite rank orders.

Middle East, in contrast to the greater security from external attack enjoyed by Americans, Canadians, and Australians.

It is possible, with the aid of Tables 3.18 and 3.19, to identify the specific values that distinguish American college men from their counterparts in Canada, Australia, and Israel. The orientation toward materialism, competition, and achievement that is so often attributed to Americans is apparent in the findings that American college men care relatively more for *a comfortable life, social recognition,* and being *ambitious* and care less for being *helpful* than do Canadian, Australian, and Israeli college men. This achievement orientation seems to be more in the service of materialism and success than in the service of personal competence. American college men (in common with Americans in general) generally place a higher value on being *ambitious* than on being *capable,* in contrast to Israeli college men who care more for being *capable* than for being *ambitious.*

Contrary perhaps to popular conception, and contrary to Lipset's speculations (1963), the data suggest that Americans are less egalitarian than Canadians, Australians, and Israelis. American college men are more *salvation*-minded, when they are compared with Canadians, Australians, and Israelis, and they are moreover less hedonistic, fun-loving, and love-oriented, as is evidenced by the findings that they care less for *an exciting life, pleasure,* and *mature love* than do Canadian, Australian, and Israeli college men.

Israelis show a markedly different value pattern. As already stated, they care more than the other three groups do for *a world at peace* and *national security,* which they rank first and second on their terminal scale of values. Also, as previously stated, Israelis care more about being *capable* than about being *ambitious,* and competence for these Israelis evidently means mainly an intellectual competence; they not only rank *capable* higher than the other national groups but also *intellectual* and *logical* higher. They are, however, less individualistic than Americans, Canadians, and Australians and more group-oriented, as is evidenced by the fact that they place generally lower values on *freedom* and on being *independent* and higher values on being *helpful, clean, polite, obedient,* and *self-controlled.* The terminal value *salvation* and the instrumental value *forgiving,* the two values that have been found to be the most distinctively Christian values, are at the bottom of their terminal and instrumental value hierarchies. Had we not been informed that the value rankings described here had been obtained for Israelis, we should have been able to guess it—from the fact that they had ranked the two main Christian values at the bottom of their value hierarchy, from the fact that they had ranked *a world at peace* and *national security* first and second among their terminal values, and from the fact that values concerning intellectual competence are more important for them than is the case with Americans, Canadians, and Australians. It is also interesting that Israeli college men place a lower value than do Americans, Canadians, and Australians on *inner harmony, true friendship, self-respect*, and on being *broadminded*. One interpretation of these findings is that they are a function of the extreme everyday conditions of stress under which Israelis live—conditions that de-emphasize modes of behavior and end-states of existence favoring personal and interpersonal over national interests.

Consider next the values that are the most distinctively Australian. The value that most notably distinguishes Australians from Americans, Canadians, and Israelis is *true friendship*, which they rank second in importance compared with fifth by Canadians, eighth by Americans, and twelfth by Israelis. Australians, too, rank *equality* higher, and this is also the case for *a sense of accomplishment*, *wisdom*, and being *broadminded* and *cheerful*. Australians seem to be somewhat less achievement-oriented than Americans but more so than Israelis and Canadians. And they rank *family security*, *happiness*, and *intellectual* lower than do the other three groups.

Lipset summarizes speculations offered by various writers on Australian culture (Taft and Walker, 1958; Ward, 1958) as follows: "Australia presents us with still different value patterns, captured in the term 'mate-ship' . . . supposedly viewed by many Australians as contradictory to the value of 'success-ship' (achievement). Mateship, then, stresses the value of particularism and egalitarianism" (1963, p. 522). The Australian value rankings provide strong support for such observations, particularly their relatively high rankings of *true friendship* and *equality*. There is, however, less support for the proposition that "mateship" and "success-ship" are contradictory values. Australians may not be quite as achievement-oriented as Americans but they are not far behind them in this respect, and they seem far ahead of the Canadians.

Finally, some comments are in order about distinctively Canadian values. Most readily apparent from Tables 3.18 and 3.19 is that Canadian students are considerably less achievement-oriented than American, Australian, and Israeli students. Canadians generally place a lower value on *a sense of accomplishment*, and *wisdom*, and on being *ambitious* and *capable*. The findings concerning the latter two values are especially noteworthy. *Ambitious* and *capable* are ranked third and fifth by Americans, sixth and eighth by Australians, seventh and fourth by Israelis, but eleventh and twelfth by Canadians. Also notable is the unusually low ranking of *logical* by Canadian college men—fourteenth, compared with third for Israelis, seventh for Americans, and twelfth for Australians. Canadian college men also seem to care less than the other three groups about being *self-controlled*, *polite*, and *obedient*. Instead, they rank relatively higher aesthetic values and values that emphasize love, peace of mind, personal happiness, honesty, and independence. Finally, Canadians seem to be about as egalitarian as Australian and Israeli college men, but they care more about egalitarianism than do American college men.

These findings are consistent with Seymour Lipset's analysis of Canadian values insofar as achievement values are concerned, but not insofar as egalitarian values are concerned. He suggests that "Canada is lower than the United States on. . . egalitarianism (and) achievement. . . . Geography, too, inhibited the spread of egalitarianism and individualism on the Canadian frontier . . . add to this a self-serving elite—that gain by keeping close ties to the Mother country—deliberately playing down egalitarianism and individualism . . ." (pp. 521–522). Lipset quotes Kaspar Naegele: "There seems to be less optimism, less faith in the future, less willingness to risk capital or reputation. In contrast to America, Canada is a country of greater caution, reserve, and restraint" (p. 522).

Tables 3.18 and 3.19 show that Canadian students are more rather than less egalitarian than American students, and also that they value *freedom* and *independence* more and *self-controlled* less than American, Australian, and Israeli students. There is thus no support here for Lipset's contention that Canadians are less egalitarian or individualistic than Americans. There is clear support, however, for his suggestion that Canadians are less achievement-oriented, but even here it is not at all clear whether their lesser achievement orientation arises from a lesser optimism or faith in the future or from a greater "caution, reserve, and restraint" or from their greater appreciation of other values: beauty, love, inner peace, and honesty.

All these cross-cultural findings must, however, be regarded as highly tentative. Although they all come from male college students in the four countries, it is difficult to say to what extent the subjects were selected in the same way or are representative of all college students in the country or even of the university tested. Nonetheless, it would seem that the data are on the whole generally consistent with what is intuitively known about Israel, Australia, Canada, and the United States. The fact that the Value Survey can readily generate such data encourages us to think that it will prove to be generally useful in cross-cultural studies no less than in studies of groups within a given culture.

CONCLUDING REMARKS

We have described in this chapter the terminal and instrumental rankings found for representative samples of adult Americans varying in sex, income, education, race, age, politics, and religion. Moreover, cross-cultural comparisons are presented for American, Canadian, Australian, and Israeli college men. The findings show that different numbers and combinations of the 36 terminal and instrumental values differentiate significantly among groups varying in demographic and cultural variables. All the findings considered together suggest that the Value Survey is sensitive to differences within and between cultural groups.

In what sense can it be said that values are social indicators of the quality of life? A social indicator is more than just another measure of some social variable. It is really a measure of where we are compared with some theoretical conception of where we ought to be. If we assess the data presented in this chapter from the standpoint of Maslow's theory of lower- and higher-order values, it becomes apparent that the data are telling us a great deal about variations in the quality of life in different segments of American society. Most particularly, they suggest that the quality of life among the poor, among the uneducated, and among black Americans is considerably lower than among the more affluent and educated, and among white Americans. In the same way, the value differences between American men and women, between Americans differing in their religious orientations, and between respondents differing in culture indicate differential strivings for lower- and higher-order values. Thus, the data presented in this chapter point in many specific ways to gaps in the quality of life characterizing various segments of American society and, to some extent also, across societies. These gaps thus inform us about how far we have yet to go toward the realization of a social order that meets human needs.

4
Values and Attitudes

The data reported in Chapter 3 demonstrate that various subsets of terminal and instrumental values differentiate in a meaningful and significant manner between cultures, and—within the American culture—between groups varying in various demographic characteristics. These findings provide evidence consistent with the general proposition that common cultural and subcultural experiences and socialization are important determinants of values. The findings moreover inform us that the particular approach to the measurement of values taken here has the various kinds of validity that Cronbach and Meehl (1955) have identified as construct, content, and predictive validity.

In this chapter and in the next our attention shifts away from an examination of values as dependent variables to their examination as independent variables. This chapter will be concerned with the functional relations between values and attitudes, and the next will discuss values and behavior. If it is indeed the case that a relatively small number of human values can be conceptualized as the core cognitive components underlying the thousands of attitudes that people hold, and the countless socially relevant behaviors they engage in, then different subsets of the 36 values included in the Value Survey should be significantly associated with virtually any attitude or behavior.

Accordingly, this chapter will contain findings on the relation between values and many different kinds of attitudes—attitudes that concern politics and religion, domestic and international issues, even attitudes that are inconsequential and, on the other extreme, more global types of attitudes that are typically called personality dispositions. In each case, the hypothesis to be tested is basically the same: Whatever the attitude, it is an expression or manifestation of and should therefore be significantly related to some subset of terminal and instrumental values.

On theoretical grounds, it should be possible to specify in advance some of but not all the values that might be related to a given attitude. Theory and knowledge in the social sciences are as yet not sufficiently developed to enable us to predict all the values that might underlie a given attitude. A given attitude held by different persons need not be in the service of the same value or the same subset of values. A favorable attitude toward socialized medicine, for instance, may serve the value of *equality* in one person and the value of *family security* in another; an unfavorable attitude toward the church may serve one person's value for *independence* and another person's value for *honesty*; a favorable attitude toward blacks may be in the service of one person's value for *equality* and another person's value for *kindness*.

Nevertheless, there are theoretical grounds for anticipating that certain values will more often be related predictably to a given attitude than other values. For one thing, there are logical relations between certain values and attitudes. For another, certain values and attitudes are within the specialized domain of specific social institutions. In general, values that can be identified as being within the specialized concern of a particular institution should be the best predictors of those attitudes and behaviors that are also within that domain. Thus, variations in what we call religious values should be most associated with variations in what we call religious attitudes and behaviors; variations in political values should be most associated with variations in political attitudes and behaviors; variations in intellectual values should be most associated with variations in intellectual attitudes and behaviors; and so on.

In presenting the data on values and attitudes, we have been mindful of Campbell and Fiske's (1959) multitrait-multimethod approach to convergent and discriminant validation. As already suggested, it may be anticipated that different values will be differentially related to specified attitudes and behaviors. Certain values should and other values should not be related to specified attitudes and behaviors. To the extent that empirical findings support such expectations, the Value Survey may be said to exhibit discriminant validity. Moreover, to the extent that certain values are significantly related to certain behaviors as well as attitudes, the Value Survey may be said to exhibit convergent validity.

The most extensive data concerning the relation between values and attitudes come once again from the national sample of adult Americans tested in April 1968. The respondents not only filled out the Value Survey but also expressed their opinions on many salient issues of the day: their reactions to the assassination of Dr. Martin Luther King, their opinions concerning various aspects of equal rights for black Americans, their views about race differences in intelligence, interracial dating and marriage, black activism, and so on. Moving beyond the race issue, the national sample of respondents also expressed their opinions about the poor in general—whether the poor should be provided with a college education, medical and dental care, a guaranteed income, and the like. Other questions elicited their opinions about the American presence in Vietnam, student protest on the nation's campuses, and the advisability of American organized churches' participation in the everyday political and social affairs of the nation.

Other findings concerning the relation between values and attitudes come from other samples, mainly from college students in the United States and abroad. Details of sampling will be presented in the appropriate context.

To save space in this chapter and in the next, we will report only the value rankings that differentiate significantly between subgroups varying on each of the attitudes or behaviors under consideration. The reader may safely assume that value rankings not reported are those that do not differentiate significantly.

CIVIL RIGHTS FOR BLACK AND POOR AMERICANS

Reactions to the Assassination of Dr. Martin Luther King

One question put to the national sample elicited reactions to the assassination of Dr. Martin Luther King which had occurred several weeks earlier in April 1968: "When you heard the news of the assassination of Dr. Martin Luther King, Jr., which one of these things was your strongest reaction? (1) sadness, (2) anger, (3) shame, (4) fear, (5) 'He brought it on himself'." About 37 percent of the white American sample reported that Dr. King had "brought it on himself." Another 11 percent reported "fear" as their main emotional reaction. The remaining 52 percent reacted more compassionately to the news of the assassination, with "sadness," "anger," or "shame." Table 4.1 shows 13 of the 36 values that differentiated significantly among respondents giving the five kinds of reactions to the assassination. The one value that best discriminates is *equality*; its composite rank is twelfth or thirteenth for those reacting with "fear" and "he brought it on himself," and its composite rank is fifth to seventh for those reacting with "sadness," "anger," or "shame." Moreover, those responding with "fear" and "he brought it on himself" are more concerned with material comfort, religious salvation, and the traditional values of cleanliness, obedience, and politeness. The values that they are less concerned about are the intellectual values—*imaginative*, *logical*, and *intellectual*. Finally, four other values show a somewhat different pattern of results: Those reporting "fear" as their main reaction place a higher value than the others do on *family security* and on being *loving*, and those reporting "shame" place a higher value than the others do on *a world at peace* and *national security*.

It is rather doubtful that all the significant value differences shown in Table 4.1 could have been predicted in advance. But at least a few of them

TABLE 4.1 SIGNIFICANT VALUES DIFFERENTIATING FIVE TYPES OF WHITE RESPONDERS TO THE QUESTION:

"When you heard the news of the assassination of Dr. Martin Luther King, Jr., which one of these things was your strongest reaction?"

	Sadness	Anger	Shame	Fear	Brought It on Himself	p*
N =	351	49	187	124	416	
Terminal Values						
A comfortable life	11.1 (13)	12.3 (14)	9.9 (12)	9.5 (9)	8.5 (8)	.001
A world at peace	3.2 (1)	3.9 (1)	2.5 (1)	3.1 (2)	3.6 (2)	.01
Equality	7.8 (7)	6.6 (5)	8.3 (7)	10.1 (12)	11.2 (13)	.001
Family security	3.6 (2)	4.1 (2)	4.2 (2)	2.6 (1)	3.8 (2)	.01
National security	9.6 (12)	10.7 (11)	7.8 (5)	10.1 (11)	8.6 (9)	.05
Salvation	9.4 (9)	14.0 (15)	8.6 (9)	6.2 (4)	7.2 (4)	.01
Instrumental Values						
Clean	10.2 (11)	13.1 (16)	9.7 (10)	8.9 (9)	7.9 (7)	.001
Imaginative	14.8 (18)	12.8 (15)	15.7 (18)	16.5 (18)	15.5 (18)	.01
Intellectual	12.5 (15)	9.4 (9)	13.3 (15)	14.3 (16)	13.4 (16)	.01
Logical	13.5 (16)	9.8 (10)	13.9 (17)	15.4 (17)	14.1 (17)	.01
Loving	8.6 (8)	10.8 (13)	10.5 (12)	7.3 (5)	9.9 (12)	.01
Obedient	13.9 (17)	15.2 (18)	13.9 (16)	12.4 (15)	13.2 (15)	.01
Polite	11.2 (14)	13.6 (17)	11.0 (13)	10.9 (14)	10.3 (13)	.01

Figures shown are median rankings and, in parentheses, composite rank orders.
* Median test.

could have been so predicted, especially the largest difference concerning *equality*, and those concerning material comfort, conformity, and anti-intellectualism. But other differences were not anticipated and will no doubt come as a surprise to many, especially the finding that those responding uncompassionately are more religious-minded. For a more detailed discussion of the results obtained with the national sample concerning religious values, see Rokeach (1969a, 1969b, 1970a, 1970b).

Several other questions concerning Dr. King's assassination yielded similar findings. "After Dr. King's death, did you feel sorry for his wife and children?"; "After Dr. King's death, did you feel angry about the murder?"; "After Dr. King's death, did you think about the many tragic things that have happened to Negroes and that this was just another one of them?" The value patterns of those responding differently to these questions are essentially the same as those shown in Table 4.1, and in all cases *equality* is the most discriminating value. Its composite rank is uniformly fourth for those agreeing strongly with these opinion statements. In contrast, it is twelfth or thirteenth for those responding to these questions with "it never occurred to me."

Attitude toward Blacks

Table 4.2 shows 12 additional and more general questions concerning civil rights for black Americans that were also asked of the national sample. They cover rather comprehensively the whole gamut of civil rights issues for black Americans: open occupancy, fair employment, desegregation in the schools, interracial contact, dating and marriage, race differences in intelligence, and black militancy. Since these findings are too voluminous to report separately, a single index of the extent to which the respondent exhibited a racist attitude was constructed on the basis of their responses to these 12 questions. They were then classified as having racist (5 to 12), in between (-4 to $+4$), and antiracist (-5 to -12) attitudes. The odd-even split-half reliability of this index corrected for length was .85. The significant value rankings of the three groups of adult white Americans so classified are shown in Table 4.3.

TABLE 4.2 CIVIL RIGHTS FOR BLACKS SCALE

	Antiracist	In between	Racist
1. How do you feel about open occupancy laws—that is, laws that make white people sell or rent to qualified Negroes, so that Negroes can move into any homes or apartments they can afford?	Strongly favor Favor	Don't know or No answer	Strongly oppose Oppose
2. How do you feel about fair employment laws—that is, laws that make white people hire qualified Negroes, so that Negroes can get any job they are qualified for?	Strongly favor Favor	Don't know or No answer	Strongly oppose Oppose
3. Do you think Negro students and white students should go to the same schools or different schools?	Same schools	Don't know or No answer	Separate schools
4. Do you think there should be laws against marriage between Negroes and whites?	No	Don't know or No answer	Yes
5. Do you think Negroes are as intelligent as white people— that is, can they learn things just as well if they are given the same education and training?	Yes, as intelligent	Don't know or No answer	No, not as intelligent
6. Which factor do you believe accounts for the failure of the Negro to achieve equality?	Restrictions imposed by white society	Don't know or No answer	Lack of initiative

TABLE 4.2 (*continued*)

	Antiracist	In between	Racist
7. All in all, do you think Negro groups are asking for too much, too little, or just about what they should be asking for?	Too little Just about what they should	Don't know or No answer	Too much
8. Negroes shouldn't push themselves where they're not wanted.	Disagree strongly Disagree somewhat	Don't know or No answer	Agree strongly Agree somewhat
9. White people have a right to keep Negroes out of their neighbourhoods if they want to, and Negroes should respect that right.	Disagree strongly Disagree somewhat	Don't know or No answer	Agree strongly Agree somewhat
10. If you were referred to a Negro doctor, would you go to him?	Yes	Don't know or No answer	No
11. What would your reaction be if a teenager of yours wanted to date a Negro boy or girl?	Not object at all	Object mildly	Object strongly
12. How do you yourself feel about the actions Negroes have taken to get the things they want?	Generally approve	Don't know or No answer	Generally disapprove

Attention should first be drawn to the fact that the racially prejudiced and unprejudiced do not differ significantly in their rankings of the following 15 values: *a world at peace, freedom, self-respect, social recognition, true friendship*, being *capable, cheerful, courageous, forgiving, helpful, honest, independent, loving, responsible*, and *self-controlled*.

But they do differ significantly on the remaining 21 of the 36 values, and many of these differences are rather sizeable. As was the case with reactions to Dr. King's assassination, the largest difference is found for *equality*, its composite rank being 4 for antiracists, 12 of those scoring in between, and 14 for racists. Feather (1970a) obtained the reactions of two samples of white college students in South Australia to the issue of continuing to keep Australia white. Consistent with the findings reported here, *equality* best predicted differences in attitude toward a white Australia.

Clean is the value that is the second best discriminator: It is ranked sixth by racists, eighth by those in between, and fifteenth by antiracists. Both of these sets of findings suggest that those scoring within the intermediate range on the 12-item attitude toward blacks scale are almost as

TABLE 4.3 SIGNIFICANT VALUE DIFFERENCES AMONG ADULT
WHITE AMERICANS VARYING IN ATTITUDE TOWARD BLACK
AMERICANS

	Antiracist	In between	Racist	
N =	255	600	340	p*
Terminal Values				
A comfortable life	12.5 (14)	9.4 (11)	7.7 (6)	.001
An exciting life	14.8 (16)	15.7 (18)	15.2 (18)	.05
A sense of accomplishment	8.0 (7)	8.7 (9)	10.0 (11)	.001
A world of beauty	12.4 (13)	13.8 (15)	13.6 (15)	.01
Equality	6.0 (4)	9.6 (12)	12.6 (14)	.001
Family security	4.6 (2)	3.3 (2)	3.5 (2)	.001
Happiness	8.6 (8)	7.4 (4)	7.1 (5)	.05
Inner harmony	9.7 (10)	10.2 (13)	11.1 (12)	.01
Mature love	11.2 (11)	12.6 (14)	11.9 (13)	.01
National security	11.3 (12)	8.6 (8)	8.6 (9)	.001
Pleasure	15.0 (17)	14.9 (17)	13.9 (16)	.01
Salvation	12.7 (15)	8.3 (7)	5.9 (4)	.001
Wisdom	6.3 (5)	8.0 (6)	8.5 (8)	.05
Instrumental Values				
Ambitious	9.5 (8)	6.5 (2)	5.7 (2)	.001
Broadminded	5.7 (2)	7.3 (5)	9.1 (8)	.001
Clean	12.2 (15)	9.0 (8)	7.9 (6)	.001
Imaginative	13.1 (17)	15.7 (18)	15.9 (18)	.001
Intellectual	11.0 (13)	13.6 (16)	13.6 (16)	.001
Logical	11.3 (14)	14.2 (17)	14.7 (17)	.001
Obedient	15.1 (18)	13.3 (15)	12.8 (15)	.001
Polite	12.9 (16)	10.6 (13)	10.4 (14)	.001

Figures shown are median rankings and, in parentheses, composite rank orders.
*Median test.

racist as those scoring more extremely, even though they are less apt to
express antiblack sentiments openly.

A more comprehensive description of the value pattern of the average
adult white American racist is as follows: He cares relatively more than
the nonracist for *a comfortable life, family security, happiness, national
security, pleasure, salvation,* being *ambitious, clean, obedient,* and *polite*;
he cares significantly less than the nonracist about *an exciting life, a sense
of accomplishment, a world of beauty, equality, inner harmony, wisdom,*
being *broadminded, imaginative, intellectual,* and *logical.* The remaining
value that shows a significant difference, *mature love,* is valued most by the
antiracists and least by those in between. It is thus seen that the value
system of the racially prejudiced places more emphasis on religion,
personal happiness, material comfort, conformity, conventional behavior,
hard work, and the security of the family and nation and less emphasis on

egalitarianism, self-actualization, inner peace, aesthetic and intellectual values, sexual love, and tolerance. This portrait of the racially prejudiced is, of course, highly consistent with other descriptions (e.g., Adorno, *et al.*, 1950; Allport, 1954), the main difference being that the present portrait is more directly and simply constructed from self-reports that require fewer inferential leaps than those based on more elaborately-constructed attitude and personality tests.

The product-moment correlation between attitude toward blacks and value for *equality* is −.40 for white Americans in the national sample; that is, the lower the value for *equality*, the greater the prejudice expressed toward blacks. This correlation increases to .52 if the *equality* and attitude toward black variables are corrected for unreliability. This estimate was arrived at by taking into account the odd-even reliability of the 12-item attitude toward black scale, which was .85, and the test-retest reliability of *equality* rankings which was estimated as .71. This latter estimate was made from the only data presently available in the United States—those shown in Table 2.1 for college students.

The multiple correlation between all 36 values on the one hand and attitude toward blacks on the other is .57. This correlation would, of course, be higher if all the value measures were corrected for unreliability.

The value pattern of racists is in many respects similar to those patterns previously reported for the poor and uneducated, as a comparison between Table 4.3 and Tables 3.3 to 3.6 will reveal. But a notable exception is *equality*. As already shown, *equality* discriminates more sharply than any of the other values between racists and antiracists. In contrast, *equality* rankings do not differentiate significantly between the poor and rich white, or between the poor and rich black. *Equality* rankings do discriminate, beyond the .05 level, between uneducated and educated whites, with the more educated ranking it higher. The same is found for uneducated and educated blacks, the latter ranking *equality* significantly higher, beyond the .01 level of significance. But the *equality* gap between racists and nonracists is far greater than the one between the educated and the uneducated, or between the poor and the rich.

Attitudes of Blacks toward Black Militancy

Willis and Goldberg (1970) have reported data on the terminal value differences between black students in the North (Lincoln University and University of Michigan) and South (Atlanta University) who varied in their attitude toward black militancy. Three values stand out as ones that discriminate significantly between black militants and nonmilitants: (1) *Salvation* is ranked sixth by Southern nonmilitants and thirteenth by Southern militants. In the North, *salvation* is ranked equally low by militant and nonmilitant black students—fourteenth to sixteenth. (2) Compared with national norms, *equality* is ranked relatively high by black students, but black militants in the North and South care less (not more) for *equality* than do black nonmilitants. This trend is notable in all samples, but it is most notable (and statistically significant) among black students at the University of Michigan where *equality* is ranked third by nonmilitant and seventh by militant blacks. It would thus appear that talk about separatism by black power advocates is more than mere rhetoric; it is actually reflected in the lower position assigned to *equality* in their militant black's value hierarchy. (3) As is the case with white college students, black students also rank *national security* toward the bottom of their value hierarchy. But nonmilitant and militant blacks nevertheless differ in their ranking of *national security*, the former ranking it fourteenth and the latter eighteenth.

Attitude toward the Poor

Another 10 statements put to the national NORC sample elicited reactions to the poor—their right to medical and dental care, an education, a minimum living standard, etc. Again, instead of presenting the results separately for each of the issues covered, a single index was computed for all the opinion statements (odd-even reliability corrected for length was .69), as shown in Table 4.4, and the respondents were then classified as pro-poor (4 to 10), in between (−3 to +3), and anti-poor (−4 to −10). The value rankings that differentiate significantly among these three groups are reported in Table 4.5.

Equality is once again the most discriminating value, although it is not nearly as discriminating as in the case of attitude toward blacks. *Equality* rankings correlate .23 with attitude toward poor as compared with a correlation of .40 with attitude toward blacks. *Equality's* composite rank is 5, 10, and 13, respectively, for those expressing attitudes that are sympathetic with, in between, and unsympathetic with the poor. More generally, the anti-poor care more on the whole for *a sense of accomplishment, national security, salvation, wisdom,* being *independent, responsible,* and *self-controlled*; they care less about *a comfortable life, a world at peace, equality, happiness,* being *cheerful, clean, helpful, loving,* and *obedient.* The multiple correlation between attitude toward the poor on the one hand and the 36 values on the other is .37, suggesting that different values rather than a few identifiable values are instrumentally related to attitude toward the poor in different people.

A comparison of Tables 4.3 and 4.5 reveals that the value patterns of those who are prejudiced against black and against poor Americans are by no means the same. Those who are racially prejudiced value *a comfortable life,* for instance, more than do those who are less prejudiced, but it is the other way around for those expressing anti- and pro-poor attitudes; it is those who are in favor of the poor who value *a comfortable life* more. To take another example, those who are prejudiced against blacks care significantly less for *a sense of accomplishment,* but those who are preju-

TABLE 4.4 ATTITUDE TOWARD THE POOR SCALE

		Pro-poor	In between	Anti-poor
1.	Should public funds be used to provide dental care?	Yes	Don't know or No answer	No
2.	Would you or wouldn't you favor the use of public funds for free dental care even if it meant a tax increase?	Favor	Don't know, Depends, or No answer	Would not favor
3.	Every capable person has a right to receive a college education even if he can't afford it.	Agree strongly Agree somewhat	Don't know or No answer	Disagree strongly Disagree somewhat
4.	Every person has a right to adequate housing even if he can't afford it.	Agree strongly Agree somewhat	Don't know or No answer	Disagree strongly Disagree somewhat
5.	Every person has a right to a minimum income which would be enough to maintain an adequate standard of living.	Agree strongly Agree somewhat	Don't know or No answer	Disagree strongly Disagree somewhat
6.	Every person has the right to free dental care if he needs it but cannot afford it.	Agree strongly Agree somewhat	Don't know or No answer	Disagree strongly Disagree somewhat
7.	Every person has a right to free medical care if he needs it but cannot afford it.	Agree strongly Agree somewhat	Don't know or No answer	Disagree strongly Disagree somewhat
8.	Which is more to blame if a person is poor—lack of effort on his own part or circumstances beyond his control?	Circumstances	Both	Lack of effort
9.	If the local government wanted to raise taxes to pay for new roads, schools, and hospitals, in general would you probably be in favor of raising the taxes or would you probably be against raising taxes?	In favor	Don't know or No answer	Against
10.	Some people say that welfare should be completely changed and what we need is new ways of getting money to the poor, such as a guaranteed income, negative income tax, or children's allowance.	Agree	Don't know or No answer	Disagree

TABLE 4.5   SIGNIFICANT VALUE DIFFERENCES AMONG ADULT
AMERICANS VARYING IN ATTITUDE TOWARD THE POOR

	Pro-poor	In between	Anti-poor	
N =	845	478	86	p*
Terminal Values				
A comfortable life	8.4 (7)	9.9 (12)	9.7 (11)	.01
A sense of accomplishment	9.4 (10)	8.3 (8)	7.1 (6)	.01
A world at peace	3.1 (1)	3.5 (1)	3.9 (2)	.05
Equality	7.5 (5)	9.5 (10)	11.1 (13)	.001
Happiness	7.3 (4)	8.0 (7)	8.8 (8)	.01
National security	10.0 (12)	9.0 (9)	9.0 (9)	.01
Salvation	9.4 (11)	6.6 (4)	7.5 (7)	.01
Wisdom	8.5 (8)	7.6 (6)	6.3 (4)	.001
Instrumental Values				
Cheerful	9.5 (10)	10.2 (12)	11.1 (12)	.05
Clean	7.9 (7)	9.5 (10)	11.5 (15)	.001
Helpful	7.9 (6)	8.4 (7)	11.3 (14)	.001
Independent	10.4 (13)	11.0 (13)	8.4 (7)	.05
Loving	9.4 (9)	9.6 (11)	11.2 (13)	.05
Obedient	13.0 (15)	13.7 (16)	14.3 (17)	.05
Responsible	7.1 (4)	6.3 (2)	4.8 (2)	.01
Self-controlled	10.2 (12)	8.9 (8)	8.2 (6)	.001

Figures shown are median rankings and, in parentheses, composite rank orders.
* Median test.

diced against the poor care significantly more for *a sense of accomplishment*.
These differences in value patterns can perhaps best be understood if we
note that those who are anti-poor more often come from the higher
socioeconomic strata of society and therefore exhibit values that are
characteristic of the affluent and the educated. Those who are anti-black,
on the other hand, are more often found to come from the lower socioeconomic strata of society and are therefore more likely to exhibit the
values of the poor and uneducated.

But the value patterns of those who are unsympathetic with or indifferent to the poor are not altogether identical to those of the affluent and
educated. In contrast with the finding that the affluent and educated are
considerably less *salvation*-minded, we find that the anti-poor and those
who are indifferent to the poor are more *salvation*-minded, despite the fact
that they exhibit on the whole the value pattern of the affluent. These
findings suggest that it is not quite accurate to say that it is the affluent
who are generally unsympathetic or indifferent to the poor, but a certain
segment of the affluent.

STUDENT PROTEST

Attitude toward Student Protest

Two questions put to the national sample concerned student protest: (1) "This country would be better off if there were less protest and dissatisfaction coming from college campuses"; (2) "The protests of college students are a healthy sign for America." Since these two questions yielded highly similar findings, Table 4.6 reports only those obtained for the first question. Sixteen values show significant relationships, with those unsympathetic to student protest caring relatively more for *a comfortable life, family security, national security, salvation, true friendship*, being *clean, obedient*, and *polite* while those expressing a sympathetic attitude toward student protest cared relatively more for *a sense of accomplishment, equality, wisdom*, being *broadminded, imaginative*, and *intellectual*. Two other values showing significant differences—*helpful* and *responsible*—are more difficult

TABLE 4.6   SIGNIFICANT VALUE DIFFERENCES AMONG RESPONDENTS EXPRESSING DIFFERENT ATTITUDES TOWARD STUDENT PROTEST

"This country would be better off if there were less protest and dissatisfaction coming from college campuses."

	Agree Strongly	Agree Some	Disagree Some	Disagree Strongly	
N =	529	469	243	155	p*
Terminal Values					
A comfortable life	8.2 (7)	8.7 (8)	10.5 (13)	10.1 (10)	.01
A sense of accomplishment	9.4 (11)	9.2 (10)	8.3 (8)	7.9 (7)	.01
Equality	10.3 (12)	8.4 (6)	7.1 (5)	6.3 (4)	.001
Family security	3.6 (2)	3.6 (2)	4.1 (2)	5.0 (2)	.01
National security	8.7 (9)	9.3 (11)	10.3 (12)	12.5 (13)	.001
Salvation	7.3 (4)	8.8 (9)	9.2 (9)	12.6 (14)	.01
True friendship	8.7 (10)	9.6 (12)	9.9 (10)	9.7 (9)	.05
Wisdom	8.6 (8)	8.4 (7)	6.9 (4)	6.6 (5)	.001
Instrumental Values					
Broadminded	8.1 (7)	7.5 (4)	7.1 (3)	6.1 (2)	.05
Clean	8.0 (6)	8.6 (7)	9.0 (8)	11.8 (14)	.001
Helpful	8.1 (8)	8.9 (8)	7.7 (6)	8.0 (6)	.05
Imaginative	15.7 (18)	16.1 (18)	14.6 (18)	12.6 (17)	.001
Intellectual	13.8 (16)	12.9 (16)	12.3 (15)	11.7 (13)	.01
Obedient	13.0 (15)	12.8 (15)	13.8 (17)	14.8 (17)	.001
Polite	10.5 (13)	10.4 (13)	11.9 (14)	12.0 (15)	.001
Responsible	7.1 (4)	6.1 (2)	6.2 (2)	7.9 (5)	.01

Figures shown are median rankings and, in parentheses, composite rank orders.
* Median test.

to interpret since they show curvilinear relationships. Thus, the value patterns underlying favorable and unfavorable attitudes toward student protest are clearly different from one another. The 70 percent of adult Americans who are unsympathetic to student protest apparently have a value pattern that is more or less typical of the poor and uneducated; they are more concerned with material comfort and affiliation, conventional values, the security of the family and nation, and religious values, and they are less concerned with intellectual values, egalitarianism, competence, and self-realization.

INTERNATIONAL AFFAIRS

Attitude toward the American Presence in Vietnam

Table 4.7 identifies 10 terminal and instrumental values that differentiate significantly among adult Americans who expressed different positions concerning the American presence in Vietnam in April 1968. Table 4.8 shows the comparable results obtained for students at Michigan State University in fall 1967. In neither case is *a world at peace* among the values that differentiate "hawks" from "doves." Its composite rank order is first for adult American hawks and doves alike, and it is tenth for both

TABLE 4.7 SIGNIFICANT VALUE DIFFERENCES AMONG ADULT AMERICANS VARYING IN ATTITUDE TOWARD U.S. INVOLVEMENT IN VIETNAM (SPRING 1968)

	Withdraw	*Continue*	*Escalate*	*Don't Know*	
N =	538	228	528	99	p*
Terminal Values					
A comfortable life	8.4 (7)	10.4 (13)	8.5 (8)	10.6 (13)	.01
An exciting life	15.2 (18)	15.7 (18)	15.1 (18)	16.4 (18)	.001
A world of beauty	13.5 (15)	12.7 (15)	14.1 (15)	13.1 (14)	.001
Equality	7.7 (5)	7.3 (4)	9.9 (12)	9.7 (11)	.001
Mature love	12.1 (14)	12.6 (14)	12.2 (14)	14.5 (15)	.001
National security	10.6 (13)	8.4 (8)	8.9 (10)	9.3 (9)	.01
Salvation	9.8 (11)	9.3 (10)	7.9 (6)	4.0 (2)	.001
Instrumental Values					
Capable	10.1 (12)	9.6 (10)	8.9 (9)	10.7 (13)	.01
Logical	14.3 (17)	13.5 (17)	14.2 (17)	15.2 (17)	.05
Responsible	7.3 (4)	6.2 (2)	6.1 (3)	8.1 (8)	.001

Figures shown are median rankings and, in parentheses, composite rank orders.
* Median test.

TABLE 4.8   SIGNIFICANT VALUE DIFFERENCES AMONG COLLEGE
STUDENTS VARYING IN ATTITUDE TOWARD WAR IN VIETNAM (FALL 1967)

	Withdraw	*Consolidate*	*Reclaim*	*Increase*	
N =	*59*	*29*	*56*	*151*	*p**
Terminal Values					
A world of beauty	12.8 (14)	12.8 (13)	14.8 (18)	14.7 (18)	.01
Salvation	16.3 (18)	10.0 (12)	11.0 (13)	11.0 (12)	.05
Social recognition	13.6 (16)	16.6 (18)	14.0 (16)	13.1 (15)	.05
Instrumental Values					
Ambitious	9.3 (11)	10.3 (11)	5.5 (3)	6.7 (4)	.05
Intellectual	7.6 (6)	9.3 (8)	8.0 (6)	10.7 (12)	.05
Loving	5.4 (2)	5.6 (2)	8.5 (10)	8.8 (8)	.05
Obedient	16.0 (18)	14.8 (18)	15.9 (18)	14.7 (18)	.05

Figures shown are median rankings and, in parentheses, composite rank orders.
* Kruskal-Wallis test.
Withdraw from Vietnam as soon as possible in a planned and orderly manner.
Consolidate our present position in the South, and fight only a defensive war.
Attempt to reclaim all of South Vietnam without escalation into the North.
Increase our war efforts, both in the North and the South, until the communists
   leave South Vietnam.

hawk and dove college students. Evidently, hawks and doves both see themselves as wanting peace.

They do, however, differ with respect to other values, and these differences give us some insight into some of the reasons that may underlie varying attitudes toward the Vietnam war. Adult Americans who advocate escalation of the war generally care more than do those who advocate withdrawal for *national security*, *salvation*, and being *capable* and *responsible*, and they care less about *a world of beauty* and *equality*.

If hawks and doves have differing value patterns, those who hold no opinion about America's involvement in Vietnam also have a distinctive value pattern, that is, a value pattern that is different from those exhibited by hawks or doves. They are more concerned with material comfort in the here and now and with eternal salvation in the hereafter; they are least concerned with love, excitement, competence, logical consistency, or responsibility.

A somewhat similar picture of hawks and doves emerges from a value analysis of American college students (Table 4.8). As before, doves care less about *salvation*, a finding that has also been replicated with college students in South Australia (Feather, 1970a). Doves are, moreover, less achievement- and conformity-oriented and they generally care more for intellectual values, and for values concerning beauty and love. Finally, it should be noted that hawks and doves both rank *social recognition* higher than do those advocating in between positions—a finding that is not readily interpretable.

Summarizing the findings obtained with adult Americans and college students, it can be concluded that doves are less religious-minded than hawks, more concerned with love and beauty, more intellectual but less achievement- and establishment-oriented. Adult American doves, moreover, seem less preoccupied with the issue of national security, and they are more egalitarian in their political orientation.

Attitude toward Communism

College students at Michigan State University indicated their attitude toward communism on a 10-item Likert scale. Each item was rated from +3 to −3, with the 0 point excluded. Even though the vast majority of the subjects in the sample were anticommunist in absolute terms, they nevertheless differed in relative terms. Respondents were categorized into upper quarter, middle half, and lower quarter on the basis of their scores—communism ratings. Twelve values differentiate significantly among these three groups, as shown in Table 4.9. Values that seem to predispose students to have a relatively more favorable attitude toward communism are *a world of beauty*, *equality* (but not *freedom*), and being *broadminded*, *imaginative*, *independent*, and *self-controlled*. On the other hand, values

TABLE 4.9 SIGNIFICANT VALUE DIFFERENCES FOR COLLEGE STUDENTS VARYING IN ATTITUDE TOWARD COMMUNISM

	Pro Communism	In between	Anti Communism	
N =	78	140	80	p*
Terminal Values				
A world of beauty	11.2 (13)	13.9 (16)	15.1 (18)	.001
Equality	9.1 (10)	9.8 (11)	12.2 (14)	.05
Salvation	16.8 (18)	10.5 (12)	9.0 (11)	.001
Social recognition	13.8 (16)	14.0 (17)	13.0 (16)	.05
Instrumental Values				
Broadminded	5.3 (2)	6.5 (4)	7.0 (4)	.05
Clean	15.8 (17)	14.3 (17)	12.7 (16)	.05
Helpful	11.2 (14)	9.6 (10)	11.6 (15)	.05
Imaginative	9.0 (8)	11.6 (15)	13.3 (17)	.001
Independent	6.4 (4)	9.5 (9)	8.5 (8)	.05
Loving	9.5 (11)	6.2 (3)	8.3 (7)	.05
Obedient	16.1 (18)	15.4 (18)	14.4 (18)	.05
Self-controlled	7.4 (5)	9.6 (11)	9.5 (10)	.05

Figures shown are median rankings and, in parentheses, composite rank orders.
* Kruskal-Wallis test.

that seem to predispose college students toward a more anticommunist position are *salvation, social recognition,* and being *clean* and *obedient.* Higher rankings on the instrumental values *helpful* and *loving* are most characteristic of students expressing an in-between position on communism. It would thus seem that a predisposition toward a more favorable attitude toward communism is more likely to be found among those rejecting religion, prestige, and conventional values on the one hand and among those accepting aesthetic and intellectual values, egalitarianism, and self-discipline on the other.

RELIGION

Attitude toward Church Activism

To assess their attitude toward the desirability of social and political activism by organized religion, the following question was put to the national sample: "In general, do you approve or disapprove of the churches' becoming involved in social and political issues such as the urban crisis, Vietnam, and civil rights?" Of the 36 values, 11 differentiate significantly between those favoring and those opposing church

TABLE 4.10 SIGNIFICANT VALUE DIFFERENCES AMONG RESPONDENTS DIFFERING IN THEIR ATTITUDE TOWARD THE CHURCH'S INVOLVEMENT IN SOCIETY

"In general, do you approve or disapprove of the churches' becoming involved in social and political issues such as the urban crisis, Vietnam, and civil rights?"

	Approve	Don't Know	Disapprove	
N =	522	54	825	p*
Terminal Values				
A comfortable life	10.0 (11)	6.5 (5)	8.3 (7)	.01
Equality	7.0 (4)	9.5 (9)	10.0 (12)	.001
Family security	4.3 (2)	4.3 (2)	3.4 (2)	.01
National security	10.6 (13)	10.1 (12)	8.8 (9)	.001
Salvation	9.8 (10)	6.5 (4)	8.1 (6)	.05
Wisdom	7.3 (5)	9.7 (11)	8.3 (8)	.05
Instrumental Values				
Clean	9.4 (8)	6.9 (4)	8.3 (8)	.05
Courageous	7.9 (6)	10.6 (13)	7.7 (5)	.05
Forgiving	7.9 (5)	6.5 (3)	6.8 (4)	.05
Imaginative	14.9 (18)	15.8 (18)	15.7 (18)	.05
Intellectual	12.0 (15)	12.5 (15)	13.8 (16)	.001

Figures shown are median rankings and, in parentheses, composite rank orders.
* Median test.

activism (Table 4.10). Those favoring it care less for *a comfortable life, family security, national security, salvation*, and being *clean* and *forgiving*, and they care more for *equality, wisdom*, and being *imaginative* and *intellectual*. Those responding "don't know" to this question care less about being *courageous* (defined as "sticking up for one's beliefs") than those approving or disapproving of church activism.

The value pattern of those opposing the church's involvement in secular affairs seems on the whole to be similar to that exhibited by those who are antiblack and anti-student protest. Their values are the conventional values of God, home, and country, antiegalitarian and anti-intellectual. The overall impression gained from these findings is that those who do not want the church to raise issues about social injustices are those who like things as they are; they possess the values of the status quo.

Perceived Importance of Religion

Michigan State University students responded to the question, "How important is your religion to you in your everyday life?" on a seven-point rating scale, with 1 representing "extremely important" and 7, "extremely unimportant." They were categorized as high (1–2), medium (3–5), and low (6–7) in perceived importance of religion. Sixteen values (Table 4.11) differentiate significantly among these three groups, the largest difference implicating *salvation*. Its composite rank is first, sixteenth, and eighteenth, respectively, for those reporting religion to be high, medium, and low in perceived importance. Moreover, those regarding religion as highly important rank *family security* higher and *a comfortable life, a sense of accomplishment, pleasure*, and *social recognition* lower. On the 10 instrumental values, those perceiving religion to be important in their daily lives consider the moral values—*forgiving, helpful, honest, loving* and *obedient*—more important, and they consider the competence and intellectual values—*ambitious, capable, independent, intellectual*, and *logical*—less important.

Intrinsic and Extrinsic Religious Orientations

Allport and Ross (1967) have suggested four basic types of religious and antireligious orientations: (1) the intrinsic religious orientation, exemplified by a person who has internalized religious teachings that guide his daily behavior; (2) the extrinsic religious orientation, exemplified by a person who employs religion in a utilitarian and opportunistic manner to advance his own personal interests and strivings for success and social status; (3) the indiscriminately proreligious orientation, exemplified by a person who uncritically accepts all proreligious ideas, whether intrinsic or extrinsic; and (4) the antireligious orientation, exemplified by a person who rejects all proreligious ideas and teachings, whether extrinsic or intrinsic. Allport and Ross have further shown that among the three types of religious orientations, (1), (2) and (3) above, the intrinsically oriented are the

TABLE 4.11 SIGNIFICANT VALUE DIFFERENCES FOR GROUPS VARYING
IN PERCEIVED IMPORTANCE OF RELIGION (COLLEGE SAMPLE)

	High	Medium	Low	
N =	92	131	75	p*
Terminal Values				
A comfortable life	13.7 (15)	11.1 (12)	11.3 (11)	.001
A sense of accomplishment	9.5 (12)	7.6 (6)	5.8 (2)	.01
Family security	7.2 (7)	8.0 (8)	10.6 (10)	.05
Pleasure	14.8 (17)	14.2 (17)	13.2 (15)	.001
Salvation	2.8 (1)	14.0 (16)	17.6 (18)	.001
Social recognition	15.1 (18)	12.8 (14)	12.8 (14)	.001
Instrumental Values				
Ambitious	9.5 (8)	5.5 (2)	7.1 (5)	.001
Capable	11.0 (12)	9.2 (8)	7.3 (6)	.001
Forgiving	7.5 (6)	10.2 (12)	11.4 (13)	.001
Helpful	7.0 (5)	11.1 (13)	12.7 (15)	.001
Honest	3.3 (1)	4.6 (1)	5.1 (1)	.05
Independent	9.8 (9)	9.6 (10)	5.6 (2)	.001
Intellectual	11.2 (13)	9.3 (9)	7.4 (7)	.01
Logical	11.8 (14)	10.0 (11)	7.7 (8)	.001
Loving	4.9 (2)	7.2 (5)	11.3 (12)	.001
Obedient	14.0 (17)	15.8 (18)	15.6 (18)	.01

Figures shown are median rankings and, in parentheses, composite rank orders.
*Kruskal-Wallis test.

least ethnically and racially prejudiced, the extrinsically oriented are more so, and the indiscriminately religious are the most ethnically and racially prejudiced.

If Allport and Ross's contentions are valid, then distinctive value patterns should be found for the four types of religious orientation. Tate and Miller (1971), employing Allport and Ross's test measuring religious orientation, classified their subjects, all members of the United Methodist Church, into the four types and compared them for similarities and differences in values. The significant findings, shown in Table 4.12 with the permission of Drs. Eugene D. Tate and Gerald R. Miller, reveal that Allport and Ross's three types of religious orientation are indeed psychologically meaningful ones, differing not only from one another but also from the antireligious orientation.

Consider first the values that clearly differentiate between the three religious orientations on the one hand and the antireligious orientation on the other. The 38 persons who show an antireligious orientation are probably not extremely antireligious. All the subjects of the Tate and Miller study were members of the United Methodist Church. As would be

TABLE 4.12 SIGNIFICANT VALUE DIFFERENCES AMONG UNITED
METHODISTS CLASSIFIED AS INTRINSIC, EXTRINSIC,
INDISCRIMINATELY PRORELIGIOUS, AND ANTIRELIGIOUS
(FROM TATE AND MILLER)

		Intrinsic	Extrinsic	Indiscriminately Proreligious	Anti religious
N =		47	50	40	38
Terminal Values					
A comfortable life		16.3 (17)	14.2 (16)	14.8 (17)	14.5 (16)
A world of beauty		12.1 (13)	13.3 (14)	12.9 (14)	14.0 (14)
Equality		6.0 (3)	7.5 (5)	8.3 (9)	6.5 (6)
Family security		4.9 (2)	3.8 (1)	6.5 (6)	4.2 (1)
Freedom		8.6 (10)	8.7 (9)	10.8 (12)	6.1 (4)
Happiness		11.4 (12)	9.2 (10)	9.4 (10)	9.3 (11)
Mature love		8.8 (11)	9.8 (11)	10.5 (11)	7.5 (8)
Pleasure		17.0 (18)	15.8 (18)	16.6 (18)	15.4 (18)
Salvation		1.3 (1)	4.5 (2)	1.4 (1)	8.0 (9)
True friendship		7.7 (8)	10.2 (12)	7.8 (8)	11.5 (12)
Wisdom		6.6 (7)	8.5 (8)	4.5 (2)	5.5 (3)
Instrumental Values					
Ambitious		12.6 (14)	7.2 (6)	11.2 (12)	10.1 (12)
Clean		14.3 (17)	10.0 (11)	10.9 (10)	15.4 (18)
Courageous		7.3 (6)	8.0 (7)	6.5 (6)	9.8 (11)
Forgiving		4.6 (3)	6.2 (2)	3.8 (2)	6.2 (4)
Helpful		6.6 (5)	9.5 (9)	5.8 (3)	8.0 (6)
Imaginative		14.1 (16)	15.8 (18)	16.2 (18)	11.7 (15)
Obedient		14.3 (18)	13.2 (17)	12.0 (14)	15.3 (17)

Figures shown are median rankings and, in parentheses, composite rank orders. All
differences are significant beyond the .05 level by the Median test, except for *equality*
and *family security*, which are significant at the .06 level.

expected, all three religious groups place a relatively high value on *salvation*
and the antireligious group places a relatively low value on it. Moreover,
the three religious groups place a greater value on *a world of beauty, true
friendship*, and being *clean, courageous*, and *obedient*, and they place a
lesser value than the antireligious group on *freedom, mature love, pleasure*,
and being *imaginative*.

Of more immediate interest, however, are the value differences found
among the three types of religious orientations that are relevant to Allport
and Ross's main thesis. The intrinsically religious rank *equality* higher than
do the extrinsically religious who, in turn, rank it higher than the indiscriminately religious. The *equality* difference between the intrinsically
and extrinsically religious is not significantly different, but the difference
between the intrinsically religious and the indiscriminately religious is

significant (Tate and Miller, 1971). These findings thus provide strong if not conclusive support for Allport and Ross's hypothesis that the intrinsically religious are the most tolerant (*equality*, as has been shown, is the value that is most related to racial tolerance) and the indiscriminately religious the least tolerant. These findings however do not obscure the fact that the antireligious United Methodists in this sample are about as tolerant as the intrinsically religious.

Moreover, the intrinsically religious differ significantly, according to Tate and Miller, from both the extrinsically religious and from the indiscriminately proreligious in ranking *imaginative* higher and in ranking *a comfortable life*, *happiness*, and being *ambitious* and *clean* lower. The intrinsically religious also value *salvation* significantly more than the extrinsically religious, but no more than the indiscriminately proreligious.

Although Allport and Ross's differentiation between the extrinsically religious and the indiscriminately proreligious is far from being conceptually clear, inspection of Table 4.12 reveals that these two groups nonetheless differ in certain values: *family security*, *freedom*, *salvation*, *true friendship*, *wisdom*, and being *ambitious*, *forgiving*, and *helpful*. It is rather difficult, however, to interpret all these differences since in some cases the indiscriminately proreligious are more like the intrinsically religious, and in other cases they are more like the extrinsically religious. Thus, the most that can reasonably be concluded from all these data is that the three religious groups have different value patterns and that the intrinsically religious are more tolerant than those who are extrinsically religious who, in turn, are more tolerant than the indiscriminately proreligious. These findings are reasonably consistent with the hypothesis put forward by Allport and Ross (1967).

PERSONALITY

Certain variables, such as the ones to be considered in this section, are ordinarily conceptualized as personality rather than as attitudinal variables. But personality variables are in principle from the same universe of discourse as attitudinal variables. Both purport to measure underlying behavioral predispositions, and both employ similar measurement procedures. There is thus no reason why personality variables should not be included in a discussion of the relations between values and attitudes.

Dogmatism

The 20-item short form of the Dogmatism scale (Troldahl and Powell, 1965) was employed to categorize Michigan State University students into three groups: low quarter, middle half, and high quarter. Six values distinguish significantly among them (Table 4.13). Subjects high in dogmatism care less for *equality*, *freedom*, and for being *broadminded*; they care more for *salvation*, *social recognition*, and for being *obedient*.

TABLE 4.13   SIGNIFICANT VALUE DIFFERENCES FOR COLLEGE STUDENTS
HIGH, MIDDLE, AND LOW IN DOGMATISM

	N =	Low 76	Middle 148	High 74	p*
Terminal Values					
Equality		9.2 (10)	9.9 (11)	12.5 (15)	.01
Freedom		4.3 (1)	4.9 (1)	6.5 (3)	.05
Salvation		16.8 (18)	10.8 (12)	9.0 (10)	.001
Social recognition		14.1 (16)	14.5 (18)	12.5 (14)	.01
Instrumental Values					
Broadminded		5.8 (2)	6.5 (3)	7.5 (3)	.05
Obedient		16.5 (18)	15.3 (18)	13.9 (18)	.001

Figures shown are median rankings and, in parentheses, composite rank orders.
* Kruskal-Wallis test.

Feather (1970a) has reported similar findings at Flinders University in South Australia. He summarizes his findings by commenting that "there may be a cluster of values associated with dogmatism or 'closed-mindedness,' a cluster in which *salvation* and *obedience* rank high in relative importance and *equality* and *broadminded* rank low in relative importance" (pp. 141–142).

But in a subsequent report comparing findings obtained in 1968, 1969, and 1970, Feather (1971b) modifies his previous conclusion (1970a), since only the value of *salvation* uniformly discriminated groups varying in dogmatism at statistically significant levels. Visual inspection of his data reveals, however, that the trends of findings for *salvation, obedient*, and *broadminded* and, to a somewhat lesser extent, for *equality* are usually in the theoretically predicted direction from one year to the next, even though they do not reach statistical significance.

Similarly, Rim (1970) has reported findings on the relation between values and dogmatism in a study conducted with male students at the Israel Institute of Technology in Haifa. Highly dogmatic students place a significantly higher (not lower) value on *equality,* and on being *honest* and *obedient*, and they place a significantly lower value on being *broadminded* and *independent*.

All three studies conducted in the United States, South Australia, and Israel identify a relatively lower value for *broadmindedness* and a relatively higher value for *obedience* as variables underlying dogmatism. But certain cultural differences should be noted: Highly dogmatic subjects in the United States and Australia uniformly rank the Christian value *salvation* significantly higher, and they usually rank the political value *equality* lower than subjects low in dogmatism. In Israel, where *salvation* is not a meaningful value, both high- and low-dogmatic subjects rank it last. More noteworthy, however, are the findings for *equality*. High-dogmatic students in the United States and Australia usually rank *equality* lower than do low-dogmatic students, but it is the other way around in Israel, where the high-dogmatic subjects rank *equality* higher. These findings confirm earlier speculations and findings (Rokeach, 1960) that there is no necessary theoretical association between authoritarianism and conservative political ideologies. Rather, the findings suggest that dogmatists may conform to whatever may be the prevailing institutional norms concerning egalitarianism.

Authoritarianism, Ethnocentrism, Intolerance of Ambiguity, and Machiavellianism

Feather (1971b) and Rim (1970) have published data on the value differences between college students at the Flinders University of South Australia and at the Israeli Institute of Technology who scored high and low on the F scale, ethnocentrism, intolerance of ambiguity, and Machiavellianism. Their findings can be briefly summarized: (1) High F scorers in Israel rank *family security*, *polite*, and *clean* significantly higher than low F scale scorers, and they rank *inner harmony*, *equality*, and being *ambitious*, *independent*, and *broadminded* significantly lower. (2) High scorers in ethnocentrism in South Australia rank *a comfortable life* and *clean* significantly higher, and *a world of beauty*, *equality*, *helpful*, and *imaginative* significantly lower. (3) In both the Israeli and South Australian studies, various values discriminated significantly between subjects scoring high and low on intolerance of ambiguity (Budner, 1962). The greatest confidence can, however, be placed in these differences that were consistent across both studies, namely, subjects scoring high in intolerance of ambiguity cared less for *inner harmony* and more for being *polite* and *obedient*. (4) Israeli subjects who were high Machiavellians (Christie and Merton, 1958) consider *equality* and being *ambitious* and *independent* significantly more important than do low Machiavellians, and *freedom*, being *courageous*, *imaginative*, and *loving* significantly less important.

INCONSEQUENTIAL ATTITUDES

If all attitudes are indeed in the service of and functionally connected with values, then even relatively inconsequential attitudes should be related to one or more values. Among the most inconsequential attitudes are surely those that people hold about alternative brand products. Two types of data are available to test this hypothesis.

Car Preferences

College students who filled out the earlier Form A of the Value Survey (12 terminal and 12 instrumental values) were also asked to indicate their preference for three automobiles within the same price range: Chevrolet, Ford, and Plymouth. A value analysis carried out separately for men and women revealed three values that significantly differentiated among those showing different car preferences. The *equality* rankings of college men preferring Chevrolets is significantly higher, followed by the rankings of men preferring Fords, and then Plymouths. College women preferring Plymouths rank *respect from others* (a value that was not retained in later versions of the Value Survey) and *politeness* significantly higher than do women preferring Fords or Chevrolets. These findings tentatively suggest that manufacturers of different automobiles in the same price range have wittingly or unwittingly projected subtle differences in value images onto their products, thus appealing differentially to people differing in certain values.

Detergent Preferences

Personal interviews were conducted by Universal Marketing Research in the homes of 767 housewives owning washing machines. Date were collected on detergent preferences as well as on Form A of the Value Survey, and these data were made available to me by Dr. Leo Bogart. Although statistical tests of significance were not available, inspection of the data showed that many values distinguished markedly among women preferring different detergents. The most sizeable differences were evident between women preferring Ivory on the one hand and Oxydol, All, and Wisk on the other. The former rank *salvation* and *clean* considerably higher, and they also rank *equality* and *broadminded* higher. Their rankings of *true friendship, courageous*, and *trustful* are, however, lower than those obtained for women having other detergent preferences. These findings suggest that the well-known Ivory image "$99\frac{44}{100}$ percent pure" has a special appeal to the *salvation-* and *clean*-minded. But the other findings, especially those suggesting that women who prefer Ivory are also more egalitarian and tolerant, are somewhat more difficult to understand. At the least, they suggest that there may be other components to the Ivory image besides pureness. In any event, these data suggest that different brands of detergents may appeal to persons with different values.

DISCUSSION

Virtually all the attitudes considered in this chapter are found to be significantly associated with some cluster or subset of terminal and instrumental values. The attitudes considered are heterogeneous in content, covering many of the major issues of contemporary life in American society: civil rights for the black and poor, black militancy, Vietnam, communism, student protest, religion, and church activism. For additional evidence concerning the functional relation between values, measured somewhat differently, and attitudes toward violence among American men, see the recent monograph published in 1972 by Blumenthal, Kahn, Andrews, and Head. At a more global level, we have had occasion to consider the values underlying more pervasive dogmatic and authoritarian personality predispositions, and those underlying ambiguity and Machiavellianism. And, at a more molecular level, we have inquired into the values underlying certain attitudes that have elsewhere (Rokeach, 1968) been called inconsequential.

All these attitudes may be regarded as a sample taken from a much larger universe numbering perhaps in the tens of thousands. This sample, admittedly selected and nonrandom, is nonetheless heterogeneous enough to allow us to test the rather broad hypothesis that virtually any attitude will be significantly associated with some subset of terminal and instrumental values. The findings generally confirm this broad hypothesis.

The findings do not reveal any simple isomorphism between any one attitude and value. Each attitude is associated with several or many values, and each value is associated with several or many attitudes. Table 4.14 presents a bird's-eye view of all the values that have been reported to be significantly associated with 11 attitudes considered in this chapter. Omitted from Table 4.14 are Feather's (1970, 1971) and Rim's (1970) cross-cultural findings and Willis and Goldberg's (1971) findings on black militancy, which are altogether too complex to present in tabular form. Also omitted, because statistical significance was not determined or because a shorter and somewhat different value scale had been employed, are the findings on inconsequential attitudes. This table shows that anywhere from 6 to 21 of the values measured are significantly related to each attitude and that anywhere from zero to 11 of the attitudes considered are significantly associated with each value. A comfortable life, equality, family security, national security, salvation, clean, imaginative, intellectual, and obedient are 9 values that turn out to be significantly related to most of these 11 attitudes. Self-respect, uniformly ranked fifth to seventh by virtually all groups and subgroups, turns out to be the only one of the 36 values that is not significantly related to any one of the 11 attitudes considered.

With 36 values always under consideration in the present research it can be expected that about two of them will turn out by chance alone to be statistically significant beyond the .05 level. It is obvious that the number of significant value differences far exceed such chance expectations. Table 4.14 shows that 146 out of a possible 396 differences—about one-third—are statistically significant. Thus, the differences found are too large and extensive to be dismissed as arising by chance. Nor can they be dismissed on the ground that the value rankings are ipsative because the degree of ipsativeness of data obtained with 18 ranked items is negligible.

We are therefore left with a rather large number of empirically obtained significant value differences that we must try to make sense of as best we can, in the hope that they will provide us with a stronger base for future theory construction. Because no theory in the social or behavioral sciences

TABLE 4.14 SUMMARY OF VALUES THAT ARE SIGNIFICANTLY ASSOCIATED WITH 11 ATTITUDINAL VARIABLES

	King Assassination	Attitude toward Blacks	Attitude toward Poor	Student Protest	Vietnam (Adults)	Vietnam (College Students)	Communism	Church Activism	Personal Importance of Religion	Extrinsic–Intrinsic Religion	Dogmatism	Number of Attitudes
Terminal Values												
A comfortable life	*	*	*	*	*			*	*	*		8
An exciting life		*		*								2
A sense of accomplishment		*	*	*					*			4
A world at peace	*		*									2
A world of beauty		*			*	*	*			*		5
Equality	*	*	*	*	*			*	*	*	*	9
Family security	*	*		*				*	*	*		6
Freedom										*	*	2
Happiness		*	*							*		3
Inner harmony		*										1
Mature love		*		*						*		3
National security	*	*	*	*	*				*			6
Pleasure		*							*	*		3
Salvation	*	*	*	*	*	*	*	*	*	*	*	11
Self-respect												0
Social recognition							*	*	*		*	4
True friendship				*						*		2
Wisdom		*	*	*				*		*		5
Instrumental Values												
Ambitious		*				*			*	*		4
Broadminded		*		*				*			*	4
Capable				*					*			2
Cheerful			*									1
Clean	*	*	*	*				*	*	*		7
Courageous									*	*		2
Forgiving								*	*	*		3
Helpful			*	*				*	*	*		5
Honest										*		1
Imaginative	*	*		*				*	*	*		6
Independent			*					*	*			3
Intellectual	*	*		*	*			*	*			6
Logical	*	*			*				*			4
Loving	*		*			*	*		*			5
Obedient	*	*	*	*		*	*		*	*	*	9
Polite	*	*		*								3
Responsible		*	*	*								3
Self-controlled		*						*				2
Number of values	13	21	16	16	10	7	12	11	16	18	6	146

is as yet sufficiently developed to permit prediction in advance of all the findings reported here, we must be content, at this stage of research, to adopt an empirical and descriptive rather than deductive approach to the study of the relations between specific attitudes and specific values. For every attitude considered, a question that may be asked is whether it is possible to identify the specific terminal and instrumental values that underlie it.

Fortunately, many of the findings make sense on intuitive grounds, and the largest value differences, at least, could have been predicted in advance on various theoretical grounds. Thus, of all 36 values, *equality* is the one that best predicts reactions to the assassination of Dr. Martin Luther King and attitude toward blacks, the poor, Vietnam, student protest, and church activism. *Salvation* is the value that is most related to perceived importance of religion, to differences in religious orientations, and to an anticommunist attitude. *Salvation* or *obedient* or both seem to be the two values that are most associated with high scores on the Dogmatism scale in the United States, Australia, and Israel. It can thus be said that present theoretical knowledge enables us to anticipate at least the major value differences that may be expected to underlie differences in any given attitude. They can be so anticipated by considering the logical relations existing between a given value and attitude, by considering the value components that are theoretically implied in such global measures of personality and ideology as the F or Dogmatism scale, by considering the common institutional influences on values and attitudes, or on the basis of sociological considerations such as those concerning the common effects of socioeconomic position on values and attitudes.

Such considerations notwithstanding, we have nonetheless encountered many sobering surprises in our research on values. Certain values that could reasonably have been expected to predict certain attitudes turned out not to predict them. For instance, *a world at peace* is just as highly valued by hawks as by doves; *national security* is ranked just as low by college students who express opposition to communism as by those expressing sympathy with communism; *broadmindedness* is ranked just as highly by those who were gleeful and fearful following Dr. King's assassination as by those who were saddened, angered, or ashamed. Yet other values that have no apparent relation to a given attitude turn out to predict it. Racists, for instance, care significantly more for *family security* and *happiness* and significantly less for *inner harmony* than do those who are less racist. As previously suggested, values are the cognitive representations of needs, and findings such as those just mentioned suggest that the needs of racists are different from the needs of nonracists, that the needs of hawks are different from the needs of doves, and so on.

Descriptive findings such as those presented in this chapter provide us with a point of departure for further investigations about the nature of the values that underlie various social attitudes. The values that people hold are conceived to be the explanations of the attitudes they hold (and the behavior they engage in), but which values underlie which attitudes (and behaviors), and why? At this stage of theory and research, we simply do not know enough about the nature of values and how they determine attitudes and behavior to answer questions of this kind satisfactorily. We are in somewhat the same position as curious astronauts exploring the moon and then the planets beyond who, before they blast off for the return trip home, will gather up as many rocks as they can and, upon returning, hand them over to others who will then undertake to describe these rocks and explain how they got to be wherever in the universe they happened to be. But the first step surely will be to describe. For there is nothing to explain unless there is first some reasonably good description of what it is one is trying to explain. And when we know enough about the structure of the universe, we should be able to predict in advance the kinds of rocks that astronauts will find in some other corner of the universe, before they even get there.

5
Values and Behavior

Values and attitudes are both intervening variables. The reason social psychologists have long been interested in them is that they are presumed to be the main genotypes that underlie or determine social behavior. In Chapter 4, a considerable body of evidence was presented suggesting that these two sets of intervening variables, one more and the other less centrally located within a person's makeup, are functionally related in certain ways: A relatively small number of terminal and instrumental values is conceived to underlie many if not all social attitudes; moreover, a given value is conceived to determine several or many attitudes and a given attitude to be determined by several or many values.

This chapter will deal with the relation between values, the more central of the two intervening variables, and behavior. If it is indeed the case that terminal and instrumental values are standards that guide actions as well as attitudes, then knowing a person's values should enable us to predict how he will behave in various experimental and real-life situations. Again, it is possible to specify in advance not all the values that will be predictably related to a given behavior, but only the main ones. Those that are the most substantively or logically related to a given behavior should be the ones that will best predict it. Thus, religious values should best predict differences in religious behavior, political values should best predict differences in political behavior, and so on.

The question arises, What can legitimately be called "behavior"? If a certain value is found to predict a specific action, say, voting for a particular candidate or cheating in a particular situation, we would have clear instance of a relation between a value and behavior. But behavior can also have a more general focus. It can range from a single, molecular act at one extreme to a whole set of acts at the other. Pursuing a certain kind of occupation, majoring in a certain kind of educational curriculum, and living a certain kind of life style are all examples of behavior that go far beyond a single specific act, and values should thus be functionally related to all kinds of molar as well as molecular behavior. Moreover, the kinds of behavior we will be especially interested in are those that are exhibited in connection with a wide variety of issues that we all confront in contemporary American society—civil rights, religion, politics, the war in Vietnam, the hippie life style, and the occupations we choose. In all cases the question we will ask in this chapter is basically the same: Is it possible to identify the value correlates of a given behavior and the behavioral correlates of a given value?

CIVIL RIGHTS

On theoretical grounds, *equality* should be the value that is most implicated in behavior concerning civil rights or discrimination against persons of different ethnic or racial background. Data are available for three kinds of molar and molecular behavior: joining or not joining a civil rights organization, participating or not participating in civil rights demonstrations, and eye contact with persons of another race.

Joining a Civil Rights Organization

A total of 408 freshmen in two residential colleges at Michigan State University were solicited by first-class letter in April 1968 and, again, a year later to join the National Association for the Advancement of Colored People (NAACP). (Three hundred and sixty-six of these subjects are the experimental or control subjects of Experiments 2 and 3, as described in Chapter 9.) Over 97 percent of these subjects were white. To join, the subject had to fill out an application form, enclose it along with a dollar in a prestamped return envelope, and post it in a United States mailbox. Forty-eight of these freshmen—about 12 percent—thus joined the NAACP, either in 1968 or 1969. The question we are most interested in here is whether a value analysis will distinguish between those who join and those who do not, and, if so, which values? Table 5.1 shows that 10 values differentiate between joiners and nonjoiners, three beyond the .10 level of confidence, four beyond the .05 level, and three more beyond the .01 level.

As may be expected on theoretical grounds, *equality* is indeed the value that best discriminates between those who join and those who do not join NAACP. Although both groups of college students rank *equality* relatively high, its median rank is 4.3 for those joining, and 7.0 for those not joining; composite rank is second and fifth, respectively. This finding is wholly consistent with many others reported in Chapter 4 showing that *equality* is the value that best discriminates among persons differing in attitude toward civil rights.

Moreover, those who join NAACP also care significantly more (or nearly significantly more) for *a world at peace, a world of beauty*, being

TABLE 5.1   VALUES THAT DIFFERENTIATE SIGNIFICANTLY BETWEEN
THOSE JOINING AND NOT JOINING NAACP

		Joined NAACP	Nonjoiners	
	N =	48	360	p*
Terminal Values				
A comfortable life		14.3 (14)	13.3 (14)	.01
A world at peace		7.0 (6)	8.4 (9)	.05
A world of beauty		10.8 (12)	12.8 (13)	.09
Equality		4.3 (2)	7.0 (5)	.001
National Security		15.4 (16)	14.2 (16)	.05
Pleasure		15.0 (15)	14.0 (15)	.05
Instrumental Values	N =	46	346	
Ambitious		11.7 (15)	9.5 (8)	.01
Helpful		7.5 (5)	9.7 (11)	.06
Honest		3.1 (1)	4.5 (1)	.05
Self-controlled		11.3 (14)	9.9 (13)	.07

Figures shown are median rankings and, in parentheses, composite rank orders.
* Median test.

honest and being *helpful.* On the other hand, those who do not join care significantly more (or nearly so) for *a comfortable life, national security, pleasure,* being *ambitious,* and being *self-controlled.* Thus, college students who are attracted to a civil rights organization such as the NAACP can be described as having a value pattern that is different in important respects from those who do not join. The former place greater priority on egalitarianism, world peace, aesthetic values, honesty in interpersonal relationships, and the welfare of others. On the other hand, nonjoiners are more materialistic and success-oriented, more patriotic and hedonistic. And, along with their greater hedonism, paradoxically, they also place greater stress on impulse control, thus suggesting a personality dynamic that has previously been found to be characteristic of the authoritarian personality (Adorno, *et al.,* 1950).

Participation in Civil Rights Demonstrations

Another sample of college students at Michigan State University were asked the following question in 1967: "In general, are you sympathetic with the aims of civil rights demonstrators?" They had three response options: (1) Yes, and I have personally participated in a civil rights demonstration; (2) Yes, but I have not participated in civil rights demonstrations; (3) No, I am not sympathetic. Table 5.2 shows about a dozen values that discriminate significantly among the three response groups, with *equality* once again being the most discriminating value. Its composite

TABLE 5.2 SIGNIFICANT VALUE DIFFERENCES AMONG COLLEGE STUDENTS VARYING IN PARTICIPATION IN CIVIL RIGHTS DEMONSTRATIONS

	Yes, and Have Participated	*Yes, but Have Not Participated*	*No, Not Sympathetic*	
$N =$	*15*	*218*	*62*	*p**
Terminal Values				
A comfortable life	15.3 (18)	12.4 (13)	9.9 (10)	.01
A world of beauty	12.6 (13)	13.5 (14)	15.5 (18)	.01
Equality	6.8 (5)	9.6 (11)	14.1 (17)	.001
Mature love	7.8 (7)	6.9 (5)	10.5 (11)	.05
National security	14.3 (17)	14.0 (17)	12.5 (14)	.05
Instrumental Values				
Broadminded	4.3 (1)	6.5 (3)	7.5 (4)	.06
Capable	11.9 (14)	9.7 (11)	7.5 (5)	.06
Clean	16.0 (18)	14.7 (17)	11.3 (13)	.001
Forgiving	8.3 (7)	9.4 (10)	11.5 (14)	.05
Helpful	10.3 (11)	10.0 (12)	13.3 (17)	.01
Loving	7.3 (4)	7.3 (5)	9.2 (9)	.05
Polite	13.9 (16)	13.4 (16)	11.2 (12)	.07
Responsible	9.3 (9)	6.3 (2)	5.0 (2)	.01

Figures shown are median rankings and, in parentheses, composite rank orders.
* Kruskal-Wallis test.

rank is fifth for participants, eleventh for those sympathetic but not participating, and seventeenth for those unsympathetic with civil rights demonstrations. *Clean* is the next most discriminating value, its composite rank being eighteenth for participants, seventeenth for sympathizers, and thirteenth for those opposed.

Civil rights participants, moreover, place a relatively greater emphasis on *a world of beauty*, *mature love*, and being *broadminded, forgiving, helpful,* and *loving,* and a relatively lesser emphasis on *a comfortable life, national security,* and being *capable, clean, polite,* and *responsible.* The value pattern of those reporting that they are unsympathetic with the aims of civil rights demonstrations is the reverse of the value pattern just described for participants, with the sympathizers typically falling in between.

Three values—*broadminded, polite,* and *capable*—do not quite reach the .05 significance level. The first two fit theoretical expectations and are consistent with other findings reported in this work. The findings for *capable* are, however, unexpected. The composite rank of *capable* is fourteenth for participants, eleventh for sympathizers, and fifth for nonsympathizers. Apparently, civil rights participants and their sympathizers are more likely to be recruited from segments of educated youth who have rejected the traditional middle-class competence values of American society.

The rather sizeable difference in the ranking of *responsible* is also noteworthy. Its composite rank is ninth for participants but second for those opposed to civil rights demonstrations. Sympathizers again fall in between but are closer to nonsympathizers than to participants. These findings suggest that the college students who refrain from participating in civil rights demonstrations, even those who are sympathetic, do so because they consciously feel that civil rights demonstrations are irresponsible. Yet the nonsympathizers who care so little for *equality* and so much for being *responsible* also care less than the others do about being *helpful* or *forgiving*. It is difficult to conclude from all this that nonsympathizers are in fact responsible people. Their value pattern suggests that they are employing *responsible* as a standard for rationalization.

When we compare the findings obtained for those joining and those not joining NAACP with those obtained for students participating in, sympathizing with, and opposing civil rights demonstrations, five values stand out in both sets of data as ones showing the same results: Those exhibiting pro-civil rights behavior value *equality, a world of beauty*, and being *helpful* relatively more, and they value *a comfortable life* and *national security* relatively less than do those exhibiting anti-civil rights behavior.

Eye Contact between Whites and Blacks

Several studies have shown that duration of eye contact is an unobtrusive measure of one's liking for someone (Argyle and Dean, 1965; Efran and Broughton, 1966; Exline and Winters, 1965; Mehrabian, 1969). In a laboratory setting, Penner (1969, 1971) measured the amount of eye contact between white subjects and white and black confederates with whom they had engaged in a 10-minute discussion. Penner obtained separate measures of eye contact for the first and second five minutes of interaction, and Table 5.3 shows with his kind permission the findings he obtained for all 18 terminal values (instrumental value rankings were not obtained).

Not one of the 18 correlations between terminal values and eye contact is significant when white subjects interact with white confederates, either during the first or second five minutes of interaction. The highest correlation obtained under this condition is .25, between *self-respect* and amount of eye contact during the first five minutes, higher rankings being associated with more eye contact. It is not statistically significant.

These findings are in marked contrast to those obtained under the condition wherein white subjects had interacted with black confederates. Consistent with the findings previously shown concerning the value differences between NAACP joiners and nonjoiners, and between participants and nonparticipants in civil rights demonstrations, the correlation

TABLE 5.3   PRODUCT-MOMENT CORRELATIONS BETWEEN VALUES
AND EYE CONTACT FOR WHITES INTERACTING WITH WHITES AND
WITH BLACKS

	White-to-White Eye Contact		White-to-Black Eye Contact	
	First 5 Minutes	Second 5 Minutes	First 5 Minutes	Second 5 Minutes
N =	20		76	
Terminal Values				
A comfortable life	−.02	.08	−.25†	−.34‡
An exciting life	.12	.00	.02	.11
A sense of accomplishment	−.07	−.23	.02	.11
A world at peace	.21	−.11	.11	.01
A world of beauty	.03	.15	.13	.18
Equality	.05	.06	.29†	.31†
Family security	.07	.16	−.26†	−.31†
Freedom	.15	.09	.06	.07
Happiness	−.11	−.21	.08	.06
Inner harmony	.06	.06	.06	.20
Mature love	−.10	−.05	.01	.00
National security	−.08	.03	.02	.01
Pleasure	.09	.11	−.16	−.21*
Salvation	.16	.15	−.12	−.01
Self-respect	.25	.18	−.03	.04
Social recognition	.14	.12	.17	.15
True friendship	−.04	.00	.03	.07
Wisdom	.10	.02	−.02	.05

* $p < .05$.
† $p < .01$.
‡ $p < .001$.

between *equality* and eye contact is .29 for the first five minutes of interaction, and .31 for the second five minutes. Both correlations are significant
beyond the .01 level.

The three other values are also significantly related to eye contact between
whites and blacks, and all of them are consistent with findings reported
earlier in this section or in the preceding chapter. White subjects who look
less at the black confederates they talk to care significantly more for *a
comfortable life, family security*, and *pleasure*.

The findings for the first and second five minutes of interaction are in
close agreement, with the correlations obtained for the second five
minutes usually being somewhat larger, though not significantly so. It
may be concluded from these data that white persons who are more
egalitarian in their value orientation engage in more authentic or intimate
interactions with black strangers. In contrast, white persons who are more

materialistic and hedonic and those who are more concerned with the security of their family seem afraid of black strangers and therefore engage in more evasive interactions with them.

RELIGION

Church Attendance

A full report on the relation between church attendance and all 36 values among adult Americans and college students are reported elsewhere (Rokeach, 1969a). Tables 5.4 and 5.5, which are taken from this report, show only the significant value differences obtained for these two samples: 12 values in the national sample and 16 values in the college sample differentiate significantly among persons varying in church attendance. Most striking is the fact that all 12 values that distinguish between church-goers and nonchurchgoers in the national sample also distinguish between churchgoers and nonchurchgoers in the college sample. There is therefore little room for doubt about the distinctive value patterns of Americans varying in their churchgoing behavior.

In both samples, *salvation* is the value that most sharply distinguishes churchgoers from nonchurchgoers. Its composite rank is third for adults attending weekly and fifteenth for those never attending; its composite rank is first for college students attending weekly and eighteenth for those never attending.

In both samples, moreover, those attending weekly place greater value than nonchurchgoers on being *helpful* and *obedient* and usually lesser value on *a comfortable life, an exciting life, freedom, pleasure*, and being *imaginative, independent, intellectual*, and *logical*. The overall impression gained from both sets of data is that churchgoers, in comparison with non-churchgoers, think of themselves as relatively less materialistic, less hedonistic, less concerned with personal freedom and independence, and less concerned with intellectual values. In contrast, they think of themselves as more conformity-oriented, more willing to forgive, more concerned with the welfare of their fellow man, and more concerned with a life hereafter. Their self-conceptions about the regard they have for their fellow man are, however, contradicted by independently obtained indices of social compassion (Rokeach, 1969b; Stark, 1971; Forbes, TeVault, and Gromoll, 1971).

In the national sample, the correlation between *salvation* rankings and church attendance was .34, and the multiple correlation between all 36 values and church attendance was .41. These findings suggest that although *salvation* is the main value underlying church attendance, there are many different values that determine why people attend church.

In addition to the 12 values just discussed, 4 other values distinguish significantly between college students who vary in frequency of church-

TABLE 5.4   SIGNIFICANT VALUE DIFFERENCES AMONG ADULT AMERICANS VARYING IN CHURCH ATTENDANCE

	Every Week	Nearly Every Week	2–3 Times Monthly	Once a Month	Several Times a Year	Once or Twice a Year	Less than Once a Year	Never	p*
N =	553	121	139	116	159	126	96	96	
Terminal Values									
A comfortable life	10.3 (13)	9.0 (11)	7.2 (4)	9.1 (8)	7.9 (6)	7.9 (6)	7.5 (5)	8.0 (7)	.01
An exciting life	15.7 (18)	15.4 (18)	15.5 (18)	15.7 (18)	14.7 (17)	14.6 (18)	14.5 (17)	14.1 (17)	.01
Freedom	5.9 (4)	5.3 (3)	5.0 (3)	5.1 (3)	5.4 (3)	5.5 (3)	7.0 (3)	4.4 (2)	.05
Pleasure	15.3 (17)	15.2 (17)	13.9 (16)	14.7 (17)	14.4 (16)	13.9 (16)	13.5 (16)	13.3 (15)	.001
Salvation	4.3 (3)	7.4 (5)	9.7 (10)	10.3 (12)	11.3 (13)	11.5 (13)	13.2 (15)	15.5 (18)	.001
Instrumental Values									
Forgiving	6.1 (2)	5.9 (3)	8.1 (6)	8.6 (7)	8.3 (7)	8.1 (6)	8.1 (7)	9.6 (11)	.001
Helpful	7.7 (6)	8.1 (7)	7.7 (4)	9.4 (9)	8.5 (8)	9.1 (8)	8.5 (8)	10.5 (13)	.001
Imaginative	16.0 (18)	15.8 (18)	15.5 (18)	15.8 (18)	14.9 (18)	14.3 (17)	15.0 (18)	13.5 (17)	.001
Independent	11.2 (14)	11.1 (14)	8.5 (7)	10.5 (13)	9.6 (11)	10.1 (12)	9.5 (10)	8.4 (5)	.05
Intellectual	13.6 (16)	12.8 (15)	11.4 (15)	12.2 (15)	12.4 (15)	13.3 (15)	14.0 (17)	10.5 (14)	.05
Logical	14.7 (17)	13.8 (17)	14.8 (17)	14.4 (17)	13.1 (16)	13.7 (16)	13.8 (16)	12.3 (16)	.05
Obedient	12.6 (15)	13.4 (16)	13.5 (16)	13.3 (16)	14.4 (17)	14.5 (18)	13.5 (15)	14.9 (18)	.001

Figures shown are median rankings and, in parentheses, composite rank orders.
* Median test.

TABLE 5.5   SIGNIFICANT VALUE DIFFERENCES AMONG COLLEGE
STUDENTS VARYING IN CHURCH ATTENDANCE

	Weekly	*Monthly*	*Rarely*	*Never*	
N =	*147*	*40*	*82*	*29*	*p**
Terminal Values					
A comfortable life	13.5 (14)	8.3 (8)	11.0 (12)	12.3 (14)	.001
An exciting life	13.6 (15)	10.5 (11)	10.5 (11)	10.8 (12)	.01
A world of beauty	14.2 (17)	14.0 (16)	14.2 (17)	9.8 (11)	.01
Freedom	6.2 (3)	3.5 (1)	5.0 (1)	3.7 (1)	.05
Pleasure	14.8 (18)	12.5 (15)	13.6 (16)	13.6 (15)	.01
Salvation	3.9 (1)	14.5 (17)	17.0 (18)	17.7 (18)	.001
Instrumental Values					
Capable	10.4 (12)	9.5 (10)	8.3 (7)	7.4 (7)	.01
Forgiving	8.4 (7)	11.0 (12)	10.4 (13)	11.3 (13)	.01
Helpful	9.2 (8)	12.5 (15)	12.1 (15)	11.6 (14)	.001
Honest	3.3 (1)	6.0 (2)	5.3 (2)	4.8 (2)	.01
Imaginative	12.9 (16)	11.5 (13)	9.8 (12)	7.8 (8)	.001
Independent	10.2 (11)	6.5 (4)	7.1 (5)	5.4 (3)	.001
Intellectual	9.9 (10)	10.5 (11)	9.4 (11)	5.7 (4)	.05
Logical	11.6 (14)	9.5 (9)	8.1 (6)	9.3 (11)	.05
Loving	5.7 (2)	7.5 (6)	9.4 (10)	11.3 (12)	.01
Obedient	14.0 (18)	16.3 (18)	16.1 (18)	16.7 (18)	.001

Figures shown are median rankings and, in parentheses, composite rank orders.
* Kruskal-Wallis test.

going. Those who are churchgoers care more for *a world of beauty* and for
being *honest* and *loving*, and they care less about being *capable*. It would
thus seem that churchgoing college students have a value pattern that is
on the whole somewhat more consistent with the teachings of Christianity
than is the case with adult churchgoers.

POLITICS

Political Activism in the 1968 Presidential
Campaign

In July, 1968, immediately before the national conventions of the Republican and Democratic parties, Bishop (1969) administered the Value Survey
to persons working actively in the various campaign headquarters of
Eugene McCarthy, Hubert Humphrey, Nelson Rockefeller, Richard Nixon,
Ronald Reagan, and George Wallace. These activists were headquartered
in various cities in Michigan—Battle Creek, East Lansing, Flint, Grand

Rapids, Lansing, Owosso, and Warren. Because of the fact that these were busy people, they were asked to rank only the terminal values. Table 5.6 shows 6 out of the 18 terminal values that significantly differentiated among them. Once again, *equality* is the value that best differentiates these groups from one another, except that this time the *equality* differences are even more striking than any of the *equality* findings reported previously. The median rank for *equality* is 4.0 for McCarthy workers at one extreme and 15.0 for Reagan and Wallace workers at the other. The composite ranks are even more striking: *Equality* is first for McCarthy activists and last for Wallace activists, with those working for the other presidential candidates following in linear fashion from left to right: Humphrey activists second, Rockefeller and Nixon activists ninth, and Reagan activists seventeenth. No other value shows as marked a linear trend from liberal to conservative, thus justifying the conclusion that rankings of *equality* are diagnostic mainly of political differences in the United States in the same way that rankings of *salvation* are diagnostic mainly of Christian devoutness. A fuller discussion of the values underlying political differences is, however, reserved for the next chapter.

Table 5.6 reveals other significant value differences among the six activist groups. Even though all groups rank *a comfortable life* relatively low, suggesting they are all of relatively high socioeconomic status (see Chapter 3), liberal activists rank it lower than do conservative activists. A similar trend is noted for *family security*, ranked thirteenth by McCarthy activists, then increasing linearly in importance to sixth or seventh for Reagan and Wallace activists. *Mature love* shows a somewhat different trend. It is ranked relatively high by McCarthy, Rockefeller, and Reagan workers and lower by the others, and lowest of all by Nixon activists. To some extent at least these *mature love* rankings are probably due to social class differences concerning the value of romantic love (see Chapter 3).

The findings for *national security*, the value of traditional concern to those who like to think of themselves as American patriots, and the findings for the religious value *salvation* parallel the linear trends found for *equality*, except that these rankings are in the other direction: *National security* and *salvation* are ranked seventeenth and eighteenth by McCarthy activists at one extreme and sixth and tenth by Wallace activists at the other extreme.

The results shown in table 5.6 can be summarized as follows: The more liberal the activist, the more egalitarian his values, the less his concern with material values or with the traditional values of God, home, and country. It is the other way around for conservative activists. However, liberal activists do have something in common with Rockefeller and Reagan activists—the importance they place on romantic love. In contrast, Wallace activists and, above all, Nixon activists accord romantic love a position of lower priority on their scale of values.

TABLE 5.6 SIGNIFICANT TERMINAL VALUES DIFFERENTIATING ACTIVIST SUPPORTERS OF SIX
PRESIDENTIAL CANDIDATES IN 1968

	McCarthy	Humphrey	Rockefeller	Nixon	Reagan	Wallace	p*
N =	30	15	30	16	11	19	
A comfortable life	15.1 (15)	15.3 (16)	14.0 (14)	10.8 (12)	11.3 (13)	11.3 (13)	.001
Equality	4.0 (1)	5.0 (2)	8.5 (9)	9.2 (9)	15.0 (17)	15.0 (18)	.001
Family security	11.9 (13)	10.0 (12)	8.5 (8)	8.0 (8)	7.8 (6)	6.7 (7)	.01
Mature love	7.1 (6)	9.8 (10)	8.0 (6)	12.5 (15)	7.0 (5)	11.0 (12)	.01
National security	15.5 (17)	13.7 (14)	15.0 (17)	7.5 (6)	9.3 (9)	6.3 (6)	.001
Salvation	17.6 (18)	16.0 (18)	16.5 (18)	17.5 (18)	14.3 (15)	10.0 (10)	.01

Figures shown are median rankings and, in parentheses, composite rank orders.
* Median test.

THE VIETNAM WAR

Antiwar Protest Behavior

Although data on the relation between values and antiwar protest behavior are not extensive, the available data are nonetheless suggestive. Parrott and Bloom (1971) requested San Francisco participants in the antiwar moratorium march of October 1969, randomly selected pedestrians in downtown San Francisco, and members of the John Birch Society in a California city to fill out a questionnaire which included a drastically reduced seven-value version of the terminal value scale. The former two groups of respondents returned the questionnaire by mail, the latter at a John Birch Society meeting. The three groups differed significantly on only two of the seven values—*a world at peace* and *national security*. The marchers, downtown pedestrians, and John Birch Society members ranked *a world at peace* 2, 3, and 5, respectively, and they ranked *national security* 7, 6, and 2, respectively.

HONEST AND DISHONEST BEHAVIOR

Returning Borrowed Pencils

Shotland and Berger (1970) gave a questionnaire that included the Value Survey to 131 female employees of a company belonging to the Mid-western Scanlon Plan Association. Upon completing the questionnaire, 39 percent of the subjects returned the scoring pencils that had been distributed to them and 61 percent did not. One question these investigators were interested in was whether these two groups of women were distinguishable from one another in their value patterns. They found four values that differentiated significantly between those returning and those not returning the pencils, as shown in Table 5.7. The median rank of *honest* is 2.0 for those returning and 4.38 for those not returning the pencils. Pencil returners, moreover, rank *salvation* and *a world at peace* significantly higher. Paradoxically, however, pencil returners also place a significantly lower value on being *helpful*, a finding that is not easily interpretable.

Cheating in the Classroom

Homant and Rokeach (1970) gave twelfth graders an opportunity to cheat under conditions of high and low motivation. The twelfth graders also ranked the following 12 instrumental values for importance: *clean, hardworking, loyal, friendly, honest, polite, brave, smart, careful, obedient, sincere,* and *calm*. Although they found no significant relation between value for *honest* and amount of cheating under the low-motivation condition, they found significant correlations of .30 and .23 between cheating and pretest rankings of *honest* in two experimental groups tested

TABLE 5.7   MEDIAN RANKS OF FOUR VALUES SIGNIFICANTLY
DIFFERENTIATING BETWEEN THOSE RETURNING AND THOSE NOT
RETURNING PENCILS

	Pencil Returners	Pencil Nonreturners	p*
Terminal Values			
A world at peace	4.08	6.20	.040
Salvation	1.41	8.88	.001
Instrumental Values			
Helpful	11.25	8.73	.005
Honest	2.00	4.38	.008

Source: Shotland and Berger (1970).
* Median test.

under high-motivation conditions. Posttest *honest* rankings obtained a
day after the experimental session also correlated significantly with
cheating—.25 and .31. Moreover, they found that *honest* rankings
correlated more highly with cheating in the classroom than did any of the
remaining 11 instrumental values—all such correlations with *honest* being
in the theoretically expected direction.

Male and Female Prison Inmates

Cochrane (1971) compared the values of inmates in state prisons in
Michigan with national samples matched for sex, age, and race. The
inmates had been convicted for a large variety of crimes: homicide, assault,
rape, armed and unarmed robbery, prostitution, forgery, and narcotics
violations. Table 5.8 shows the values that significantly differentiate male
and female inmates from matched males and females selected from the
national sample. Five values discriminate significantly in both sets of
comparisons. Although *honest* generally ranks relatively high in the
instrumental value hierarchy of those inside as well as outside prison, male
and female inmates nonetheless rank it significantly lower. Its median is
6.0 or more for men and women in prison but it is under 4.0 for those
outside prison.

Surprisingly, however, the value that turns out to be the best discriminator between those in and out of prison is *wisdom*. Male and female
inmates rank it second or third in importance compared with those outside,
who rank it eighth. Is *wisdom* ranked high by inmates because it is a virtue
they do not possess, a virtue which, had they possessed more of it, would
have kept them out of jail? Or, is it a virtue they perceive themselves as
possessing and therefore able to outsmart society and the police? We do
not know, since preprison values are not available for these subjects.

TABLE 5.8 SIGNIFICANT VALUE DIFFERENCES BETWEEN PRISON
INMATES AND NATIONAL SAMPLES MATCHED FOR SEX, AGE,
AND RACE

	Male Prison Inmates	Male National Sample	p*	Female Prison Inmates	Female National Sample	p*
N =	363	100		98	91	
Terminal Values						
An exciting life	—	—	—	14.8 (18)	16.4 (18)	.05
A sense of accomplishment	—	—	—	8.1 (8)	9.9 (9)	.05
A world at peace	9.0 (9)	4.3 (3)	.001	7.4 (7)	3.4 (1)	.001
Equality	8.5 (8)	6.5 (4)	.01	—	—	—
Freedom	—	—	—	3.3 (1)	4.9 (3)	.01
Happiness	6.5 (4)	8.1 (7)	.05	—	—	—
Inner harmony	—	—	—	8.8 (10)	10.7 (12)	.01
National security	13.9 (16)	11.6 (14)	.001	13.5 (14)	11.6 (14)	.05
Pleasure	12.9 (14)	14.4 (18)	.05	—	—	—
Salvation	15.1 (18)	11.2 (11)	.001	13.7 (15)	10.6 (11)	.001
Wisdom	5.2 (2)	8.2 (8)	.001	5.0 (3)	9.1 (8)	.001
Instrumental Values						
Broadminded	—	—	—	5.7 (1)	8.9 (9)	.05
Capable	8.1 (7)	9.7 (11)	.05	—	—	—
Helpful	—	—	—	10.6 (12)	8.6 (7)	.01
Honest	6.2 (2)	3.8 (1)	.01	6.0 (3)	3.9 (1)	.01
Independent	—	—	—	8.5 (8)	10.3 (12)	.05
Intellectual	—	—	—	11.0 (13)	12.9 (16)	.05
Logical	—	—	—	12.7 (16)	14.8 (17)	.01
Self-controlled	6.9 (3)	9.7 (10)	.01	—	—	—

Figures shown are median rankings and, in parentheses, composite rank orders.
* Median test.

Moreover, prison inmates are evidently less religious than noninmates, both males and females ranking *salvation* rather low on their terminal value scale. They are also less concerned with broader social issues: They rank *a world at peace* seventh or ninth compared with matched noninmates, who rank it first or third; and they rank *national security* as less important.

Other values discriminate significantly only between male inmates and noninmates or only between female inmates and noninmates. Male inmates care less than their outside counterparts do for *equality* and more for *happiness*, *pleasure*, and being *capable* and *self-controlled*. This value pattern suggests a self-centered concern with hedonism accompanied by a lesser concern with religion, the plight of others, their nation, or the world beyond. At the same time, the male inmates seem to be telling us that competence, maturity, and impulse control are salient problems for them, as if to say that if only they had more of these qualities, they might not be in their present predicament.

The value differences between women inmates and noninmates suggest a somewhat different set of dynamics. Instead of a greater hedonism, we discern a relatively greater desire in women inmates for excitement compared with women noninmates with whom they are matched. This desire for excitement is, however, accompanied by a relatively greater desire for inner peace. And compared with matched women from the national sample, women in prison also place a greater value on autonomy, tolerance, and self-fulfillment: They rank *a sense of accomplishment, freedom*, and being *independent, broadminded, intellectual*, and *logical* significantly higher. Without additional information about these women, it would be premature to speculate about the meaning of all these differences or whether the value pattern they exhibit is an antecedent or consequence of their incarceration. These findings are puzzling and invite further research.

Although it was not possible to predict beforehand all the differences observed, the difference in value for *honesty* between inmates and non-inmates is especially noteworthy because it is consistent with theoretical expectations. When these findings are considered alongside those reported for pencil returners and nonreturners and for schoolchildren who cheat and do not cheat in the classroom, it can be concluded that value for *honesty* is at least to some extent a valid predictor of honest and dishonest behavior. At the same time, the findings suggest that honest or dishonest behavior is related to other values as well. Thus, the present findings provide somewhat more support for the generality of behavior than that provided in the classical study by Hartshorne and May (1928).

INTERPERSONAL CONFLICT

Conflict between College Roommates

Sikula (1970) selected 50 pairs of college roommates who stopped being roommates because they had been in conflict with one another. He compared them with another 50 pairs of roommates who got along well and therefore had continued to room together. Value Survey data for these two groups were first analyzed to ascertain to what extent compatibility between roommates was a function of similarity of value systems. The measure of such similarity was the rho correlation between the value rankings of the two roommates.

Compatible and incompatible roommates do not differ significantly in the extent to which their instrumental value systems are similar. The rho correlations are rather low for both groups—a mean of .21 for compatible roommates, and .16 for incompatible roommates. But Sikula found that the two kinds of roommates did differ significantly in terminal value system similarity. The mean correlation is .41 between compatible room-mates and .26 between incompatible roommates. These findings suggest that similarity of terminal but not of instrumental values is a significant determinant of compatibility between college roommates.

Sikula's research also informs us about the particular values that are implicated as determinants of compatibility between roommates. Certain values (Table 5.9) show significant correlations between rankings of compatible roommates; others show significant correlations between incompatible roomates. All seven of these concern terminal values, as would be expected from Sikula's findings concerning the role of terminal value similarity as a determinant of roommate compatibility.

Comparing the two sets of correlations shown in Table 5.9, it would seem that compatible roommates share similar views concerning the relative importance of *an exciting life*, *equality*, *mature love*, and, especially, *wisdom*. In contrast, incompatible roommates seem to share similar views about the relative importance of *social recognition*. It seems reasonable to suggest that when roommates are both concerned with *social recognition* they will compete, and therefore each will find the other threatening. Finally, religion seems to be a less crucial determinant of compatibility, since rankings of *salvation* are significantly correlated in both sets of roommates, although the correlation is somewhat higher among com-patible roommates.

BEHAVIOR IN THE COUNSELING SITUATION

Counselor Effectiveness

S. Danish compared the values of graduate students in counseling psy-chology who had been judged by their peers to be effective or ineffective counselors (unpublished data). The more effective counselors, he found, valued *equality*, being *broadminded*, and being *loving* significantly more, and *national security* and being *independent* significantly less than did ineffective counselors. These findings suggest that the Value Survey may be a useful diagnostic tool for identifying those who behave in such a way that they will be judged by their peers to be potentially successful or unsuccessful counselors.

Continuing or Discontinuing Counseling

It is reasonable to suppose that a student's decision to continue or dis-continue counseling would to some extent at least be a function of his values and of the degree of their similarity to the counselor's values. Employing the 12-item Form B version of the Value Survey, Shotland (1968) compared the values of clients at the Counseling Center at Michigan State University who terminated or continued the counseling sessions

TABLE 5.9   CORRELATIONS BETWEEN RANKINGS OF TERMINAL
VALUES BY COMPATIBLE AND INCOMPATIBLE ROOMMATES (N = 50
IN EACH GROUP)

Value	Compatible Roommates	Incompatible Roommates
An exciting life	.36†	−.16
Equality	.27*	−.10
Mature love	.42†	.07
Salvation	.49†	.33*
Social recognition	−.02	.30*
Wisdom	.61†	−.15

* p < .05.
† p < .01.

following the first interview. Those terminating counseling valued *salvation*
and *clean* significantly more than did those continuing beyond the first
session, and they valued *a world at peace*, *respect for others*, and being
tender significantly less. But it is not clear from Shotland's data whether
it is the values of the client as such or the similarity between client and
therapist values that is more crucial to the client's decision to continue or
discontinue counseling. The median correlation between the terminal value
rankings of clients terminating counseling after the first interview and their
counselors was .37; the median correlations between the terminal value
rankings of clients continuing beyond the first session and their counselors
was .60. This difference is a statistically significant one. Whichever interpretation may turn out to be the more tenable one, it would seem that
a client's terminal values is, in any event, a significant variable that
affects one's decision to continue or discontinue counseling.

Another finding of Shotland's study is that clients who either did or
did not continue counseling did not differ in the extent to which their
instrumental value systems were similar to that of their counselors. The
median correlation between the instrumental value system of terminating
clients and their counselors was .25, and that between continuing clients
and their counselors was .26. These findings are wholly consistent with
Sikula's study of value similarity between compatible and incompatible
roommates. Similarity of terminal value systems but not of instrumental
value systems seems to be an important factor affecting both compatibility
between roommates and the continuation of the client-counselor relationship. It would thus seem that what matters more to persons interacting with
one another is each one's perception of the other's terminal rather than
instrumental value system. It will be interesting to see if similar results are
obtained for other kinds of dyadic relationships, for instance, marriage,
scientific collaborations, business partnerships, and so on.

ACADEMIC PURSUITS

Academic Major

The best data currently available concerning value differences among academic majors comes from Feather's (1970a) comparison of 463 first-year students at Flinders University in South Australia. These students were enrolled in the humanities (drama, English, fine arts, French, music, philosophy, Spanish), social sciences (American studies, economics, education, geography, history, politics, psychology, social administration), and the physical sciences (applied mathematics, chemistry, Earth sciences, mathematics, physics, biology). He found eight values that differentiated significantly among these three rather broad groups, as shown in Table 5.10.

It is apparent from a visual inspection of Table 5.10 that the social and physical science majors are, on the whole rather similar, and that the main differences are found, generally, between humanities majors and social and physical science majors. As might be expected, humanities majors care more for *a world of beauty* and for being *forgiving* and *imaginative*. What may be surprising, however, is the finding that humanities majors also place a relatively higher value on being *intellectual*. Social and physical science majors, however, place a significantly higher value on *a comfortable life* and on being *ambitious, capable,* and *self-controlled.*

TABLE 5.10 SIGNIFICANT VALUES DIFFERENTIATING HUMANITIES, SOCIAL SCIENCES, AND PHYSICAL SCIENCES MAJORS AT FLINDERS UNIVERSITY IN SOUTH AUSTRALIA

		Humanities	*Social Sciences*	*Physical Sciences*	
	$N =$	*103*	*162*	*198*	*p**
Terminal Values					
A comfortable life		14.4 (17)	13.3 (14)	12.2 (13)	.001
A world of beauty		10.9 (13)	13.0 (13)	12.9 (15)	.001
Instrumental Values					
Ambitious		10.8 (14)	7.8 (6)	7.8 (6)	.01
Capable		10.1 (12)	8.7 (11)	8.0 (7)	.05
Forgiving		7.8 (6)	8.2 (9)	9.7 (12)	.05
Imaginative		8.4 (7)	12.8 (16)	12.4 (16)	.001
Intellectual		9.1 (10)	11.4 (14)	11.5 (15)	.05
Self-controlled		10.2 (13)	8.1 (8)	7.7 (5)	.05

Figures shown are median rankings and, in parentheses, composite rank orders.
* Kruskal-Wallis test.

Thus, humanities majors seem more appreciative of aesthetic values, a life of fantasy and intellect, and a forgiving attitude toward others, whereas social and physical science majors seem more interested in material comfort, achievement, and impulse control. It remains to be seen whether these value differences between majors in an Australian university will be replicated elsewhere. A comparable analysis of value differences conducted with Michigan State University students is not as clear as the Flinders University findings, and will therefore not be presented here. The main reason the Michigan State University data are more ambiguous is that there were too many majors (agriculture, arts and letters, business, communication, education, engineering, home economics, natural science, social science, and no preference) resulting in small numbers of cases. Although many distinctive value differences were noted in these data, many of them were not statistically significant, probably because of small numbers of cases.

LIFE STYLE

Hippie and Nonhippie Values

In summer 1968, Raymond Merriman, assisted by Helen Zettig and Elizabeth Ihrig, all having previously participated in the hippie subculture, collected data from 78 persons identified as hippies. They lived in the communes of Ann Arbor, East Lansing, Detroit, and Birmingham; their physical appearance was distinctive—long hair, beards, hippie-style clothing; they used drugs more or less regularly. Of the 78 hippies, 50 were men, 28 were women. Forty-eight of them had been to college or had recently graduated from college. Tables 5.11 and 5.12 show the results for this hippie sample and compares them with those obtained for 275 nonhippie students at Michigan State University.

Twelve terminal and eleven instrumental values distinguish at statistically significant levels between hippies and nonhippies. The largest difference among the terminal values is found for *a world of beauty*, its composite rank being eighth for hippies and sixteenth for nonhippies. The largest instrumental value difference is found for *responsible*, hippies ranking it twelfth and nonhippies ranking it second.

The many significant differences shown in Tables 5.11 and 5.12 are consistent with what is generally known about hippie culture and enable us to pinpoint the values that distinguish hippie from nonhippie culture. Hippies place a generally higher value on certain end-states—*an exciting life, a world at peace, a world of beauty, equality*, and *pleasure*—and they place a higher value on certain modes of behavior—being *broadminded, cheerful, forgiving, imaginative, independent*, and *loving*. Nonhippies, in contrast, project a very different image: They care significantly more about

TABLE 5.11 TERMINAL VALUE MEDIANS AND COMPOSITE RANK
ORDERS FOR HIPPIES AND NONHIPPIES

		Nonhippies	Hippies	
	$N =$	275	78	p^*
A comfortable life		12.0 (13)	14.6 (15)	.001
An exciting life		11.6 (12)	9.9 (11)	.001
A sense of accomplishment		7.8 (6)	11.1 (12)	.001
A world at peace		8.4 (9)	5.7 (3)	.001
A world of beauty		13.7 (16)	7.2 (8)	.001
Equality		10.6 (11)	6.8 (7)	.001
Family security		8.4 (10)	13.4 (14)	.001
Freedom		5.1 (1)	5.1 (2)	—
Happiness		6.2 (2)	6.7 (6)	—
Inner harmony		8.3 (8)	6.5 (5)	—
Mature love		7.3 (5)	5.6 (1)	—
National security		13.8 (17)	16.8 (17)	.001
Pleasure		14.1 (18)	12.1 (13)	.001
Salvation		12.7 (14)	17.1 (18)	.001
Self-respect		6.6 (4)	8.6 (10)	.001
Social recognition		13.6 (15)	15.3 (16)	.01
True friendship		7.9 (7)	7.5 (9)	—
Wisdom		6.4 (3)	6.1 (4)	—

Figures shown are median rankings and, in parentheses, composite rank orders.
* Median test.

*a comfortable life, a sense of accomplishment, family security, national
security, salvation, self-respect,* and *social recognition,* and they place a
higher value on being *ambitious, obedient, polite, responsible,* and *self-
controlled.*

These results are for hippies and nonhippies tested in Michigan.
Comparable data has also been obtained for two other hippie samples,
the first still unpublished and the second published. Roberta Koons
(personal communication) tested a sample of hippies and nonhippies in
Ohio; Cross, Doost, and Tracy (1970) tested hippies and nonhippies in
Connecticut. Results from all three studies are highly similar. Hippies are
less concerned with the traditional middle-class values of God, home, and
country, material success, achievement, competence, and strivings for
self-actualization. Hippie youths value the present more than the future,
a life of fantasy and hedonism more than a responsible and disciplined
life. They prefer egalitarian, communal social arrangements to the competition of the marketplace. The hippie emphasis on everyone's "doing his
own thing" is reflected in the greater emphasis hippies place on values of
being *broadminded* and *independent.* A content analysis of hippie values

TABLE 5.12 INSTRUMENTAL VALUE MEDIANS AND COMPOSITE
RANK ORDERS FOR HIPPIES AND NONHIPPIES

		Nonhippies	*Hippies*	*p**
	N =	275	78	
Ambitious		7.0 (4)	13.6 (15)	.001
Broadminded		6.7 (3)	4.9 (4)	.01
Capable		9.4 (10)	10.1 (11)	—
Cheerful		11.0 (14)	9.3 (10)	.01
Clean		14.1 (17)	14.7 (16)	—
Courageous		8.2 (7)	8.1 (8)	—
Forgiving		9.7 (11)	8.0 (7)	.05
Helpful		10.5 (13)	8.8 (9)	—
Honest		4.3 (1)	4.4 (2)	—
Imaginative		11.5 (15)	4.0 (1)	.001
Independent		8.1 (6)	6.4 (5)	.001
Intellectual		9.1 (9)	7.7 (6)	—
Logical		10.1 (12)	11.3 (13)	—
Loving		8.0 (5)	4.7 (3)	.01
Obedient		15.2 (18)	17.0 (18)	.001
Polite		13.0 (16)	15.4 (17)	.001
Responsible		6.0 (2)	10.9 (12)	.001
Self-controlled		9.0 (8)	11.7 (14)	.05

Figures shown are median rankings and in parentheses, composite rank orders.
* Median test.

found in the underground press generally supports these findings (Levin
and Spates, 1971).

But also evident in the value pattern of hippies are signs of defensiveness,
anxiety, and alienation from society. *Self-respect* is not among their most
cherished values. Neither is *a sense of accomplishment*. All three hippie
groups that have been studied rank *inner harmony* ahead of *happiness*, in
contrast to nonhippie students of the same age who care more about being
happy than about being tranquil. All these findings suggest that hippies are
being recruited more often from among those who feel strongly the pressure
of society and parents to achieve success and that their main motivation in
adopting the hippie life style is to restore peace of mind.

Homosexual Values

It is widely assumed that homosexual life styles are very different from
those characterizing others in the general population. Presumably, such
differences in life style should also be reflected in their value patterns. Data
are available for 35 male homosexual members of the Homophile Society
based at a Canadian university, and these data were compared with those

TABLE 5.13 SIGNIFICANT VALUE DIFFERENCES BETWEEN MALE
HOMOSEXUALS AND HETEROSEXUALS

	N =	Homosexuals 35	Heterosexuals 125	p*
Terminal Values				
Family security		11.4 (12)	7.5 (8)	.001
True friendship		5.6 (2)	7.1 (6)	.05
Instrumental Values				
Clean		11.8 (15)	15.4 (17)	.05
Independent		11.0 (13)	6.9 (5)	.05
Loving		3.4 (2)	6.5 (4)	.01
Polite		10.8 (11)	14.7 (16)	.001
Responsible		8.1 (6)	5.6 (2)	.05

Figures shown are median rankings and, in parentheses, composite rank orders.
* Median test.

obtained for a roughly comparable group of heterosexual males at the same university. Table 5.13 shows, surprisingly, that male homosexuals and heterosexuals do not differ all that extensively from one another. Homosexuals and heterosexuals differ significantly from one another on only 2 of the 18 terminal values, and on only 5 of the 18 instrumental values.

The value differences that are significant can reasonably be explained as consequences of a life style forced upon homosexuals by a society that ridicules, persecutes, and despises them. Although *mature love* is ranked about as high by homosexuals as by heterosexuals—it is ranked first by homosexuals and third by heterosexuals—*true friendship* is ranked second by homosexuals and sixth by heterosexuals, a significant difference. *Family security* and being *responsible* are less highly valued by homosexuals. The significantly higher ranking of *loving* by homosexuals can be interpreted as a consequence of society's making it so difficult for them to satisfy their love and affection needs. Moreover, homosexuals place a higher value on being *clean*, which some might interpret as a reaction formation or which others might interpret as suggesting that by a process of identification with the aggressor homosexuals have internalized society's stereotype of homosexuality as dirty. Their higher rankings of *polite* can be interpreted as an attempt to adapt to the majority by placating them. Finally, homosexuals place a lesser value on being *independent*, a finding that can either be interpreted psychoanalytically, as a manifestation of feminine passivity, or sociologically, as a consequence of the fact that society has forced homosexuals to become excessively dependent on one another, thereby inhibiting them from developing normal needs for independence.

OCCUPATIONAL ROLES AND CHOICES

To what extent can terminal and instrumental values be regarded as determinants of occupational roles and choices? Data are available for college professors, police (Rokeach, Miller, and Snyder, 1971), Catholic priests, and laymen in Canada (Hague, 1968); business executives, scientists writers, and artists in India (Beech, undated); and service station dealers and oil company salesmen in the United States.

Academic Values

At Michigan State and Wayne State universities, 212 faculty members with the rank of assistant professor or higher filled out the Value Survey in summer 1969. They were selected from the following five fields: biological sciences (biology, botany, biochemistry), physical sciences (physics, chemistry, geology), social sciences (psychology, sociology, political science, anthropology, economics), the arts (music, drama, painting), and business. Although it cannot be asserted that this sample is an altogether representative one, there is no reason to think that the data thus obtained are unrepresentative. They provide us with at least a rough approximation of what academic values in the United States are like.

The findings are shown in Tables 5.14 and 5.15 and, for comparative purposes, the findings for the adult American NORC sample are also shown. Median tests comparing all six groups reveal that only two terminal values, *freedom* and *pleasure*, and only four instrumental values, *courageous*, *honest*, *loving*, and *responsible*, are not statistically significant. The remaining 30 values are. But this is not really a surprising finding, in view of the large number of cases in the national sample (Bakan, 1966). In the final analysis, we are more interested in the magnitude than in the statistical significance of value differences.

Considering first the terminal value findings, the largest differences between American adults' values and values of academicians are as follows: The composite rank of *a sense of accomplishment* is tenth for adult Americans and first to third for college professors; adult Americans rank *salvation* eighth and college professors rank it eighteenth; adult Americans rank *a comfortable life* ninth and college professors rank it from thirteenth to sixteenth; adult Americans rank *an exciting life* last and college professors rank it anywhere from seventh to fourteenth.

For instrumental values, the largest difference is obtained for *clean*, with adult Americans ranking it eighth and academicians ranking it seventeenth or eighteenth. This difference as well as the large difference obtained for *a comfortable life* is probably attributable to socioeconomic factors (Tables 3.3 and 3.4). Other large differences are noted for *logical*, *imaginative*, and *intellectual*, which are ranked virtually at the bottom of the hierarchy by adult Americans but much higher by academicians, who rank *intellectual* anywhere from first to fourth, *logical* from fifth to eighth,

TABLE 5.14 TERMINAL VALUE MEDIANS AND COMPOSITE RANK ORDERS FOR FIVE ACADEMIC FIELDS AND FOR ADULT AMERICANS

	Adult Americans	Business	Biological Science	Physical Science	Social Science	Arts	$p*$	$p†$
N =	1,409	38	51	51	50	22		
A comfortable life	9.0 (9)	11.8 (13)	14.8 (16)	14.7 (15)	14.9 (15)	14.1 (15)	.001	—
An exciting life	15.3 (18)	9.8 (9)	9.2 (8)	8.0 (7)	8.5 (8)	12.5 (14)	.001	—
A sense of accomplishment	9.0 (10)	5.0 (3)	2.8 (1)	4.0 (1)	3.3 (1)	3.2 (2)	.001	—
A world at peace	3.3 (1)	8.3 (6)	7.1 (6)	9.0 (9)	7.3 (7)	8.0 (6)	.001	—
A world of beauty	13.6 (15)	13.5 (14)	11.3 (12)	10.3 (11)	11.3 (12)	7.0 (5)	.001	—
Equality	8.5 (7)	8.9 (7)	7.2 (7)	8.4 (8)	5.0 (3)	8.0 (7)	.001	.001
Family security	3.8 (2)	4.2 (1)	5.1 (4)	5.3 (4)	5.5 (5)	8.0 (7)	.001	—
Freedom	5.5 (3)	4.8 (2)	6.4 (5)	4.3 (2)	5.7 (6)	8.5 (8)	.001	—
Happiness	7.6 (4)	9.8 (10)	10.6 (11)	11.8 (13)	12.3 (13)	8.5 (9)	—	.05
Inner harmony	10.5 (13)	9.3 (8)	9.4 (9)	7.3 (6)	9.0 (9)	11.2 (12)	.001	—
Mature love	12.5 (14)	10.5 (11)	11.6 (13)	9.6 (10)	9.3 (10)	4.8 (3)	.01	—
National security	9.5 (12)	14.5 (17)	13.7 (15)	15.3 (17)	9.3 (10)	9.5 (10)	.001	.05
Pleasure	14.6 (17)	14.3 (15)	16.1 (17)	14.9 (16)	16.5 (17)	15.5 (17)	.001	—
Salvation	8.8 (8)	15.5 (18)	17.3 (18)	17.7 (18)	15.1 (16)	14.8 (16)	—	—
Self-respect	7.7 (5)	5.5 (4)	4.3 (2)	5.0 (3)	4.3 (2)	5.5 (4)	.001	—
Social recognition	14.4 (16)	14.5 (16)	12.9 (14)	14.3 (14)	12.3 (14)	12.5 (13)	.001	—
True friendship	9.3 (11)	11.5 (12)	9.8 (10)	11.1 (12)	11.1 (11)	11.0 (11)	.01	—
Wisdom	8.0 (6)	5.8 (5)	5.0 (3)	5.6 (5)	5.3 (4)	1.5 (1)	.001	.01

Figures shown are median rankings and, in parentheses, composite rank orders.

* Comparing all 6 groups by Median test.

† Comparing 5 academic groups only by Median test.

TABLE 5.15 INSTRUMENTAL VALUE MEDIANS AND COMPOSITE RANK ORDERS FOR FIVE ACADEMIC FIELDS AND FOR ADULT AMERICANS

	Adult Americans	Business	Biological Science	Physical Science	Social Science	Arts	p*	p†
N =	1,409	38	51	51	50	22		
Ambitious	6.5 (2)	7.8 (8)	7.1 (6)	9.6 (11)	10.5 (11)	11.5 (12)	.001	—
Broadminded	7.5 (5)	7.5 (6)	8.9 (9)	6.1 (2)	5.0 (1)	6.2 (5)	.05	.05
Capable	9.5 (9)	6.5 (3)	6.6 (5)	6.3 (3)	5.4 (3)	6.3 (6)	.001	—
Cheerful	9.9 (12)	13.1 (15)	12.8 (14)	12.8 (15)	13.9 (15)	14.0 (15)	.001	—
Clean	8.7 (8)	16.0 (17)	15.7 (17)	15.9 (17)	16.5 (17)	16.6 (18)	.001	—
Courageous	7.8 (6)	7.8 (7)	6.4 (4)	7.3 (6)	8.0 (9)	9.2 (10)	—	—
Forgiving	7.2 (4)	11.5 (14)	11.1 (12)	10.7 (12)	11.1 (13)	11.5 (13)	.001	—
Helpful	8.2 (7)	9.5 (11)	10.0 (11)	9.6 (10)	9.2 (10)	10.9 (11)	.01	—
Honest	3.3 (1)	3.8 (1)	3.2 (1)	3.3 (1)	5.2 (2)	4.5 (2)	—	—
Imaginative	15.4 (18)	9.0 (10)	8.4 (8)	6.6 (5)	7.0 (5)	6.0 (3)	.001	—
Independent	10.5 (13)	8.0 (9)	9.0 (10)	8.0 (9)	7.5 (7)	8.9 (9)	.001	—
Intellectual	13.0 (15)	6.5 (4)	6.3 (3)	6.4 (4)	5.7 (4)	4.0 (1)	.001	—
Logical	14.2 (17)	7.5 (5)	7.6 (7)	7.6 (8)	7.8 (8)	6.5 (7)	.001	—
Loving	9.7 (11)	11.5 (13)	13.3 (15)	11.3 (13)	11.0 (12)	12.8 (14)	—	—
Obedient	13.3 (16)	17.0 (18)	16.7 (18)	17.6 (18)	17.3 (18)	15.5 (17)	.001	—
Polite	10.8 (14)	15.0 (16)	14.0 (16)	15.5 (16)	15.5 (16)	14.9 (16)	.001	—
Responsible	6.7 (3)	6.2 (2)	4.8 (2)	7.3 (7)	7.0 (6)	6.0 (4)	—	—
Self-controlled	9.6 (10)	10.5 (12)	11.4 (13)	12.7 (14)	11.5 (14)	8.2 (8)	.001	.05

Figures shown are median rankings and, in parentheses, composite rank orders.

* Comparing all 6 groups by Median test.

† Comparing 5 academic groups only by Median test.

and *imaginative* from third to tenth. All these rather large differences can perhaps best be summarized by saying that college professors place considerably more value on intellectual competence and self-actualization than do adult Americans, whereas adult Americans generally care considerably more for God, home, country, and material values.

There are other findings shown in Tables 5.14 and 5.15 that deserve special mention: (1) The average professor, who is, of course, white, ranks *equality* anywhere from third to eighth in importance, which is considerably higher than the average white American's composite ranking of eleventh (Table 3.7). It can thus be said that college professors are more liberal on the whole than the national sample of white Americans. (2) Contrary to popular conception, world peace seems to be less salient for academicians than for the man in the street. The composite rank of *a world at peace* is anywhere from sixth to ninth for college professors, whereas it is first for adult Americans. Similarly, *national security* is ranked twelfth by adult Americans but fifteenth to seventeenth by academicians. These findings lead us to wonder about the reasons for the greater involvement of college professors in the widespread antiwar protests of the late 1960's. One interpretation is that their greater involvement was not so much a function of preoccupation with world peace as it was a function of their belief that the security of their country was not being threatened. They were evidently not worried about *national security*, and therefore *a world at peace* was not so salient for them either. Similar findings are noted for college students whose composite ranks are tenth for *a world at peace* and sixteenth for *national security* (Table 3.13). The greater involvement of the academic community in the antiwar protest movement was apparently a function of the relation between these two terminal values, combined perhaps with the greater emphasis that the academic community places on self-actualization values. These findings may be contrasted not only with the findings for the adult American sample but also with those previously reported for Israeli students, who rank *a world at peace* first and *national security* second. It would probably not be possible to mount an antiwar protest movement among persons or groups for whom both these two values are salient.

(3) Professors value *an exciting life* more than does the average American, but this difference cannot be interpreted to mean that professors are more hedonistic, since *pleasure* is ranked equally low by both groups. Recall that *an exciting life* was defined in the Value Survey as a "stimulating, active life." (4) Adult Americans care considerably more for *happiness* than for *inner harmony*, but it is the other way around for college professors. Adult Americans are more like college students in this respect, whereas college professors are more like the hippies reported on earlier. (5) Adult Americans care more about being *ambitious* than about being *capable*, which they rank second and ninth, but it is again the other way around for professors, who rank *ambitious* anywhere from sixth to twelfth and *capable* anywhere from third to sixth. Ambitiousness has to do with working hard

to earn a living, whereas being *capable* concerns a motivation to achieve by becoming competent. College professors perhaps take their ambitiousness for granted and are now striving for competence, which is a higher-order value. (6) *Courageous*, defined as "standing up for your beliefs," is no more a value of the academic community than of other Americans: It ranks sixth for the American people as a whole and about eighth for professors. It would therefore seem that the greater political activism of college professors in recent years is not so much a function of their having more courage, but of other values that differentiate them from adult Americans and which they perhaps feel are being threatened. (7) The differences in *forgiving* parallel the differences in *salvation*, with college professors ranking both as less important than adult Americans rank them. Thus, the former are seen to be less devout than the latter, at least in the organized Christian sense.

Finally (8) professors and adult Americans feel very differently about the importance of being *logical*: It is ranked seventeenth by the latter and from fifth to eighth by the former. As previously stated, these findings should be of special interest to social psychologists in view of their widespread interest in consistency theories (Abelson, *et al.*, 1968). The need for logical consistency that social psychologists so often assume to be motivating for human subjects is evidently a projection of values existing among college professors onto the man in the street.

Consider next the value patterns found for the five academic fields, which are arranged in Tables 5.14 and 5.15 in the order of their overall similarity to the national sample. This was determined by simply summing the composite rank differences between each of the five academic fields and the national sample. Calculating the rho correlations leads to the same result. Professors specializing in business have a value pattern that is most similar to that of the national sample, followed by professors of biological science, physical science, and social science. Professors in the arts (music, painting, and drama) show a value pattern that is most unlike that of the national sample.

Nonetheless, it can be said that the value patterns obtained for the five academic fields are, on the whole, rather similar, with each of them varying far more from the national sample's than from one another's. There are, however, several significant differences among faculty in the five academic fields. Social scientists care more than the others do for *equality*, *mature love*, and being *broadminded* and less for *national security*. Professors in business rank *equality*, *a world of beauty*, and *wisdom* lower than do the others. Professors in the arts care more than the others do for *a world of beauty*, *wisdom*, and being *self-controlled*. Professors in the biological sciences are more preoccupied with *national security* and less with *mature love* or being *broadminded*. Finally, the only value that can be said to be distinctive for professors in the physical sciences is that they place a lower value than do all the others on being *self-controlled*.

One-way analysis of variance, which is perhaps a more sensitive test with a relatively small number of cases, shows three additional values that discriminate significantly among the five groups. *Happiness* and *pleasure* are most valued by professors of business. *Imaginative* is least valued by professors in business and most valued by professors in the arts.

The Value Survey, then, reveals that professors in different areas are distinguishable in certain respects. This conclusion is consistent with the findings of Nevitt Sanford's study in which interview procedures were employed as the main research tool. "There is nothing to indicate," Sanford writes (1970, p. 18), "that professors in psychology or other social science departments are different, on the significant dimensions, from professors in other departments. They are first of all academic men—participants in academic culture." As already shown, the five academic groups are relatively homogeneous in their value patterns, differing little from one another yet differing markedly from the national sample of adult Americans.

The question may be raised whether the values of younger professors differ in any significant respect from those of older professors. It is reasonable to expect that a major determinant of academic values is socialization within the academic subculture and that with increasing socialization academic values will become increasingly evident. But an analysis of the value rankings obtained from assistant, associate, and full professors shows remarkably similar value patterns. The differences are small in magnitude and the few significant ones obtained—4 of 36—could easily have arisen by chance. It would thus seem that academic values are determined by selective factors that predispose one to an academic career or by socialization in graduate school rather than after recruitment to a faculty position. This conclusion is essentially similar to the one reached in studies of the determinants of the values of police and Catholic priests, to be discussed shortly.

A final question is whether the values of professors are uniquely academic values or more generally the values that are characteristic of the relatively affluent or educated. Since we did not collect data on the income of the professors, and since the professors were at an educational level far above even the most educated in the national sample, it was not possible to compare the value rankings of professors with those of others matched on income or education. Instead, comparisons were made between professors and adult Americans in the national sample who were the most educated and affluent.

A comparison of professors with the most highly educated subsample of adult Americans—those attending graduate and professional schools (see Tables 3.5 and 3.6)—reveals statistically significant differences for 10 of the 36 values. Academicians place a significantly higher value than do the most educated Americans in the national adult sample on *an exciting life, pleasure, self-respect, social recognition*, and being *capable, intellectual* and *logical*, and they place a significantly lower value on *a world at peace*, *salvation*, and being *obedient*. Comparing professors with the most affluent segment of American society—persons earning $15,000 a year or more (see Tables 3.3 and 3.4)—we find 16 values that differentiate significantly between them, and the magnitude of these differences is generally greater than that found between professors and the most educated. Virtually all the same values (except *pleasure*) distinguish significantly between professors and the most affluent, and in addition professors rank *a sense of accomplishment, mature love*, and being *imaginative* higher and *family security, happiness, national security*, and being *clean* lower. These analyses clearly show, then, that the value pattern of college professors is distinctive of the academic community and, moreover, cannot be accounted for by saying that it is merely the value pattern of the educated or affluent.

Police Values

The values of a sample of 153 male, white policemen in a midwestern city of about 150,000 have been reported by Rokeach, Miller, and Snyder (1971). Comparing these with values obtained for the national sample, police were found to differ markedly and significantly from white and black Americans on many values, as shown in Table 5.16. Since these differences have already been reported and discussed in detail elsewhere only a brief summary will be presented here.

Most noteworthy is the large and significant difference between the police and the policed on *equality*, its composite rank being fourteenth for police, twelfth for white, male Americans, and third for black, male Americans. The difference between police and each of the two national samples is statistically significant. Police rankings of *equality* are closest to those obtained for Wallace supporters in the 1968 presidential campaign. This discrepancy in value for *equality* appears to be the most significant component of the value gap between the police and the policed.

Police are more concerned than are white and black Americans in the national sample with certain personal values. They care more about *a sense of accomplishment* and about being *capable, intellectual*, and *logical*. These findings suggest an image of the policeman as a person who, contrary to popular conception, sees himself as striving to perform his occupational functions in a professionally competent and responsible manner. But this professional orientation has a special quality to it that distinguishes it from role conceptions prevailing in other professions. Paradoxically, value priorities by police concerning self-actualization, achievement, and competence exist side by side with a relatively higher value for obedience to authority, a devaluing of autonomy, and a punitive and unsympathetic orientation toward people in general. Police place a relatively high value on self-fulfillment, but one that exists within the framework provided by an authority-dominated and rule-oriented social organization—one that

TABLE 5.16 VALUES THAT DIFFERENTIATE SIGNIFICANTLY BETWEEN POLICE AND NORC SAMPLES OF MALE WHITE AND MALE BLACK AMERICANS

	1	2	3		
	Police	NORC Whites	NORC Blacks	1–2	1–3
N =	153	561	93	p*	p*
Terminal Values					
An exciting life	12.9 (15)	14.5 (18)	15.1 (18)	.05	.01
A sense of accomplishment	7.3 (5)	8.1 (5)	10.6 (11)	—	.01
A world at peace	5.3 (2)	3.6 (1)	4.1 (1)	.01	—
A world of beauty	16.0 (18)	13.4 (15)	14.6 (17)	.01	.01
Equality	11.7 (14)	10.1 (12)	4.3 (3)	.05	.01
Family security	2.9 (1)	3.7 (2)	4.7 (4)	—	.05
Mature love	10.2 (10)	12.3 (14)	13.4 (15)	.01	.01
National security	11.1 (12)	8.8 (9)	10.9 (13)	.01	—
Social recognition	14.4 (17)	13.9 (16)	12.9 (14)	—	.05
Instrumental Values					
Broadminded	8.8 (7)	7.0 (4)	7.4 (6)	.05	—
Capable	7.7 (5)	8.6 (8)	10.1 (11)	.05	.01
Cheerful	12.6 (17)	10.3 (11)	10.6 (13)	.01	—
Forgiving	10.3 (10)	8.2 (6)	8.3 (8)	.01	—
Helpful	11.6 (13)	8.4 (7)	8.2 (7)	.01	.01
Honest	2.6 (1)	3.3 (1)	4.2 (1)	—	.05
Independent	11.8 (14)	10.4 (12)	9.6 (9)	.05	—
Intellectual	11.0 (11)	12.9 (15)	12.2 (15)	.05	—
Logical	10.2 (9)	13.3 (16)	14.5 (17)	.01	.01
Obedient	11.9 (15)	13.7 (17)	12.4 (16)	.01	—
Responsible	5.0 (2)	6.6 (3)	6.8 (4)	.05	—
Self-controlled	6.3 (4)	9.7 (9)	9.9 (10)	.01	.01

Figures shown are median rankings and, in parentheses, composite rank orders.
* Median test.

provides a framework for dealing with people in an impersonal manner according to previously formulated bureaucratic rules.

We note a somewhat larger value gap between white police and black Americans than between white police and white Americans, but the value gap is considerable in both cases. Of the 36 values, 21 show consistent differences (with one or both of the differences being statistically significant) between police and the national samples of blacks and whites. Of these 21, 13 show larger differences between police and blacks, and eight show larger differences between police and whites.

Given these differences in value patterns, what can be said about the personal or social "etiology" of police values? Do such patterns originate with unique personality factors that predispose certain individuals to enter law enforcement work? Or are they merely a reflection of the fact that police are recruited, as Lipset (1969) has suggested, from a working-class background that is characterized by similar values? Or are they, perhaps, a reflection of a socialization process that takes place after recruitment to law enforcement agencies?

As was the case with college professors, police of varying age, rank, and experience on the police force do not differ in value patterns, thus suggesting that socialization after recruitment is not a determinant of police values. To find out to what extent personality and working-class background can affect police values, a subgroup of the national sample of male whites was matched with the police sample for education and age. In contrast to the 17 values out of the 36 that show statistically significant differences between police and whites (Table 5.16), now only 8 out of 36 values are found to be statistically significant, or nearly significant, suggesting that police have value patterns that are indeed more homogeneous with those held by white American males of the same age and education. These findings lend some support to Lipset's contention that police derive their conservatism from the working-class background that they originate from. But this is evidently not the whole story. Police still differ in certain important respects from other whites, even from other whites of comparable age and social status. Within the less-educated social strata from which police are traditionally recruited, recruitment is more likely to take place selectively from among white males who value significantly less *freedom*, *equality*, and being *independent* and significantly more being *obedient* and *self-controlled*, thus reminding us of the dynamics Erich Fromm wrote about thirty years ago in his book *Escape from Freedom* (1941). Moreover, police differ from other white males of the same age and social background in caring significantly less about *a world of beauty* and significantly more about *a comfortable life* and *pleasure*. We may hesitate to suggest that such a value pattern is tantamount to saying that police, by virtue of the way they are recruited, have a predisposition toward corruptability, but we may also hesitate not to put it forward as a tenable hypothesis.

All in all, the data indicate that socialization after recruitment is not an important factor in police recruitment, whereas personality and social background are. Both personality and social status seem to operate together to draw persons with a certain kind of value pattern into law enforcement work. It now remains to be seen whether police in other parts of the United States, and in other countries, have similar value patterns and to what extent social background, personality, and socialization determine recruitment into law enforcement occupations. Data compiled by Dr. Eugene Tate, as yet unpublished, show similar value patterns for a sample of Royal Canadian Mounted Police in Saskatchewan.

Catholic Priests and Seminarians

William Hague (1968) compared the values of Catholic priests and seminarians in a city in western Canada with students attending Catholic colleges and with committed lay members and participants in Catholic organizations. The terminal and instrumental value means and composite ranks for these four groups are shown in Tables 5.17 and 5.18 with Dr. Hague's permission, together with a statement of the level of statistical significance between the two groups showing the largest mean differences.

Priests and seminarians have very similar terminal and instrumental value systems. Only 3 of the 18 terminal values and only 2 of the 18 instrumental values show statistically significant differences. These differences typically are not large and could easily be due to chance or to age variations. The fact that priests and seminarians are so much alike in their values suggests once again that the values distinctive of Catholic priests result from initial selection rather than from changes following socialization. This finding is consistent with previous ones concerning academic and police values.

TABLE 5.17   TERMINAL VALUE MEANS AND COMPOSITE RANKS FOR
CATHOLIC PRIESTS, SEMINARIANS, COLLEGE STUDENTS, AND LAYMEN

	Priests	Seminarians	College	Laymen	
N =	80	80	68	41	p*
A comfortable life	15.9 (18)	15.5 (17)	12.6 (15)	12.8 (14)	.01
An exciting life	11.6 (13)	12.9 (14)	11.4 (13)	11.9 (13)	—
A sense of accomplishment	6.3 (4)	8.9 (10)	6.1 (2)	7.9 (9)	.01
A world at peace	9.0 (10)	9.1 (11)	9.7 (12)	7.9 (8)	—
A world of beauty	12.3 (15)	12.9 (15)	13.5 (16)	13.1 (15)	—
Equality	8.8 (9)	8.0 (7)	9.2 (11)	7.6 (5)	—
Family security	11.2 (12)	10.1 (12)	8.5 (9)	4.3 (1)	.01
Freedom	8.1 (7)	8.4 (8)	8.2 (8)	7.7 (6)	—
Happiness	6.3 (3)	6.5 (5)	7.3 (5)	9.9 (12)	.01
Inner harmony	7.0 (6)	6.1 (4)	8.5 (10)	7.3 (4)	.01
Mature love	10.5 (11)	7.6 (6)	6.7 (4)	7.7 (7)	.01
National security	12.8 (16)	14.4 (16)	14.9 (18)	13.9 (16)	.01
Pleasure	15.7 (17)	15.6 (18)	14.0 (17)	15.2 (18)	.01
Salvation	3.7 (1)	3.1 (1)	6.7 (3)	5.5 (2)	.01
Self-respect	8.8 (8)	8.9 (9)	7.7 (7)	9.0 (10)	—
Social recognition	11.9 (14)	12.3 (13)	12.6 (14)	14.1 (17)	.05
True friendship	6.5 (5)	6.0 (3)	7.6 (6)	9.1 (11)	.01
Wisdom	4.4 (2)	4.8 (2)	5.7 (1)	6.0 (3)	—

* Newman-Keuls test (Winer, 1962). Significance of differences are shown here only for the two means showing the largest differences.

TABLE 5.18   INSTRUMENTAL VALUE MEANS AND COMPOSITE RANKS
FOR CATHOLIC PRIESTS, SEMINARIANS, COLLEGE STUDENTS, AND LAYMEN

	Priests	*Seminarians*	*College*	*Laymen*	
N =	80	80	68	41	p*
Ambitious	13.2 (17)	11.1 (12)	8.3 (8)	10.5 (12)	.01
Broadminded	8.6 (8)	8.4 (8)	7.9 (5)	9.4 (8)	—
Capable	9.0 (9)	9.9 (10)	10.2 (14)	9.3 (7)	—
Cheerful	8.3 (7)	9.4 (9)	9.8 (11)	9.9 (10)	—
Clean	14.3 (18)	14.8 (18)	14.3 (18)	13.2 (18)	—
Courageous	7.6 (5)	8.4 (7)	9.2 (9)	7.0 (4)	—
Forgiving	6.6 (4)	6.3 (3)	8.0 (6)	7.0 (5)	—
Helpful	6.1 (3)	6.6 (4)	8.3 (7)	7.2 (6)	.05
Honest	5.0 (1)	5.4 (1)	5.7 (2)	5.2 (1)	—
Imaginative	12.7 (16)	12.8 (17)	12.4 (15)	11.2 (14)	—
Independent	12.3 (15)	12.4 (16)	10.0 (12)	10.4 (11)	.05
Intellectual	10.7 (12)	11.3 (13)	10.1 (13)	11.3 (15)	—
Logical	10.3 (11)	12.4 (15)	9.7 (10)	10.8 (13)	.01
Loving	8.1 (6)	6.8 (5)	7.2 (4)	7.0 (3)	—
Obedient	11.0 (13)	10.0 (11)	13.3 (17)	13.2 (17)	.01
Polite	12.2 (14)	12.0 (14)	13.2 (16)	12.2 (16)	—
Responsible	5.4 (2)	5.9 (2)	5.1 (1)	5.9 (2)	—
Self-controlled	9.1 (10)	7.8 (6)	7.2 (3)	9.7 (9)	.05

* Newman-Keuls test (Winer, 1962). Significance of differences are shown here only
for the two means showing the largest differences.

The main differences between Catholic clergy and committed Catholic
laymen are as follows: Clergy care more than do laymen for *happiness,
inner harmony, salvation, social recognition, true friendship, wisdom,* and for
being *helpful* and *obedient*; they care less for *a comfortable life, family
security, pleasure,* and for being *ambitious* and *independent*. There are other
significant value differences shown in Tables 5.17 and 5.18 which need not
concern us here because they can more readily be interpreted as a function
of age (e.g., *mature love, self-controlled*) or other factors. All in all, the
value pattern of Catholic clergy seems to conform to a priori expectations.

Of special interest is the fact that the composite rank of *salvation* is
first for Catholic clergy and second and third for committed Catholic
college students and older laymen. *Salvation* also ranks first for Catholic
college students at Michigan State University, but it is ranked thirteenth
by adult Catholics in the United States (Rokeach, 1969a). These findings
are puzzling, not because Catholic priests, seminarians, and committed lay
Catholics rank *salvation* high but because Catholic students in a secular
state university also rank it high, whereas adult Catholics in the American
population rank it much lower. No sensible reason for these findings comes
to mind. Whatever the explanation may turn out to be, it would seem from

Hague's data that *salvation* is just as important a value for the Roman Catholic church as it is for more fundamentalist Protestant churches.

Business Executives, Scientists, Writers, and Artists

Beech (undated) has reported data on the values of business executives, scientists, writers, and artists in Calcutta, India. They were selected by nomination from members of the academic community in Calcutta, research and management institutions, or by subjects previously interviewed by Beech. They were all at home with the English language and were therefore tested in English with Form C of the Value Survey. Table 5.19 shows the significant value differences found for these four professional groups. The most discriminating value is *a world of beauty*, ranked third on the average by Bengalese artists, ninth by writers, and fourteenth by scientists and business executives. These findings demonstrate that *a world of beauty* is indeed diagnostic of an aesthetic orientation and, moreover, that this value is to the creative arts what *salvation* is to the Christian

TABLE 5.19   SIGNIFICANT VALUE DIFFERENCES BETWEEN BUSINESSMEN, SCIENTISTS, WRITERS, AND ARTISTS IN CALCUTTA, INDIA

	Business Executives	Scientists	Writers	Artists	
N =	25	25	25	25	p^*
Terminal Values					
A comfortable life	8.8 (8)	13.6 (16)	14.0 (16)	13.9 (16)	.01
A world at peace	8.0 (7)	9.0 (10)	8.3 (6)	5.1 (4)	.05
A world of beauty	12.1 (14)	11.8 (14)	9.0 (9)	4.6 (3)	.001
Family security	5.0 (2)	7.7 (7)	8.0 (5)	10.6 (12)	.001
Happiness	7.0 (6)	7.3 (6)	10.3 (12)	10.7 (13)	.01
Mature love	13.9 (16)	12.3 (15)	9.3 (10)	10.4 (11)	.05
Salvation	17.8 (18)	17.9 (18)	17.5 (18)	17.7 (18)	.05
Instrumental Values					
Capable	7.3 (5)	7.8 (6)	11.6 (12)	11.3 (12)	.01
Courageous	8.7 (8)	9.8 (11)	4.3 (2)	5.0 (2)	.01
Forgiving	13.8 (16)	14.7 (17)	8.3 (6)	10.0 (10)	.05
Helpful	11.8 (13)	9.4 (10)	8.6 (7)	10.1 (11)	.05
Imaginative	10.3 (12)	8.3 (7)	5.3 (3)	7.6 (7)	.01
Loving	14.1 (17)	12.0 (13)	8.8 (8)	13.0 (15)	.001
Obedient	12.3 (14)	16.1 (18)	16.6 (18)	14.0 (17)	.05
Responsible	4.3 (1)	4.8 (2)	8.9 (9)	7.4 (6)	.01
Self-controlled	7.8 (6)	9.0 (8)	9.4 (11)	6.0 (3)	.05

Figures shown are median rankings and, in parentheses, composite rank orders.
* Kruskal-Wallis test.

religion, what *equality* and *freedom* (as will be shown in the next chapter) are to the world of politics, and what intellectual values are to the academic world.

Successful business executives are distinguishable from scientists, writers, and artists in caring more for *a comfortable life, family security, happiness*, and being *capable, obedient*, and *responsible* and in caring less about *a world of beauty, mature love*, and being *helpful, imaginative*, and *loving*. The businessman of Calcutta thus seems to be more materialistic and conforming to traditional middle-class values, less aesthetically inclined, and less inclined to a life of the imagination or to a concern with the love or welfare of others.

The scientists look more like Calcutta's business executives than its writers or artists. About the only ways in which they are distinctively different from the other three groups is that they place a lower value than do the others on *a world at peace* and on being *courageous* and *forgiving*.

Writers in Calcutta care more than do the others for values that concern interpersonal affectional relationships—*mature love* and being *loving, forgiving*, and *helpful*—and for values that are surely idealized by writers everywhere—being *courageous* and *imaginative*. They care less than do the others about *a comfortable life* and being *capable, obedient, responsible*, and *self-controlled*. In general, Calcutta writers are, in their values, more like the artists than like the business executives or scientists of Calcutta.

Finally, artists, as already stated, care more than do the other three groups for *a world of beauty*. They also rank *a world at peace* and being *self-controlled* higher and they rank *family security, happiness*, and being *capable* lower. Especially noteworthy is that artists value more than do the other three groups being *self-controlled*, suggesting that impulse control is a necessary prerequisite for the artistic life. That the writers rank *self-controlled* lowest of the four groups is puzzling, however. Also puzzling is the finding that writers and artists place a lower value on being *capable* than do scientists and business executives. Further research with other national groups of artists, writers, and so on should throw more definitive light on the importance of these values for such occupational groups.

Small Entrepreneurs and Salesmen

Value data were collected by a marketing research organization on a national sample of white service station dealers and company salesmen for an American oil company. These data were compared with national samples of adult Americans, matched for sex, race, age, and type of employment. The dealers were up to seventy years of age. The salesmen were, for the most part, between twenty-one and forty, and most of them were college graduates. The findings are reported in Tables 5.20 and 5.21.

In general, service station dealers and salesmen differ in essentially similar ways from the national samples of adult Americans with whom they are matched. Both dealers and salesmen generally place a higher value

TABLE 5.20   TERMINAL VALUE MEDIANS AND COMPOSITE RANKS FOR
SERVICE STATION DEALERS AND OIL COMPANY SALESMEN COMPARED
WITH A NATIONAL SUBSAMPLE MATCHED ON SEX, RACE, AGE,
EDUCATION, AND EMPLOYMENT STATUS

	Service Station Dealers	National Subsample	p*	Oil Co. Salesmen	National Subsample	p*
N =	235	470		69	41	
A comfortable life	4.54 (2)	8.43 (8)	.001	7.13 (5)	11.88 (13)	.01
An exciting life	10.96 (10)	14.40 (17)	.001	8.42 (8)	10.00 (10)	—
A sense of accompl.	5.83 (4)	7.82 (4)	.001	3.91 (2)	6.00 (4)	—
A world at peace	8.93 (8)	3.62 (2)	.001	12.63 (14)	6.20 (5)	.001
A world of beauty	14.63 (17)	13.58 (15)	.05	15.33 (16)	11.89 (14)	.01
Equality	12.54 (14)	10.13 (12)	.001	13.92 (15)	8.13 (8)	.001
Family security	2.26 (1)	3.50 (1)	.001	2.89 (1)	5.75 (3)	.05
Freedom	7.18 (6)	4.70 (3)	.001	8.40 (7)	3.69 (1)	.001
Happiness	5.52 (3)	8.06 (5)	.001	6.56 (4)	10.67 (12)	.01
Inner harmony	11.47 (12)	10.95 (13)	—	9.22 (9)	10.38 (11)	—
Mature love	11.62 (13)	11.91 (14)	—	8.38 (6)	7.63 (7)	—
National security	13.63 (16)	9.00 (9)	.001	15.88 (18)	13.00 (15)	.01
Pleasure	11.36 (11)	14.52 (18)	.001	12.25 (13)	15.29 (17)	.01
Salvation	14.67 (18)	9.93 (11)	.001	15.63 (17)	16.80 (18)	—
Self-respect	6.24 (5)	8.29 (7)	.001	5.00 (3)	6.92 (6)	.05
Social recognition	12.94 (15)	13.94 (16)	—	10.82 (12)	14.44 (16)	.001
True friendship	8.97 (9)	9.79 (10)	—	9.69 (11)	10.00 (9)	—
Wisdom	8.88 (7)	8.17 (6)	—	9.25 (10)	5.44 (2)	—

Figures shown are median rankings and, in parentheses, composite rank orders.
* Median test.

than do other Americans on personal values centering around individual
achievement, strivings for independence, material success and comfort,
hedonism, and the security of the family. Both groups generally rank the
social values—*a world at peace, a world of beauty, equality, freedom,* and
national security—lower than do other Americans. Both also value
relatively less intimacy, affection, and the welfare of others.

This is not to say, however, that the value patterns of service station
dealers and salesmen are identical. Separate statistical analyses reveal that
salesmen are even more achievement-, status-, and competence-oriented
and more concerned with personal values than are dealers, and they are
less concerned with such conventional moral values as being *clean,
forgiving, obedient,* and *polite.* We are not able to say whether this is a
difference between the value patterns of the two occupations or whether,
instead, it is a difference between a younger and more educated group of
salesmen who have not yet achieved the status, success, and independence
they are striving for and an older, somewhat more secure group of entre-

TABLE 5.21 INSTRUMENTAL VALUE MEDIANS AND COMPOSITE RANKS FOR SERVICE STATION DEALERS AND OIL COMPANY SALESMEN COMPARED WITH A NATIONAL SUBSAMPLE MATCHED ON SEX, RACE, AGE, EDUCATION, AND EMPLOYMENT STATUS

	Service Station Dealers	National Subsample	p*	Oil Co. Salesmen	National Subsample	p*
N =	235	470		69	41	
Ambitious	2.96 (1)	5.60 (2)	.001	2.81 (1)	6.00 (4)	.01
Broadminded	7.59 (5)	7.12 (4)	—	7.35 (5)	4.63 (2)	—
Capable	7.14 (4)	8.61 (8)	.05	4.75 (3)	9.13 (10)	.001
Cheerful	9.81 (10)	10.58 (13)	—	11.56 (14)	13.38 (16)	—
Clean	8.00 (7)	10.07 (10)	.01	12.00 (15)	14.00 (17)	—
Courageous	9.63 (9)	7.74 (5)	.01	9.60 (8)	7.08 (6)	—
Forgiving	10.82 (12)	8.50 (6)	.05	13.14 (16)	12.00 (14)	—
Helpful	10.85 (13)	8.60 (7)	.01	10.13 (10)	9.88 (11)	—
Honest	3.52 (2)	3.15 (1)	—	4.06 (2)	2.75 (1)	—
Imaginative	13.58 (16)	14.16 (18)	—	10.43 (12)	8.00 (7)	—
Independent	7.77 (6)	10.26 (11)	.01	9.75 (9)	7.00 (5)	—
Intellectual	12.93 (15)	12.89 (15)	—	10.38 (11)	11.33 (13)	—
Logical	13.63 (17)	13.18 (16)	—	7.42 (6)	8.67 (8)	—
Loving	12.67 (14)	10.46 (12)	.01	13.75 (17)	10.88 (12)	.05
Obedient	14.97 (18)	13.75 (17)	.01	16.54 (18)	16.00 (18)	—
Polite	10.12 (11)	10.96 (14)	—	11.09 (13)	13.00 (15)	—
Responsible	6.57 (3)	6.38 (3)	—	4.80 (4)	5.56 (3)	—
Self-controlled	9.18 (8)	9.55 (9)	—	8.88 (7)	9.00 (9)	—

Figures shown are median rankings and, in parentheses, composite rank orders.
* Median test.

preneurs who have achieved a greater measure of reward from the free enterprise system.

DISCUSSION

Supplementing the findings reported in Chapter 4 which show that values are significantly related to all kinds of attitudes, the findings reported in this chapter show that values are also significantly related to all kinds of behavior. These behaviors range from the very specific to the very general, and the differences observed reflect important behavioral differences with respect to many salient issues in contemporary society.

In this chapter, as in the preceding one, we have reported far more significant relationships than could have been predicted in advance on theoretical grounds. But it is important to stress that certain values which on a priori grounds could reasonably have been anticipated to predict certain kinds of behavior typically turn out to be the clearest discriminators.

Thus, *equality* is the value that is the most predictive of behavior involving interracial relations—joining NAACP, participating in a civil rights demonstration, eye contact between whites and blacks, and partisan political activity; *salvation* is the value that best predicts churchgoing; *a world of beauty* best discriminates between artists and other professional groups; the intellectual values—*imaginative, intellectual,* and *logical*—best predict whether one will become a professor, and so on.

When the findings reported in this chapter are considered alongside those reported in Chapter 4, it becomes evident that a certain orderliness pervades both bodies of data. Not only certain kinds of attitudes but also certain kinds of behavior are significantly predicted by certain values. *Equality* rankings, for instance, differentiate among those manifesting not only attitudinal differences but also behavioral differences in the area of race relations and politics; *salvation* rankings differentiate not only among those showing behavioral differences in churchgoing but also among those showing differences in attitude toward religion. Thus, the findings reported in both chapters suggest that values are determinants of those attitudes and behaviors that are substantively or logically related to them.

Parallel to data in Table 4.14 in the preceding chapter, the data in Table 5.22 provide a convenient summary of all the values that have been found to differentiate significantly between the various kinds of behavior considered in this chapter. Included in this table are the data obtained only with the 18 terminal and 18 instrumental values. Excluded from this table are data obtained with earlier, shorter, or different versions of the Value Survey. Over one-third of all the value-behavior relationships are significant—252 out of a possible 684—a finding that is similar to that reported in Chapter 4 for value-attitude relationships. Moreover, terminal and instrumental values turn out to be significant about equally often. Of the significant findings, 54 percent concern terminal values, whereas 46 percent concern instrumental values.

A comparison of Table 5.22 with Table 4.14 reveals that three values in particular—*a comfortable life, equality,* and *salvation*—are significantly related to half or more of all the behaviors as well as to most of the attitudes considered in Chapter 4. This finding suggests that socioeconomic, political, and religious values are the most powerful determinants of attitude and behavior. Other values—being *clean, obedient,* and *polite*—predict attitudes more often than they predict behavior. Yet other values predict behavior more frequently than they predict attitudes—*an exciting life, a world at peace, mature love, pleasure,* and being *capable, forgiving, helpful, honest,* and *self-controlled.* Finally, certain values—*self-respect* and *true friendship*—seem to be the least frequently predictive of attitudes and behavior, at least, of the kinds of attitudes and behaviors that have been considered in Chapters 4 and 5.

It is difficult to tell to what extent such findings are a function of the

TABLE 5.22 SUMMARY OF VALUES THAT ARE SIGNIFICANTLY ASSOCIATED WITH VARIOUS KINDS OF BEHAVIOR

Terminal Values	Joining NAACP	Eye Contact with Blacks	Civil Rights Participation	Church Attendance (NORC)	Church Attendance (College)	Partisan Politics Activism	Returning Pencils	Male Prisoners	Female Prisoners	Compatible Roommates	College Majors	Hippies	Homosexuals	Professors	Police vs. White	Police vs. Black	Priests, Catholic Laymen	Businessmen, Scientists, Writers, & Artists	Small Entrepreneurs	Salesmen	Number of Behaviors
A comfortable life	*	*	*	*	*	*					*	*		*			*	*	*	*	13
An exciting life				*	*				*	*		*		*				*	*	*	9
A sense of accomplishment	*											*		*	*	*	*		*		6
A world at peace					*			*				*		*		*	*	*	*	*	9
A world of beauty							*			*	*	*		*	*	*		*	*	*	10
Equality	*	*	*			*						*	*	*	*	*		*	*	*	12
Family security				*	*							*		*	*	*	*	*	*	*	10
Freedom												*				*	*		*	*	5
Happiness														*		*	*	*	*	*	6
Inner harmony									*	*				*							3
Mature love			*					*	*			*		*	*		*	*			8
National security	*		*			*						*		*	*	*	*	*	*	*	11

																				Total
Pleasure																				9
Salvation																				11
Self-respect																				4
Social recognition																				5
True friendship																				3
Wisdom																				4
Instrumental Values																				
Ambitious																				7
Broadminded																				4
Capable																				9
Cheerful																				3
Clean																				4
Courageous																				2
Forgiving																				9
Helpful																				11
Honest																				6
Imaginative																				6
Independent																				9
Intellectual																				6
Logical																				7
Loving																				7
Obedient																				8
Polite																				3
Responsible																				5
Self-controlled																				8
Number of Values	7	4	10	12	16	6	4	10	14	5	8	23	7	30	16	12	17	15	22	14	252

Instrumental values not tested.

particular attitudes and behaviors that happened to be selected for inclusion in this chapter. But should such findings be confirmed in future research, they would suggest that certain values are employed equally often as standards guiding attitude and behavior, that others are mainly employed as standards guiding attitudes, and that yet others are mainly employed as standards guiding behavior. There is no reason to think that all values must serve equally as standards to guide attitudes and actions.

Finally, there is no reason to expect that any one value or attitude should predict behavior perfectly. As has been discussed in considerably more detail elsewhere (Rokeach, 1968b; Rokeach and Kleijunas, 1972), behavior toward a particular object in a particular situation is a function of the cognitive interaction between the attitude activated by the object and the attitudes activated by the situation within which the object is encountered. These attitudes toward object and situation are each functionally related to a subset of values that are activated by the attitude object on the one hand and by the situation on the other. Thus, the evidence that has been presented in this chapter merely demonstrates that different subsets of 36 values are predictive of various kinds of gross behaviors. More precise predictions will, however, require more precise specifications of the actions to be predicted, the objects toward which the action is directed, the situations within which the objects are encountered, and the values and attitudes that are activated by the object and situation.

PART THREE
Values and Politics

6
A Two-value Model of Political Ideology

Social scientists and political theorists have long thought that variations in political orientation are ordered along a single continuum—a continuum variously identified as the liberalism-conservatism, left-right, or conservatism-radicalism continuum. Whichever of these concepts one may prefer, there seems to be good consensus that the consensus concerning their definitions is poor. Thus, Levinson writes: "It would be helpful . . . if the purely political meaning of the terms 'conservative' and 'radical' were clearly defined and widely agreed upon. This is, unfortunately, not the case" (1968, p. 22). McClosky, referring to liberalism-conservatism, admits that it is not his purpose "to resolve the questions of its 'real' definition" (1958, p. 28). Caute complains that "the Left is as frequently invoked as it is rarely defined. And when it is defined it is usually defined wrongly, without historical perspective" (1966, p. 9).

Nevertheless, there are many definitions of this elusive phenomenon. Smith defines liberalism as a "belief in and commitment to a set of methods and policies that have as their common aim greater freedom for individual men" (1968, p. 276). Caute offers "popular sovereignty . . . as a term descriptive of the central creed of the Left" (1966, p. 32) and subsumes under it many other ideals such as liberty, equality, optimism about man, rationalism, antimilitarism, sympathy for the oppressed, and social reform. Mannheim (1953) distinguishes between "natural" conservatism or traditionalism and "modern" conservatism. McClosky (1958) describes conservatism as an identifiable pattern of many interrelated variables which all together add up to a coherent conservative philosophy of man, a coherent philosophy that McClosky has attempted to measure with a single unidimensional scale ranging from liberal to conservative. Similarly, Tompkins describes the left-right dimension as including a pattern of at

165

least ten interrelated "polarities," the most important being "man is an end in himself versus man is not an end in himself" (1963, p. 400). Levinson (1968) equates conservatism and radicalism with right and left and then characterizes the right as supporting the status quo, tradition, stability, and a hierarchical social order and the left as critical of the status quo and as seeking social and economic equality.

Despite such variations in definition, there seems to be general agreement that, whatever the components may turn out to be (as discovered perhaps by multivariate methods of analysis), there is a single continuum along which the major ideological orientations and political parties can be arranged. Much empirical research over the past half century, based on this assumption of a single continuum, attempts to measure it and to study its determinants and correlates. For an early review of this work see Murphy, Murphy, and Newcomb (1937). For more recent treatments, see Adorno (1950), Levinson (1968), McClosky (1958), Rokeach (1960), Rossiter (1968), and Tompkins (1963).

One purpose of this chapter is to draw attention to several difficulties inherent in the liberalism-conservatism concept and in other, similar concepts that would limit their usefulness as descriptive ones in the behavioral sciences. A second purpose is to ask whether the major varieties of political ideology can indeed be meaningfully ordered along a single dimension. A third purpose—the major one—is to propose an altogether different approach to an understanding of differences in political ideology that avoids and denies the reality of a unidimensional liberalism-conservatism continuum.

One difficulty inherent in the liberalism-conservatism and in related concepts is that they cannot be employed ahistorically or cross-culturally. A Stalinist conservative's political orientation is very different from a Goldwater conservative's, and both are different from that of a Czarist conservative. Unlike other concepts in the natural or behavioral sciences, like momentum, force, habit, or conditioned response, such descriptive terms as "liberal" and "conservative" cannot be meaningfully employed across cultures or across historical time. Time and place must always be specified. It is therefore not surprising that in empirical research on liberalism-conservatism, then, we focus on comparisons between individuals and groups within a given culture at a specified time. It thus seems relatively easy to decide, for example, that George McGovern is more liberal than Richard Nixon or, in the year 1968, that Czechoslovakia's Dubček was more liberal than Poland's Gomulka. But it becomes more difficult to decide whether Gomulka and Dubček are more liberal or more conservative than McGovern and Nixon or to decide how all four should be ordered along a liberalism-conservatism dimension.

A second difficulty arises from the fact that there is little or no agreement on the exact number of defining attributes of liberalism-conservatism. In the absence of such agreement, it becomes possible to shift back and forth arbitrarily or unwittingly between one attribute and another when comparing two persons or groups for liberalism or conservatism. Stalin, for example, might be considered a liberal when compared with Goldwater and a conservative when compared with Dubček. But it is doubtful that the same criterion is employed in making the two comparisons. When comparing Goldwater with Stalin, the criterion used may be their difference on social and economic equality; when comparing Dubček with Stalin, an altogether different criterion may be used, say, their difference over the issue of individual freedom. And if we combine the results of such paired comparisons, we are not confident that it will lead to an overall ordering on liberalism-conservatism with which everyone will agree. Thus, if Goldwater is more conservative than Stalin and if Stalin is more conservative than Dubček, then the ordering from conservative to liberal is Goldwater-Stalin-Dubček. Intuitively, this ordering does not seem quite right to us.

A third difficulty is that the liberalism-conservatism concept is ambiguous because ideological and stylistic attributes are mixed together. If we define a liberal as one who is critical of the status quo—a stylistic attribute —and, moreover, as one who supports social and economic equality—an ideological attribute—it becomes difficult to decide whether a particular member of the Soviet Politburo is a liberal or a conservative: He may favor social and economic equality yet resist changing the status quo because Russia, in his view, has provided more social and economic equality than any other country. If we were to follow this line of reasoning to its logical limits, we would have to conclude, paradoxically, that all the happy citizens of a classless Utopian society are conservatives, because they like the status quo, and liberals, because they like the classless society they live in.

A fourth difficulty with the liberalism-conservatism concept is that it is often confused with the authoritarian-antiauthoritarian concept. McClosky (1958) and Tompkins (1963), especially, define conservatism, or the "right," in ways that are uncomfortably similar to the classic description of the authoritarian personality: Man is basically evil or wicked; there is an emphasis on tradition, conformity, authority, discipline, order, and anti-intellectualism; there is a firm belief in a hierarchically organized society and in the status quo. But authoritarianism is conceptually and empirically independent of liberalism-conservatism (Rokeach, 1960).

A fifth difficulty becomes apparent when we try to compare two political orientations that are both to the left or both to the right of the hypothetical center of the liberalism-conservatism continuum. Is communism more or less liberal than socialism? Is fascism more or less conservative than free-enterprise capitalism? To address ourselves to questions such as these, we are forced to extend the unidimensional liberalism-conservatism continuum at both ends by adding, ad hoc, radicalism at one extreme and reaction at the other. The major difficulty with such an extended conception, however, is that it assumes that radicalism and reaction are but more extreme or more intense manifestations of the very same dimension identified as liberalism-conservatism. But does a radical really believe in the same ideology as a liberal, only more so, and does a reactionary really believe in the same ideology as a conservative, only more so?

It is unlikely that the liberalism-conservatism concept can be rescued from all such ambiguities. What seems to be required is a clearer, more systematic way of thinking about ideological variations—a frame of reference that, it is hoped, would enable us to make comparisons easily across historical time and cultural space, a frame of reference that would enable us to envision the kinds of ideological orientations that are theoretically possible in the future or even in some unknown social system on some other planet that spacemen may someday discover.

To be offered here is an alternative, value approach to the study of political ideology in the hope that it will enable us to overcome the shortcomings of traditional conceptions. Is there some identifiable set of values that must necessarily underlie variations in political ideology? If so, which values?

If political variations are to arise, there must first exist two or more persons or subgroups within a differentiated social group wherein power, however it might be defined—in terms of scarce resources, physical, political, social power, or control of the means of production or communication—is unequally distributed and is so perceived by individual members and subgroups. We may reasonably assume that individual members or subgroups, whether they possess greater or lesser power, will have a cognitive need to justify in exhortatory, ideological terms whatever satisfactions or dissatisfactions they may have about the differential distribution of power. The function of such exhortation is to justify to self and to others either the desire to reinforce or to remain entrenched in one's position of greater power or the desire to improve on one's position of lesser power. Such exhortations, provided that they are socially permitted, will be carried forward in language designed to appeal to others in order to persuade others to share one's own viewpoint and to engage in supportive political action.

The language of values is an ingenious language admirably suited to the enhancement of all kinds of self-interest, whether enlightened or unenlightened, selfish or altruistic. It permits rational justification of self-interest, and, insofar as it is necessary, the language of values can also be employed as an Aesopian language to permit rationalized justification of self-interest.

Those with either greater or lesser power can reasonably be assumed to perceive that those with the greater power are more free to live and behave in accord with their biological and social needs and to think and speak as they wish. Moreover, many will perceive a relation of inequality to exist within the social group, with these having the greater power being thought to possess status superior to that of those having the lesser power.

Given an unequal distribution of power, a condition that surely prevails to one degree or another in all existing societies, strong differences in perceived self-interest are bound to arise. Differences in political orientation are manifestations of social conflict arising from differences in perceived self-interest. Such differences in political orientation are really competing proposals to solve existing social and economic problems, which are asserted by some and denied by others to be the consequences of an unequal distribution of power. If such differences in perceived self-interest are permitted ideological expression (and in many social systems they will not be permitted), it will most likely take the form of expressed satisfaction or dissatisfaction with the differential amounts of freedom and inequity existing within the social system.

Since ideological expression is typically couched in idealistic terms, a question arises whether certain ideals or values will be singled out for special consideration or mention by all political ideologies. It may be hypothesized that all major varieties of political orientation will have to take an explicitly favorable, a silent, or an explicitly unfavorable position with respect to two values in particular—*freedom* and *equality*—not only ideologically to advance one's own perceived self-interest but also to oppose perceived competing interests. Thus, the major variations in political ideology are hypothesized to be fundamentally reducible, when stripped to their barest essence, to opposing value orientations concerning the political desirability or undesirability of freedom and equality in all their ramifications. The reason these two values rather than others are being singled out as distinctive to the domain of politics is that a condition of unequal distribution of power implies, as already suggested, an ongoing social system wherein the group members will perceive that some members have greater freedom than others and, moreover, that a relation of superiority-inferiority exists among individuals or subgroups. It is reasonable to assume that those possessing the greater power—aided by those who may, for whatever reason, identify themselves with the possessors of power—will seek to maintain or even enhance their greater freedom and superior status in society. Conversely, those possessing the lesser power—along with those who may, for whatever reason, identify themselves with the less powerful—will seek to decrease status differences and to increase freedom.

Why one political orientation rather than another will appeal to a particular person or group is an independent question requiring further research and does not concern us here. What does concern us here is to formulate a frame of reference for defining the domain of politics by identifying the minimum number of variables that will adequately describe all major political variations across historical time and cultural space.

Let us see whether variations in two values alone, *freedom* and *equality*, can be conceptually coordinated with the major varieties of political orientation in a meaningful manner. If we think of these two values as variables ranging from high to low, four extreme types of value orientation are conceivable: (1) *freedom* and *equality* are both judged to be high in value; (2) *freedom* and *equality* are both judged to be low in value; (3) *freedom* is judged to be high and *equality* low in value; and (4) *freedom* is judged to be low and *equality* high in value.

As we try to identify the main varieties of political orientations existing in the contemporary world, we also come up with four major types: communism, socialism, capitalism, and fascism. The question now arises whether the four types of political orientation can be coordinated with the four types of value orientation. Assuming that *freedom* and *equality* are two independent dimensions, the four extreme value types can be located at the extreme corners of the four quadrants shown in Figure 6.1. We represent socialism at the corner of quadrant I, because it places a high value on both *freedom* and *equality*, and fascism at the corner of quadrant III, because it places a low value on *freedom* and *equality*. Communism is represented at the corner of quadrant II, because it places a high value on *equality* and a low value on *freedom*, and capitalism at the corner of quadrant IV, because it places a high value on *freedom* and a low value on *equality*.

The preceding can be regarded as a theory of what politics is mainly about, namely, a fundamental concern or a studied lack of concern with *equality* and *freedom*. To what extent, it may now be asked, is this a valid theory?

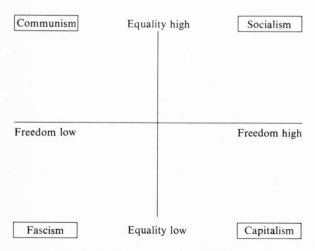

Figure 6.1 A Freedom–Equality Model of Political Variations.

PROCEDURE

To determine the validity of the two-value model, we selected 25,000-word samples from writings representing the four major ideological orientations, and we counted the absolute and relative frequency of positive or negative references therein to all terminal and instrumental values. Although our main theoretical interest is with the relative frequency of mention of the two terminal values, *equality* and *freedom*, we also obtained data on other terminal and instrumental values. All such data will be reported here.

The samples were taken from Lenin, Hitler, and Goldwater and from socialist writings. The reason we selected several socialist writers rather than just one writer was that we did not consider any one socialist's writings to be sufficiently representative of socialist ideology. To ensure comparability across all four sets of writings, the Hitler and Lenin samples were selected from periods before they took political power. More specifically, the following writings were selected for content analysis:

Socialism

> Bottomore, T. B. "Industry, work and socialism." In Erich Fromm (Ed.), *Socialist humanism: An international symposium.* Garden City, N.Y.: Doubleday (Anchor Books), 1966, pp. 393–402.

> Fromm, E. *Let man prevail: A socialist manifesto and program.* New York: The Call Associates, 1960, pp. 4–36.

> Medow, P. "The humanistic ideals of the enlightenment and mathematical economics." In Erich Fromm (Ed.), *Socialist humanism: An international symposium.* Garden City, N.Y.: Doubleday (Anchor Books), 1966, pp. 405–417.

> Thomas, N. "Humanistic socialism and the future." In Erich Fromm (Ed.), *Socialist humanism: An international symposium.* Garden City, N.Y.: Doubleday (Anchor Books), 1966, pp. 347–357.

> Titmuss, M. "Social welfare and the art of giving." In Erich Fromm (Ed.), *Socialist humanism: An international symposium.* Garden City, N.Y.: Doubleday (Anchor Books), 1966, pp. 377–392.

Communism

> Lenin, V. I. *Collected works.* Moscow: Progress Publishers, 1964.
> volume 10, pp. 71–74.
> volume 11, pp. 17–19, 96–101.
> volume 14, pp. 187–197.
> volume 20, pp. 144–146, 172.
> volume 25, pp. 71–74, 305–310, 323–365, 464–470.

Fascism

> Hitler, A. *Mein Kampf* (trans. Ralph Manheim). Volume II. Boston: Houghton-Mifflin, 1943, pp. 374–451.

Capitalism

> Goldwater, B. *The conscience of a conservative.* New York: McFadden, 1960, p. 127.

With the sentence as the unit of analysis, a frequency count was made of all terminal and instrumental values, with separate counts kept of positive and negative mentions. The frequency for any given value was the total number of positive minus the total number of negative mentions. Any given sentence might contain no reference to values (e.g., "A meeting was called last August") or might contain one or more references to values (e.g., "Our goal is a world where truth, beauty, justice, and freedom reign supreme").

A list of value categories was drawn up and agreed upon in advance by two judges. The term "value category" is employed here to emphasize that the two judges engaged in more than simple word count; they had to decide which value terms could be considered more or less synonymous. Thus, the total count for the terminal value *freedom* also included references to "liberty," "voluntary association," and "not dominated"; the total *equality* count also included references to "brotherhood," "equal rights," and "one man–one vote."

To determine reliability, the two judges independently conducted content analyses of yet other 2,000-word passages selected to represent the four ideological positions. Rank-order (rho) correlations between the frequencies obtained by the two judges were then computed for each of the four ideological samples for all values combined and for the terminal and instrumental values considered separately. The data are shown in Table 6.1.

For all values combined, the reliabilities of the four sets of writings range from .68 to .88. For the terminal values the reliabilities range from .84 to .97 and, for the instrumental values, from .52 to .88. The instrumental value reliabilities tend to be lower than the terminal value reliabilities, a finding that can perhaps be attributed to the fact that fewer instrumental values were mentioned in the writings or to the fact that instrumental values are inherently less reliable than terminal values, as has been shown

TABLE 6.1 CORRELATIONS (RHO) BETWEEN TWO JUDGES IN RANKING VALUE SYSTEMS FOUND IN FOUR SETS OF IDEOLOGICAL WRITINGS

Author	*All Values*		*Terminal Values*		*Instrumental Values*	
	Number	*Rho*	*Number*	*Rho*	*Number*	*Rho*
Socialists	29	.88	13	.85	16	.85
Lenin	21	.80	12	.93	9	.68
Hitler	20	.68	11	.84	9	.52
Goldwater	13	.88	10	.97	3	.88

in Chapter 2. On the whole, the findings demonstrate, in agreement with those presented by White (1949, 1951), that it is possible by content analysis to assess reliably the value systems contained within relatively small samples of political writings.

The first judge then proceeded to analyze the four 25,000-word samples that had been selected from socialist, communist, fascist, and capitalist writings. When the value counts were completed, we were left with the problem of what to do with those values that had been infrequently mentioned, say, once or twice in one of the 25,000-word samples and not at all in the remaining samples. To end up with a reasonably short list of values on which all four sets of writings could be meaningfully compared, we employed the following rule: A given value is retained in the analysis if it is mentioned a minimum of five times across all four samples; otherwise, it is eliminated from further consideration. By proceeding in this way, we ended up with 17 terminal and 23 instrumental values, across which the four sets of ideological writings could be compared. By varying this rule it is possible to end up with different numbers of values. But the basic results on *equality* and *freedom* to be reported here are essentially the same regardless of the number of values retained in the analysis.

TERMINAL VALUE DIFFERENCES AMONG THE FOUR IDEOLOGIES

Table 6.2 shows the similarities and differences in 17 terminal values for the socialists, Hitler, Goldwater, and Lenin. The data of main theoretical interest are, of course, those concerning *equality* and *freedom*. Together, *equality* and *freedom* account for about 45 percent of all the terminal values mentioned. On the basis of this finding alone it can be argued that *equality* and *freedom* are the two values that are the most distinctively political. More important, however, are the relative rather than the absolute frequencies obtained for these two values. The socialist frequency score for *freedom* is 66 (favorable mentions minus unfavorable mentions) and it ranks first among 17 terminal values. *Equality* ranks second. For Hitler, *freedom* ranks sixteenth and *equality* seventeenth. For Goldwater, *freedom* ranks first and *equality* sixteenth among the 17 values, and for Lenin the order is reversed, *equality* ranking first and *freedom* last.

The only deviation from a result that is in perfect agreement with the two-value model is that *equality* ranks sixteenth instead of seventeenth for Goldwater. But this deviation is more apparent than real. Seventeenth on Goldwater's scale of terminal values is *state power*, a value that is the converse of *freedom*. Similar negative relations between *state power* and *freedom* are found for the remaining three sets of ideological writings. When *freedom* is highly valued, *state power* is devalued; conversely, when *freedom* is devalued, *state power* is valued highly.

In contrast, a positive relation is apparent between *individuality* and

TABLE 6.2 FREQUENCY OF MENTION AND RANK ORDER OF 17 TER-
MINAL VALUES FOUND IN WRITINGS BY SOCIALISTS, HITLER,
GOLDWATER, AND LENIN

Values	Socialists		Hitler		Goldwater		Lenin	
	f	Rank	f	Rank	f	Rank	f	Rank
Beauty	6	10	5	6.5	0	12	0	11.5
Comfortable life	27	3.5	3	8	− 1	15	1	9
Equality	62	2	−72	17	−10	16	88	1
Freedom	66	1	−48	16	85	1	−47	17
Group unity	14	7	5	6.5	0	12	5	6
Health	5	11	24	2	0	12	0	11.5
Individuality	10	8	− 5	13	11	5	− 6	16
Justice	7	9	2	9	9	6.5	2	8
National defense	− 8	16	9	5	22	3	6	5
National superiority	− 6	15	12	4	18	4	− 5	15
Orderly world	0	13.5	−12	14	24	2	− 3	14
Peace	18	6	− 1	12	2	9	4	7
Progressive society	4	12	0	10.5	0	12	9	4
Racial purity	0	13.5	57	1	0	12	0	11.5
Self-fulfillment	21	5	0	10.5	3	8	0	11.5
State power	− 15	17	23	3	− 36	17	12	3
Wisdom	27	3.5	− 17	15	9	6.5	14	2

freedom. Goldwater and the socialists, ranking *freedom* high, also rank *individuality* high; Hitler and Lenin, ranking *freedom* low, also rank *individuality* low.

The rank orderings shown are, of course, relative rather than absolute. But the absolute frequencies yield additional information of great interest. Even though *equality* ends up at the bottom of both Goldwater's and Hitler's terminal value scales, Goldwater is not nearly so expressly antiegalitarian as Hitler. *Equality* ends up at the bottom of Goldwater's scale mainly because he soft-pedals *equality.* For the most part, he is silent about it in his writings, and he concentrates instead on *freedom.* Hitler, on the other hand, overtly expresses an antipathy for *equality.*

Although *equality* and *freedom* differentiate the four sets of writings to the maximum extent possible, they do not, of course, exhaust all the terminal value differences found. Other values differentiate one set of writings from the remaining three, or two sets from the remaining two. Hitler, who cares least for *equality* and *freedom*, is most preoccupied with *racial purity*, a value that leads his list of terminal values; the other three never mention it. *Health* counts second for Hitler; Goldwater and Lenin never mention it, and the socialists refer to it only occasionally. In contrast, Hitler places a low value on *wisdom*—fifteenth—whereas the other three value it much more highly.

If *racial purity* and *health* are highly positive values for Hitler, then an *orderly world* is a highly positive value for Goldwater, and a *comfortable life* is highly valued by the socialists. *National defense* has little value for the socialists but high value for Hitler, Goldwater, and Lenin. *National superiority*, however, has a low value for Lenin as well as for the socialists, but has a high value for Hitler and Goldwater.

So far, we have been dealing with similarities and differences in terminal values taken one at a time. It is also possible to assess overall differences or similarities in systems of values by intercorrelating the rankings obtained for the 17 terminal values across the four samples. The findings are shown in Figure 6.2. If the liberalism-conservatism or left-right continuum is indeed a unidimensional one ranging from communism to socialism to capitalism to fascism, we should expect to find positive correlations between ideologies adjacent to one another on the continuum and decreasing correlations between ideologies farther apart. But this is clearly not the case. All the terminal value system correlations (rho) are either negligible or negative. Moreover, the two largest negative correlations shown in Figure 6.2 suggest that the ideology that is most different from fascism is socialism (rho = −.71) and that the ideology that is most different from communism is capitalism (rho = −.53). These findings are inconsistent with a unidimensional conception of ideological variation.

INSTRUMENTAL VALUE DIFFERENCES
AMONG THE FOUR IDEOLOGIES

Table 6.3 shows the instrumental value findings obtained for the four sets of writings. As already suggested, instrumental values were less frequently mentioned by the writers than terminal values: There are many more zero entries in Table 6.3. Nonetheless, many instrumental values differentiate

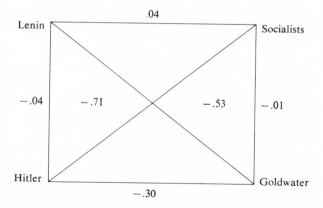

Figure 6.2   Correlations (rho) between the Terminal Value Systems of Socialists, Hitler, Goldwater, and Lenin.

TABLE 6.3 FREQUENCY OF MENTION AND RANK ORDER OF 23 INSTRUMENTAL VALUES FOUND IN WRITINGS BY SOCIALISTS, HITLER, GOLDWATER, AND LENIN

Values	Socialists		Hitler		Goldwater		Lenin	
	f	Rank	f	Rank	f	Rank	f	Rank
Active	7	9	15	5	6	7	16	4
Altruistic	9	6	0	21.5	0	18.5	0	18
Competent	10	5	11	10.5	0	18.5	4	12
Concerned	4	15	1	20	5	9.6	0	18
Conviction	0	19.5	23	3	2	13	18	2
Courageous	3	16	12	7	4	11.5	9	8.5
Creative	20	2	4	17.5	0	18.5	0	18
Efficient	0	19.5	0	21.5	6	7	9	8.5
Forceful	− 5	22	37	2	1	14	20	1
Honest	5	12.5	4	17.5	10	2.5	11	6
Intellectual	29	1	− 9	23	6	7	8	10
Idealistic	8	7.5	12	7	− 2	23	− 3	22
Loyal	5	12.5	18	4	4	11.5	16	4
Moral	12	4	2	19	8	5	4	12
Noble	0	19.5	6	14.5	0	18.5	0	18
Patriotic	0	19.5	11	10.5	0	18.5	16	4
Persevering	0	19.5	11	10.5	0	18.5	10	7
Practical	5	12.5	12	7	0	18.5	10	7
Productive	8	7.5	10	13	9	4	0	18
Responsible	14	3	6	14.5	10	2.5	4	12
Silent	0	19.5	5	16	0	18.5	− 7	23
Spiritual	5	12.5	11	10.5	5	9.5	0	18
Strength of will	6	10	48	1	12	1	2	14

among the four sets of writings. Before considering these, however, let us first note the ones that turn out to rank highest in the four sets of writings. The socialists consider *intellectual, creative,* and *responsible* the three most important instrumental values. Hitler values *strength of will, forceful* behavior, and *conviction* most highly. Goldwater, like Hitler, values most *strength of will,* but *forceful* behavior and *conviction* are considerably less important for him. Instead, Goldwater ranks *honest* and *responsible* second and third in importance. Lenin is similar to Hitler in considering *forceful* behavior and *conviction* among the most important, but he regards *strength of will* as much less important.

We are not able to identify any combination of instrumental values that distinguishes the four political orientations in a distinctive manner that is comparable to *equality* and *freedom.* The largest difference noted in Table 6.3 is for *intellectual,* which is considered most important by the socialists, seventh by Goldwater, tenth by Lenin, and twenty-third by

Hitler. Both Hitler and Lenin stress *forceful* very often—first or second—whereas Goldwater stresses it much less—fourteenth—and the socialists stress it least of all—twenty-second.

Altruistic, creative, and *competent* seem to be most favored by the socialists, and *perseverance* seems to be most favored by Lenin. Both Lenin and Hitler seem to share the high values they place on *conviction* and being *forceful, loyal, practical,* and *courageous*; in contrast, these values occupy considerably lower positions in Goldwater's and in the socialists' instrumental value hierarchy. Conversely, Goldwater and the socialists stress the importance of being *moral, intellectual, productive,* and *responsible.*

The socialists and Hitler share a high value for *idealistic* behavior whereas Goldwater and Lenin deemphasize it. On the other hand, it is Goldwater and Lenin who share an admiration for being *efficient* and *honest,* values that are deemphasized by the socialists and Hitler. None of these values seem to be distinctive in the sense that they would be found in the writings of all communists, fascists, socialists, and capitalists. They seem to be more the private values of individual ideologists rather than shared values that underlie ideologies.

As was the case with the terminal value systems, indices of overall similarity in instrumental value systems are also informative. In contrast to the findings shown in Figure 6.2 for terminal value systems, we see in Figure 6.3 that half of the instrumental value correlations are positive in direction. Whatever similarities may exist among the four major political ideologies, they are on instrumental rather than terminal value systems or, put another way, on means rather than ends. But these similarities are only moderate at best. The largest positive correlation is between Lenin's and Hitler's instrumental value systems (rho = .41), and the largest negative

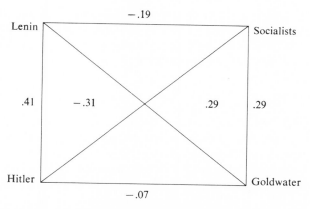

Figure 6.3   Correlations (rho) between the Instrumental Value Systems of Socialists, Hitler, Goldwater, and Lenin.

correlation is between Hitler's and the socialist's (rho = .31). Moreover, Goldwater's instrumental value system, which is probably widely believed to be opposite to communist and socialist conceptions about desirable behavior, is, instead, positively correlated with these conceptions. Goldwater's instrumental value system shows small positive correlations both with Lenin's (rho = .29) and with the socialists' (rho = .29) instrumental value systems.

When we consider these results alongside those obtained for the terminal value systems, the only consistent finding is that the fascist value systems are the most different from socialist value systems, with respect to both means and ends. In contrast, communist and capitalist instrumental value systems are positively correlated, even though their terminal value systems are negatively correlated.

Eckhardt, employing White's method of value analysis (1949, 1951a, 1951b), has also reported on the values of fascism (1968), communism (1970), liberalism, and conservatism (1965, 1967). He summarizes his main findings as follows: "The Fascist system of values was significantly different from that of Communism, Conservatism, and Liberalism, whose value-systems were not significantly different from each other" (1965, p. 356).

A comparison of Eckhardt's findings with those presented here reveals many similarities. For instance, his general description of fascist and communist values is compatible with the present description, and Eckhardt also found that *freedom* is Goldwater's "most frequently mentioned value" (1967, p. 445). But there are also major differences between Eckhardt's and the present methods and findings. One major difference is the parsimony of the *equality-freedom* scheme. A second difference is that in the present study the comparisons reveal similarities as well as differences not just between fascism on the one hand and the remaining three ideologies on the other, but among all four ideologies. As Campbell and Fiske (1959) might have preferred to put it, the four sets of ideological writings are convergent with one another in certain respects, and they are discriminant of one another in other respects.

A BLIND REPLICATION

One possible alternative explanation of the *equality-freedom* findings reported above is that they arise from "experimenter bias." The reliability study and content analysis had been carried out by graduate assistants who were aware of the main hypothesis. Such awareness may have influenced their count of *equality* and *freedom*. Rosenthal (1966) has shown that prior knowledge of hypothesis can affect the research outcome.

To ascertain whether this alternative interpretation is a tenable one, a third judge blindly repeated the content analysis. She was provided at the outset with a list of the value categories along with the following instruction: "Here is a list of values which have been used in the past to analyze similar material. This does not mean that all the values listed will be mentioned in any particular set of materials. You are free to add other values not contained in this list." She was then trained (by the first judge) to identify terminal and instrumental values on other materials taken from writings by John F. Kennedy, Herbert Hoover, Senator Fulbright, and others. After scoring this material, differences in value categorization were discussed and resolved. After the training period was over, the third judge then proceeded over a three-month period to analyze independently the same set of writings originally analyzed by the first judge. All identifications of author and title had been removed from these writings. Far more important, the third judge was not informed of the special interest we had in the data concerning *equality* and *freedom*.

Table 6.4 shows that there is generally high agreement between the first and third (blind) judges in the rankings they assigned to the four ideologists' instrumental and terminal values. These data are in good agreement with those shown in Table 6.1 concerning the reliability of the first and second judges, both of whom were familiar with the *equality-freedom* hypothesis.

TABLE 6.4   CORRELATIONS (RHO) BETWEEN FIRST AND THIRD (BLIND) JUDGES IN RANKING VALUE SYSTEMS FOUND IN FOUR SETS OF IDEOLOGICAL WRITINGS

Author	*Terminal Values* N = 17	*Instrumental Values* N = 23
Goldwater	.85	.39
Hitler	.87	.78
Socialists	.94	.63
Lenin	.97	.90
All Authors	.87	.53

Table 6.5 shows the frequencies and rankings obtained by the third judge for *equality* and *freedom*. Although the absolute frequencies differ markedly from those obtained by the first judge, it is apparent that the relative orderings of *equality* and *freedom* among the 17 values are highly similar to those shown in Table 6.2. On the basis of these findings we can confidently reject the "experimenter bias" hypothesis as an alternative explanation of the *equality-freedom* findings. More generally, these findings demonstrate that the value rankings extracted from a set of writings can proceed objectively regardless of individual variations among content analysts.

TABLE 6.5   FREQUENCY OF MENTION AND RANK ORDER OF
EQUALITY AND FREEDOM FOUND BY "BLIND" JUDGE IN WRITINGS
BY SOCIALISTS, HITLER, GOLDWATER, AND LENIN

	Socialists		Hitler		Goldwater		Lenin	
Value	f	Rank	f	Rank	f	Rank	f	Rank
Equality	34	1	−42	17	− 16	15	103	1
Freedom	28	2.5	−25	16	118	1	− 39	17

ADDITIONAL EVIDENCE FOR THE
TWO-VALUE MODEL

Additional data that are relevant to the validity of the two-value model
are available for various groups of known political identification. Recall
that in April 1968 a national sample of adult Americans had stated their
preferences for seven presidential candidates and had also filled out Form
D of the Rokeach Value Survey (Chapter 3). The composite rankings of
equality and *freedom* by the seven groups of presidential supporters are
shown in Table 6.6.

TABLE 6.6   COMPOSITE RANK ORDERS FOR EQUALITY AND FREEDOM
OBTAINED FROM A NATIONAL SAMPLE OF SUPPORTERS OF SEVEN
PRESIDENTIAL CANDIDATES, 1968

	Kennedy	McCarthy	Johnson	Rockefeller	Nixon	Reagan	Wallace
N =	273	149	221	129	291	52	118
Equality	4	6	4	9	12	10	14
Freedom	3	3	3	3	3	3	3

All seven groups are uniformly high on *freedom* but differ systematically
on *equality*. If they are arranged from liberal to conservative, as shown in
Table 6.6, it is seen that as we proceed from the liberal to the conservative
pole the patterns change from *equality* high–*freedom* high to *equality* low–
freedom high. Relating these results to those considered earlier, these
patterns represent variations from socialist to capitalist. Communist and
fascist patterns are not evident.

In Chapter 5 reference was made to the research by Bishop (1969) in
which the values of activist supporters of six presidential candidates in the
1968 campaign had also been measured. Their *equality-freedom* rankings
are shown in Table 6.7. The results are similar to those shown in Table 6.6
except for the fact that they are even more extreme. McCarthy supporters

TABLE 6.7 COMPOSITE RANK ORDERS FOR EQUALITY AND
FREEDOM OBTAINED FROM ACTIVE SUPPORTERS OF SIX PRESIDENTIAL
CANDIDATES, 1968

	McCarthy	Humphrey	Rockefeller	Nixon	Reagan	Wallace
N =	30	15	30	16	11	19
Equality	1	2	9	9	17	18
Freedom	2	4	2	2	1	1

rank *equality* and *freedom* first and second, and the Wallace supporters
rank them eighteenth and first.

The data shown in Table 6.6 and 6.7 are clearly consistent with the
two-value model. They also suggest that the liberalism-conservatism
dimension in American politics is really an *equality* dimension: The major
ideological differences evident in American politics are reducible to
variations in one value alone—*equality*—rather than in two values. What
seems to be missing from the present American scene are political groupings large enough to support viable political candidates for the presidency
who place a low value on *freedom*.

A third body of data, shown in Table 6.8, describes the *equality-freedom*
patterns obtained for 298 Michigan State University students who rated
themselves on a seven-point liberalism-conservatism scale. These self-
styled liberals (1–2), moderates (3–5), and conservatives (6–7) vary in
equality rankings but uniformly rank *freedom* among their top four values.
These patterns are, of course, consistent with those shown in Tables 6.6
and 6.7, and again suggest that variations from liberal to conservative in
the United States are mainly variations in value for *equality*.

TABLE 6.8 COMPOSITE RANK ORDERS FOR EQUALITY AND FREEDOM
BY SELF-STYLED LIBERALS, MODERATES, AND CONSERVATIVES AT
MICHIGAN STATE UNIVERSITY

	Liberals	Moderates	Conser- vatives
N =	54	216	27
Equality	7	11	15
Freedom	2	1	4

DISCUSSION

Although the two-value model presented here is probably new, several others have drawn attention to the dynamic, interacting relation between *equality* and *freedom*. Robin Williams has observed:

> Values do not emerge in experience as sharply separated unitary standards, each self-contained in its monadic independence from other coexisting values. Instead, the actual content and boundaries of any particular value will be affected by its changing relations to other values. In one group or society men may conceive of "freedom" only within the limits set by commitment to a principle of submission to a hierarchical order of authority; in another society, freedom is closely tied to egalitarian values. The two societies will not experience the same "freedom" (1968, p. 286).

Rossiter takes note of "the conservative preference for liberty over equality" (1968, p. 293), and political columnist Sydney Harris comments:

> The underdog demands "equality" and the upperdog demands "liberty" and neither can see that unless these two concepts are held in a just equilibrium, both are capable of wrecking the social fabric (*Detroit Free Press*, August 10, 1967).

In a similar vein, a student leader at Iowa State University described his transition from conservative to liberal in the following way:

> In 1964 I would have voted for Goldwater had I been old enough. At that time I felt the conservatives did most to further the cause of personal freedom. Later I saw the light. When conservatives talk about personal freedoms they really mean their own, not mine (*Lansing State Journal*, March 7, 1967).

The earliest reference to *equality* and *freedom* as distinctively different values may perhaps be found in de Tocqueville's *Old Regime and the French Revolution*, originally published in 1858. De Tocqueville writes:

> Readers of this book who have followed carefully my description of eighteenth-century France will have noticed the steady growth amongst the people of two ruling passions, not always simultaneous or having the same objectives. One of these, the more deeply rooted and long-standing, was an intense indomitable hatred of inequality. This inequality forced itself on their attention, they saw signs of it at every turn; thus it is easy to understand why the French had for so many centuries felt a desire, inveterate and uncontrollable, utterly to destroy all such institutions as had survived from the Middle Ages and, having cleared the ground, to build up a new society in which men were as much alike and their status as equal as was possible, allowing for the innate differences between individuals. The other ruling passion, more recent and less deeply rooted, was a desire to live not only on an equal footing but also as free men. . . .
>
> On several occasions during the period extending from the outbreak of the Revolution up to our time we find the desire for freedom reviving, succumbing, then returning, only to die out once more and presently blaze up again. This presumably will be the lot for many years to come of a passion so undisciplined and untutored by experience; so easily discouraged, cowed and vanquished, so superficial and short-lived. Yet during this same period the passion for equality, first to entrench itself in the hearts of Frenchmen, has never given ground; for it links up with feelings basic to our very nature. For while the urge to freedom is forever assuming new forms, losing or gaining strength according to the march of events, our love of equality is constant and pursues

the object of its desire with a zeal that is obstinate and often blind, ready to make every concession to those who give it satisfaction. Hence the fact that the French nation is prepared to tolerate in a government that favors and flatters its desire for equality practices and principles that are, in fact, the tools of despotism (In Gusfield, 1970, pp. 81–83).

All the preceding suggest that there is not only an interaction between *freedom* and *equality* but, more important, that the meaning of *freedom* and *equality* is to be sought in their relation to one another within a particular scale of values. Perhaps better than anyone else, Karl Mannheim (1953) has analyzed in detail the differences between conservative and liberal conceptions of *freedom* and *equality*:

> Revolutionary liberalism understood by liberty in the economic sphere the release of the individual from his medieval connections with state and guild. In the political sphere they understood by it the right of the individual to do as he wishes and thinks fit, and especially his right to the fullest exercise of the inalienable Rights of Man. Only when it encroaches on the liberty of fellow citizens does man's freedom know any bounds according to this concept. Equality, then, is the logical corollary of this kind of liberty—without the assumption of political equality for all men it is meaningless. Actually, however, revolutionary liberalism never thought of equality as anything more than a postulate. It certainly never took it as a matter of empirical fact, and indeed never demanded equality in practice for all men, except in the course of economic and political struggles. Yet conservative thought twisted this postulate into a statement of fact, and made it appear as if the liberals were claiming that all men were in fact and in all respects equal (Mannheim, 1953, pp. 105–106).

On the other hand:

> Political necessity compelled the conservatives to develop their own concept of liberty to oppose that of the liberals, and they worked out what we may call the qualitative idea of liberty to distinguish it from the revolutionary egalitarian concept. The counter-revolutionary opposition had a sound enough instinct not to attack the idea of freedom as such; instead, they concentrated on the idea of equality which stands behind it. Men, they claimed, are essentially unequal, unequal in their gifts and abilities, and unequal to the very core of their beings. Freedom therefore can only consist in the ability of each man to develop without let or hindrance according to the law and principle of his own personality. A. Muller for instance says: "nothing could be more inimical to freedom as I have described it . . . than the concept of an external equality. If freedom is simply the general striving of the most varied natures for growth and development, nothing more contradictory to this could be conceived than a false notion of freedom which would remove all the individual peculiarities, i.e. all the heterogeneity of these natures" (Mannheim, 1953, p. 106).

Obviously, then, *freedom* cannot mean the same thing to socialists and to capitalists even though both may insist that they value it very highly. It is one thing to value *freedom* highly and ignore or be silent about *equality*, and it is quite another thing to insist that *freedom* is not truly possible unless it goes hand in hand with *equality*. To American conservatives, *freedom* probably means lack of restraint on individual initiative and the *freedom* to achieve superior status, wealth, and power; to socialists, *freedom* probably means sufficient restraint on individual initiative to ensure greater *equality* for all. To American conservatives, social *equality* is perhaps seen as a threat to individual *freedom*; to socialists, there can be no *freedom* for the citizenry without social *equality*. Similarly, both communism and fascism place a low value on *freedom* and advocate instead the supremacy and power of the state. But to fascists, the power of the state is seen to be a weapon to coerce inequality, whereas to communists it is a weapon to coerce *equality*.

Our results clearly show that the traditional left-right dimension turns out to be a two-dimensional one. If we nonetheless insist on representing the four ideological orientations along the traditional single dimension, we may quickly ascertain how the four ideologies have been found here to differ by referring to Figure 6.4.

The moderate left differs from the moderate right only with respect to *equality*. The extreme left differs from the moderate left and the extreme right differs from the moderate right only with respect to *freedom*. The extreme left differs from the moderate right and the extreme right differs from the moderate left with respect to both *freedom* and *equality*. Finally, the extreme left differs from the extreme right only with respect to *equality*. These findings cannot be reconciled with a unidimensional conception of ideological variation, even with a unidimensional conception that factor analysis has shown to have components, because such components are typically correlated components.

When comparing any two persons or groups in a given time or place, it is generally easy to decide which one is the more liberal and which one is the more conservative. Such paired comparisons may implicate differences in *freedom*, differences in *equality*, or both. When we speak of liberalism

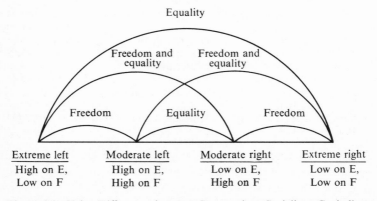

Figure 6.4   Value Differences between Communism, Socialism, Capitalism and Fascism.

and conservatism within, say, an American context, we are apparently referring to differences in value for *equality*. But when we speak of liberals and conservatives within, say, a Russian context, we are evidently referring to differences in value for *freedom*. As long as we conduct research on liberalism-conservatism in one country, say, the United States, it is possible to preserve the illusion of a single dimension when in fact there is a second political dimension that has been overlooked. Our data show that *equality* alone can differentiate among the major political groupings in the United States. But it cannot be concluded from this finding that all varieties of political ideology can therefore be ordered along a single dimension because not all ideological variations are sufficiently represented in the body politic of American life.

What about other variations of the four major political ideologies, such as Maoism, Stalinism, the Students for a Democratic Society, the John Birch Society, or the Ku Klux Klan? All such groups can be similarly described either by locating them on the same two dimensions or, if they do not differ from one another with respect to *equality* and *freedom*, by determining their differences with respect to other values.

To illustrate, supporters of liberal Congressional candidates Boulding and Vivian in the 1968 Democratic primary in Michigan were extremely high in both their *equality* and *freedom* rankings and were therefore not distinguishable with respect to these two values. But supporters of Mrs. Boulding, an anti-Johnson peace candidate, ranked *courageous* significantly higher than did Vivian supporters. The latter, on the other hand, ranked *responsible* significantly higher.

It should be pointed out that the four sets of political writings analyzed here came originally from different cultural areas of Europe and America, were written at different times within the twentieth century, and were originally written in three different languages—German, Russian, and English. The fact that we could nevertheless obtain the results we did strongly suggests that the present approach to a content analysis of values can indeed be applied across history and across cultures. All that seems to be required is a set of documents to be compared on a common list of values and a rank ordering of the value frequencies thus obtained.

It is perhaps worth noting in this connection that a content analysis of the values contained in the *New Program of the Communist Party U.S.A.* published in 1966, yields an *equality-freedom* pattern that is similar to that found for Lenin's works which antedate 1917. For 9 terminal values extracted from this work, *equality* is the one most frequently mentioned whereas *freedom* is sixth down the list.

Attention should also be drawn to a recent and rare cross-cultural study by Inglehart (1971) who measured the "hierarchy of politically relevant values" in representative national samples in Great Britain, Germany, Belgium, The Netherlands, France, and Italy. Respondents were asked to select two of the following four values as the most desirable: (1) maintaining order in the nation, (2) giving the people more say in important political decisions, (3) fighting rising prices, and (4) protecting freedom of speech. Inglehart refers to those who select the first and third as having "acquisitive" values and to those who select the second and fourth as having "post-bourgeois" values. He then describes many interesting and apparently significant relationships between these two types of value orientations and other attitudinal and demographic variables. Inglehart's post-bourgeois value orientation seems to be equivalent to an "*equality* high, *freedom* high" value orientation, and his acquisitive value orientation seems to be equivalent to an "*equality* low, *freedom* low" value orientation. His mixed value types can similarly be thought to represent mixed *equality-freedom* value orientations. Thus Inglehart's six value types obtained by selecting two out of a possible four values seem to be readily reducible to the four *equality-freedom* value types that have been discussed here.

The objection may be raised, however, that the two-value model is not an ahistorical one. The *equality-freedom* orientations underlying the ideologies selected for study here, it may be argued, can surely not be generalized to ideologies or political orientations that prevailed a thousand years ago or to those that might prevail a thousand years hence. But there is no good theoretical reason why the four types of value orientations should describe only the four major ideologies that happen to prevail in the twentieth century. Whatever ideologies or social orders may have existed in earlier periods of history are also hypothesized to be expressions of differences in the uneven distribution of power and, consequently, of differences in underlying orientations toward *equality* and *freedom*. Thus, feudalism and the doctrine of the divine right of kings can be seen as earlier functional counterparts of modern fascist ideology, namely, a political ideology with a low value for *equality* and *freedom* at its ideological core.

A brief comment is now in order about some other uses of the method of value analysis employed here. The documents we analyzed happen to be political documents, but there seems to be no reason why the present method cannot be extended to extract the values in other kinds of documents—historical, literary, biographical, and so on. This approach has proved to especially useful in the settling of questions of disputed authorship. A value analysis of the disputed Federalist papers (Rokeach, Homant, and Penner, 1970) confirms findings obtained by altogether different methods (Mosteller and Wallace, 1964) that it was James Madison rather than Alexander Hamilton who was the author of the disputed Federalist papers.

SOME ALTERNATIVE INTERPRETATIONS

The two-value model presented here most resembles Eysenck's hypothesis (1954) that the four major ideological orientations can best be differentiated in terms of two orthogonal traits—a liberalism-conservatism dimension and a tough-tender-mindedness dimension. Various questions have been raised whether Eysenck's findings are replicable and, indeed, whether Eysenck's own research supports his two-trait hypothesis. The interested reader is referred to Christie (1956a, 1956b), Rokeach and Hanley (1956), Hanley and Rokeach (1956), and Eysenck (1956a, 1956b) for an extensive discussion of the many issues involved. For a more recent report of a failure to confirm Eysenck's two-trait hypothesis, see Eckhardt (1971).

Despite the fact that Eysenck's two-trait hypothesis has not survived critical scrutiny or replication, he nonetheless came close to solving the problem of empirically distinguishing the four major ideological orientations. He did not succeed in solving the problem because his two traits, liberalism-conservatism and tough-tender-mindedness, were not conceptually clear enough or operationally adequate to distinguish among the four ideologies.

A more recent and more promising line of research that provides a fresh perspective on liberalism-conservatism is Kerlinger's (1970, 1972). Kerlinger has proposed, in agreement with the present view, that liberalism-conservatism cannot be viewed as a single bipolar dimension but as two dimensions, liberalism and conservatism, which are independent of one another. In line with his theory of criterial referents (1967), Kerlinger has argued that for the conservative private property, religion, educational subject matter, and certain other referents are criterial, whereas such referents as social change and civil rights, not normally criterial to the conservative, are criterial to the liberal (Kerlinger, 1972). His findings confirm the hypothesis; separate measures of liberalism and conservatism are indeed found to be independent of one another. Kerlinger concludes from this and other studies that the accepted assumption of bipolarity, or of a single liberalism-conservatism dimension is a doubtful one. Arguing from a very different point of departure about the party identifications of the Detroit electorate, Segal and Hikel have arrived at a similar conclusion: "liberalism vs. conservatism . . . is relevant for only a minority of the Detroit electorate. We believe that we must move beyond the simplified conception of our political system inherent in the traditional unidimensional approach to politics" (pp. 23–24).

Close examination of Kerlinger's two scales reveals, however, that his liberalism scale is concerned mainly (but not solely) with *equality* issues, and his conservatism scale is concerned mainly (but not solely) with *freedom* issues. Thus, his liberalism scale addresses itself to *equality*-related attitudes concerning such topics as racial purity, Jews, Negroes, children, the aged, the sick, the poor, the United Nations, equal opportunity in education, and the Supreme Court as a protector of equal treatment for all. Kerlinger's conservatism scale, on the other hand, is concerned mainly with *freedom*-related issues: freedom to deal in private property or real estate; freedom of religion; a concern with the security, sovereignty and traditions of the United States, the land of free enterprise. Seen in this way, Kerlinger's finding that liberalism and conservatism are independent dimensions is completely consistent with the present view and with present findings that *equality* and *freedom* are independent dimensions. Recall from Chapter 2 that these two values have a correlation of only .14 in the national adult sample.

An empirical test of the present reinterpretation of Kerlinger's findings would not be difficult. If the present view is correct, liberalism, as Kerlinger would measure it, should be highly correlated with value for *equality*, but not with value for *freedom*. Conversely, conservatism, as Kerlinger would measure it, should be highly correlated with value for *freedom*, but not with value for *equality*. In Kerlinger's terms, *equality* is criterial for liberals, whereas *freedom* is criterial for conservatives.

CONCLUDING COMMENT

The most remarkable empirical finding of the present research is that we have succeeded in identifying two words in the English, German, and Russian languages and close synonyms of these two words that differentiate to a maximum extent the ideological positions of communist, socialist, capitalist, and fascist ideologists. The theoretical point of departure leading to this finding was an analysis of the role that values must play in social groups differentiated with respect to power and an identification of the two values that must be especially implicated when there is ideological conflict among individuals and groups jockeying to maintain or enhance their positions of power.

7
Some Implications of the Two-value Model of Politics

At least two major implications seem to follow from the fact that two values alone, *equality* and *freedom*, underlie similarities and differences in major ideological orientations. One concerns the question: Does a particular *equality-freedom* orientation represent a predisposition to become differentially receptive to competing ideologies? The other concerns the question: Do the two political values play a special role in political activism? An empirical answer to the first question requires us to determine whether politically naïve persons who exhibit different *equality-freedom* orientations also hold systematically different attitudes toward various ideologies. An empirical answer to the second question requires us to determine whether politically active individuals and groups differ in some systematic way from politically less active individuals and groups in the importance they place on *equality* and *freedom*.

EQUALITY-FREEDOM ORIENTATIONS
AS IDEOLOGICAL PREDISPOSITIONS

The classic work by Adorno, Frenkel-Brunswik, Levinson, and Sanford (1950) has already familiarized us with the idea that a certain kind of personality structure may unconsciously predispose a person to become selectively receptive toward certain political ideologies. The F scale, a 30-item summated-rating scale having no explicit ideological content, and purporting to measure deep-lying personality predispositions toward fascist authoritarianism, has been repeatedly shown to be related to variations in attitude toward political conservatism and ethnocentrism.

In analogous fashion, the present theory suggests perhaps an even more parsimonious principle: A differential receptivity to political ideology

189

is a function of the relative importance a person has learned to place on the two distinctively political values—*equality* and *freedom*. We know little as yet about the determinants of different *equality-freedom* orientations. It may be supposed that personality factors such as these considered by Adorno, *et al.* (1950) and by Rokeach (1960) will probably turn out to play an important determining role. At the same time, it also seems likely that various social and cultural factors will also be found to play important determining roles. In whatever way these two values might have been originally acquired, once acquired they should predispose a person to accept or reject, express sympathy for or antipathy to, or actively support or oppose ideological concepts, political figures, and political organizations that reinforce, support, and legitimize his own *equality-freedom* orientation. Thus, if we know nothing more about a person than where he stands with respect to the two distinctively political values we should be able to predict his position with respect to all the major ideologies and toward the major reference persons and groups associated with the major ideologies.

This sweeping hypothesis, that a particular *equality-freedom* orientation represents a predisposition to political ideology, goes beyond the hypotheses considered in Chapters 4 and 5; it asserts that his having certain values alone may predispose a person to have particular attitudes or to engage in particular behaviors. Variations in *equality* alone, for instance, have been shown to be significantly related to all sorts of attitudes and behaviors concerning civil rights, the poor, Vietnam, student protest, and church activism. The hypothesis that *equality-freedom* orientations represent ideological predispositions cannot be empirically validated by demonstrating that people with different value orientations hold different attitudes toward such selected issues as these because such differences can readily be attributed to variations in one value alone. An adequate test of the hypothesis requires us to examine a considerably broader body of data that implicates both values at once.

A closely related question is: How accurately will a politically unsophisticated person with a particular political value orientation preceive the value orientations of others that are similar and dissimilar to his own? In line with an old hypothesis in cognitive psychology (Bruner and Postman, 1949; Postman, Bruner, and McGinnies, 1948), it may be conjectured that a person will be more accurately attuned toward persons who would support his own value orientation and will misperceive those who would threaten to disconfirm it. Thus, *equality-freedom* orientations are not only hypothesized to be predispositions to political ideology but also to result in ideological positions that are mediated by accuracy of perception of the *equality-freedom* orientations of significant others.

Subjects and Procedure

To find out whether these hypotheses are valid, data were gathered in summer 1968 from about 600 students taking social science and business courses at Michigan State University. They first ranked the 18 terminal values "in order of their importance to YOU, as guiding principles in YOUR life." They then ranked the same 18 terminal values in four other ways: "This time fill it out as you think NIKOLAI LENIN (NORMAN THOMAS, BARRY GOLDWATER, ADOLPH HITLER) would have filled it out." Since many of the subjects had never heard of Norman Thomas they were offered an additional explanation: "Norman Thomas has been a Socialist Party candidate for President of the United States six times." In this way the subjects provided us with data about their perceptions of the terminal values held by the four major ideologists as well as about their own terminal values. Of greatest theoretical interest, of course, are the subjects' own rankings and perceptions of the *equality* and *freedom* positions of the four major ideologies.

The subjects then indicated how much they liked or disliked various ideological stimuli, shown in Table 7.2. These stimuli included the major ideological concepts, political figures, and political organizations associated with the major ideologies of our time. The subjects rated each of these on a nine-point scale, 1 indicating "like very much" and 9 indicating "dislike very much."

Of the 600 subjects, 547 completed all the questionnaire materials, the five sets of terminal value rankings, and the ratings of 25 ideological stimuli. They moreover provided us at the end of the session with additional information concerning their political identification and level of political sophistication. These will be discussed later.

On the basis of the subject's own terminal value rankings, each one was classified as high, middle, or low in *equality* and *freedom*, depending on whether he had ranked them in the upper third (1–6), middle third (7–12), or lower third (13–18) of the ranking scale.

Distribution of Equality-Freedom Orientations among American College Students and Adult Americans

A first question that concerned us was whether we would be able to find enough college students having each of the four extreme *equality-freedom* orientations. As already reported in the last chapter, Americans of all political persuasions, whether liberal, moderate, or conservative, are generally alike in caring a great deal about *freedom*, varying mainly in the importance they place on *equality*. Two out of every three adult Americans in the national sample rank *freedom* ahead of *equality*. (For adult white Americans, 69.5 percent rank *freedom* above *equality* and 30.5 percent rank *equality* as more important. For adult black Americans, only 48 percent rank *freedom* ahead of *equality*, and 52 percent rank *equality* ahead of *freedom*.) Sixty percent of adult Americans rank *freedom* in the upper third of their terminal value hierarchy, but only about a third rank *equality* in the upper third. Conversely, less than 10 percent of adult Americans rank *freedom* in the bottom third of their terminal value hierarchy, whereas three times as many—30 percent—rank *equality* in the bottom third. For an independent confirmation of the findings concerning the relatively greater value placed on *freedom* compared with *equality* among Americans, see Blumenthal, Kahn, Andrews, and Head (1972). It may be conjectured that the reason the total spectrum of viable political parties is not found in American politics as it is found in, say, French or Italian politics is that there are simply not enough Americans possessing values that would support political parties which openly advocate government restrictions on individual freedom.

The *equality-freedom* findings for college students are virtually identical to those obtained for the national adult sample. Table 7.1 shows that only about 2 percent of college youth and adult Americans exhibit a Leninist type of value orientation: *equality* ranked high and *freedom* ranked low. Twice this number—about 4 percent—exhibit a fascist type of value orientation: *equality* and *freedom* both ranked low. Taken together, these two types describe only about 6 percent of all the respondents tested in the two samples. Should it turn out, however, that value orientations are indeed ideological predispositions, the data shown in Table 7.1 suggest that fascism presently has roughly twice the receptive audience that communism has in the United States.

TABLE 7.1 PERCENT OF ADULT AMERICANS AND COLLEGE STUDENTS EXHIBITING DIFFERENT TYPES OF EQUALITY-FREEDOM ORIENTATIONS

Value Orientation	*Type of Ideological Orientation*	*% Adult Americans* $N = 1,409$	*% College Students* $N = 547$
High E, low F	Communist	2.4	1.8
High E, high F	Socialist	24.2	25.2
Middle E and/or F	Middle American	54.9	55.4
Low E, high F	Capitalist	14.5	13.0
Low E, low F	Fascist	4.0	4.6

Table 7.1 shows further that about one out of every four Americans places a high value on both *equality* and *freedom*—a socialist type of value orientation—compared with the finding that one out of seven places a high value on *freedom* but a low value on *equality*—a capitalist type of value orientation. This may seem surprising, considering that the United States is considered to be the major citadel of capitalism. Why should the number of Americans showing a socialist type of value orien-

tation be almost twice as numerous as those showing a capitalist type? Several reasons come to mind as possible explanations. Ever since the days of Franklin Delano Roosevelt, Americans have increasingly come to accept the idea of the government assuming obligations for social welfare and equal opportunity—old age security, "soak the rich" programs, medicare for the aged and poor, equal opportunity laws protecting minority groups, unemployment insurance, aid to dependent mothers, and so on. The ideological climate in America has changed sufficiently in the past few decades so that it now seems to be only a matter of time until socialized medicine and a guaranteed annual income will be extended to all. These changes in a more egalitarian direction are still a far cry from classical socialist notions about state ownership of the means of production, but they can, regardless, be steps in that direction. The slogans of free enterprise capitalism notwithstanding, an increasing number of Americans would seem to be receptive to socialist values if not to a socialist ideology.

A second reason the socialist value orientation is found to be more prevalent than the capitalist, at least in the national adult sample, is that black Americans are more often found in the socialist than in the capitalist camp. Twice as many black as white Americans are found in the *equality* high-*freedom* high cell—42 percent against 21 percent, a highly significant difference. Conversely, only 7 percent of black Americans, compared with 16 percent of white Americans, are in the *equality* low-*freedom* high cell. In other words, in April 1968 about six times as many black Americans held socialist value orientations as compared with capitalist value orientations. The comparable figure for white Americans is 21 to 16, which is a considerably more equal distribution into the socialist and capitalist camps.

A third possible reason for the greater frequency of the socialist compared with capitalist value orientations is that despite the competitive notions so dear to free enterprise capitalism, *equality* is just as essential a component as individual *freedom* in the American heritage and traditions. Both are legitimized by the Bill of Rights; both have been reinforced by recent Supreme Court decisions.

The four extreme *equality-freedom* types discussed thus far, however, account for only 45 percent of college and adult American respondents. The remaining 55 percent exhibit a value orientation that might best be called middle American, middle in the sense that they rank *equality* or *freedom* or both in the middle of the terminal value hierarchy. These middle Americans are not altogether homogeneous since they still vary considerably in the relative importance they place on *equality* and *freedom*. They are nonetheless moderate with respect to at least one of the two values under consideration, and it is this majority which is presumably the "silent majority" that has the most say at election time in determining the composition of national and local legislative bodies in the United States.

Political Value Orientations as Ideological
Predispositions

The findings reported in Table 7.1 show, then, that all four extreme types of political value orientation are found in the college sample, although the number showing fascist and, especially, communist value orientations are rather small from a statistical standpoint. These observed frequencies for college students are nonetheless quite representative of those found in the adult American population as a whole. We may now ask what these various types of value orientations really signify. Do they, as hypothesized, represent different predispositions to accept and reject various ideological alternatives? If so, then we should expect systematic differences in patterns of sympathy and antipathy expressed concerning various ideological symbols, personages, and organizations. The pertinent findings are shown in Table 7.2.

It is necessary to keep the following in mind when examining these findings: (1) Five rather than four *equality-freedom* groups are compared, the fifth being composed of college students who had ranked both *equality* and *freedom* as middle values, that is, from 7 to 12. (2) The number of subjects who exhibit communist and fascist types of value orientation are extremely small—only 10 out of 573 subjects had ranked *equality* high and *freedom* low; only 25 subjects had ranked both *equality* and *freedom* in the lower third of their terminal value hierarchy. As already stated, the reason these numbers are small is that these value orientations are relatively rare in the United States. (3) Like most college students in midwestern universities, the great majority of the students tested were politically naïve, as will be independently demonstrated later. (4) The ratings of the 25 stimuli shown in Table 7.2 took place within an American context, a context which is for the most part inhospitable to a favorable espousal of communist or fascist ideology. It is therefore not to be expected that our subjects would express favorable attitudes toward communist or fascist symbols in any absolute sense. It is nonetheless reasonable to look for and to expect different degrees of negative feelings toward communist and fascist symbols among our subjects.

For convenience of presentation, the 25 concepts have been classified under five categories. *Communism*, Lenin, Marx, Stalin, and Mao Tse-Tung clearly represent the extreme left. The Students for a Democratic Society (SDS) proved to be somewhat more difficult to classify because it has so many factions within it, but after much thought SDS was also placed in the extreme left category, mainly because most Americans would probably think it belonged there. *Socialism*, Norman Thomas, Humphrey, McCarthy, and the Democratic Party have all been classified as moderate left.

The two black leaders—Martin Luther King and Malcolm X—were difficult to categorize either as moderate or extreme left because both of these political figures had been mainly concerned with the single issue of civil rights. For this reason the data concerning these two have been

	Equality High Freedom Low	Equality High Freedom High	Equality Middle Freedom Middle	Equality Low Freedom High	Equality Low Freedom Low	One-way Analysis of Variance	
N =	10	138	68	71	25	F	p
Attitude toward the Extreme Left							
Communism	5.50 (9.5)	6.58 (16.0)	7.16 (17)	7.46 (19)	7.64 (23.5)	5.96	.0005
Nikolai Lenin	5.80 (13.5)	6.47 (15.0)	6.88 (15)	6.94 (16)	6.83 (18.0)	1.71	.146
Karl Marx	4.80 (5.5)	5.46 (8.0)	6.16 (12)	6.48 (13)	6.20 (14.0)	3.64	.006
Joseph Stalin	6.80 (19.5)	7.27 (18.0)	7.53 (21)	7.76 (22)	7.08 (19.0)	1.99	.096
Mao Tse-Tung	6.40 (18.0)	7.25 (17.0)	7.68 (22)	7.76 (22)	7.64 (23.5)	2.54	.040
Students for a Democratic Society	5.00 (7.0)	5.59 (10.0)	6.43 (13)	6.62 (15)	6.25 (15.0)	3.38	.010
Attitude toward the Moderate Left							
Socialism	4.80 (5.5)	4.92 (5.0)	5.09 (7)	6.13 (12)	5.64 (11.0)	4.44	.002
Norman Thomas	5.30 (8.0)	5.32 (7.0)	6.15 (11)	6.01 (10)	6.00 (12.0)	3.23	.013
Hubert Humphrey	5.80 (13.5)	5.25 (6.0)	5.19 (8)	5.68 (9)	5.48 (9.0)	0.77	.545
Eugene McCarthy	2.70 (2.0)	3.00 (2.0)	3.31 (2)	3.37 (1)	3.16 (1.0)	0.79	.530
Democratic Party	4.00 (3.0)	4.02 (3.0)	3.99 (4)	4.25 (4)	4.68 (7.0)	0.97	.424
Attitude toward the Civil Rights Movement							
Martin Luther King	2.10 (1.0)	2.42 (1.0)	2.69 (1)	4.17 (3)	4.72 (8.0)	20.99	.0005
Malcolm X	5.89 (15.0)	5.96 (12.0)	6.47 (14)	7.49 (20)	7.48 (20.0)	6.46	.0005
Attitude toward the Moderate Right							
Conservatism	6.30 (17.0)	5.94 (11.0)	5.22 (9)	5.14 (7)	4.60 (5.5)	4.05	.003
Barry Goldwater	6.80 (19.5)	6.09 (13.5)	5.04 (6)	5.13 (6)	4.60 (5.5)	6.13	.0005
George Wallace	7.70 (22.0)	7.93 (23.0)	7.28 (19)	6.11 (11)	5.60 (10.0)	16.05	.0005
Ronald Reagan	5.70 (12.0)	6.09 (13.5)	5.42 (10)	5.36 (8)	4.12 (4.0)	5.15	.0005
Richard Nixon	5.50 (9.5)	5.58 (9.0)	4.75 (5)	5.04 (5)	4.04 (3.0)	3.29	.012
Republican Party	4.60 (4.0)	4.67 (4.0)	3.88 (3)	4.10 (2)	3.44 (2.0)	3.44	.009
Attitude toward the Extreme Right							
Fascism	7.30 (21.0)	8.17 (24.0)	7.99 (24)	8.17 (25)	7.52 (21.5)	2.78	.027
Adolf Hitler	8.00 (24.5)	8.46 (25.0)	8.43 (25)	8.14 (24)	8.12 (25.0)	1.31	.265
Benito Mussolini	8.00 (24.5)	7.84 (22.0)	7.91 (23)	7.76 (22)	7.52 (21.5)	0.51	.732
Francisco Franco	5.55 (11.0)	7.31 (19.0)	6.89 (16)	6.95 (17)	6.56 (16.0)	4.05	.003
George Lincoln Rockwell	6.00 (16.0)	7.68 (20.0)	7.25 (18)	6.96 (18)	6.79 (17.0)	4.51	.001
John Birch Society	7.90 (23.0)	7.70 (21.0)	7.30 (20)	6.53 (14)	6.16 (13.0)	9.06	.0005

separately classified under the category "Attitude toward the civil rights movement."

Under "attitude toward the moderate right" are included the findings on attitudes held by the various *equality-freedom* groups toward *conservatism*, Goldwater, Wallace, Reagan, Nixon, and the Republican Party. Finally, the data on *fascism*, Hitler, Mussolini, Franco, and George Lincoln Rockwell have all been included together under the category "attitude toward the extreme right." Included here also are the ratings given to the John Birch Society, on the assumption that most Americans would probably see the John Birch Society as an extreme right-wing organization if not a fascist organization, just as they might see SDS as an extreme left-wing organization.

These five categories are, however, nothing more than categories constructed for convenience of presentation. Regardless of possible agreements or disagreements with these categorizations, out main interest is in the determination of similarities and differences in ratings of the 25 ideological stimuli by the five *equality-freedom* groups. Let us now examine these findings in more detail.

The most favorable attitudes are generally expressed by all five *equality-freedom* groups toward Martin Luther King and Eugene McCarthy and toward the Democratic and Republican Parties; the least favorable attitudes are usually expressed toward *fascism*, Hitler, Mussolini, Stalin, and Mao Tse-Tung. Moderate and domestic ideologies and ideologists are thus seen to be the most popular; extremist and foreign ones are the least popular. Despite such gross similarities, the five *equality-freedom* groups differ significantly in their ratings of 18 of the 25 concepts. They differ significantly in their ratings of the four ideological concepts, *communism*, *socialism*, *conservatism*, and *fascism*, and they differ significantly in their ratings of most of the political figures and parties that are associated with these four ideological positions.

Those exhibiting a communist value orientation—*equality* high, *freedom* low—express a more favorable attitude toward *communism* than any of the other groups, and increasingly unfavorable attitudes are expressed toward *communism* by those exhibiting socialist, middle American, capitalist, and fascist value orientations. Similar linear trends are apparent for Lenin, Marx, Stalin, Mao Tse-Tung, and SDS, except for the fact that those showing capitalist and middle American value orientations are usually somewhat more extreme in their opposition to these stimuli than those showing a fascist value orientation.

Roughly similar trends are also noted for *socialism* and Norman Thomas. Those exhibiting a communist value orientation express the most favorable attitude, followed by those exhibiting a socialist value orientation. Those exhibiting middle American, capitalist, and fascist value orientations express attitudes that are decreasingly favorable toward *socialism* and toward Norman Thomas. No significant differences are, however, found among the five *equality-freedom* groups in attitudes expressed toward Hubert Humphrey, Eugene McCarthy, or the Democratic Party.

Differences in ratings of Martin Luther King by the five groups are noteworthy because they are rather large. On a nine-point scale, subjects exhibiting communist, socialist, middle American, capitalist, and fascist value orientations rate him 2.10, 2.42, 2.69, 4.17 and 4.72, respectively. These findings follow the same trend as those evident in ratings of the stimulus, *communism*. Attitude toward Malcolm X shows a similar trend, except that Malcolm X is uniformly more disliked than Martin Luther King by all groups.

Attitudes toward the moderate right are opposite in direction to those observed for the extreme left, and moderate left, and toward the two civil rights leaders. This time it is those exhibiting a fascist value orientation who uniformly show the most favorable attitude. Those exhibiting capitalist and middle American value orientations express somewhat less favorable attitudes, and those who exhibit socialist and communist value orientations express the most negative attitudes toward the moderate right. In some instances, it is those with a communist value orientation who show the most negative attitude—toward *conservatism* and Goldwater. In other instances, it is those with a socialist value orientation who express the most negative attitude—toward George Wallace, Reagan, Nixon, and the Republican Party.

We come now to the most surprising and puzzling findings of the study—the ratings given by the five *equality-freedom* groups to the extreme right concepts. Table 7.2 shows that those having a communist value orientation on the average express a more favorable attitude than do the other groups toward *fascism*, Hitler, Franco, and George Lincoln Rockwell and that those having a fascist value orientation typically express the next most favorable attitude toward those stimuli. The most unfavorable ratings given to these extreme right stimuli come from those having a socialist value orientation. A notable exception, however, are the findings concerning the right-wing John Birch Society. The most negative attitude toward the John Birch Society is expressed by those exhibiting a communist value orientation, and this attitude becomes increasingly more positive as we proceed from communist to socialist, to middle American, to capitalist and, finally, to fascist value orientation. These findings concerning the John Birch Society are most closely parallel to those observed for *conservatism* and Barry Goldwater and least resemble trends observed for *communism* and Martin Luther King.

To some extent, but not altogether, the significant differences found for the extreme right stimuli, *fascism*, Franco, and Rockwell, may arise for purely methodological reasons. Those exhibiting a communist value pattern rate all 25 stimuli somewhat more favorably than do the other four groups, and it is thus possible that a difference in frame of reference might have led them to give consistently more positive ratings to these extreme right stimuli also. A look at the relative ordering of the 25 ideological concepts by each *equality-freedom* group is instructive in this respect. These orderings are shown in parentheses in Table 7.2. All five groups rate *fascism*, Hitler, and Mussolini far more negatively than they rate the remaining concepts. These stimuli uniformly are among the five most disliked concepts. Thus, the differences in the mean *fascism* ratings among the five *equality-freedom* groups, although statistically significant, are not all that impressive since all groups perceive *fascism* in an extremely negative way. More puzzling, however, are the findings that Franco and George Lincoln Rockwell are more favorably regarded by all five groups than are *fascism*, Hitler, and Mussolini and, moreover, that those who exhibit a communist value orientation rate Franco and Rockwell substantially higher. Franco is the eleventh best-liked among the 25 choices, and Rockwell is the sixteenth best-liked. An explanation of these findings for the communist-oriented subjects will become more apparent when we examine additional data about their general level of political sophistication and, more specifically, about their level of understanding of the nature of fascism. These data will be reported shortly.

Returning to the rankings shown in parentheses in Table 7.2, it is obvious that subjects exhibiting a communist value orientation feel far more favorably than the other groups about stimuli representing the political left. For these subjects, *communism*, Marx, *socialism*, and SDS are among the 10 most popular items. These stimuli decrease steadily in relative popularity for subjects exhibiting socialist, middle American, capitalist, and fascist value orientations. Differences in attitude toward *communism* are especially noteworthy: It is among the 10 best-liked concepts for those exhibiting a communist value orientation, and it then decreases steadily in popularity as we proceed from left to right; it is rated almost at the bottom by the subjects who exhibit a fascist value orientation.

Equally noteworthy are the relative orderings of certain moderate right concepts. *Conservatism* is seventeenth on the list of preferences for subjects expressing a communist value orientation, and its rating increases steadily to about fifth in popularity for those having a fascist value orientation. Attitude toward Barry Goldwater shows a similar trend. Goldwater is about twentieth on the list among those exhibiting a communist value orientation but his is the sixth most popular name for subjects exhibiting a fascist value orientation. Similarly, George Wallace is rated twenty-second or twenty-third on the list by those having communist and socialist value orientations, nineteenth by middle Americans, and eleventh or tenth by subjects expressing capitalist and fascist orientations. Finally, similar trends are noted for the mean ratings given to Nixon and Reagan and the Republican Party, except that these ratings are on the whole more positive.

Findings concerning attitude toward the John Birch Society resemble most closely those obtained for George Wallace, with the Society being rated twenty-third by subjects on the extreme left and thirteenth by subjects on the extreme right. These findings, along with those concerning the six moderate right concepts, are all internally consistent with one another and they are all statistically significant. The trends are linear proceeding from left to right, that is, proceeding from communist to socialist to middle American to capitalist to fascist types of values.

Summarizing all these findings, we find the conclusion inescapable that there are indeed pervasive differences in attitudes toward the major ideologies among persons having different *equality-freedom* orientations. But, as has been pointed out, these patterns do not fit theoretical expectations quite as neatly as had been anticipated. The reason they do not will become clearer as we examine the subjects' perceptions of the four ideologists' political value orientations.

Perceived Value Orientations of Lenin, Thomas, Goldwater, and Hitler

Recall that all subjects had ranked not only their own terminal values but also those that they perceived to be held by Lenin, Norman Thomas, Goldwater, and Hitler. To what extent do persons with varying *equality-freedom* orientations accurately perceive the *equality-freedom* orientations of these major ideological figures, and how do these perceptions affect attitudes toward the four major ideological positions? The results are shown in Table 7.3.

It is readily apparent that each of the four extreme *equality-freedom* groups accurately perceives the *equality-freedom* orientation of the ideological figure whose value orientation is known on independent grounds to be most similar to its own. Subjects who exhibit a communist value orientation accurately perceive Lenin as ranking *equality* high and *freedom* low, subjects who exhibit a socialist value orientation accurately perceive Thomas as ranking *equality* and *freedom* high, and so on. But they are considerably less accurate in perceiving the *equality-freedom* orientations of the remaining ideological figures.

If we assume, on the basis of findings reported in Chapter 6, that Lenin, Thomas, Goldwater, and Hitler would have ranked *equality* and *freedom* 1–18, 2–1, 18–1, and 18–17, respectively, it is possible to estimate for each group the amount of error in perception of the *equality-freedom* orientations of the four ideologists. Subjects exhibiting communist and fascist value orientations are evidently the most misinformed of the five groups, as also shown in Table 7.3. Although communist-minded subjects perceive the *equality-freedom* orientation of Goldwater as well as Lenin's with reasonable accuracy, they grossly misperceive Norman Thomas's and Hitler's. If we take these misconceptions into account, their attitudes toward ratings of the various ideologies become somewhat more understandable. Subjects exhibiting a communist value orientation perceive Norman Thomas as having an *equality-freedom* orientation very much like

TABLE 7.3 PERCEPTIONS OF LENIN'S, THOMAS'S, GOLDWATER'S, AND HITLER'S COMPOSITE RANKINGS ON EQUALITY AND FREEDOM BY FIVE EQUALITY-FREEDOM GROUPS

		Equality High Freedom Low	Equality High Freedom High	Equality Middle Freedom Middle	Equality Low Freedom High	Equality Low Freedom Low	Error Score
N =		10	138	68	71	25	
Lenin	Equality (1)	5	4	13	12	16	45
	Freedom (18)	16	17	17	17	17	6
Thomas	Equality (2)	4	1	1	1	3	6
	Freedom (1)	17	5	9	7	14	47
Goldwater	Equality (18)	16	8	8	13	9	36
	Freedom (1)	7	2	4	2	2	12
Hitler	Equality (18)	18	18	18	18	18	0
	Freedom (17)	9	15	16	15	16	14
Error Score		40	22	36	27	41	166

Lenin's—in fact, slightly more Leninist than Lenin's. This misperception can account for the fact that communist-oriented subjects rate Norman Thomas and *socialism* as well as *communism*, Lenin, Marx, Stalin, Mao, and SDS uniformly higher than do subjects exhibiting a socialist value orientation. These subjects apparently are not able to distinguish between communism and socialism, and they therefore rate them both with about equal favor.

Notice, however, that subjects exhibiting a communist value orientation also perceive Hitler as having cared more for *freedom* than he actually did care for it. In fact, these subjects perceive Hitler very much as they perceive Goldwater, except that they see Hitler as a somewhat more extreme Goldwater. Both are thought to have cared little for *equality*, and both are thought to have cared considerably more for *freedom*. If this misperception of Hitler also applies to *fascism* and to Franco and George Lincoln Rockwell, it becomes possible to offer a reasonable explanation of the somewhat higher ratings they generally assign to the fascist concepts. It is based upon a gross misconception on their part of the nature of fascism. More specifically, it is based upon their misperception of fascism as representing not the totalitarianism and inhumanity for which it is feared the world over, but merely a somewhat more extreme form of Goldwaterism.

Subjects with socialist value orientations are, in contrast, considerably more accurate in their perceptions. Their major misperception, however, concerns Goldwater, who is seen as having a greater dedication to *equality* than he actually possesses, thereby transforming Goldwater to look more like a Norman Thomas than a Goldwater. It thus becomes apparent that these subjects' attitudes toward Norman Thomas and *socialism* are more favorable than their attitudes toward most of the other ideological stimuli because these stimuli stand for *equality-freedom* orientations that are most like their own. Moreover, their attitudes toward Goldwater and *conservatism* are the next most favorable because these are perceived to stand for *equality-freedom* orientations that are the next most similar to their own. Lenin's and *communism*'s *equality-freedom* orientation are perceived to deviate more markedly, and Hitler's and *fascism*'s even more markedly from their own. Thus, favorable and unfavorable ratings seem to be assigned by these socialist-minded subjects on the basis of perceived similarity with their own *equality-freedom* orientation.

There is, however, an important difference in the pattern of attitudes expressed by those exhibiting communist and socialist value orientations. Communist-minded subjects think more highly of *communism* and Lenin than of *conservatism* and Goldwater. The reverse is true for socialist-minded subjects, who think more highly of *conservatism* and Goldwater than of *communism* and Lenin. These findings can also be explained as a function of perceived similarity.

Now what about the perceptions of subjects who rank *equality* and *freedom* in the middle of their value hierarchy? These people perceive Hitler's value orientation quite accurately but they show sizeable errors in perceiving Lenin's, Norman Thomas's, and Goldwater's. Middle Americans perceive Lenin as having a low value for *equality* as well as for *freedom*, thus making him look more like Hitler. They perceive Norman Thomas as caring less for *freedom* than he in fact did, thus giving him a middle American stand on *freedom* that is more congruent with their own *freedom* rankings. And they perceive Goldwater as caring more for *equality* and less for *freedom* than he actually does, thus transforming Goldwater to look the most like themselves, that is, middle American.

Middle American ratings of the ideological concepts are on the whole consistent with their perceptions and misperceptions. They regard Barry Goldwater more highly than Lenin, Thomas, or Hitler because they perceive him as having a value orientation most similar to their own. They regard Norman Thomas next most favorably because they perceive Thomas as the one next most dedicated to middle American values. They reject Lenin because Lenin is perceived to deviate more from the middle American values they identify themselves with. Finally, they dislike Hitler the most because he is perceived to deviate the most from their own middle American values.

Considering next the perceptions of those having capitalist value orientations, it is evident from Table 7.3 that their major misperceptions concern Lenin, whose value for *equality* they downgrade, thus making Lenin look more like Hitler. To a lesser extent, Norman Thomas's value for *freedom* is also downgraded. Taking these misperceptions into account, their attitudes toward these four political figures become more (although not completely) consistent with their perceptions. Goldwater, who is seen to have a value orientation that is the most similar to their own is the most positively regarded. Norman Thomas, Lenin, and Hitler, who have less similar *equality-freedom* orientations, are less positively regarded.

We have thus far considered the perceptions of the subjects exhibiting communist, socialist, middle American, and capitalist value orientations, and how such perceptions might have affected their attitudes toward the four major ideologies. Differences in attitude expressed toward the various ideological stimuli can now be largely explained as a joint function of their own *equality-freedom* orientation and their perceptions of the extent to which the *equality-freedom* orientations of the major ideologies are similar to their own.

This sort of explanation, however, does not altogether hold for the subjects exhibiting a fascist value orientation. Even though these subjects perceive Hitler's values quite accurately, they are clearly misinformed about the remaining three ideological figures. They perceive Lenin as having essentially the same value orientation as Hitler—a fascist value orientation; they perceive Norman Thomas as having a Leninist value orientation—*equality* high, *freedom* low; and they perceive Goldwater as caring more for *equality* than he actually cares for it. Unlike the other *equality-freedom* groups, their attitudes toward the four ideological figures are not compatible with their perceptions of these ideologists' value orientations. In fact, their attitudes are in inverse proportion to perceived similarity. Hitler, who has an *equality-freedom* orientation most similar to their own, is the least admired of the four political figures. Goldwater, whose value orientation is incorrectly perceived to be the most unlike Hitler's or their own, is the most admired of the four political figures. In absolute terms, these fascist-minded subjects reject *fascism*, but they reject *communism* even more strongly. It is the only one of the five groups that rejects *communism* more than *fascism*. It is the group that is the most favorably disposed toward capitalist symbols—*conservatism*, Goldwater, Reagan, Nixon, the Republican Party—and it is also the most favorably disposed toward right-wing George Wallace and the John Birch Society. There can thus be no doubt that these subjects who exhibit a fascist value orientation also exhibit a pattern of ideological attitudes that is distinctively different from those exhibited by the remaining four *equality-freedom* groups.

At this point, we can only speculate about the reasons why their attitudes toward the four ideologists are not consistent with their perceptions of these ideologists' value orientations. It is reasonable to suppose that these subjects, who, we must remind ourselves, are American subjects, need to protect themselves against the shock of recognition that their own value orientation is also Hitler's value orientation. Different processes of distortion seem to be at work in this group from those in the other groups considered. The attitudes that these fascist-minded subjects express toward the various ideological positions not only seem to be a function of their own value orientation and their misperceptions about others' value orientations but also seem to be a function of repression or denial of their own value orientation. Further research is needed to clarify the different processes of distortion that may be at work.

Political Sophistication of Subjects Exhibiting
Different Equality-Freedom Orientations

The data reported in Table 7.3 strongly suggest that our subjects were politically unsophisticated. Additional evidence provides further support for this interpretation. At the end of the study, they were all asked: "How would you describe your own political orientation?" and Table 7.4 shows how they identified themselves. Not a single one of the 10 subjects exhibiting a communist value orientation identified himself as a "communist" or "radical" or even as a "leftist." One called himself a "socialist," another a "liberal," and another, a "moderate conservative." Three merely identified themselves by giving their political party affiliation. Finally, four responded that they were "confused," "undecided," and so forth or gave no response. It is thus evident that these 10 college students who exhibit a

TABLE 7.4 POLITICAL ORIENTATIONS CLAIMED BY FIVE EQUALITY-FREEDOM GROUPS (IN PERCENT)

	Equality High Freedom Low	Equality High Freedom High	Equality Middle Freedom Middle	Equality Low Freedom High	Equality Low Freedom Low
N =	10	138	68	71	25
Radical, leftist	0	6.5	3	0	0
Socialist, liberal, moderate liberal	20	34.0	34	22	16
Moderate, independent	0	14.5	9	17	4
Moderate conservative, conservative	10	13.0	10	20	28
Identified themselves as Democrat or Republican	30	8.0	9	6	4
Confused, undecided, uninformed, detached, apathetic, indifferent, no response, misunderstood question, unclassifiable	40	24.0	35	35	48
Total Percent	100	100	100	100	100

Leninist value orientation are not really able to articulate their own political identity or value position.

Even less political sophistication is apparent among those exhibiting a fascist value orientation. About half identified themselves as politically "undecided," "confused," or "uninformed." The remaining half identified themselves variously with political labels ranging from "liberal" to "conservative." Two identified themselves as "liberal," another two as "moderate liberal," one as an "independent," five as "moderate conservative," and two more as "conservative." One subject merely responded with his party affiliation. It would not have been possible to predict from these responses that we are describing 25 college students whose value orientation most resembles Hitler's. They are at best unconscious fascists.

Those with socialist value orientations are on the whole most accurate in the way they label themselves. A third identify themselves as "socialist," "liberal," or "leftist," and another 15 percent consider themselves "moderate" or "independent." But one out of every four of these subjects still reports confusion or indecision about his political identity.

Middle Americans and those showing a capitalist value orientation also betray an absence of political sophistication. A third of each group again report confusion or indecision about their political identity. Another third of the middle American students and one in five of the capitalist-oriented students identify themselves with such terms as "socialist," "liberal," "moderate liberal," and, occasionally, even as "radical." Only 19 percent of the middle Americans and 37 percent of the capitalist-oriented students think of themselves as "moderate," independent," "moderate conservative," or "conservative."

The hypothesis that variations in *equality-freedom* orientations represent ideological predispositions can be confirmed or disconfirmed only if the sample tested is known to be a politically unsophisticated one. The data just presented provide us with independent evidence about the political naïveté, indeed, political ignorance, of our subjects, and confirm the findings presented earlier suggesting that American college students in general and students exhibiting communist and fascist value orientations in particular are the most confused and misinformed about ideological matters. We can thus be reasonably assured that the relation between *equality-freedom* orientation and ideological position is not attributable to the fact that the subjects studied happened to be knowledgeable about the world of politics.

Further Discussion

All the findings presented here support the proposition that variations in *equality-freedom* orientations represent ideological predispositions. But the question may be raised whether a two-value model of politics is really needed to account for the differing patterns of attitudes. Cannot *equality* alone adequately account for the findings?

If variations in *equality* alone were adequate, no differences should be expected between the two value orientations that are equally high on *equality*—the communist and socialist value orientations—or between the two value orientations that are equally low on *equality*—the capitalist and fascist value orientations. Instead, we would expect increasing or decreasing trends in attitudes from communist and socialist value orientations at one pole, to middle American, and to capitalist and fascist value orientations at the opposite pole. The data do not conform to such a one-value model:

1. Subjects with communist and socialist value orientations differ systematically in many ways despite the fact that they rank *equality* relatively highly. Communist-oriented subjects (as defined by their *equality-freedom* orientation) have more favorable attitudes than socialist-oriented subjects toward the two black leaders, Martin Luther King and Malcolm X. They have uniformly more favorable attitudes toward the extreme left—communism, Lenin, Marx, Stalin, Mao Tse-Tung, and the Students for a Democratic Society. Communist-oriented subjects show a greater antipathy to capitalism, especially as exemplified by the concepts *conservatism* and Goldwater, and they also show a greater antipathy to the extreme right wing, as exemplified by the John Birch Society. Finally, those with communist value orientations also express the most favorable attitudes toward most of the fascist stimuli, whereas those with socialist value orientations generally express the least favorable attitudes. These differences between subjects exhibiting communist and socialist types of value orientation could not have arisen as a function of value for *equality*, for the two groups do not differ on *equality*.

2. Those with capitalist and fascist value orientations, who both care little for *equality*, nonetheless show systematic differences in attitude. Fascist-oriented subjects express more negative attitudes than the capitalist-oriented subjects toward Martin Luther King and *communism* and more favorable attitudes toward capitalist symbols—*conservatism*, Goldwater, Wallace, Reagan, Nixon, and the Republican Party. Fascist-oriented subjects, moreover, express a more favorable attitude toward the John Birch Society. Again, such systematic differences between fascist- and capitalist-minded subjects, could hardly have arisen if they were a function of value for *equality* alone.

At the same time, it is not possible to argue that the two-value model could have generated all the findings. Other variables must also be taken into account, especially level of political sophistication, subjects' conceptions about their own *equality-freedom* position, and the accuracy of their perceptions about value positions held by various ideologists. Taking such variables into account, it seems reasonable to conclude from the findings presented—even though they are not altogether satisfactory from the standpoint of sample size—that variations in *equality-freedom* orientation, even among politically unsophisticated people, can be taken to be predispositions that permit prediction of position toward the major ideological issues of contemporary society.

A LAW OF POLITICAL ACTIVISM

A second major implication of the two-value model, now to be considered, concerns the possible role that *equality* and *freedom* might play in political activism. Why should persons or groups decide to become political activists in the first place? How strongly must they hold to certain values if they are to lead to a sustained political activism? If one engages in political activity is it likely to lead to value change, and if so, which values might be expected to undergo change?

If it is indeed the case that the world of politics is distinctively concerned with ideas about the desirability and undesirability of *equality* and *freedom*, then persons or groups that are politically active should have a more extreme regard for one or both of the two political values when compared with politically less active persons or groups. The two-value model suggests, in other words, that there would be little motivation for a person to become politically active unless he held an intense belief in the desirability or undesirability of at least one or both of the two distinctively political values.

A low ranking on any particular value may mean either that it is unimportant or that it is undesirable. The findings presented in Chapter 6, especially those concerning the values of Lenin and Hitler and, possibly, also Goldwater, suggest that low rankings of the two political values, *equality* and *freedom*, can safely be assumed to mean that these are politically undesirable rather than merely unimportant.

Proceeding on this assumption, the *equality* and *freedom* rankings of many individuals and groups known to be politically active and inactive were examined to ascertain whether they are consistent with this hypothesis. The relevant data are shown in Table 7.5.

Direct comparisons between activists and nonactivists are possible in some cases but not in others. Political figures such as Lenin and James Madison can be assumed to be activists and should therefore exhibit extreme rankings on one or both values. Similarly, certain groups shown in Table 7.5, such as Catholic priests and service station dealers, can generally be assumed to be politically inactive, and they should therefore exhibit less extreme rankings. Other data enable us to compare directly the politically active and inactive supporters of certain political figures, for instance, persons working actively for George Wallace in the 1968 presidential campaign (Bishop, 1969) and adults in the national sample who simply stated a preference for Wallace. We should expect Wallace activists to show more extreme rankings than Wallace nonactivists on one or both values.

Lenin, the socialist writers, Goldwater, and Hitler—all activists—show

TABLE 7.5 EQUALITY-FREEDOM RANKINGS OF POLITICALLY ACTIVE
AND INACTIVE PERSONS AND GROUPS

Individual or Group	Activists		Nonactivists	
	Equality	Freedom	Equality	Freedom
Lenin	1	17	—	—
Socialists	2	1	—	—
Goldwater	16	1	—	—
Hitler	17	16	—	—
James Madison	5	1	—	—
Alexander Hamilton	7	1	—	—
Boulding supporters, 1968	2	3	—	—
Vivian supporters, 1968	2	3	—	—
Kennedy supporters, 1968	—	—	4	3
Johnson supporters, 1968	—	—	4	3
Humphrey supporters, 1968	2	4	—	—
McCarthy supporters, 1968	1	2	6	3
Rockefeller supporters, 1968	9	2	9	3
Nixon supporters, 1968	9	2	12	3
Reagan supporters, 1968	17	1	10	3
Wallace supporters, 1968	18	1	14	3
John Birch Society	7	1	—	—
S.F. antiwar marchers vs. pedestrians	4	1	4	2
Black vs. white adult Americans	2	3	11	3
Secular vs. Catholic students	11	1	11	8
Pro- vs. anti-church activism	4	3	12	3
All adult Americans	—	—	7	3
Adult Americans: Democrats	—	—	6	3
Adult Americans: Republicans	—	—	10	3
Adult Americans: Independents	—	—	7	3
Prison inmates	—	—	8	3
Catholic priests	—	—	9	7
Police	—	—	14	3
Actors (students)	—	—	5	6
Actresses (students)	—	—	15	4
Service station dealers	—	—	14	6
Oil company salesmen	—	—	15	7

extreme value rankings on both political values, as already discussed.
James Madison and Alexander Hamilton, two activists of an earlier era of
American history, exhibit an extreme regard for *freedom*. These data come
from Rokeach, Homant, and Penner's content analysis of the Federalist
papers (1970) which yielded 13 terminal values. Three values—*government
security*, *national security*, and *public security* were excluded in calculating

the *equality-freedom* rankings shown in Table 7.5 because the main purpose of the Federalist papers was to persuade the American people that ratifying the U.S. Constitution was instrumental to the realization of these three values. Thus, the *equality-freedom* rankings shown in Table 7.5 for Madison and Hamilton are based on 10 rather than 13 terminal values.

Boulding and Vivian were two contenders for a Congressional seat in the 1968 Democratic primaries in the Ann Arbor, Michigan, area. Mrs. Boulding was a peace candidate running against incumbent Democrat Congressman Vivian, who was a progressive on civil rights and other domestic issues but a supporter of President Johnson's Vietnam policies. Boulding and Vivian supporters were tested with the Value Survey following the publication of their names in political advertisements identifying them as supporters of one or the other candidate. Both of these activist groups showed extreme rankings on *equality* and *freedom*—second and third—rankings that are exceeded only by *a world at peace*.

Next shown in Table 7.5 are the *equality* and *freedom* rankings for various nonactive as well as active supporters of the several presidential candidates in April 1968. These data are perhaps more decisive for our hypothesis because they permit direct comparison of the *equality* and *freedom* rankings given by activist and nonactivist supporters, at least, for five of the eight presidential candidates of 1968.

Inspection of these data reveals, without exception, that activist supporters rank at least one of the two political values more extremely than do nominal supporters. Activists working for Eugene McCarthy ranked *equality* and *freedom* first and second, compared with rankings of sixth and third for nominal McCarthy supporters. Thus, McCarthy activists were more extreme in their regard for both political values. Similarly, activist supporters of George Wallace and Ronald Reagan were more extreme than nonactivist Wallace and Reagan supporters in their low regard for *equality* and in their high regard for *freedom*. In the case of Rockefeller and Nixon supporters, however, activists were more extreme than nonactivists only with respect to *freedom*.

Next shown in Table 7.5 are the *equality-freedom* rankings obtained by Parrott (1971) for activist John Birch Society members. Their composite rankings are seventh and first, respectively. Both of these rankings are at the extremes since, as stated earlier, Parrott had employed a drastically reduced ranking scale composed of only seven values.

Parrott (1971) has also reported the rankings obtained on the same seven-value scale for San Francisco participants in the 1969 antiwar "moratorium" march as compared with downtown San Francisco pedestrians. Moratorium marchers are assumed to be activists and pedestrians, nonactivists. The antiwar marchers show composite rankings of fourth and first for *equality* and *freedom*, and pedestrian nonmarchers show rankings of fourth and second. Thus, marchers were found to be more extreme than nonmarchers in their value for *freedom*.

Black American adults can be assumed to be more activist on the whole than white American adults, and therefore they should show more extreme value rankings. The data shown in Table 7.5 confirm this expectation: Although black and white Americans tested in 1968 did not differ in *freedom* rankings, the more activist black Americans were more extreme in their *equality* rankings.

Similarly, it is reasonable to assume that college students at a large secular university in the Midwest had been more actively involved in campus protest in the late sixties than students at a Catholic college in Canada (Hague, 1968). The findings again confirm this expectation: Although the two groups do not differ with respect to *equality*, the secular students rank *freedom* more extremely.

The next comparison between activists and nonactivists comes from the national NORC study. One question put to the national sample was designed to elicit indications of their attitude toward the church's active involvement in the social and political affairs of contemporary society. If our hypothesis is valid, we should expect to find that those favoring involvement will be more extreme on one or both political values than those opposing church involvement. This expectation is again borne out by the data. Although the two groups do not differ with respect to *freedom* rankings, church activists show more extreme rankings on *equality*.

Finally, Table 7.5 show the *equality-freedom* rankings of a number of groups that can reasonably be assumed to be politically inactive. All these groups have already been discussed in earlier chapters, with the exception of the actors and actresses, who were tested by Dr. Lloyd A. Borstemann (unpublished). In virtually all these cases the *equality-freedom* rankings are less extreme than those obtained for politically active individuals and groups. In no case are the composite rankings higher than 3 or lower than 15. In contrast, most of the activist individuals and groups show more extreme rankings on one or both values.

Further Discussion

When evaluating these data the reader should bear in mind that they were obtained with scales of varying length. Those shown for Lenin, the socialist writers, Goldwater, and Hitler are based on 17 terminal values; the Madison and Hamilton data are based on 10 terminal values; the data for the John Birch Society and for antiwar marchers and nonmarchers are based on seven terminal values; the remainder are based on 18 values. Regardless of such differences in length of scale, the findings consistently show that political activists have a more extreme regard for at least one of the two political values. In some cases, the differences between activists and nonactivists are small and, in other cases, large. In virtually all cases, however, the differences are in the theoretically expected direction.

Attention should also be given to the fact that political activists are not necessarily more extreme on both political values. Activist supporters of Nixon and Rockefeller show more extreme rankings than do nonactivist supporters only on *freedom*; activist supporters of McCarthy, Reagan, and Wallace show more extreme rankings than do nonactivist supporters on both values. All that can be concluded from the data is that political activists are more extreme in their regard for one or two values, and that these two values can be specifically identified as *equality* and *freedom*.

The findings moreover suggest that the hypothesis is valid for political activism of the left, center, and right and also that it is valid in other cultures and in other historical periods. Lenin and Hitler were politically active in Russia and Germany, and the remaining persons and groups were politically active in the United States. Lenin and Hitler and Madison and Hamilton had been politically active in earlier historical periods; the others are more contemporary political activists.

The finding that activists of all political persuasions have a more extreme regard for either one or both of these political values does not, of course, tell us anything about causal relationships. It is not possible to ascertain from the data whether the extreme value positions found for political activists are antecedents or consequences of their activism. Theoretically, it is possible to argue that polarization of political value orientation can be a consequence as well as an antecedent. A person who engages in a political act, for whatever fleeting reason—for example, protesting desegregation or busing in one's community, the American presence in Vietnam, or Lieutenant Calley's conviction—will, as a result of a process of politicization, come to place a more extreme emphasis on either or both of the political values. Cognitive change often follows behavior (Festinger, 1957; Abelson *et al.*, 1968), in order to reduce the discrepancy between behavior that one has engaged in for whatever reason and the values that one holds. Conversely, polarization of political values can precipitate a more sustained political activism since values are standards that determine and guide action.

Thus, whatever *equality* and *freedom* may mean to different individuals and groups the available data suggest the operation of some principle or law which can be tentatively called a law of political activism: A more extreme regard for either one or both of the two political values, *equality* and *freedom*, is a minimum condition for sustained political action and is also a minimum consequence of political action.

The question now arises whether there are perhaps other values that may become distinctively implicated in some extreme way as determinants of activism in other domains. Why not also a law of religious or ecological or aesthetic activism? Further research is obviously needed to determine whether the proposed law of political activism is only a specific instance of some more general principle.

PART FOUR

Long- and Short-term Change in Values, Attitudes, and Behavior

8
A Theory of Cognitive and Behavioral Change

Conceptual distinctions have already been drawn in Chapter 1 between beliefs and attitudes, attitudes and values, and instrumental and terminal values. All these conceptually distinct components—the countless beliefs, their organizations into thousands of attitudes, the several dozens of hierarchically arranged instrumental values, and the several handfuls of hierarchically arranged terminal values—are organized to form a single, functionally interconnected belief system, wherein terminal values are more central than instrumental values and instrumental values are more central than attitudes. The reason it is a functionally interconnected system is that the objects and situations around which a person organizes his attitudes arouse various instrumental values (Katz and Braly, 1933; Gilbert, 1951; Scott, 1965) which are perceived to be instrumental to the attainment of various terminal values (Woodruff and DiVesta, 1948; Smith, 1949; Peak, 1955; Rosenberg, 1956; Carlson, 1956; Fishbein, 1966; Homant, 1971; Hollen, 1972).

Attention must now be directed, however, to another class of beliefs that are even more central to a person than his values. We are referring to the many conceptions or cognitions that a person has about himself—what Mead (1934), Cooley (1956), Rogers (1959), Hilgard (1949), and many others have identified as the self or self-concept. Self-conceptions include all one's cognitions, conscious and unconscious, about one's physical image; intellectual and moral abilities and weaknesses; socioeconomic position in society; national, regional, ethnic, racial and religious identity; the sexual, generational, occupational, marital, and parental roles that one plays in society; and how well or poorly one plays such roles. In short, a person's total conception of himself is an organization of all the distinctive cognitions, negative as well as positive, and the affective connotations of

215

these cognitions that would be displayed if a full answer to the question "Who am I?" (Kuhn, 1960) were forthcoming. All these conceptions that a person has about himself are highly socialized ones, closer perhaps to Mead's and Cooley's social conception of the self than to Rogers' and Hilgard's more personological conception. All such self-cognitions can reasonably be represented at the innermost core of the total belief system, and all remaining beliefs, attitudes, and values can be conceived of as functionally organized around this innermost core.

As previously stated, the functions served by a person's values are to provide him with a comprehensive set of standards to guide actions, justifications, judgments, and comparisons of self and others and to serve needs for adjustment, ego defense, and self-actualization. All these diverse functions converge into a single, overriding, master function, namely, to help maintain and enhance one's total conception of oneself. This self-conception is not necessarily a positive one. Every person attempts at the very least to maintain and, insofar as possible, to enhance whatever self-conception he has managed to develop as a result of socialization within the framework of a particular culture and society, society's institutions, primary groups, and personal experience. In other words, the ultimate purpose of one's total belief system, which includes one's values, is to maintain and enhance what McDougall (1926) has called the master of all sentiments, the sentiment of self-regard.

This sentiment or attitude of self-regard must be accorded a more central status within the total belief system than other attitudes or values for at least two reasons. First, it has a self-reflexive quality about it that other attitudes and values do not possess. More important, self-conceptions are activated in virtually every situation a person may find himself in; one's performance in every situation is more or less routinely judged for its bearing on self-conceptions. In contrast, other attitudes and values are activated only by certain relevant objects and situations and are otherwise not activated.

Since the total belief system is a functionally interconnected system, a change in any part of it should affect other parts and should moreover affect behavior. The more central the part affected by an induced change, the more enduring and far-reaching should be its effects, not only on other parts of the cognitive system but also on behavior. Thus, an induced change in self-conceptions, which is claimed to take place as a result of various experiences such as therapy, religious conversion, hypnosis, psychedelic drugs, surgical intervention, thought control, and brain-washing, should lead to changes in terminal and instrumental values, in functionally related attitudes, and in behavior. An induced change in a particular terminal value should lead to systematic changes in other terminal values in the hierarchy, functionally related instrumental values, functionally related attitudes, and behavior and should ultimately affect self-conceptions as well.

A major reason social psychologists have concentrated their attention on theory and research concerning attitude change rather than value change is that they have assumed that the centrally located values are more resistant to change than attitudes. There are numerous demonstrations of attitude change in the scientific literature that can be attributed to some persuasive communication or to the fact that a person had been induced to engage in behavior discrepant with some attitude. But such changes are typically short-lived, their effects usually dissipating or decaying within a matter of hours or days. The reason attitude changes are typically short-lived is that the more central values underlying them have been left intact. The changed attitude, now more consistent with the discrepant communication or behavior, is, paradoxically, now also more inconsistent with the underlying values that have not changed. The change in attitude can, therefore, be only a short-lived change. The inconsistency between intact values and changed attitude produces tension, and to reduce tension the changed attitude typically reverts to its earlier, original position of consistency with the intact values. The decay of a changed attitude is an active process of restoring an earlier consistency between the attitude and its underlying values—a rubber band effect—and it is probably not a passive process that can be explained away as occurring because of "lack of reinforcement" or other such learning concepts. Thus, it has been found that attitudes are easier to change than values, but such changes seem theoretically doomed to an extremely short half-life because of the underlying values that remain intact.

This theory suggests, paradoxically, that under certain conditions values may be easier to change than attitudes. Values are less central than self-conceptions but more central than attitudes. If a person's values are in fact standards employed to maintain and enhance self-conceptions, then a contradiction between values and self-conceptions can be most effortlessly resolved by changing the less central values. A value that contradicts self-conceptions is more likely to undergo change than an attitude that is discrepant with persuasive communications or behavior. A value should undergo enduring change if maintenance or enhancement of self-conception is at stake, and its having undergone change should lead to systematic changes in other related cognitions within the belief system and should then culminate in behavioral change.

A MATRIX OF POSSIBLE CONTRADICTIONS
WITHIN THE TOTAL BELIEF SYSTEM

A question now arises as to how changes with the total belief system can be initiated. All contemporary theories in social psychology would probably agree that a necessary prerequisite to cognitive change is the presence of some state of imbalance within the system. A comprehensive theory of cognitive and behavioral change, one that would allow us to compare and contrast various contemporary theories of change, requires us first to identify all the parts or subsystems of the total cognitive system that could conceivably undergo change as a result of contradictions within or between subsystems. Seven such subsystems have already been identified in an earlier formulation (Rokeach, 1968b):

> It is now possible to discern the outlines of at least four separate subsystems within the value-attitude system just described, and we may concern ourselves with problems of measurement, organization, and change within any one of these subsystems considered separately. First, several beliefs may be organized together to form a single attitude focused on a specific object or situation. Second, two or more attitudes may be organized together to form a larger attitudinal system, say, a religious or political ideology. Third and fourth, two or more values may be organized together to form an instrumental or a terminal value system.
>
> This description of a person's value-attitude system is incomplete, however, unless we also represent within it at least three additional kinds of cognitions or beliefs that are continually fed into the value-attitude system, in order to provide it with the raw materials for growth and change. Coordinated with the four subsystems just mentioned there are, fifth, the cognitions a person may have about his own behavior (or commitments to behavior); sixth, the cognitions he may have about the attitudes, values, motives, and behavior of significant others; and seventh, the cognitions he may have about the behavior of physical objects. All such cognitions may be experienced by a person as being consistent or inconsistent to varying degrees with one another or with one or more of the attitudes or values within his value-attitude system (pp. 162–163).

The present formulation extends the earlier one in two main respects: (1) An eighth subsystem, cognitions about self, will now also be represented within the total belief system; (2) "Cognitions about significant others' attitudes, values, motives, or behavior" has been separated into three separate subsystems for reasons that will soon become apparent. All together, 10 subsystems are now represented within the belief system, and 55 different types of contradictions within and between subsystems are possible, as shown in Table 8.1.

The diagonals depict 10 types of possible contradictions within subsystems. Type AA, for instance, represents a contradiction between two cognitions concerning oneself; type EE represents a contradiction between two beliefs concerning a single attitude object or situation; type FF represents a contradiction between two cognitions concerning behavior. The remaining 45 types describe possible contradictions between subsystems. Type AB, for instance, represents a contradiction between a cognition about oneself and a terminal value; type EF represents a contradiction between an attitude and a cognition about a behavior one has engaged in.

With the aid of Table 8.1 it now becomes possible to identify and then compare various personality, cognitive, and behavioral theories of change for similarities and differences in conceptions and approaches they have taken to the induction of change. Psychoanalytic, rational, and reality therapies, emotional role playing and nondirective therapy, various theories of group psychotherapy, and sensitivity training all share the common objective of bringing about changes in personality or self-conceptions, but they differ in methods advocated to bring about such changes. Psychoanalysis, perhaps the earliest of all balance theories, seeks to effect personality change by giving a patient insight and by helping him work through contradictions among id, ego, and superego. Such contra-dictions can readily be represented as contradictory cognitions, for the most part unconscious, of type AA. Rational (Ellis, 1962) and reality (Glasser, 1965) therapy and emotional role playing as conceived by Janis and his co-workers (Janis and King, 1954; Janis and Gilmore, 1965; Janis and Mann, 1965; Mann, 1967; Mann and Janis, 1968) attempt to bring about change in self-conceptions by confronting a person with contradic-tions of type AF, between self-conceptions and cognitions about behavior. Nondirective therapy (Rogers, 1959) attempts to effect change in self-conceptions by confronting the client with the contradictions between the negative attitude he has about himself and the therapist's unqualified positive regard for him, type AG. Encounter groups (Burton, 1969), T groups (Campbell and Dunnette, 1968), and psychodrama (Moreno, 1946) attempt to bring about changes in personality and self-conceptions by making a person aware of discrepancies between self-conceptions and cognitions about the needs and values of other people, type AH. To perhaps a lesser extent, group psychotherapies also attempt to make a person aware of type AG contradictions—between self-conceptions and other's attitudes toward oneself.

All these theories assume, of course, that changes in personality and self-conceptions will culminate in value, attitude, and behavioral change. Whether or not this turns out to be the case, however, the main focus of the therapist's attention is on changing personality and self-conceptions and not on changing particular values, attitudes, or behavior.

In contrast to all these theories of personality and therapy, the other theories shown in Table 8.1 are more modest in aim. They are more modest in the sense that what they try to act upon is not the centrally located self-conceptions but specified behaviors, attitudes, or values. Bandura's theory of modeling and observational learning describes how a person can be induced to modify his behavior by observing the rewards accruing to others whose behavior differs from his own and then modeling his behavior after theirs in order to reap the same rewards—type FI. Behavioral change brought about in this way is assumed to generalize to other, similar behaviors, and does not concern itself with cognitive or personality change.

The remaining theories shown in Table 8.1 are cognitive theories, mainly about attitude change. They do not for the most part address themselves to problems of personality change or changes in self-concep-

TABLE 8.1 MATRIX OF CONTRADICTORY RELATIONS POSSIBLE WITHIN THE TOTAL

Organization of:	A	B	C	D
A. Cognitions about self	Psychoanalysis			
B. Terminal value system				
C. Instrumental value system				
D. Attitude system				Congruity theory Belief congruence
E. Attitude				
F. Cognitions about own behavior				
G. Cognitions about significant others' attitudes				
H. Cognitions about significant others' values or needs				
I. Cognitions about significant others' behavior				
J. Cognitions about behavior of nonsocial objects				

BELIEF SYSTEM

E	F	G	H	I	J
	Rational therapy Reality therapy Emotional role playing	Nondirective therapy	Encounter groups T-groups Psychodrama		
Cognitive-affective consistency					
	Achievement motivation				
		Balance theory			
Syllogistic analysis of attitudes	Dissonance theory Attribution theory	Communication and persuasion Innoculation theory Assimilation-Contrast theory			
				Modeling and observational learning	

tions, and their concern with behavioral change is secondary. Attitudes are, of course, theoretically assumed to be a major mediator of behavior, and consequently, attitude change is assumed to mediate behavioral change. But in actual practice researchers rarely study the effects of attitude change on behavioral change, and, as Festinger (1964) has shown, the few efforts to study these effects by and large have been unsuccessful.

The various cognitive theories differ in approaches advocated to bring about attitude change. Abelson and Rosenberg's theory of cognitive-affective consistency (1958) can be conceptualized as dealing with contradictions of type BE. Their cognitive component deals with the perceived instrumentality of an attitude object for the realization of terminal values of varying importance. Their affective component deals with favorable or unfavorable attitudes toward objects.

McClelland and Winter's theory (1969) can be conceptualized as an attempt to bring about change in the achievement motive by making a person aware of a contradiction between achievement-related instrumental values and cognitions about behavior, a type CF contradiction. Osgood and Tannenbaum's congruity theory (1955) is apparently concerned with contradictions of type DD since it makes predictions about the outcome of incongruities between two attitudes linked together by an assertion. Heider's (1958) and Newcomb's (1959) theory can be conceptualized as dealing with type DG contradictions, that is, with contradictions between an attitude system (P has attitudes toward O and X), and a cognition about a significant other's attitude (O has an attitude toward X). McGuire (1960), in his syllogistic analysis of attitude and in his research on the Socratic effect, is dealing with type EE contradictions between two beliefs concerning one attitude object. Dissonance theorists (Festinger, 1957; Brehm and Cohen, 1962; Kiesler, 1971) and attribution theorists (Jones and Davis, 1965; Bem, 1967; Kelley, 1967) all seem to be dealing with contradictions of type EF, between an attitude and a cognition about behavior. Finally, the work of Hovland and his associates (1953, 1957), Sherif and Hovland (1961), Sherif, Sherif, and Nebergall (1965), and McGuire's work on innoculation (1964) all seem to be concerned with type EG contradictions, between one's own attitude and the perceived attitude of significant others, or with the conditions under which the consequences of such contradictions can be resisted.

Even though it is unlikely that there will be complete agreement with the way all the cited theories have been located in the matrix, comparing them for similarities and differences suggests the following:

1. Theories of personality and therapy all attempt to induce enduring change by making a person aware of contradictions that chronically exist within his own belief system below the level of awareness. These contradictions directly implicate self-conceptions. Insight into these contradictions are believed to lead to changes in self-concep-

tions. Such theories further assume that a change in self-conceptions will inevitably lead to changes in values, attitudes, and behavior. Their aim is education and re-education (Lewin and Grabbe, 1946) rather than persuasion, enhancement of the self-concept rather than its maintenance, growth and self-actualization rather than the mere removal of imbalanced states.

Such theories of change have obvious limitations. Therapy is often time consuming and costly. It is extremely difficult to establish by objective procedures that one therapeutic theory approach is superior to another (Eysenck, 1961) or whether, as a result of therapy, temporary or enduring changes in personality, self-conceptions, values, attitudes, or behavior have indeed taken place. Moreover, it is difficult to determine either the direction of change or whether the insights gained by a patient or client have indeed helped him or, instead, have done more harm than good.

2. Cognitively oriented theories in social psychology have typically not concerned themselves with changes in personality or self-conceptions or values because these variables are considered to be too complex, central, or ill-defined to be subject to demonstrable change as a result of situational and experimental variation. They have instead concerned themselves mainly with the problem of organization and change in attitude, on the assumption that social attitudes are the distinctive concern of social psychology and are susceptible to change as a result of situational and experimental variation, and on the assumption that attitude change leads to behavioral change. Such changes can therefore be effected by inducing inconsistencies between two components of an attitude or between two attitudes; between attitude and behavior; or between one's own attitudes and those of significant others.

Attitude changes are, however, typically found to be short-lived rather than enduring. Such changes are expected to affect closely related attitudes but not remotely related attitudes, or behavior, values, self-conceptions, or personality. A change in attitude is explained in learning theory as a function of incentive, and in consistency theory as a restoration of a previously disrupted state of consistency. In contrast to theories of personality and therapy, cognitive theories in social psychology have not asked whether an attitude change merely restores the consistency held at an earlier level or represents a higher or lower, more or less integrated, or mature or self-actualized level of consistency.

3. The kind of change that behavioral theories are mostly concerned with is, of course, behavioral change. Traditionally, behavior theorists have rejected cognitive and personality approaches to change as mentalistic and therefore unscientific. Bandura's theory of observational learning, which is more cognitive and more socially oriented

than other behavior theories (which is why it is possible to represent it within the belief system matrix), has been demonstrated to be an effective method for bringing about behavioral change which may generalize to other, related behaviors. But the kind of change it deals with is limited to behavior. It is not held to lead to changes in attitudes, values, self-conceptions, or personality. There is, moreover, some question about the extent to which behavioral changes thus effected are situation-specific (Goranson, 1969).

That the various theories can be represented within so many different cells in the matrix shown in Table 8.1 suggests that they are not so much competing as supplementary theories. Although they are all theories of change, they differ in the kind of change focused upon—change in personality, self-conceptions, values, attitudes, or behavior. They differ in methods advocated to bring about change, in the anticipated duration of the change, in the specificity or generality of change, and in the ease or difficulty of assessing change.

None of the theories discussed can be regarded as a comprehensive theory of change. A comprehensive theory should ideally be able to address itself to the conditions that will lead to long-range as well as short-range change, behavioral change as well as cognitive change, personality change as well as cognitive and behavioral change, and a raising or lowering of self-conceptions as well as their maintenance. A major objective of this book is to build a theoretical framework that will, it is hoped, address itself to such issues, one that at least attempts to bridge the current gap between various personality, social-psychological, and behavior theories that for the most part do not speak to each other. It attempts to bridge this gap by placing a far greater emphasis on the crucial missing link, the values within a person's cognitive system that are so essential to self-conceptions on the one hand and to attitudes and behavior on the other. A glance at the matrix reveals that what has been relatively neglected thus far in the various theories of change are the contradictions that exist between two or more values and between values and self-conceptions, values and attitudes, and values and behavior. A study of such contradictions and how such contradictions are resolved should be equally relevant to theories of personality change, cognitive change, and behavior change. It is difficult to conceive of a person in therapy who does not suffer from some contradiction implicating his value system. It is also difficult to conceive of his genuinely changing as a result of therapy without that change being somehow reflected as some change in his value and attitude system.

THE NATURE OF COGNITIVE INCONSISTENCY

Contradictions probably exist, and may also be induced to exist, within all human cognitive systems. They may be consciously experienced or they may exist below the level of conscious awareness because of intellectual limitations, repression, ego defense, or a need to conform to contradictory norms or demands of society. The more a person becomes consciously aware of a contradiction and the more it implicates his self-conceptions, the greater the likelihood that it will lead to cognitive change and, as a consequence, to behavioral change.

In traditional approaches, any two cognitions that are asserted to be in an inconsistent relation—say, E and F in Table 8.1, an attitude and a cognition about behavior—are assumed to give rise to inconsistency reducing forces that should lead to change. In our theory, a contradiction within the cognitive system may be assumed to have no psychological import unless it implicates self-cognitions, in which case the inconsistency that generates a process of change is not between any two inconsistent cognitions, say, E and F in Table 8.1, but between cognitions about oneself, A, and cognitions about one's total performance, EF. More precisely, it is a contradiction between A and E or between A and F rather than a contradiction between E and F. It is what one's perceived performance in a given situation implies about self-conceptions that is crucial in determining whether a contradiction will be affectively experienced and, consequently, in determining whether it will lead to cognitive and behavioral change. Does my engaging in this particular behavior while holding this particular value or attitude imply anything about the sort of person I am? Does it imply that I am incompetent or immoral in some way? If so, then my total performance or, at least, some particular feature of my total performance is logically contradictory to my conception of myself.

Since people vary markedly in self-conceptions, an inconsistency between any two given cognitions may be motivating for one person but not for another. A professor of psychology who takes pride in his ability to be logical might be upset to discover that his students consider his lectures illogical. Such a discovery would violate his conception of himself. A minister who takes pride in his ability to be moral might not care all that much if his sermons are illogical but might care very much whether his behavior is morally compatible with the values and attitudes he espouses. Similarly, the kind of contradictions an artist might care about may be a matter of indifference to a housewife, a peasant, a hippie, a nine-year-old, a deprived person in the ghetto, or a soldier on the battlefield. Thus, there is no compelling theoretical reason why any two specified cognitions should routinely be judged inconsistent or consistent for all persons and, thus, a motivating force for change or stability.

Certain contradictions within the cognitive system are more likely than others to implicate self-conceptions and thus be more important as determinants of cognitive and behavior change. Contradictions involving values are especially likely to implicate self-conceptions, since values are employed as the standards for evaluating oneself as well as others. Contradictions involving a person's more important values should implicate self-conceptions more than those involving less important values. The more a contradiction implicates self-conceptions, the more it produces tension and, consequently, the more it should lead to efforts to reduce the tension.

A question often arises whether contradictions are logical or psychological inconsistencies. A great deal has been written on this subject and, no doubt, a great deal more will be written in the future. It will perhaps suffice to observe here that any human behavior judged by an external observer to be *psychologically* inconsistent will also turn out to be *logically* inconsistent if all related cognitions were taken into account. Henle (1962) goes a step further when she contends that all cognitions are logically consistent with one another when all of a person's unstated premises are known. Whether or not others will agree with this viewpoint, however, it is difficult to see how a contradiction between a self-conception and some other component of the belief system can be anything other than a logical contradiction. Only this type of logical contradiction is postulated to require reduction or alleviation, or to constitute pressure for cognitive and behavioral change.

SELF-DISSATISFACTION AS A DETERMINANT
OF CHANGE

John Dewey has once said that all education begins with a "felt difficulty." This "felt difficulty" is a more or less consciously experienced affective state of self-dissatisfaction, a dissatisfaction arising from some cognitive discrepancy between self-conceptions and performance in a given situation or class of situations. Does my total performance in this situation—what I said, what I did, and most important, what it signifies about myself— measure up to whatever conception I have of myself as a competent person? as a moral person? Most, if not all, activities a person engages in end, at least implicitly, with some evaluation of his performance. To the extent that a person perceives a discrepancy between self-conceptions and performance, he experiences it emotionally as a "felt difficulty" or state of self-dissatisfaction.

The more a contradiction implicates self-cognitions, the more it will be experienced as a state of self-dissatisfaction. It is such an affective experience rather than a cognitive contradiction per se that is postulated here to be the basic motivation for cognitive or behavioral change. Not all cognitive contradictions are necessarily experienced as a state of self-dissatisfaction, but only those in which and only to the extent that self-conceptions are implicated.

Once a person experiences such a state of self-dissatisfaction, he is motivated to reduce or eliminate it. To do so, he must first try to identify the source of the self-dissatisfaction. This is usually a difficult task. Sources of self-dissatisfaction typically elude identification because of their complexity and because of a need for self-deception. As a result, a great deal of trial-and-error effort is expended by human beings in unsuccessful attempts to locate sources of self-dissatisfaction.

A diffuse state of self-dissatisfaction is a common enough human experience. A person who experiences such states as anxiety, internal conflict, disaffection, self-alienation, alienation from society, or confusion over self-identity may be suffering from some affective state of self-dissatisfaction, but one too ill-defined to generate a process of cognitive or behavioral change. A person in such a state may desperately want to change but will not perceive what it is that needs changing. A person seeking therapy is, in effect, saying to the therapist that he is in some state of self-dissatisfaction arising from some contradiction implicating his conceptions of himself, but finds himself unable to put his finger on the exact nature of the contradiction. He is in effect asking the therapist to diagnose the source of his self-dissatisfaction, in, he hopes, language plain enough and specific enough to enable him to do something about it. Different therapists respond to this request for help in different ways depending on the therapeutic approach they favor. Whatever the differences in approach, they all have the common objective of locating the source of the self-dissatisfaction as clearly as possible and then removing it.

Under various conditions, a person is able consciously to identify the source of his self-dissatisfaction, sometimes correctly and perhaps more often incorrectly, by various means—trial and error, one or another degree of sudden insight, therapy, a process of education, drugs, or perhaps through religious conversion. Whether correct or incorrect, a more or less conscious identification of the components of a person's performance that contradicts self-conceptions will motivate him to remove the source of the self-dissatisfaction by modifying one or more of the components of his belief system so that all the components will become more compatible with his self-conceptions.

Cognitive and behavioral change can best be brought about if a person is able to identify the strategically located values that are inconsistent with self-conceptions. Once he is able to do so, the affective state of self-dissatisfaction will become highly specific rather than general or diffuse, and it should provide a motive for changing cognitions and behavior.

Self-dissatisfaction and Self-esteem

The concept of self-dissatisfaction is conceptually different from the concept of self-esteem. Level of self-esteem is a more or less enduring characteristic of any person. Self-satisfaction or dissatisfaction, however, is specific to a situation and will vary from one situation to another. Regardless of the general level of a person's self-esteem, he is motivated in any situation to perform no less competently and no less morally than he can, than his conception of himself, however high or low it may usually be, demands that he perform. To the extent that he meets or exceeds such expectations, he will be reasonably satisfied with himself; to the extent that he fails to do so, he will be dissatisfied with himself.

In the final analysis, self-dissatisfaction is always situationally determined. Regardless of general level of self-esteem, change should take place to the extent that the sources of situationally produced self-dissatisfaction are located and removed.

General and Specific Sources of Self-dissatisfaction

Situationally determined sources of self-dissatisfaction have both a general and a specific aspect. A person may feel dissatisfied in a general way with his performance in a situation and what it implies about him without necessarily being able to articulate to himself which aspect of his total performance he feels dissatisfied with. A person can, moreover, feel dissatisfied with specific aspects of his total performance. He may, if asked or prodded, be able to pinpoint the extent of his satisfaction or dissatisfaction with this or that feature of his total performance. The more easily a person is able to identify the specific contradictory components that lead him to be dissatisfied with himself in a particular situation, the more that identification should lead to cognitive and behavioral change.

DETERMINANTS OF SELF-DISSATISFACTION

A question may now be raised about the determinants or conditions under which a person might become dissatisfied with himself. As already suggested, feelings of self-dissatisfaction arise mainly over issues concerning morality and competence (Bramel, 1968), more or less universal human strivings that have elsewhere been identified as strivings for goodness and greatness (Rokeach, 1964). A person defines himself as incompetent in a given situation to the extent that he sees his performance to be deficient in skill, ability, intelligence, ability to appraise reality correctly, or in ability to play assigned roles in society successfully. A person defines himself as immoral to the extent that he sees himself as harming himself or others or as deficient in exercising impulse control over his thoughts or feelings.

A contradiction within one's cognitive system engages self-conceptions and thus leads to self-dissatisfaction to the extent that it implies that one is incompetent or immoral. What will you think of me, and how will I face myself, if I become aware that I espouse this and in the next breath also espouse the opposite, or if I espouse this and in the next moment do the opposite? Cognitive and behavioral change is initiated whenever such feelings are aroused, in the direction of reducing or eliminating the sources of displeasure with oneself.

In the final analysis, society and its agencies have the most say in defining general standards of competence and morality and, in particular, the conceptions that a person has about his own competence and morality. Society defines the many different ways of becoming competent and moral, rewards their positive manifestations, and punishes their negative manifestations. Society moreover defines the roles that people play, sets standards of competence and morality in playing these roles, and rewards and punishes conformity and nonconformity to such standards. A person learns to evaluate his own performance and those of others for competence and morality by social comparison processes described by various theorists (Festinger, 1954; Deutsch and Gerard, 1955; Kelley, 1952; Thibaut and Strickland, 1956; Jones and Gerard, 1967). The end result of such comparison processes is an affective state ranging along a continuum from self-satisfaction at one end to self-dissatisfaction at the other. Cognitive and behavioral change begins when a social comparison process ends in some identifiable affective state of self-dissatisfaction concerning competence or morality.

MODES OF REDUCING SELF-DISSATISFACTION

One alternative open to a person who becomes consciously aware of a cognitive contradiction implicating self-conceptions is denial or repression. This restores the contradiction to its former tenure within the cognitive system below the level of awareness. But the more clear and unambiguous one's awareness of a contradiction the more difficult it should be to ignore, deny, or re-repress it. How then can a person resolve conscious contradictions that can no longer be ignored or repressed?

At first glance, it might seem reasonable to propose, on both theoretical and intuitive grounds, that a conscious contradiction between a more central and less central cognition will be resolved by changing the less central, hence less resistant, cognition. Thus, if there is a contradiction between a value and attitude, the less central attitude should change, in a direction that will make it consistent with the value. Yet, if a value and an attitude are contradictory, the situation will lead to self-dissatisfaction only to the extent that the contradiction implicates self-conceptions. The person is motivated to remove the contradiction between the self-conception and the value or between the self-conception and the attitude rather than the contradiction between the value and the attitude. If the attitude is inconsistent with self-conception and the value is consistent, the attitude should change to become more consistent with the value. However, if it is the value that is inconsistent with self-conception and the attitude is consistent, *the value should change*, in a direction that will make it more consistent with the attitude. Thus, a contradiction between an attitude and a value will be resolved not necessarily by changing the attitude but by changing whichever one contradicts self-conceptions.

According to traditional formulations, if two cognitions are consistent with one another, no cognitive change is anticipated. In our formulation, two values or attitudes that are logically consistent may both contradict self-conceptions, in which case changes in the two consistent cognitions are expected to take place in a direction that will bring both of them more into line with self-conceptions—even if in the process the two cognitions become more inconsistent with one another.

What is crucial, then, in determining which of two cognitions will change is not so much whether the two are consistent with one another, but whether either of them is inconsistent with self-conceptions. Cognitive contradictions within the belief system, such as those mentioned above and all others represented in Table 8.1, should be resolved in accordance with a simple principle: Contradictions are resolved so that self-conceptions will, at the least, be maintained and, if at all possible, enhanced.

MAJOR DIFFERENCES BETWEEN THE PRESENT THEORY AND OTHER BALANCE THEORIES

The present approach differs in a number of theoretical and methodological respects from other contemporary approaches in social psychology. Four major conceptual differences are identified and discussed below:

1. *Conception of Inconsistency.* As already stated, a major way in which the present approach differs from other contemporary approaches in social psychology is in the fundamental conception of what it means for a person to be in a state variously described as one of imbalance, inconsistency, dissonance, or incongruity. To address themselves to such states, various contemporary theorists have typically identified two or more cognitive elements, X and Y, that are said to be in some inconsistent or imbalanced relation to one another. These cognitive elements may refer to beliefs; attitudes; values; cognitions about one's behavior; or cognitions about the values, attitudes, or behavior of significant others. Thus conceived, X and Y will vary from one situation to another and must, consequently, be assessed anew in each situation. Cognitions X and Y must first be identified, by correctly extracting them from all other cognitions that may be present in a given situation, and then assessed for extent of consistency. The extraction of X and Y is guided solely by theory and inference without benefit of independent observation and measurement.

A different conception of X and Y has been proposed here. As already stated, X refers to a cognition about oneself, and Y refers to a cognition about one's performance in a given situation. Thus, X and Y are not only defined differently but are also conceived to be invariant, thus obviating the need to identify them anew in every situation. Even if an observer were unaware of the particular situation a subject might find himself in, the observer could still ascertain by appropriate procedures the extent to which the subject is satisfied or dissatisfied with whatever his performance may have been in that situation.

Social psychologists have devoted a good deal of attention to an analysis of the meaning of psychological consistency. Many contributors to a recent book (Abelson, *et al.*, 1968), grappling with this problem, have expressed dissatisfaction with conventional formulations. An increasing number of them have attempted to arrive at some other formulation of the nature of inconsistency that includes the self-concept. In their interpersonal theory of congruency, Secord and Backman (1965), although they have not assigned to the concept of values the same status as that accorded here, have nonetheless proposed a systematic position very similar to that taken here. They too assign a central role to the self-concept, view the self as a socially defined and learned self, see the self-concept as involved in various kinds of congruency relations, and view "stability and change . . . as arising both from intra-individual processes and from forces in a sense external to interacting individuals" (p. 91). Aronson (1969) has discussed in considerable detail the role of the self-concept in dissonance theory, and Nel, Helmreich, and Aronson (1969) have perhaps come closest to the present identification of the two components that are in a contradictory relation when they write: "in the clearest experiments performed to test dissonance theory, dissonance did not arise between any two cognitions—rather, dissonance arose between a cognition about the self and a cognition about a behavior which violated this self-concept" (p. 118). The present conception differs from Nel, Helmreich, and Aronson's view in suggesting that dissonance may arise not only between a cognition about the self and a cognition about behavior, but also between a cognition about the self and any other cognition represented within the matrix shown in Table 8.1.

2. *From Attitudes to Values.*   Although the main theoretical focus in contemporary social psychology is on the concept of attitude and on theories of attitude change, the present focus is on the concept of value and on a theory of value change. This is not to suggest, however, that attitudes are no longer considered to be important as determinants of social behavior, but only that values are considerably more important. Values have more implications for self-conceptions because they are the standards employed to evaluate oneself as well as others. Moreover, values determine attitudes as well as behavior.

A shift from attitudes to values becomes scientifically possible only if clear conceptual and operational distinctions can be made between the two concepts. Despite the fact that values seem intuitively to be deeper structures than attitudes, the two concepts have typically been employed interchangeably in psychology and sociology. A clear distinction between the value and attitude concepts is as indispensable for the behavioral sciences as the distinction between genes and chromosomes is for biology and genetics.

3. *Short-term and Long-term Cognitive Change.*   A third major

difference concerns the issue of long-term and short-term change. Although most cognitive theories in social psychology turn out, upon closer scrutiny, to be theories about conditions leading to short-term change, the present theory attempts to address itself to long-term cognitive change as well. It attempts to understand better the conditions under which both kinds of change can be expected.

Another reason for the present shift of emphasis to long-term change is a methodological one. The research findings concerning short-term attitude change are often ambiguous because they are extraordinarily vulnerable to alternative interpretations. The closer a posttest following an experimental treatment, the more difficult it is to rule out alternative interpretations of findings concerning demand characteristics (Orne, 1962), evaluation apprehension (Rosenberg, 1965), or other unwanted methodological biases (Rosenthal and Rosnow, 1969). Consequently, a great deal of effort has been expended on investigating the validity of alternative interpretations and on methodological issues concerning the social psychology of the social-psychological experiment. Long-term changes are less susceptible to alternative interpretations. The more removed in time a posttest is from an experimental treatment, the more likely that the changes will be genuine ones.

4. *Behavioral Change Following Cognitive Change.*   A major reason social psychologists have long been interested in cognition is that cognition is assumed to mediate behavior, and cognitive change is assumed to mediate behavioral change. But the experimental evidence for these assumptions is still regarded to be weak (Wicker, 1969; Festinger, 1964). This state of affairs can be interpreted to mean either that attitudes are not important determinants of behavior or that our theories and methods are as yet not advanced enough to enable us to understand in what ways and under what conditions attitudes will indeed determine behavior.

The present formulation suggests that so long as the values underlying a changed attitude remain intact, there is no compelling theoretical reason why a short-term attitude change should lead to behavioral change. The forces acting upon a person not only dissipate whatever change in attitude has taken place but also maintain behavior at previous levels so that they will remain consistent with intact values. Thus, attitude change cannot theoretically be expected to lead to behavioral change. Value change, however, should lead to behavioral change.

Closely related to the four theoretical differences discussed above are two methodological differences between the present approach and other contemporary approaches in social psychology.

1. *The Measurement of Self-dissatisfaction.*   A major methodological difficulty encountered by contemporary balance theories is that a state of inconsistency cannot readily be independently ascertained. Such states are

typically attributed to persons studied by social psychologists on the basis of various theoretical considerations about human motivation. Post-experimental interviews are designed to obtain an "independent check of the experimental manipulation" rather than to obtain an independent check of whether a subject did in fact experience a state of inconsistency.

In the present formulation, a psychological state of self-dissatisfaction is posited to be the central mechanism that triggers cognitive and behavioral change. A feeling of self-satisfaction or self-dissatisfaction is a tangible enough human experience which can be routinely measured by the same procedure at the end of any experiment. Can the person tell us whether he is satisfied or dissatisfied with whatever he may have said or done or found out about himself in a particular situation? If a state of self-dissatisfaction is reported to be experienced, it can be assumed to be a manifestation of some contradiction within the total belief system, implicating self-conceptions.

This is not to suggest, however, that a person will necessarily tell himself or others the truth about whether he is satisfied or dissatisfied with himself in a given situation. He may, for example, be reluctant to admit to self-dissatisfaction for reasons of ego defense. Self-reports about states of self-satisfaction–dissatisfaction must be accepted warily just like self-reports about any other state. Their validity will depend on the methods employed to elicit them and on the conditions under which they are elicited.

2. *Method for Inducing Cognitive and Behavioral Change.*   McGuire's review of several hundred attitude change studies (1969) reveals that virtually all of them can be categorized as falling into two groups, according to the procedure employed to induce attitude change: (*a*) A person may be exposed to information about the cognitions or behavior of a significant other that is discrepant with his own cognitions or behavior. (*b*) A person may be induced to engage in behavior that is discrepant with his own cognitions.

A third method for inducing change is to expose a person to information about his own belief system, or to selected features of it, in order to make him consciously aware of certain contradictions that chronically exist within it below the level of awareness. The effects of exposing a person to information about possible contradictions within his own belief system should be similar to the effects of a medical examination that exposes a person to information about possible malfunctions in his biological system. Information about biological malfunctions, if serious enough, is often sufficient by itself and without benefit of additional persuasion to motivate changes in cognitions and behavior that will reduce the biological imbalance. For instance, a person may, as a result of such information, undergo surgery, move to another climate, retire before the usual retirement age, or give up smoking. Analogously, information about contradictions within one's belief system that is perceived to be incompatible with self-conceptions should motivate cognitive and behavioral change that will remove or reduce incompetent or immoral self-conceptions.

The third method for inducing change differs in certain important respects from the first two methods. Exposing a person to persuasive communications and inducing him to behave in ways inconsistent with his cognitions are persuasion- rather than education-oriented. Such exposures and inductions emphasize the discovery of principles about inducing change in arbitrarily selected attitudes rather than the discovery of principles about initiating changes in others that might facilitate their growth, self-esteem, or self-actualization. In persuasion-oriented research, the subject is merely a person who "receives the experimental manipulation." The incompleteness of social psychological theory (Argyris, 1969), the "fun-and-games" approach to experimental research that social psychologists have been accused of (Ring, 1967), and the judgment that social psychological experiments are "experiments in a vacuum" (Tajfel, 1972), are perhaps consequences of the fact that social psychology's cognitive theories of change are persuasion- rather than education-oriented. They are thus more relevant to the fields of propaganda, public opinion, communication, and advertising, and they are less relevant to the fields of education, rehabilitation, therapy, and counseling.

Although the third method can also be employed for persuasion, it is basically education-oriented. Its purpose is to induce changes that will not only alleviate self-dissatisfaction but also enhance self-conceptions and facilitate personal growth and self-actualization. It is based on an assumption that unconscious contradictions within a person's total belief system are psychologically maladaptive in the long run and consequently undesirable. It is also based on the assumption that a person who becomes consciously aware of such contradictions will often, if not always, be motivated to remove them because it violates his conception of himself as a competent and moral person who strives for yet higher levels of competence and morality. Informing a person about the relations existing within his cognitive system will serve his need to know himself, even if it hurts, in much the same way that a medical examination serves his need to know his physical state, even if it, too, hurts.

9
Procedures for Inducing and Assessing Long-term Change

In this chapter I will describe the procedures that were followed in investigating long-term changes in values, attitudes, and behavior. In view of the crucial role that the values of *equality* and *freedom* play as determinants of political attitudes, ideological predispositions, and behavior, these two terminal values were selected as the target values to be focused upon. Feedback procedures were invented to help a person become aware of possible contradictions involving his values of *equality* and *freedom* and related attitudes. More important, the feedback procedures were designed to arouse self-dissatisfaction concerning possible contradictions between these two values and related attitudes on the one hand and self-conceptions on the other.

If a person is to become conscious of certain contradictions within his own belief system, he must obviously be provided with certain information about himself. Ideally, feedback of such information should be simple and unambiguous, providing the person with nontechnical, easily understandable data about his own values and attitudes, the relations between them, and how they might reflect upon his self-conceptions. Moreover, the person's attention must somehow be directed toward contradictions that might exist within himself in a manner that would make them highly credible and that would, at the same time, minimize reactions of withdrawal, rationalization, or ego defense.

Accordingly, subjects were first given information about their own values and attitudes, followed immediately by similar information, with which they could compare themselves, concerning others. Their attention was drawn not only to comparable descriptive data concerning the values and attitudes of significant others, but also to certain relations between these values and attitudes that previously had been found in significant

235

others. They were also offered brief interpretations on these data, designed to draw attention to certain contradictions existing in significant others and, by implication, possibly within their own belief systems.

GENERAL PROCEDURE

Three experiments, to be called Experiments 1, 2, and 3, will be reported here. All three experiments were designed to induce a state of self-dissatisfaction within the subject, and the long-term cognitive and behavioral effects of such an affective state were objectively ascertained. The general procedure in the three experiments was basically the same, as described below.

The experimental subjects were first asked to rank their own terminal values. In Experiment 1, the subjects ranked 12 terminal values (Form B); in Experiments 2 and 3 they ranked 18 terminal values (Form E). They then indicated the extent of their value commitment on an eleven-point rating scale, with 1 indicating "I care very much about the order in which I ranked these values" and 11 indicating "It does not make much difference which order I put them in." They then ranked the same list of terminal values the way they thought "Michigan State University students on the average would rank them."

The experimental subjects were then shown "Table 1," giving the

TABLE 9.1 "TABLE 1" SHOWN TO EXPERIMENTAL SUBJECTS IN
EXPERIMENTS 1, 2, AND 3

Experiment 1	*Experiments 2 and 3*
Table 1: Rank order of importance to 444 Michigan State Students	*Table 1:* Rank order of importance to 298 Michigan State Students
10 A comfortable life	13 A comfortable life
2 A meaningful life	12 An exciting life
3 A world at peace	6 A sense of accomplishment
6 Equality	10 A world at peace
1 Freedom	17 A world of beauty
8 Maturity	11 Equality
11 National security	9 Family security
9 Respect for others	1 Freedom
7 Respect from others	2 Happiness
12 Salvation	8 Inner harmony
4 True friendship	5 Mature love
5 Wisdom	16 National security
	18 Pleasure
	14 Salvation
	15 Social recognition
	4 Self-respect
	7 True friendship
	3 Wisdom

comparable rankings on the 12 or 18 values that had been obtained previously for Michigan State University students. Table 9.1 shows the "Table 1" that was displayed in Experiments 1, 2, and 3.

The experimenter then drew the subject's attention particularly to the data concerning the two target values *equality* and *freedom*:

> One of the most interesting findings shown in Table 1 is that the students, on the average, felt that *Freedom* was very important—they ranked it 1; but they felt that *Equality* was considerably less important—they ranked it 6 (11, in Experiments 2 and 3).

Then, to arouse a state of self-dissatisfaction, the experimenter offered a brief interpretation of these findings:

> Apparently, Michigan State Students value *Freedom* far more highly than they value *Equality*. This suggests that MSU students in general are much more interested in their own freedom than they are in freedom for other people.

Experimental subjects were then invited to compare their own value rankings with the composite value rankings of Michigan State University students:

> Feel free to spend a few minutes comparing your own rankings on the preceding page with those of the 444 (298) students shown in Table 1.

"Table 1" was presented in order to arouse a state of self-dissatisfaction concerning a possible contradiction between self-conceptions and terminal values. Then, to arouse an additional state of self-dissatisfaction, this time concerning possible contradictions between self-conceptions and values and attitudes, the experimental subjects were asked to record their position with respect to civil rights demonstrations.

> We have one other finding which we think is unusually interesting. In order to make this finding more meaningful and relevant to you personally, you should first answer honestly the following question on civil rights: Are you sympathetic with the aims of civil rights demonstrators?

Subjects responded on a mimeographed form by checking off one of the following three options:

> ＿＿ Yes, and I have personally participated in a civil rights demonstration.
> ＿＿ Yes, but I have not participated in a civil rights demonstration.
> ＿＿ No.

The subjects were then informed that the previously tested students had been asked the identical question and, depending on which option they chose, were divided into three groups; they were then compared for *equality* and *freedom* rankings. The results were then presented to the subjects in all three experiments as "Table 2." "Table 2" displays a highly significant relation between position on civil rights demonstrations and value for *equality*, as shown in Table 9.2.

Since most persons, college students included, cannot be expected to be

TABLE 9.2 "TABLE 2" SHOWN TO EXPERIMENTAL SUBJECTS IN
EXPERIMENTS 1, 2, AND 3

Table 2: Average Rankings of *Freedom* and *Equality* by Michigan State
University Students for and against Civil Rights

		Yes, and Have Participated	Yes, but Have Not Participated	No, not Sympathetic to Civil Rights
Experiment 1	FREEDOM	1	1	2
	EQUALITY	3	6	11
	DIFFERENCE	2	5	9
Experiments 2 and 3	FREEDOM	6	1	2
	EQUALITY	5	11	17
	DIFFERENCE	+1	−10	−15

too interested in data displayed in tabular form, special pains had to be
taken to ensure that the subjects saw what the experimenter wanted them
to see. The experimenter commented in some detail about what "Table 2"
showed, as described in Appendix C.

Then again, in order to arouse a feeling of self-dissatisfaction, the
experimenter offered the following interpretation of the findings shown
in "Table 2":

> This raises the question whether those who are *against* civil rights are really
> saying that they care a great deal about *their own* freedom but are indifferent
> to other people's freedom. Those who are *for* civil rights are perhaps really
> saying they not only want freedom for themselves, but for other people too.
> What do you think?

The experimental subject was then given an opportunity to agree or
disagree with the experimenter's interpretation, using a rating scale
ranging from 1, "I agree strongly with this interpretation," to 6, "I'm not
sure," to 11, "I disagree strongly with this interpretation." He was then
once more invited to compare his own value rankings with the results
shown.

The last part of the experimental session was designed to elicit the
subjects' reactions to the experimental procedure. Various measures that
were obtained at this time are discussed below under the "measurements"
section. The experimental session lasted from 40 to 50 minutes.

It should perhaps be emphasized that all instructions and interpretations
were given in written form as well as orally, to ensure that the subjects
understood the information. The written material was incorporated into
seven pages of mimeographed materials. A copy of the mimeographed
material employed in Experiments 2 and 3 is reproduced in Appendix C

for the benefit of those who might wish to replicate our experimental procedures for research or teaching purposes. The material employed in Experiment 1 was identical, except for the fact that it was based on 12 rather than 18 values.

Experimental subjects were then dismissed with the following remarks, which were given orally:

> In closing . . . I hope that all of you learned something today about the process of learning by the Method of Active Participation. As I see it, the role of the teacher is to set the conditions for a learning experience to take place. I presented you today with some new facts. In addition, I asked each of you to think about yourself—about the things you value. One result of this may be a change in your conception of the world around you. But that is up to you. A teacher may present new facts, he may ask students to think about themselves, he may even say things that disturb them, all in an effort to arouse their interest so that they will learn and grow intellectually. But no teacher can tell students what to think or what to believe. All he can do, as I have said, is to set the conditions of learning. I have told you some things which are of deep concern to me. How you react to them is your own private business. I only hope that I have caused each of you to think seriously about your own values.
>
> Your values and what things in life are really most important to you are matters which merit serious consideration not only during your college career, but throughout your lifetime.

Control Groups

The control subjects merely filled out the first two pages of the mimeographed material. The first page gave the list of terminal values, arranged alphabetically, which they were asked to rank. They then ranked the values of the average Michigan State University student on the second page. They were not shown "Table 1," "Table 2," or the accompanying commentaries and, thus, were not given the opportunity to become aware of possible contradictions within their belief system. Attention was in no way drawn either to their own or to others' *equality-freedom* rankings. Control groups were usually finished in about 15 to 20 minutes and were dismissed with the following remarks:

> In closing . . . I hope that all of you learned something today about your own system of values. As I see it, the role of the teacher is to set the conditions for a learning experience to take place. One way we can do this is by getting people to examine what they believe or what is important to them. Your values and what things in life are really most important to you are matters which merit serious consideration not only during your college career, but throughout your lifetime.

THE THREE EXPERIMENTS

Experiments 1, 2, and 3 differed in several important respects:

1. Subjects in Experiment 1 ranked 12 terminal values, whereas subjects in Experiments 2 and 3 ranked 18 terminal values.

2. Experiment 1 included a control group and two experimental groups, to be called E_1 and E_{12}. Group E_1 was shown only "Table 1," which was designed to make the subjects conscious of contradictions between their values and self-conceptions. Group E_{12} was shown "Table 2" as well as "Table 1," the former designed to make the subjects aware of contradictions between their values and attitudes and their self-conceptions. In Experiments 2 and 3, only the second type of experimental group, E_{12}, was employed. Thus, the experimental groups in the second and third experiment are comparable to group E_{12} in the first experiment.

3. The long-term effects of the experimental treatment in Experiment 1 were determined for values and attitudes, but not for behavior. In Experiments 2 and 3, however, long-term behavioral effects were determined as well as effects on values and attitudes.

4. In Experiment 1, posttest measures of values and attitudes were obtained 3 weeks and 3 to 5 months after the experimental treatment; in Experiments 2 and 3, posttest measures of values, attitudes, and behavior were obtained 3 weeks, 3 to 5 months, 15 to 17 months, and 21 months afterward. More exact details will be presented in Chapters 10 and 11.

5. All subjects in Experiment 1 were informed of the true purpose of the experiment by means of a written report mailed to each subject after the first posttest. This report was mailed out a week or two after the first posttest, which was administered 3 weeks after the experimental treatment. The effects of this debriefing on the second posttest, given 3 to 5 months after the experimental treatment, were ascertained. In Experiments 2 and 3, debriefing occurred only after all posttests had been completed—about 22 months after the experimental treatment.

6. Finally, Experiments 2 and 3 were identical in all respects save one. Experiment 2 was conducted with entering freshmen who were uniformly interested in the social sciences, whereas subjects in Experiment 3 were entering freshmen uniformly interested in the natural sciences.

THE SUBJECTS

The subjects in all three experiments were students at Michigan State University, 97 percent of whom were white.

Experiment 1

This experiment was initiated in summer 1966 and was concluded 3 to 5 months afterward. The subjects were for the most part Michigan State University freshmen taking required core courses in Natural Science. Ten classes of varying size, ranging from 15 to 75 students, participated. Three classes were assigned to the control condition (N = 67); another three classes (N = 135) were assigned to experimental condition E_1, that is, they were shown only "Table 1"; and the remaining four classes were assigned to experimental condition E_{12} (N = 178). Our having larger sizes for the two experimental groups was deliberate, thereby enabling us to determine the amount of value and attitude change occurring in various experimental subgroups varying initially in values and attitudes. The proportion of men to women was 43 to 57 percent in the control group, 62 to 38 percent in group E_1, and 56 to 44 percent in group E_{12}.

Experiments 2 and 3

These two studies, which were carried out concurrently, were identical in all respects except for type of student sample. In fall 1967 two new residential colleges were founded at Michigan State University: James Madison College, for freshmen indicating an interest in the social sciences (Experiment 2), and Lyman Briggs College, for freshmen indicating an interest in the natural sciences (Experiment 3). The entire entering freshmen classes in the two colleges were the subjects in Experiments 2 and 3. Pretests and experimental treatments were administered in early 1968, in regularly scheduled classes ranging in size from 20 to 25. Each class was randomly assigned to a control condition (N = 99 in Experiment 2 and N = 70 in Experiment 3) or to experimental condition E_{12} (N = 98 in Experiment 2 and N = 99 in Experiment 3). Altogether, there were 11 sections that were assigned to the experimental condition and 8 to the control condition. In Experiment 2, the proportion of men to women was 49 to 51 percent for the control and also for the experimental group. In Experiment 3, the natural science college, the proportion of males was much higher—69 percent in the control group and 86 percent in the experimental group. Separate analysis by sex in Experiment 1 showed no differences on the dependent variables.

THE MEASUREMENTS

Various pretest and posttest measures were obtained for values, attitudes, and behavior; in addition, a number of other measures were obtained during the experimental session. These are all described below:

Attitudes

One week before the experimental session, the subjects filled out Likert-type questionnaires which were designed to obtain pretest measures of three attitudes: (1) equal rights for blacks, (2) equal rights for people in general, and (3) the American presence in Vietnam. All attitude items were rated on scales ranging from -5 (strongly disagree) to $+5$ (strongly agree), with the zero point excluded. Posttest measures of these attitudes were obtained in all three experiments: 3 weeks, and 3 to 5 months after the experimental treatment in Experiment 1; and 3 weeks, 3 to 5 months, and 15 to 17 months afterward in Experiments 2 and 3.

Equal Rights for Blacks.   This attitude was measured by the following five items: (1) I am in favor of open housing laws which should legally forbid discrimination against Negroes in buying or renting houses and apartments. (2) If necessary, Negro children should be "bused" to white schools to insure that they get a better education. (3) Negroes protesting discrimination are justified in using sit-in and lie-in tactics. (4) People who wish to date or marry others of a different race should have the right to do so if they wish. (5) Negroes protesting discrimination are justified in using demonstrations and picket lines as means of protest.

Equal Rights for All.   The following 10 items were used to measure attitude toward equal rights for all people: (1) The U.S. foreign aid program to help underdeveloped countries is a waste of money and should be reduced. (2) All young males should have the same chance of being drafted, and no one should be deferred. (3) Poor people should get medical aid. (4) Public schools should stop having Christmas programs because some children of minority religions feel left out. (5) Demonstrations and picketing are useful and legitimate means of political and social protest. (6) Those who truly cannot afford legal fees should be provided free legal counsel in court cases. (7) There should be more vocational retraining for the unemployed. (8) I am in favor of reapportionment to insure that every person's vote will have the same weight (one man–one vote). (9) Poor people are not getting a fair chance to obtain a college education. (10) People have a right to be homosexuals if they want to be.

Attitude Toward the U.S. Presence in Vietnam.   This attitude was measured by the following five items: (1) I approve of the way President Johnson handled the Vietnam war. (2) The United States should increase the intensity of its attacks in order to bring North Vietnam to the conference table. (3) The United States should not use napalm and should not burn villages in Vietnam. (4) The United States should withdraw completely from Vietnam now. (5) The United States should completely cease its bombing of North Vietnam.

Values

Pretest measures of terminal values were obtained immediately prior to the experimental treatment (not a week before, as was the case for the attitude measurements). Posttest measures of terminal *and* instrumental values were obtained 3 weeks and 3 to 5 months afterward in Experiment 1, and 3 weeks, 3 to 5 months, and 15 to 17 months afterward in Experiments 2 and 3.

Behavioral Measures

In Experiments 2 and 3, three behavioral measures were employed to assess the effects of the experimental treatment:

Behavioral Responses to Solicitation by the National Association for the Advancement of Colored People (NAACP). Letters of solicitation by NAACP were sent to all experimental and control subjects in Experiments 2 and 3. Each subject received a first-class, individually-typed letter on an NAACP letterhead and an envelope addressing the subject by first name, signed by the President of NAACP:

> The Lansing branch of the National Association for the Advancement of Colored People is presently engaged in a recruiting drive. Our target is the M.S.U. campus. Considerably less than 1% of the M.S.U. students are members of *any* civil rights organization. We invite you to join us in our fight for equal rights and equal opportunity for all people, especially in jobs, in education, and in housing.
>
> We are offering you a one-year membership for only $1.00. Every little bit helps to finance our struggle. Please fill out the enclosed form, and return it in the stamped envelope which we have provided.

To join, the recipient had to fill out the application blank, enclose one dollar, and drop the prestamped return envelope into a United States mailbox.

These letters were mailed 3 to 5 months after the experimental treatment, in spring 1968. A full year later, in spring 1969, 15 to 17 months since the experimental treatment, each subject received a second letter stating that "once again the Lansing branch of NAACP is engaged in a recruiting drive . . ." and again inviting the recipient to join by paying one dollar. Those who had joined the year before received a slightly different letter: "I am writing you for the purpose of asking you to renew your membership in the Lansing branch of the NAACP. . . . The cost of a membership renewal is $1.00. . . ."

The nonobtrusive NAACP solicitation was, of course, experimentally invented, and employed with the full knowledge and cooperation of the local NAACP chapter. I would like to express my appreciation to Mr. Stuart Dunnings, President in 1968 of the Lansing NAACP chapter, for his cooperation in sending out the letters of solicitation. Needless to say, NAACP kept the money but turned over to us the membership applications that had arrived in the mail in response to the solicitation.

In addition, it was possible to assess the long-term behavioral effects of the experimental treatment by taking advantage of two unanticipated natural events:

Majoring in Ethnic Core Program. Subjects in Experiment 2, who were all students in the social science residential college, were requested five months after the experimental treatment to declare a major in one of the following five "core" areas: (1) ethnic and religious intergroup relations, (2) international relations, (3) justice, morality, and constitutional democracy, (4) socieconomic regulatory and welfare policy problems, or (5) urban community policy problems. Knowledge of this request did not reach us until two years had elapsed following the experimental treatment. At that time, we ascertained the number of experimental and control subjects in Experiment 2 who had declared majors in the various "core" areas five months after the experimental treatment, and we furthermore ascertained the number officially enrolled in the five core areas in September 1969, 21 months after the experimental treatment.

Changes in Academic Career. Finally, experimental and control subjects in Experiments 2 and 3 were compared for frequency of dropout from school and change to other academic curricula in the year and a half following the experimental treatment.

For the sake of completeness it should be reported that other behavioral measures were also tried out but were not considered adequate for various reasons: (1) A membership solicitation from the American Civil Liberties Union; (2) Participation in the door-to-door primary Wisconsin campaign of Eugene McCarthy in 1968; (3) Signing an open housing petition; and (4) participation in a five-mile open housing march from the East Lansing campus to the Capital Building in Lansing. The ACLU solicitation yielded very few responses and could therefore not be analyzed for statistical significance. Behaviors (2), (3), and (4) were confounded by other variables, most particularly by the influence of friends who had also participated or had not participated, etc. Experimental subjects generally participated more in these activities than control subjects, but the differences can only be said to represent trends. They were not statistically significant.

Reactions to the Experimental Situation

As already indicated in the "general procedure" section, several measures were obtained during the experimental session that were designed to assess: (1) value commitment, (2) perceived values of Michigan State University students, and (3) extent of agreement with the experimenter's interpretation. Several additional measures of reactions to the experimental treatment were obtained at the end of the session:

General Measure of Self-dissatisfaction. Experimental subjects (but not control subjects) reported their general feeling of self-dissatisfaction by responding to the question: "Right now, how satisfied do you feel about the way you have ranked the 12 (18) values?" The subjects rated themselves on an eleven-point scale, with 1 signifying "extremely satisfied" and 11 signifying "extremely dissatisfied."

Specific Measures of Self-dissatisfaction. All subjects were also asked to report their feelings of self-dissatisfaction with their rankings of each value—12 values in Experiment 1, and 18 in Experiments 2 and 3:

> Now look again for a moment at your own rankings on the first page. Which rankings do you now feel satisfied or dissatisfied with? (Please indicate whether you now feel satisfied or dissatisfied for each one, by a check mark or an X).

The subjects then checked "I am satisfied with my ranking of" or "I am dissatisfied with my ranking of" each one of the terminal values.

Hypocrisy. At the end of the experimental session the subjects in Experiments 2 and 3 (but not in Experiment 1) rated themselves on an eleven-point rating scale in response to the question: "Do you feel that your responses were somewhat hypocritical?" with 1 indicating "Yes, very hypocritical" and 11 indicating "No, not at all hypocritical."

Perceived Validity of Data. Experimental subjects in all three experiments responded with a "yes" or "no" to the question: "In your own opinion, do you think that the Michigan State findings I have described to you are scientifically valid?"

Ego-involvement. The subjects also rated, on eleven-point scales, the extent to which they found the experimental materials "thought provoking" and the extent to which the experimental materials would lead them "to do some more thinking about your own values." Responses to these two rating scales were assumed to be an index of ego-involvement.

Recall of "Table 1" and "Table 2"

In Experiment 1 only, measures of recall were obtained during the first posttest, three weeks after the experimental treatment. Experimental group E_1 was asked to reproduce the rankings shown in "Table 1." Experimental group E_{12} was asked, in addition, to reproduce the numbers shown in "Table 2." In both instances, the subjects were given the tables exactly as before, except for the fact that the numbers were missing. They filled in the numbers from memory and were encouraged to guess if necessary.

Dogmatism

In Experiment 1 only, all subjects filled out the short form of the Dogmatism Scale (Troldahl and Powell, 1965) during the pretest session that had been scheduled seven days before the experimental session.

10
Long-term Value and Attitude Change

To be reported in this chapter are the changes in values and attitudes that were observed 3 weeks, 3 to 5 months, and 15 to 17 months after the experimental subjects had received feedback about their own and others' values and attitudes. Findings concerning behavioral change will be reported in Chapter 11, and those concerning the process of change will be reported in Chapter 12.

A number of testable hypotheses can be derived from the theory presented in Chapter 8. Experimental groups, given feedback concerning their own and others' values and attitudes, are more likely to become aware of contradictions within themselves and should, therefore, undergo systematic long-term changes in values and attitudes, in a direction designed to reduce or eliminate such contradictions. Control groups, receiving no such feedback, should have no reason to undergo cognitive change.

Our theory allows us, moreover, to specify in considerably greater detail what should happen as a result of the experimental treatment. Feedback about one's own and others' values and attitudes should lead experimental subjects but not control subjects to (1) increase significantly their regard for *equality* and *freedom*, (2) exhibit systematic changes in other values within their terminal value system, (3) exhibit greater change in the value system considered as a whole, and (4) exhibit greater change in value-related attitudes. Moreover, (5) value change should be followed by attitude and behavioral change.

Not all subjects are, however, expected to manifest long-term value and attitude change as a result of the experimental treatment. The experimental subjects should exhibit different degrees of value and attitude change, depending on the extent to which their values or attitudes contradict their self-conceptions. Thus, experimental subjects who initially place a relatively

248

high value on *equality* and *freedom* should have less reason to modify these values since their value positions are less likely to contradict self-conceptions. On the other hand, experimental subjects who place a lower value on *equality*, *freedom*, or both should, upon becoming conscious of their value positions, perceive them as contradicting their conceptions of themselves as fair-minded, unselfish, tolerant, compassionate, or non-hypocritical persons—self-conceptions which, it is reasonable to assume, all or at least most of our subjects possessed. They should consequently show larger and more enduring increases in one, or the other, or both values. Similarly, experimental subjects who discover that they care a good deal for *equality* and civil rights for blacks should have little or no reason to alter their value or attitude positions. But experimental sub-groups that place a lower value on one, or the other, or both are more likely to perceive such value or attitude positions as contradicting self-conceptions, regardless of whether their value and attitude positions are logically consistent with one another. They should, consequently, undergo more enduring long-term change, in whichever cognitive components are seen as contradicting self-conceptions, in a direction that would reduce or eliminate such contradictions.

Finally, experimental group E_{12} in Experiment 1 is expected to show larger experimental effects than experimental group E_1, since experimental group E_{12} had been shown "Table 2" as well as "Table 1." Experimental group E_{12}, exposed to information of Type BE as well as Type BB (Table 8.1), had been put into a position of being able to discover possible contradictions between self-conceptions and attitudes as well as between self-conceptions and values. Such a double exposure should lead more E_{12} subjects to become dissatisfied with themselves than E_1 subjects. The former should consequently show greater experimental effects than the latter.

PRETEST COMPARISONS OF EXPERIMENTAL AND CONTROL GROUPS

Before considering the effects of the experimental treatment, it is first necessary to assure ourselves that the experimental and control groups did not differ initially in their values or attitudes. The findings are shown in Table 10.1.

Consider first the findings of Experiments 2 and 3. No significant pretest differences between experimental and control groups are evident for *equality* or *freedom* or for any of the three attitudes—toward blacks, toward all people, or toward Vietnam. Additional analyses reveal that these experimental and control groups did not differ significantly either on the remaining 16 terminal values.

Three significant pretest differences are, however, evident in Experiment 1. The control group, for some unexplained reason, had ranked *equality*

TABLE 10.1 PRETEST MEANS ON VALUES FOR EQUALITY AND FREEDOM AND ATTITUDES FOR EXPERIMENTAL AND CONTROL GROUPS IN THREE EXPERIMENTS[a]

	Experiment 1				Experiment 2 (Madison)			Experiment 3 (Briggs)		
	Control	Group E_1	Group E_{12}	p*	Control	Experimental	p	Control	Experimental	p
N =	67	135	178		99	32		70	99	
Equality	6.13	6.93	7.46	<.01	7.61	7.88	n.s.	9.67	10.65	n.s.
Freedom	3.69	4.03	4.07	n.s.	5.76	4.96	n.s.	5.71	6.61	n.s.
Attitude toward blacks	37.25	32.31	32.52	<.01	39.21	39.33	n.s.	33.55	33.76	n.s.
Attitude toward all	68.69	67.16	65.97	n.s.	67.07	67.16	n.s.	61.91	61.79	n.s.
Vietnam	24.22	20.47	23.35	<.05	24.92	25.64	n.s.	23.51	21.35	n.s.

* Obtained by analysis of variance.

[a] *Explanatory note concerning N's.* In Experiment 1, subjects were defined as control or experimental subjects providing they (a) had been present for the experimental session which included the value pretest and (b) had been present for the attitude pretest and (c) had returned one or both posttest questionnaires and had (d) completed all value and attitude tests. Approximately equal numbers of experimental and control subjects, not meeting these criteria, were discarded. In Experiments 2 and 3, because of smaller numbers of cases to start with, a less rigorous definition was employed: Subjects were defined as control or experimental subjects providing they had been present for (a) the experimental session and (b) for one or more of the three posttests. Thus, not all experimental and control subjects were necessarily present for the attitude pretest nor did they necessarily fill out all the attitude tests. All comparisons were made for whatever N's were available. For the three attitude measures shown in Table 10.1, the N's for the control group in Experiment 2 are 66, 62, and 60, respectively, and the N's for the experimental group are 69, 67, and 67, respectively. The comparable N's for Experiment 3 are 42, 42, and 43, respectively, for the control group and 71, 66, and 69, respectively, for the experimental group.

initially higher than experimental group E_1 or E_{12} and had also scored more liberally with respect to attitudes toward blacks and Vietnam. To overcome this initial noncomparability, 47 of the 67 control subjects were matched in values and attitudes with experimental groups E_1 and E_{12} so that they no longer differed. These 47 control subjects were then compared with the two experimental groups for magnitude of pretest-to-posttest value and attitude change following the experimental treatment. This matching procedure was necessarily only in Experiment 1, since the experimental and control subjects in Experiments 2 and 3 did not differ initially in values or attitudes. It should perhaps also be pointed out that this matching procedure was unnecessary when posttest comparisons of experimental and control groups were made, since the groups were equated for initial position by analysis of covariance.

LONG-TERM CHANGES IN EQUALITY AND FREEDOM

Tables 10.2 and 10.3 show the experimental effects on *equality* and *freedom* rankings for the control and experimental groups in all three experiments. They also show the experimental effects obtained for the remaining terminal values, which will be discussed in the next section. In examining these two tables, we will first pay attention to the consistency of the value changes obtained across all three experiments, then to the significance levels obtained for pretest-to-posttest changes in the experimental and control groups considered separately and, finally, to the significance levels obtained for posttest-only comparisons between the experimental and control groups, determined by analysis of covariance. The latter, shown in parentheses in Table 10.2 and 10.3 following the data on pretest-to-posttest change, are generally regarded as more sensitive tests of the effects of the experimental treatments (Campbell and Stanley, 1963; Cronbach and Furby, 1970).

Tables 10.2 and 10.3 show that all experimental groups increased their *equality* and *freedom* rankings from pretest to posttest to a greater extent than did their respective control groups. These results are remarkably consistent from experiment to experiment and from posttest to posttest. Moreover, all the pretest-to-posttest increases in *equality* are statistically significant and, with one exception, all the pretest-to-posttest *freedom* increases are also significant. In contrast, not one of the control groups shows significant pretest-to-posttest increases in *equality* or *freedom*. In fact, in Experiment 1, the control group had significantly decreased its *freedom* ranking from the pretest to the second posttest. This decrease cannot be explained except as having arisen by chance.

Finally, the posttest only comparisons between the experimental and their respective control groups are on the whole consistent with the pretest-to-posttest comparisons. The posttest differences in *equality*

TABLE 10.2   MEAN CHANGES IN VALUES FOR CONTROL AND
EXPERIMENTAL GROUPS 3 WEEKS AND 3 TO 5 MONTHS LATER:
EXPERIMENT 1

		Experimental Group E_1	Experimental Group E_{12}	Control Group
		$N =$		
	3 wks	135	178	47
	3 mos	93	120	32
Equality	3 wks	1.47‡ (.11)	1.72‡ (.09)	.79
	3 mos	1.47‡ (.06)	1.68‡ (.04)	.44
Freedom	3 wks	.78† (.005)	.70‡ (.002)	− .47
	3 mos	.48 (.008)	.46* (.002)	−1.19†
A comfortable life	3 wks	− .48*	− .34	.17
	3 mos	− .57	− .61*	.09
A meaningful life	3 wks	− .39	− .29	− .23
	3 mos	− .44 (.10)	− .20 (.05)	.25
A world at peace	3 wks	.61*	.18	.34
	3 mos	.62*	.30	.19
Maturity	3 wks	− .10	− .13	− .04
	3 mos	− .10 (.008)	− .17 (.02)	1.16
National security	3 wks	.41	.55†	.36
	3 mos	.65	.54*	.31
Respect for others	3 wks	.16	− .11	.11
	3 mos	− .03 (.06)	.33	.75
Respect from others	3 wks	− .09	− .11	.13
	3 mos	− .52	.14	.03
Salvation	3 wks	− .21	− .48†	.15
	3 mos	− .27	− .53*	.09
True friendship	3 wks	−1.06‡	−1.05‡	− .83*
	3 mos	− .52*	−1.12‡	− .72
Wisdom	3 wks	− .99‡	− .61†	− .55
	3 mos	− .72*	− .90†	− .28

* $p < .05$.
† $p < .01$.
‡ $p < .001$.
t test for correlated measures employed in pretest-to-posttest comparisons; shown in
parentheses are significance levels for posttest comparisons between experimental and
control group, obtained by analysis of covariance.

rankings are statistically significant or nearly significant for groups E_1 and
E_{12} in Experiment 1 for both posttests. (If one-tailed significance tests are
preferred, on the ground that direction of change was predicted in advance,
the significance levels shown in Table 10.2 should be halved.) These same
differences are, moreover, statistically significant for all three posttests

TABLE 10.3   MEAN CHANGES IN VALUES FOR CONTROL AND EXPERIMENTAL GROUPS 3 WEEKS, 3 TO 5 MONTHS, AND 15 TO 17 MONTHS LATER: EXPERIMENTS 2 AND 3

		Experiment 2 (Madison)		Experiment 3 (Briggs)	
		Experimental Group	Control Group	Experimental Group	Control Group
	3 wks	77	77	76	52
	3 mos	44	63	65	45
	15 mos	49	64	66	39
Equality	3 wks	1.43‡ (.005)	.10	2.45§	1.10
	3 mos	2.84‡ (.01)	.98	3.46§ (.001)	.07
	15 mos	2.67§ (.001)	.53	2.68§ (.02)	− .03
Freedom	3 wks	1.21† (.01)	.53	1.99‡ (.07)	− .04
	3 mos	1.14*	.84	1.40†	− .24
	15 mos	1.02*	.48	2.02† (.09)	− .21
A comfortable life	3 wks	− .97*	.25	−1.68†	− .33
	3 mos	.07	− .27	−2.48§	− .56
	15 mos	− .92	− .50	−2.71§	− .56
An exciting life	3 wks	− .49	.75	− .47	.42
	3 mos	−1.70*	− .43	− .65	.16
	15 mos	− .96	.16	− .80 (.05)	.92
A sense of accomplishment	3 wks	− .90	− .44	− .58	− .50
	3 mos	− .67 (.06)	− .22	− .68	− .44
	15 mos	− .45	− .30	.09	− .33
A world at peace	3 wks	.13	.06	.16	.50
	3 mos	.41	.37	1.25*	.38
	15 mos	1.36*	1.34	.88	− .11
A world of beauty	3 wks	.87	.55	.34	.73
	3 mos	.59	.24	− .26	− .02
	15 mos	.40	.27	− .14	− .18
Family security	3 wks	− .26	− .45	− .05	− .62
	3 mos	− .18	− .05	− .40 (.08)	− .04
	15 mos	.78 (.06)	−1.05	.17	− .15
Happiness	3 wks	− .42	− .58	.49	.33
	3 mos	− .64	− .71	.23	− .33
	15 mos	−2.04† (.005)	.41	−1.17	− .38
Inner harmony	3 wks	.96*	.81	.30	1.56*
	3 mos	.98 (.09)	.63	.42	.71
	15 mos	1.31	2.25†	.53	.79
Mature love	3 wks	.09	− .08	.34	.35
	3 mos	− .45	.03	.58	.91*
	15 mos	.18	.22	1.32†	1.15*
National security	3 wks	.78	− .34	.39 (.08)	.55
	3 mos	1.48*	.71	.52	.02
	15 mos	1.18	− .17	− .33	.03

TABLE 10.3 (Continued)

| | | Experiment 2 (Madison) | | Experiment 3 (Briggs) | |
		Experimental Group	Control Group	Experimental Group	Control Group
	3 wks	77	77	76	52
	3 mos	44	63	65	45
	15 mos	49	64	66	39
Pleasure	3 wks	.78	.35	− .18	− .49
	3 mos	.16	− .75	.48	.38
	15 mos	−1.14 (.05)	.50	− .52	− .21
Salvation	3 wks	−1.21‡	− .95*	−1.20†	− .98*
	3 mos	−1.29‡	−1.83‡	−1.28*	− .58
	15 mos	−1.02* (.05)	−2.88§	−2.38‡	−1.15
Self-respect	3 wks	.22	.04	− .36	− .71
	3 mos	−1.00 (.01)	.44	−1.31*	.04
	15 mos	.16	− .42	.06	.36
Social recognition	3 wks	−1.00*	− .52	−1.03*	−1.35*
	3 mos	− .73 (.07)	.29	− .54	.31
	15 mos	− .38	− .95*	.06	.36
True friendship	3 wks	− .95* (.09)	− .06	− .76	− .41
	3 mos	−1.00	−1.37†	.18	− .38
	15 mos	−2.20‡ (.02)	− .33	.17	.67
Wisdom	3 wks	− .27	− .01	− .13	−1.24*
	3 mos	.18 (.09)	1.08*	.34	− .38
	15 mos	.02	.50	.21	− .87

* $p < .05$.
† $p < .01$.
‡ $p < .001$.
§ $p < .0001$.
t test for correlated measures employed in pretest-to-posttest comparisons; shown in parentheses are significance levels for posttest comparisons between experimental and control group, obtained by analysis of covariance.

in Experiment 2, and for the last two posttests in Experiment 3. As for *freedom*, it is seen that both of the posttest differences between experimental group E_1 and the control group, and also between experimental group E_{12} and the control group, are highly significant. This is also the case in Experiment 2 for the first posttest comparison. Finally, in Experiment 3, two of the three posttest differences between experimental and control groups are significant, at least beyond the .09 level (at least beyond the .05 level, if one-tailed significance tests are preferred).

Taking into account the consistency of findings from experiment to experiment, from the pretest-to-posttest comparisons, and from the posttest-only comparisons, it seems reasonable to conclude that as a result of the treatments, the various experimental groups had undergone long-term increases in the importance they attached to the two political values *equality* and *freedom.*

It will be noticed, however, that the increases in *freedom* rankings in all experimental groups are without exception smaller than the *equality* increases. Moreover, the *freedom* increases typically dissipated somewhat with successive posttests. No such dissipation is apparent for the *equality* changes.

The fact that these *equality* increases were uniformly greater than the *freedom* increases is to be expected. As may be seen in Table 10.1, *freedom* is typically ranked higher than *equality* to begin with, not only in all the samples presently under consideration but also, as previously shown, in the American population at large.

Finally, a comment is in order about the *equality* and *freedom* increases found for experimental groups E_1 and E_{12} in Experiment 1. While these increases were rather sizeable for both experimental groups, they are of about the same magnitude. The *equality* increases were slightly larger for group E_{12}, and the *freedom* increases were slightly larger for group E_1. These differences are, however, not significant, suggesting that the experimental effects were of about the same magnitude in both experimental groups.

Over and above the matter of magnitude of increase, it would be helpful to know the number of experimental and control subjects who had increased their rankings of *equality* and *freedom.* Across all experiments and all posttests, approximately two-thirds of the experimental subjects had increased their *equality* rankings from what it was before the experiment. In contrast, only 45 percent of the control subjects had done so, the remaining ones showing either no change or decreases in *equality* rankings. The comparable figures for *freedom* are, however, not as marked because, as previously stated, *freedom* was usually ranked higher to begin with: About 48 percent of the experimental subjects in all three experiments, compared with 40.5 percent of the control subjects, had increased their *freedom* rankings as a result of the experimental session.

LONG-TERM CHANGES IN OTHER VALUES

Since ranking procedures are ipsative, changes in *equality* and *freedom* must necessarily be accompanied by changes in remaining values. If these changes were purely random ones, they should all decrease to about the same extent as a result of increases in *equality* and *freedom.* If such an array of results were found, it would suggest that the *equality-freedom* changes in the experimental subjects did not bring about any meaningful changes in the other terminal values in the system. Moreover, it would open the door to suspicion that the *equality-freedom* changes may not be altogether genuine—a result perhaps of methodological artifacts arising from demand characteristics (Orne, 1962), or evaluation apprehension (Rosenberg, 1965), or experimenter bias (Rosenthal and Rosnow, 1969). If, however, the changes in remaining values were systematic rather than random in nature, it would be more difficult to explain the *equality-freedom* increases away on such methodological grounds, and it would suggest that the experimental treatment had led not only to changes in *equality* and *freedom* but also to a systematic reorganization of the whole terminal value system.

In Experiment 1 (Table 10.2), two other values besides *equality* and *freedom* increased consistently in both of the experimental groups, and six values decreased consistently. The two that increased—*a world at peace* and *national security*—are social values; the six that decreased consistently—*a comfortable life, a meaningful life, maturity, salvation, true friendship*, and *wisdom*—are personal values. A number of these increases and decreases are statistically significant, sometimes by pretest-to-posttest comparisons and sometimes by posttest-only comparisons. These consistent trends suggest that the experimentally induced increases in *equality* and *freedom* led to increases in certain other social values, and to decreases in certain personal values. No such systematic pattern of change is evident for the control group.

Yet, it is difficult to identify the particular social and personal values that had increased or decreased as a result of the experimental treatments. If consistency of findings is the criterion, we can identify two social values as having increased and six personal values as having decreased. If consistency of pretest-to-posttest significance levels is the criterion, then at least *true friendship* and *wisdom* can be identified as the personal values that underwent change as a result of the *equality-freedom* changes. If consistency of posttest-only significance levels is the criterion, then at least *a meaningful life* and *maturity* can be identified as the personal values undergoing systematic change. Whichever criteria one prefers to adopt, it is still possible to conclude that the remaining values within the terminal value system underwent systematic rather than purely random change.

One additional finding may be noted in Table 10.2. As was the case with the *equality* and *freedom* changes, no marked differences between experimental groups E_1 and E_{12} are apparent with respect to changes in the remaining values. Both experimental groups show changes of about the same magnitude.

The comparable findings for Experiments 2 and 3 (Table 10.3) are, however, not quite as clear as those obtained in Experiment 1, perhaps because the subjects participating in these two experiments were asked to rank 18 rather than 12 values, thus possibly diluting whatever effects the experimental treatment may have had on the remaining values. Nonetheless, certain systematic effects are still apparent. *A world at peace* and *national security*, both social values, again show consistently greater ranking increases in the two experimental groups than in the two control groups, with some of them reaching a statistical significance. On the other hand, certain personal values—*a comfortable life*, *an exciting life*, and *happiness*—usually show decreases for one or both experimental groups, with some of these also being significant, either by pretest-to-posttest or by posttest-only comparisons. These findings, when considered alongside those obtained in Experiment 1, again suggest that the remaining values in the terminal value system changed systematically rather than randomly.

LONG-TERM VALUE SYSTEM CHANGES

The experimental treatment had affected not only individual values but also the value system considered as a whole. The correlation (Pearson r) between pretest and posttest rankings can be taken as an index of change in the total value system, with smaller correlations representing greater change and larger correlations, greater stability. Table 10.4 shows the amount of value system change obtained at various posttest periods following the experimental treatment.

The terminal value system correlations usually decreased over time, in control as well as in experimental groups. This is to be expected, since the reliability or stability of any test should decline over time. In Experiments 1 and 3, however, the amount of change in the value system is significantly, or nearly significantly, greater on all posttests for the experimental than for the control groups. This was not found in Experiment 2, however, for reasons that are not altogether clear. Thus, the hypothesis that the experimental treatment led to greater value system change is confirmed in two of the three experiments.

LONG-TERM ATTITUDE CHANGE

If a person undergoes value change, it should further lead him to undergo change in associated attitudes. The attitudes should undergo change after the values change—a "sleeper" effect. Significant changes are expected in those attitudes that are functionally related to egalitarian values—in attitude toward civil rights for blacks and, more generally, in attitude toward civil rights for all. Other attitudes that are less clearly related to egalitarian values, such as attitude toward the American presence in Vietnam, should, however, show less change or no change as a result of the experimental treatment. Table 10.5 shows the mean amounts of change found in these three attitudes as a result of the experimental treatment.

Equal Rights for Blacks

"Backlash" Effects.   Three weeks after the experimental treatment, all control and experimental groups without exception showed backlash effects which are highly consistent, although not one of them is statistically significant. The fact that backlash was observed in all control as well as

TABLE 10.4   MEAN CHANGES IN TERMINAL VALUE SYSTEM FOR EXPERIMENTAL AND CONTROL GROUPS
FROM PRETEST TO 3 WEEKS, 3 TO 5 MONTHS, AND 15 TO 17 MONTHS LATER

Correlation between pretest and posttest rankings obtained at:	Experiment 1				Experiment 2 (Madison)			Experiment 3 (Briggs)		
	Control	Group E_1	Group E_{12}	$p*$	Control	Experimental	p	Control	Experimental	p
3 weeks	.74	.64	.67	.05	.69	.71	n.s.	.71	.66	.07
3 to 5 months	.69	.59	.57	.05	.67	.66	n.s.	.72	.62	.05
15 to 17 months	—	—	—	—	.58	.62	n.s.	.70	.58	.01

* Determined by analysis of variance rather than t test.

TABLE 10.5 MEAN CHANGES IN ATTITUDES FOR CONTROL AND EXPERIMENTAL GROUPS 3 WEEKS, 3 TO 5 MONTHS, AND 15 TO 17 MONTHS LATER[a]

Attitude	Experiment 1			Experiment 2 (Madison)		Experiment 3 (Briggs)	
	Group E_1	Group E_{12}	Control	Experimental	Control	Experimental	Control
Attitude toward blacks							
3 wks	-1.14	-.12	-.19	-.79	-.57	-.15	-.86
3 mos	.15	1.58*	.81	.72	.17	2.98† (.06)	.23
15 mos	—	—	—	1.87*	.55	3.44†	1.34
Attitude toward all							
3 wks	-1.34 (.02)	.48	1.21	3.09†	3.96‡	.78	2.21
3 mos	-.53	2.12*	.70	6.45‡	6.69‡	4.88†	2.51†
15 mos	—	—	—	3.00‡	2.88‡	3.49‡	2.46†
Vietnam							
3 wks	1.69† (.08)	.28	.61	.01	-1.06	-.24	.92
3 mos	.43	.44	.68	.37	2.09	2.02*	2.14
15 mos	—	—	—	-.36	.50	.44	-.24

* $p < .05$.
† $p < .01$.
‡ $p < .001$.

t test for correlated measures employed in pretest-to-posttest comparisons; shown in parentheses are significance levels for posttest comparisons between experimental and control group, obtained by analysis of covariance.

[a] *Explanatory note concerning N's.* The N's differ across attitudes and across posttests because of failure of all subjects to respond to all posttests and to all attitude questions, either in the pretest or the several posttests. In Experiment 1, the N's for attitude toward blacks and toward all are almost the same as those shown in Table 10.1 but the N's for Vietnam attitude are lower—from 76 to 91 percent of the N's shown in Table 10.1. N's for Experiments 2 and 3 vary, however, for the three attitudes and for the three posttests. In Experiment 2, the N's vary from 56 to 40 in the control group and from 57 to 32 in the experimental group. In Experiment 3, the N's for the control group vary from 39 to 24, and for the experimental group from 59 to 48.

in all experimental groups suggests that it was perhaps a result of having to respond repeatedly to a test of prejudice against blacks rather than a result of the experimental treatment itself. An alternative interpretation is that these are merely regression-toward-the-mean effects rather than backlash effects. If this were the case, we would also expect to find such an outcome in the remaining two attitudes. Inspection of Table 10.5 shows that this is not the case.

"Sleeper" Effects.   The backlash effects did not persist beyond the first posttest. In all experiments without exception, attitude toward blacks had become more favorable on the second posttest, coming 3 to 5 months after the experimental treatment and, in Experiments 2 and 3, it was even more favorable on the third posttest, coming 15 to 17 months afterward. These trends toward a more favorable attitude are just as evident in all the control groups as in all the experimental groups, even though they never reach statistical significance in the control groups. They can most reasonably be interpreted as a function of social pressures upon both control and experimental subjects from a liberal midwestern academic environment in the middle and late sixties—social pressures to reduce discrimination against blacks on university campuses and, more generally, in American society.

The consistent trends observed in the various control groups toward a more favorable racial attitude are, however, not accompanied by similar trends toward higher rankings of *equality* and *freedom* (Tables 10.2 and 10.3). Thus, the fact that these control groups manifested somewhat more tolerant racial attitudes as time went on can be interpreted as a result of compliance or identification with the academic community rather than as representing a genuinely internalized change in value orientation (Kelman, 1961). Newcomb and his co-workers (1943, 1967) have suggested that such attitude changes are often brought about by changes in reference groups and social norms, and that they will dissipate unless there is continued social support from such reference groups.

Further inspection of Table 10.5 reveals that the pretest-to-posttest changes in racial attitude are uniformly greater for all the experimental groups than for their respective control groups. In contrast to the fact that none of the pretest-to-posttest increases in any of the control groups are significant, significant changes were obtained in three of the four experimental groups. The experimental group that did not show a significant change was group E_1 in Experiment 1, suggesting that mere exposure to "Table 1" did not affect attitudes. But the remaining three experimental groups, all exposed to "Table 2" as well as to "Table 1," do show statistically significant pretest-to-posttest changes. In Experiment 1, group E_{12} had increased 1.58 units 3 to 5 months after the experimental treatment; this is significant beyond the .05 level. The findings in Experiments 2 and 3 are highly consistent with this finding: There was a reasonably steady increase in favorable racial attitude from first to last posttest. In Experiment 2, the change from pretest to third posttest (15 to 17 months later) is significant, and in Experiment 3 the changes from the pretest to the second posttest (3 to 5 months later) and also to the third posttest (15 to 17 months later) are significant. That the increases are somewhat smaller in Experiment 2 than in Experiment 3 can perhaps best be explained by noting once again that the subjects in Experiment 2 were social science students, whereas the Experiment 3 subjects were natural science students; the former had significantly higher egalitarian values and attitudes to begin with (Table 10.1).

These changes in racial attitude, which gradually became more favorable on successive posttests, and which reached statistical significance on the second or third posttest, suggest a sleeper effect—an attitude change that became larger with the passage of time.

Finally, we must consider the results of the posttest comparisons between experimental and control groups. Inspection of Table 10.5 reveals that the magnitude of posttest differences between experimental and control groups is on the whole smaller than the magnitude of pretest-to-posttest differences found for the various experimental groups. The reason these posttest differences are smaller is that all control groups had also, to some small extent, become consistently more favorable in their racial attitude because of social pressures emanating from the academic community.

A comparison of the posttest-only differences between experimental and control groups, corrected for initial position on racial attitude by analysis of covariance, revealed that all experimental groups were consistently more favorable in posttest attitude than their respective control groups. But these differences did not reach statistical significance, in marked contrast to the consistent and significant posttest differences between experimental and control groups for the two values *equality* and *freedom*. The only posttest difference that is nearly significant is the one obtained for the second posttest in Experiment 3, which is beyond the .06 level (or beyond the .03 level, if a one-tailed significance test is preferred).

How, then, are we to interpret the empirical finding that the pretest-to-posttest analyses for the various experimental groups show significant long-term changes in attitude toward blacks, whereas the posttest-only comparisons do not? In view of the fact that all the control groups also showed small, yet consistent increases in favorable attitudes toward blacks, the most reasonable interpretation is that the experimental groups (but not the control groups) had undergone significant long-term changes in racial attitude; but the magnitude of changes obtained was a joint function of the experimental treatment plus mild social pressures from the academic community demanding greater racial tolerance from all students. The extent to which this interpretation is tenable will become more apparent when we report additional findings in this and in succeeding chapters.

Generalization to Other Attitudes

Equal Rights for All. An experimental treatment that leads to an increase in value for *equality* and to more favorable attitudes toward black Americans should also lead to a more favorable attitude toward the civil rights of others who are discriminated against—other minorities, the poor, the unemployed, and homosexuals. The effects of the experimental treatment on this more general attitude are, however, more ambiguous. First, no consistent backlash effect is evident here as it was in the case of attitude toward blacks. Second, in Experiments 2 and 3, control as well as experimental groups had increased markedly and significantly from pretest-to-posttest in sympathy for the civil rights of all. These increases are evident on virtually all posttests. How can we account for these significant long-term changes in control as well as in experimental groups? One plausible explanation is that they were a result of a new protest climate that pervaded the American campus during the period of the Madison and Briggs experiments, 1968–69, which, in contrast to an earlier academic climate that had focused primarily on equal rights for blacks, now emphasized equal treatment for all, with respect to draft deferment, a student voice in academic affairs, a more humane attitude toward homosexuals, free education, medical and legal aid for the poor, and so forth.

Experiment 1, in contrast, had been conducted two years earlier, before such more extensive protests had become a dominant feature of campus life. Here, a significant increase in equal rights for all was found in experimental group E_{12}, 3 to 5 months after the experimental treatment. But once again, the control group had also increased slightly in its sympathy toward equal rights for all, and for this reason the posttest-only comparison is not significant. Thus, these findings warrant the same conclusion as before: This particular experimental group had undergone significant long-term change in its attitude concerning equal rights for all as a joint function of the experimental treatment and some social pressure from within the academic community. These findings moreover suggest that exposure to "Table 1" and "Table 2" had greater effects on attitudes than exposure to "Table 1" alone. Yet, evidence for generalization to attitudes beyond civil rights for blacks is not as strong as evidence for the other hypotheses that have been considered.

Attitude toward the American Presence In Vietnam. Since Vietnam-related attitudes are not as clearly related to the two values that had been the focus of the experimental treatment, there is little theoretical ground for expecting that it should also have been affected by the experimental treatment. The findings confirm this expectation. The data shown in Table 10.5 provide little or no evidence that the experimental treatment alone, or in combination with other factors, had stably or enduringly altered the subjects' attitude toward the American presence in Vietnam.

TEMPORAL SEQUENCE OF VALUE AND ATTITUDE CHANGE

A comparison of the value change data shown in Tables 10.2 and 10.3 with the attitude change data shown in Table 10.5 reveals that value change had clearly preceded attitude change. A similar conclusion is reached from an inspection of Table 10.7, which will be considered in greater detail in the next section. Significant value changes were found 3 weeks after the experimental treatment and persisted; they were no less evident 3 to 5 months and 15 to 17 months afterward. Significant attitude change was, however, not apparent 3 weeks after the experimental treatment, becoming apparent only 3 to 5 months afterward in Experiments 1 and 3, and 15 to 17 months afterward in Experiment 2. It would thus appear that the sleeper effect noted earlier—racial attitudes becoming more favorable over time—is, in whole or in part, dependent upon the previously induced value changes.

VALUE AND ATTITUDE CHANGES IN VARIOUS EXPERIMENTAL SUBGROUPS

The theory of cognitive change presented in Chapter 8 further enables us to predict that certain experimental subjects are likely to undergo greater change than others. A process of cognitive change is initiated not by discrepancies between two values (or between a value and attitude), but by a discrepancy between a self-conception and some other cognition that a person may have. A person who defines himself as fair-minded, democratic, tolerant, and so on will increase his regard for such values and attitudes as *equality, freedom*, and civil rights if he discovers that the positions he holds about them contradict his self-conceptions, *regardless of the internal consistency of these values or attitudes with one another*. Thus, a person who discovers that his values or attitudes are consistent with his self-conceptions would have no reason to change. But whenever a person discovers that his values or attitudes are inconsistent with self-conceptions he should undergo change in whichever values or attitudes are inconsistent with his self-conceptions, in a direction of greater compatibility with those self-conceptions.

Effects of Initial Position on Equality and Freedom

To test this hypothesis, experimental subjects were first classified as high or low on *equality* and *freedom*, depending on whether they had ranked these initially in the upper or lower half of the ranking scale. Thus, "high" and "low" were defined in Experiment 1 by rankings of 1 to 6 versus 7 to 12, and in Experiments 2 and 3 by rankings of 1 to 9 versus 10 to 18. This yielded four experimental subgroups—high on both values, high on one and low on the other, and low on both values. These four subgroups were

TABLE 10.6   MEAN CHANGES IN EQUALITY AND FREEDOM FOR FOUR
EXPERIMENTAL SUBGROUPS VARYING INITIALLY ON EQUALITY
AND FREEDOM

		Equality High Freedom High	Equality High Freedom Low	Equality Low Freedom High	Equality Low Freedom Low
				$N =$	
Experiment 1:	3 wks	55	4	52	24
(Group E_1)	3 mos	35	2	36	20
Equality	3 wks	.76*	−1.75	1.98‡	2.54‡
	3 mos	.23	−2.50	2.28‡	2.60†
Freedom	3 wks	.20	5.25†	− .21	3.50‡
	3 mos	− .26	3.00	− .53	3.35‡
				$N =$	
Experiment 1:	3 wks	61	8	78	31
(Group E_{12})	3 mos	41	7	54	18
Equality	3 wks	.31	.13	2.82‡	2.13‡
	3 mos	.37	− .43	3.42‡	1.94†
Freedom	3 wks	.33	3.63	.12	2.13‡
	3 mos	− .27	4.43*	− .39	3.11‡
				$N =$	
Experiment 2:	3 wks	49	3	16	9
(Madison)	3 mos	23	2	13	6
	15 mos	28	3	13	5
Equality	3 wks	.27	1.33	4.31§	2.67
	3 mos	.57	.00	5.61§	6.50†
	15 mos	.93*	3.00	4.69‡	7.00†
Freedom	3 wks	.04	3.00*	1.18	7.00‡
	3 mos	.04	1.00	.69	6.33†
	15 mos	.29	4.33	− .23	6.40†
				$N =$	
Experiment 3:	3 wks	27	4	25	19
(Briggs)	3 mos	24	3	21	16
	15 mos	21	4	23	17
Equality	3 wks	.22	−1.00	4.40§	3.68‡
	3 mos	1.75*	1.00	3.95†	5.44§
	15 mos	.05	2.50	3.30†	5.00‡
Freedom	3 wks	− .07	4.25	.16	6.74§
	3 mos	.04	3.33†	− .48	5.44§
	15 mos	− .14	4.00	− .57	8.12§

* $p < .05$.
† $p < .01$.
‡ $p < .001$.
§ $p < .0001$.
t test for correlated measures employed in pretest-to-posttest comparisons.

264

then compared for magnitude of pretest-to-posttest changes in *equality* and *freedom* following the experimental treatment. The findings are shown in Table 10.6.

It is worth noting that the numbers of subjects in the four subgroups are rather uneven. The *equality* high-*freedom* low subgroup is always the smallest, and the *equality* low-*freedom* low subgroup is always the next smallest. The remaining two subgroups contain considerably more subjects, with the *equality* high-*freedom* high subgroups being somewhat larger on the whole than the *equality* low-*freedom* high subgroup. These findings are consistent with those presented in Chapter 7 showing the distribution of the several *equality-freedom* orientations in adult American society and among college students. But it should be noticed that the cutoff point defining "high" and "low" in the present research is upper and lower half, compared with upper and lower third in the research discussed in Chapter 7.

In all experiments, the *equality* high-*freedom* high subgroups manifested pretest-to-posttest changes in *equality* and *freedom* that were usually small in magnitude. The *equality* increases are nevertheless consistent, and three of them (out of the ten shown across all experiments and posttests) are significant. The *freedom* changes are, however, small, inconsistent in direction, and nonsignificant. These findings suggest that even the *equality* high-*freedom* high subgroups had enduringly increased their regard for *equality* to some small extent as a result of the experimental treatment.

The *equality* high-*freedom* low subgroups, however, consistently increased their *freedom* rankings from pretest-to-posttest. Four of these increases are significant, despite the unusually small numbers of cases. In contrast, the pretest-to-posttest *equality* changes of these subgroups are small, inconsistent in direction, and never reach statistical significance.

The converse is found for the *equality* low-*freedom* high subgroups. These subgroups uniformly increased in their *equality* but not their *freedom* rankings from pretest-to-posttest. In all experiments and for all posttests the *equality* ranking increases were large, consistent, and significant, at least beyond the .01 level. This time, though, all the *freedom* changes were small, inconsistent in direction, and statistically nonsignificant.

At first glance, the findings presented thus far might be interpreted to mean that whenever there is a discrepancy between the two political values, the antidemocratic one will change to become more compatible with the democratic one. Such an interpretation will not, however, fit the findings obtained for the experimental subgroups that had ranked both values low to begin with. Although these subgroups exhibited no discrepancy in ranking the two political values (no dissonance), in experiment after experiment they increased their rankings of both values as a result of the experimental treatment. These increases were very large, consistent, and almost always significant, usually beyond the .01 level of confidence. These increases moreover persisted and often became larger as the months passed.

But note that the *equality* low-*freedom* low subgroups typically increased their *freedom* rankings even more than their *equality* rankings. In Experiment 3, to take an extreme example, the *equality* low-*freedom* low subgroup had increased their *equality* rankings an average of five units and their *freedom* rankings an average of over eight units on the third posttest. For all experimental groups considered as a whole, however, the *equality* rankings had increased more than the *freedom* rankings, as is evident in Tables 10.2 and 10.3.

In summary, certain experimental subgroups increased the importance they attached to both *equality* and *freedom*, other subgroups increased their rankings of one but not the other value, and yet other subgroups increased their value rankings either slightly or not at all. Posttest-only comparisons, between each experimental subgroup and its comparable control subgroup, are wholly consistent with the data reported here. Many of these posttest differences were statistically significant despite the small number of subjects in the various experimental and, especially, in the various control subgroups, and despite the declining numbers of subjects from posttest to succeeding posttests.

Effects of Initial Position on Value and Attitude

According to traditional formulations, if a person has two cognitions that are inconsistent, cognitive readjustments should take place so that they will become more consistent. If one of these cognitions is more important than the other, the less important one should change in a direction of greater consistency with the more important one. Thus, if one of the cognitions is a value and the other an attitude, the less central attitude should change to become more consistent with the more central value.

The present theory, however, leads us to a rather different prediction. When an attitude and value are inconsistent, cognitive change will take place in whichever one is incompatible with self-conceptions, regardless of whether it is more or less central. Thus, if it is the value rather than the attitude that is inconsistent with self-conceptions, the value should change, and if it is the attitude that is inconsistent with self-conceptions, the attitude should change. And, if both the value and attitude are inconsistent with self-conceptions, they should both undergo change in a direction that will make both of them more consistent with self-conceptions, even if, to begin with, they had both been consistent with one another.

To test these predictions, the subjects in all the experimental groups were again classified into four subgroups, this time depending on whether they had scored high or low on *equality* (as before) and whether their attitude toward blacks was favorable or unfavorable. Pro- and anti-black were defined by scores above or below the mean on the pretest measure of attitude toward blacks. The amount of change in value for *equality* and attitude toward blacks for these four subgroups is shown in Table 10.7.

The numbers of cases in the four subgroups again deserve special notice because they inform us about the proportion of students at a midwestern university whose value for *equality* and attitude toward blacks are logically consistent in their everyday life. Approximately 30 percent of all the subjects had ranked *equality* high and also had a favorable attitude toward blacks. Another 40 percent had attitudes toward blacks that are logically inconsistent with their value for *equality*, either ranking *equality* high and scoring anti-black (15 percent) or, more often, ranking *equality* low and scoring pro-black (25 percent). Finally, about 30 percent of the subjects had consistently ranked *equality* low and had also scored as anti-black. Little or no cognitive change is theoretically expected among the 30 percent of the experimental subjects who had consistently ranked *equality* highly and were pro-black in attitude. But as a result of the experimental treatment, substantial changes are expected in the remaining 70 percent of the subjects, who should be vulnerable because they had a value and attitude that either separately or together were incompatible with self-conceptions. Let us now see how these four subgroups were affected by the experimental treatment.

Effects on Subjects High on Equality and Pro-black. The subjects in the several experiments who had initially ranked *equality* high and were pro-black did not show enduring change, either in value for *equality* or in attitude toward blacks. No significant changes were evident at any time in group E_{12} in Experiment 1 or in Experiment 3. In group E_1 of Experiment 1 and again in Experiment 2, however, these subjects had manifested a significant increase in *equality* and a significant backlash in attitude toward blacks on the occasion of the first posttest. But these significant effects did not persist, being evident neither on the second nor on the third posttest. An inspection of the findings shown in Table 10.7 across all experiments reveals that subjects who had initially ranked *equality* high and were pro-black had only a slightly higher value for *equality* and about the same attitude toward blacks 15 to 17 months after the experimental treatment as they had started out with.

Effects on Subjects High on Equality and Anti-black. Consider next the value and attitude changes occurring among subjects whose anti-black attitude was inconsistent with their high value for *equality*. Subjects of this type did not consistently or enduringly change their value for *equality*, but did manifest enduring and often significant increases in favorable racial attitude. The findings are significant in group E_{12}, and in Experiment 2. Although they are not significant in group E_1 of Experiment 1 or in Experiment 3, they are in the same direction, and the most likely reason why they are not significant is the small number of cases. When the results of all the experiments are inspected visually, it seems obvious that subjects who had an initially high regard for *equality* and were at the same time anti-black had changed their antidemocratic attitude and had not changed their egalitarian values.

TABLE 10.7 MEAN CHANGES IN VALUE FOR EQUALITY AND ATTITUDE TOWARD BLACKS FOR FOUR EXPERIMENTAL SUBGROUPS VARYING INITIALLY ON THEIR VALUE ATTITUDE 3 WEEKS, 3 TO 5 MONTHS, AND 15 TO 17 MONTHS LATER

	Equality High, Pro-black		Equality High, Anti-black		Equality Low, Pro-black		Equality Low, Anti-black	
	(N)	Mean Change	(N)	Mean Change	(N)	Mean Change	(N)	Mean Change
Experiment 1:								
(Group E₁)								
Equality								
3 wks	(42)	1.17‡	(15)	− .67	(31)	2.61‡	(44)	1.86‡
3 mos	(28)	.39	(9)	− .44	(20)	2.85‡	(35)	2.20‡
Attitude								
toward blacks								
3 wks	(41)	−4.22‡	(15)	.73	(31)	− .97	(44)	.98
3 mos	(28)	−2.79	(9)	5.22	(20)	−2.30	(35)	2.60*
Experiment 1:								
(Group E₁₂)								
Equality								
3 wks	(43)	.49	(26)	− .04	(51)	3.35‡	(57)	2.04‡
3 mos	(29)	− .52	(19)	− .16	(31)	3.94‡	(40)	2.48‡
Attitude								
toward blacks								
3 wks	(43)	−1.09	(26)	3.27*	(50)	−1.88*	(57)	.61
3 mos	(29)	− .72	(19)	6.68†	(31)	− .74	(40)	2.63*
Experiment 2:								
(Madison)								
Equality								
3 wks	(25)	1.20†	(17)	− 47	(8)	5.50†	(8)	4.25*
3 mos	(13)	1.62	(8)	− .13	(6)	5.33*	(6)	6.00†
15 mos	(15)	.93	(12)	.75	(4)	3.75	(8)	6.38‡
Attitude								
toward								
blacks								
3 wks	(24)	−2.38†	(17)	− .12	(8)	− .50	(8)	2.25†
3 mos	(13)	−1.92	(8)	3.38*	(6)	− .83	(6)	4.50†
15 mos	(14)	−1.64	(12)	4.83†	(4)	−1.23	(8)	5.13†

Experiment 3:

(Briggs)								
Equality								
3 wks	(19)	.79	(7)	− .43	(15)	4.00†	(18)	2.89†
3 mos	(17)	1.35	(6)	2.83†	(12)	3.50*	(16)	3.44†
15 mos	(15)	1.33	(6)	.50	(13)	3.62*	(19)	4.84‡
Attitude toward blacks								
3 wks	(19)	− .42	(7)	1.71	(15)	−1.87	(18)	.39
3 mos	(16)	1.00	(6)	3.00	(12)	.67	(16)	6.56†
15 mos	(15)	.33	(6)	1.50	(13)	− .69	(20)	9.05‡

Experiments 2 & 3:

(Combined)								
Equality								
3 wks	(44)	1.02*	(24)	− .46	(23)	4.52‡	(26)	3.31‡
3 mos	(30)	1.47*	(14)	1.14	(18)	4.11‡	(22)	4.14‡
15 mos	(30)	1.13	(18)	.67	(17)	3.65†	(27)	5.30‡
Attitude toward blacks								
3 wks	(43)	−1.51*	(24)	.42	(23)	−1.39	(26)	.96
3 mos	(29)	− .31	(14)	3.21†	(18)	.17	(22)	6.00‡
15 mos	(29)	− .62	(18)	3.72*	(17)	− .82	(28)	7.93‡

* $p < .05$.
† $p < .01$.
‡ $p < .001$.

t test for correlated measures employed in pretest-to-posttest comparisons.

Note: *Equality* high if ranked 1 to 6 (1 to 9 in Experiments 2 and 3); *Equality* low if ranked 7 to 12 (10 to 18 in Experiments 2 and 3). High and low on attitude toward equal rights for blacks is defined as above or below group mean pretest score.

Effects on Subjects Low on Equality and Pro-black.   Findings from all experiments reveal that such persons had uniformly increased their *equality* rankings. These increases were evident 3 weeks after the experimental treatment and they persisted at about the same level 3 to 5 months and 15 to 17 months afterward. But their racial attitude did not change significantly during this period, although consistent backlash effects were evident for these subjects, especially on the first posttest. Thus, experimental subjects who were initially pro-black but cared little for *equality* had consistently changed their value but not their attitude.

Effects on Subjects Low on Equality and Anti-black.   Experimental subjects who on the pretest had ranked *equality* low and were at the same time anti-black changed both their value and their attitude. This finding was obtained in all experiments and it is a theoretically crucial one because it demonstrates that it is not the inconsistency between two cognitions—in this instance, an inconsistency between a value and attitude—that generates a process of change. An anti-black attitude is logically consistent with a low value for *equality*. Nevertheless, both the anti-black attitude and the low value for *equality* were significantly and enduringly altered during the long course of the research program. These findings suggest that the experimental treatment did not realign values with attitudes or attitudes with values, but realigned values and attitudes with self-conceptions. These findings also suggest that the single experimental session had enduringly affected those subjects whom some might call "conservative" and whom others might call "reactionary" so that they became more genuinely "liberal" in outlook; that is, they developed more egalitarian values as well as more tolerant attitudes toward blacks.

Systematic posttest-only comparisons revealed differences in value and attitude between experimental subgroups and the comparable control subgroups that, in all experiments, were wholly consistent with the findings just discussed. However, in contrast to the many *equality* differences between experimental and control subgroups reaching statistical significance, only a few of the attitude differences did so. An explanation of these discrepant findings has already been offered: The various control subgroups also showed small, consistent increases in pro-black attitudes over time which were not accompanied by parallel increases in *equality* rankings, thus resulting in consistent and often significant posttest-only *equality* differences from experiment to experiment, and in consistent, yet nonsignificant differences in racial attitude from experiment to experiment.

Summarizing all these findings, both values and attitudes were found to undergo long-term change as a result of feedback of information about one's own and others' values and attitudes in the context of an academic environment. These changes did not, however, proceed according to the simple principle of restoring consistency between two inconsistent cognitions or of changing the less important one so that it would become more consistent with the more important one. Rather, the data suggest that values and attitudes changed in a direction of greater consistency with self-conceptions. Thus, subjects who became aware that they possessed an antidemocratic value changed their antidemocratic value, and subjects who became aware that they possessed an antidemocratic attitude changed their antidemocratic attitude. Finally, subjects who became aware that they possessed both an undemocratic value and attitude changed both of them. In all instances, the law or principle that the subjects seemed to be obeying was to initiate a change or changes in a direction of greater consistency with self-conceptions.

EFFECTS OF VALUE CHANGE ON ATTITUDE CHANGE

We are not entitled to conclude from the data presented in Tables 10.2, 10.3, and 10.5 that value change leads to attitude change. All that can be reasonably concluded is that the experimental treatment, carried out in an academic context, had significant long-term effects on values and attitudes and that value change preceded attitude change. But such changes may not necessarily have occurred in the same persons. Is it not possible that some experimental subjects had undergone value change, to realign values with attitudes and that other experimental subjects had undergone attitude change, to realign attitudes with values? The data shown in Table 10.7 suggest, however, that certain subjects had undergone both value and attitude change and, moreover, that attitude change followed value change. In all experiments, those subgroups initially ranking *equality* low and having anti-black attitudes first increased their *equality* rankings significantly on the first posttest. Change in attitude toward blacks was, however, usually manifested later on, on the second posttest. Only in Experiment 2 did these subjects manifest changes in attitude as well as in value on the first posttest. But even here, attitude toward blacks became more favorable with the passage of time. Thus, the data suggest that the experimental treatment led certain subjects to first change their value for *equality*; in the same subjects, this change was followed by a change in attitude toward blacks.

The next question that concerns us is whether the experimental treatment also had long-term behavioral effects. This is the subject of the next chapter.

11
Long-term Behavioral Change

Given the present state of theory and knowledge in the behavioral sciences, it hardly seems likely that a single experimental session could have produced the extensive and long-lasting changes in values and attitudes that have been reported in the last chapter. If these are to be regarded as genuine rather than mere paper-and-pencil changes, more convincing evidence is required. The cognitive changes, if this is what, indeed, they are, should have demonstrable behavioral consequences. Accordingly, we set about in Experiments 2 and 3 to assess the long-term effects of the experimental treatment on behavior as well as on cognition.

The three kinds of behavioral effects reported in this chapter are rather far removed in time and space from the research setting and were all assessed by rather unobtrusive measures of behavior in real-life settings (Webb, et al., 1966). Subjects (1) responded to direct solicitations for membership by NAACP; (2) registered in various core courses offered by one of the two residential colleges, which included core courses in ethnic and race relations; and (3) stayed on at or resigned from their residential colleges.

BEHAVIORAL RESPONSES TO NAACP SOLICITATIONS

The First NAACP Solicitation

Three to five months after the experimental session, all control and experimental subjects in Experiments 2 and 3 received first-class, individually typed letters inviting them to join the National Association for the Advancement of Colored People. These letters were sent on NAACP stationery from its headquarters in Lansing and were signed by NAACP's president. To join, a subject filled out the application form, enclosed it

272

along with a dollar in a prestamped return envelope, and deposited it in a United States mailbox.

The number of experimental and control subjects responding to this solicitation is shown in Table 11.1. In Experiment 2, 23 subjects joined NAACP; 15 of these were experimental subjects, and 8 were control subjects. Another four wrote favorable letters asking for additional information about NAACP; three of these were experimental and one was a control subject. Thus, two-thirds of all the subjects responding to the solicitation were experimental subjects. This difference between experimental and control groups is statistically significant ($p < .05$).

In Experiment 3, 17 subjects joined NAACP. Fourteen of these were experimental subjects; only three were control subjects. Nine others wrote favorable letters; of these, seven were written by experimental and only two by control subjects. Thus, in Experiment 3 about three times as many experimental as control subjects had responded to the NAACP solicitation. This difference between experimental and control groups is also significant ($p < .01$).

Combining the findings from both experiments, 40 of the 366 subjects, or about 11 percent, had joined NAACP, and an additional 13 subjects

TABLE 11.1 NUMBER OF PERSONS RESPONDING TO FIRST NAACP SOLICITATION 3 TO 5 MONTHS AFTER EXPERIMENTAL TREATMENT

	Joined NAACP	Wrote Positive Letter Asking for More Information about NAACP	No Response	Total	χ^2	p
Experiment 2 (Madison)						
Experimental	15	3	80	98		
Control	8	1	90	99		
Total	23	4	170	197	2.84*	.05
Experiment 3 (Briggs)						
Experimental	14	7	78	99		
Control	3	2	65	70		
Total	17	9	143	169	5.20	.01
Experiments 2 and 3 Combined						
Experimental	29	10	158	167		
Control	11	3	155	199		
Total	40	13	313	366	8.82	.002

* Those writing letters were combined with NAACP joiners in calculating chi square (1 *d.f.*, one-tail test).

wrote favorable letters. All told, 53 subjects, about 14.5 percent, had responded to the NAACP solicitation. Of these 53, 39 were experimental subjects, and 14 were control subjects. Thus, almost $2\frac{1}{2}$ times as many experimental as control subjects in both experiments had responded to the solicitation. This difference is also statistically significant ($p < .002$).

Some explanation is in order about the rather high return rate to a mail solicitation. First, it was probably due to the fact that NAACP is a civil rights organization that has traditionally appealed to and welcomed white liberals. (Recall that 97 percent of all subjects were white.) Second, the high response rate was probably also affected by the assassination of Dr. Martin Luther King, which had occurred just a few weeks before the solicitation. This tragedy cannot, of course, explain the differences in response rates between experimental and control groups, since the subjects in both groups had been solicited at the same time.

The Second NAACP Solicitation

A full year later, 15 to 17 months after the experimental treatment, 323 of the 366 experimental and control subjects were still enrolled at Michigan State University. All these were again solicited by NAACP, in the same way as they had been the year before. Those who had joined the previous year were invited to renew their membership simply by paying their annual dollar dues. Responses to this second solicitation were classified as one of the following five types: (1) joined NAACP; (2) wrote positive letter asking for more information; (3) renewed membership; (4) wrote letter complaining he had joined the previous year but had not heard from NAACP all year; (5) no response. The findings are shown in Table 11.2.

This time only 25 of the 323 students still in school responded—a 7.7 percent response rate compared with the 14.5 percent response rate of the year before. For the two experiments combined, six additional students had joined NAACP—five experimental subjects and one control subject. Eleven additional subjects wrote letters asking for more information— seven experimental and four control subjects. Six students renewed their membership of the year before; half were experimental and half were control subjects. Finally, 2 students, both experimental subjects who had joined the year before, wrote indignant letters complaining that they had not heard from NAACP all year long and therefore refused to renew their membership. All together, 17 experimental subjects and 8 control subjects had responded to the second NAACP solicitation, a result that falls short of statistical significance ($\chi^2 = 1.44$, significant at about .12 level). In Experiment 2 considered alone, however, 17 subjects had responded—12 experimental and 5 control subjects. This difference is significant at the .06 confidence level ($\chi^2 = 2.49$).

Results from Both NAACP Solicitations

When the results of both solicitations were combined, we obtained the

TABLE 11.2 NUMBER OF PERSONS RESPONDING TO SECOND NAACP SOLICITATION 15 TO 17 MONTHS AFTER EXPERIMENTAL TREATMENT

	Joined NAACP	Wrote Positive Letter Asking for More Information about NAACP	Renewed Membership	NAACP Member Wrote Letter Complaining He Had Not Heard from NAACP All Year	No Response	Total	χ^2	p
Experiment 2 (Madison)								
Experimental	4	4	2	2	76	88		
Control	0	4	1	0	85	90		
Total	4	8	3	2	161	178	2.49*	.06
Experiment 3 (Briggs)								
Experimental	1	3	1	—	83	88		
Control	1	0	2	—	54	57		
Total	2	3	3	—	137	145	.07	n.s.
Experiments 2 and 3 Combined								
Experimental	5	7	3	2	159	176		
Control	1	4	3	0	139	147		
Total	6	11	6	2	298	323	1.44	n.s.

* The first four types of responses were combined in calculating χ^2 (1 $d.f.$, one-tail test).

findings shown in Table 11.3. In each of the two experiments, the response rate for experimental subjects was over 25 percent, whereas the response rate for control subjects was about 10 percent—a ratio of about $2\frac{1}{2}$ to 1. In Experiment 2, about twice as many experimental as control subjects had responded to the solicitations, and in Experiment 3 the ratio was about 3 to 1. All the differences shown in Table 11.3 are statistically significant for the two experiments considered both separately and together. The findings strongly suggest, therefore, that the experimental treatment had long-term behavioral as well as long-term cognitive effects in each of the two experiments.

TABLE 11.3 NUMBER OF PERSONS RESPONDING TO FIRST AND SECOND NAACP SOLICITATIONS

	Responded to NAACP Solicitation	No Response	Total	χ^2	p
Experiment 2 (Madison)					
Experimental	26	72	98		
Control	12†	87	99		
Total	38	159	197	5.68*	.009
Experiment 3 (Briggs)					
Experimental	25	74	99		
Control	6	64	70		
Total	31	138	169	6.54	.005
Experiments 2 and 3 Combined					
Experimental	51	146	197		
Control	18	151	169		
Total	69	297	366	12.80	.001

* One degree of freedom, one-tail test.
† One of these subjects wrote letters requesting more information in response to both NAACP solicitations, thus accounting for this N's being one less than the N's reported for the two solicitations separately.

Value Differences between Those Joining and Not Joining NAACP

Since NAACP is primarily an *equality*-oriented organization, it is reasonable to expect that those joining would differ from those not joining with respect to the value they had placed on *equality*, which should predict such behavior better than any other value. Other social values should also differentiate those who joined from those who did not join. The values differentiating NAACP joiners from nonjoiners were presented in Chapter 5, which concerns the relation between values and behavior, and so they are only briefly summarized here.

Table 5.1 shows that a total of 408 students in the residential colleges had been solicited by NAACP. Of these, 366 had participated as experimental and control subjects in Experiments 2 and 3. The remaining 42 students were not defined as subjects because they were not present either for the pretest or for the experimental session.

Of the 36 values, 10 differentiated significantly or nearly significantly between those joining and those not joining NAACP. *Equality* is the value that best differentiated between them, the difference being significant beyond the .001 level. Joiners also cared more than nonjoiners for the terminal values *a world at peace* and *a world of beauty*—both social values—and they cared less for *a comfortable life, national security,* and *pleasure.* As for the instrumental values, those joining NAACP cared significantly less about being *ambitious* and *self-controlled* and more about being *helpful* and *honest.* It would thus seem that relatively higher rankings on certain social values and relatively lower rankings on certain personal and achievement-oriented values had predisposed certain subjects to respond favorably to the NAACP solicitations. A single exception is *national security,* a social value that was ranked lower by those joining NAACP. This value is at best, however, an ethnocentric or nationalistic social value.

The findings in Table 5.1 concern all subjects who had joined or not joined NAACP. Separate comparisons of experimental and control subjects who had joined with those who had not joined yielded essentially the same results. Experimental subjects who joined NAACP differed most from experimental subjects who did not join on *equality*; control subjects who joined also differed most on *equality* from control subjects who did not join.

Pretest and Posttest Differences between
Experimental and Control Subjects
Joining NAACP

Both experimental and control subjects who joined NAACP were equally egalitarian at the time of joining, as shown in Table 11.4. They did not differ significantly in their mean posttest value levels for *equality* or *freedom,* their mean attitude toward blacks, or even with respect to other values or attitudes.

But the 32 experimental subjects who had joined NAACP manifested a significantly increased regard for *equality* between pretest and posttest. These experimental subjects had a lower regard for *equality* to begin with, but, mainly as a result of the experimental treatment, had caught up with and had even surpassed the subjects in the control group who had joined NAACP. Similar trends are evident in the *freedom* rankings, although they are not as marked. Here too we note that the experimental subjects who had joined NAACP had a lower regard for *freedom* to begin with, but had manifested an increased value for *freedom* following the experimental

TABLE 11.5   NUMBER OF STATED PREFERENCES AND ACTUAL ENROLLMENTS IN ETHNIC CORE AND OTHER PROGRAMS BY EXPERIMENTAL AND CONTROL GROUPS IN MADISON COLLEGE 5 AND 21 MONTHS AFTER EXPERIMENTAL TREATMENT

	Preferences: 5 Months Later			Enrollments: 21 Months Later		
	Ethnic Core Program	Other Core Programs	Total	Ethnic Core Program	Other Core Programs	Total
Experimental group	14	66	80	28	39	67
Control group	14	60	74	14	50	64
	n.s.			$\chi^2 = 5.12^*$, $p < .02$		

* One degree of freedom, one-tail test.

as many experimental as control subjects were enrolled in the ethnic core program 21 months after the experimental treatment—a difference that is significant beyond the .02 level of confidence. Thus, despite the absence of differences in stated preference 5 months after the experimental treatment, a long delayed behavioral "sleeper" effect became evident 21 months afterward. Since the experimental and control groups in Experiment 2 did not differ initially in their pretest values, in their attitudes, or in their interests, it can reasonably be concluded that the experimental treatment had resulted in a doubling of student enrollments in the ethnic core courses.

DROPOUTS AND TRANSFERS

That the ethnic courses offered by James Madison College had attracted significantly more experimental than control subjects suggested that the experimental treatment might also have differentially affected the subjects' academic careers in other ways. The end of the spring term in 1969 marked the end of two years of academic work by the students in the two residential colleges, and a year and a half had passed since they had participated in the experimental session. By that time approximately 33 percent of the subjects in Experiment 2 (Madison) and 44 percent of the subjects in Experiment 3 (Briggs) were no longer enrolled in their respective residential colleges. They had either dropped out of school altogether or had transferred to other curricula within the university. About as many experimental as control subjects had resigned from each of the two residential colleges, as shown in Table 11.6.

More crucial, however, is what had happened to these experimental and control subjects after they had resigned from their respective residential colleges. In the social science-oriented Madison College, just as many control as experimental subjects had transferred and had dropped out. But in the natural science-oriented Briggs College, almost two-thirds of the control subjects had dropped out of school altogether (22 out of 35) and a third had transferred (13 out of 35), compared with a third of the experimental subjects who had dropped out (14 out of 43) and two-thirds who had transferred (29 out of 43). This difference between experimental and control subjects is significant beyond the .01 level.

It would thus seem that whereas both experimental and control subjects had left the natural science-oriented Briggs College at about the same rate, considerably more of the experimental subjects had merely transferred to another curriculum, and considerably more of the control subjects had dropped out of the university altogether. No such difference between experimental and control subjects was evident in the social science-oriented Madison College, where the experimental subjects had enrolled in the ethnic core curriculum about twice as often as the control subjects.

Although the fate of those who had left the university is unknown, it was possible to trace the changes in major of the experimental and control

TABLE 11.6 NUMBER OF EXPERIMENTAL AND CONTROL SUBJECTS IN THE TWO RESIDENTIAL COLLEGES TRANSFERRING WITHIN THE UNIVERSITY AND LEAVING IT ALTOGETHER

	Experiment 2 (Madison)			Experiment 3 (Briggs)		
	Transferred	Dropped Out	Total	Transferred	Dropped Out	Total
Experimental group	19	14	33	29	14	43
Control group	20	16	36	13	22	35
Total	39	30	69	42	36	78
		n.s.			$\chi^2 = 5.96^*$, $p < .01$	

* One degree of freedom, one-tail test.

TABLE 11.7 NUMBER OF EXPERIMENTAL AND CONTROL SUBJECTS IN THE TWO RESIDENTIAL COLLEGES WHO TRANSFERRED TO A SOCIAL SCIENCE OR EDUCATION MAJOR

	Experiment 2 (Madison)			Experiment 3 (Briggs)		
	Transferred to Social Science or Education	Transferred to Other Majors	Total	Transferred to Social Science or Education	Transferred to Other Majors	Total
Experimental group	10	9	19	16	13	29
Control group	11	9	20	2	11	13
		n.s.			$\chi^2 = 4.29^*$, $p < .02$	

* One degree of freedom, one-tail test.

subjects who had transferred elsewhere within the university. These subjects were classified as having changed either to a social science or education major or to some other major which included natural science, organic and natural resources, engineering, human medicine, arts and letters, communication arts, home economics, business, and the University College. The frequency of such transfers for the experimental and control subjects of Experiments 2 and 3 is shown in Table 11.7.

Once again, no differences were found between the experimental and control subjects who had transferred out of Madison College; slightly more than half of each group had simply transferred to a social science or education major elsewhere within the university. But the results were quite different for the subjects in Briggs College. A majority of the transferring experimental subjects—16 out of 29—had transferred out of their natural science-oriented residential college in order to major in social science or education. In contrast, only 2 out of the 13 transferring control subjects had transferred to a social science or education major. This difference is significant beyond the .02 level.

Since the experimental and control groups within each of the two colleges did not differ initially with respect to their values, attitudes, or academic interests, one may conclude that the differences between them in registration figures for the ethnic courses, in dropouts and transfers, and the differences in major among those transferring elsewhere within the university must have resulted from the differences in experimental treatment that they had been exposed to.

A final bit of evidence that tends to support the above conclusion concerns the relative frequency of resignations from the two residential colleges of the 40 subjects who had joined NAACP in response to the first solicitation. These data are shown in Table 11.8. In the social science college, 19 of the 23 subjects who had joined NAACP continued on in the social science college. In the natural science college, only 6 of the 17 subjects who had joined NAACP continued on, the remaining subjects having left the college. This difference is significant beyond the .01 level.

TABLE 11.8   DROPOUTS FROM SOCIAL SCIENCE AND NATURAL SCIENCE COLLEGES BY STUDENTS JOINING NAACP

	Type of College	Still in Residential College	Left Residential College	Total	χ^2	p
Experiment 2 (Madison)	Social science	19	4	23		
					7.43*	.01
Experiment 3 (Briggs)	Natural science	6	11	17		

* One degree of freedom, one-tail test.

Presumably, the majority of the subjects from the social science college who had joined NAACP remained satisfied with their academic career and therefore stayed where they were, whereas the majority of the subjects from the natural science college who had joined NAACP became dissatisfied with their academic pursuits and therefore left their residential college.

SUMMARY

The long-term behavioral effects described in this chapter can now be summarized. Consistent with the long-term changes in values and attitudes that we reported in the preceding chapter are the following:

1. Significantly more experimental than control subjects in the social science and natural science residential college had responded favorably to the NAACP solicitations. These behavioral effects were observed 3 to 5 months after the experimental treatment. Similar effects were also observed 15 to 17 months afterward, although these data did not reach statistical significance.
2. Significantly more of the experimental than control subjects were registered in ethnic core courses in the social science-oriented Madison College 21 months after the experimental treatment.
3. Experimental and control students generally did not differ in resignation rate from their respective residential colleges; but in the natural science-oriented college, most of the resigning control subjects had dropped out of the university altogether, whereas most of the resigning experimental subjects had simply transferred elsewhere within the university.
4. After transferring out of the natural science residential college, a majority of the experimental subjects but only a minority of the control subjects had changed to a social science or education major.

12
The Process of Change

This chapter concerns the psychological processes underlying the cognitive and behavioral changes reported in Chapters 10 and 11. Data about the change process come mainly from three sources: (1) independent reports by experimental subjects about their affective states, (2) interviews with experimental and control subjects after all the posttests had been completed and (3) findings from other experiments specifically designed to answer certain questions about the process of change.

As suggested in Chapter 8, the basic mechanism that initiates a process of change is an affective state of self-dissatisfaction, which is induced when a person becomes aware of certain contradictions in his total belief system. The more such contradictions implicate self-conceptions, the more likely that they will induce self-dissatisfaction and the more likely that the ensuing changes will endure. Self-dissatisfaction will not arise if such contradictions do not exist or do not become apparent or, should they become apparent, they are denied or repressed. But if a person perceives such contradictions within himself as credible, his perception should generate self-dissatisfaction. To reduce or eliminate such self-dissatisfaction, a person will often find it necessary to realign values with self-conceptions. Value change should in turn lead to a cognitive reorganization of the remaining values in the system and changes in functionally related attitudes, and it should culminate finally in behavioral change.

EFFECTS OF CONTRADICTION ON SELF-DISSATISFACTION

These considerations lead us to expect that persons who are experimentally made aware of the fact that their value and attitudes contradict self-conceptions will more often experience self-dissatisfaction. Recall from Chapter 9 that measures of specific and general self-dissatisfaction had been obtained from experimental subjects at the end of the experimental session. They indicated whether they were "satisfied" or "dissatisfied"

286

with their rankings of each of the terminal values, and they reported the extent to which they felt generally satisfied with or hypocritical about their value rankings.

Effects of Initial Value Positions on Specific Self-dissatisfaction

Table 12.1 shows the proportion of experimental subjects varying initially in *equality* and *freedom* rankings who reported satisfaction or dissatisfaction with their rankings of these values. The data are shown for each experiment separately and for all experiments combined. "High" and "low" rankings of *equality* and *freedom* were defined as before: rankings in the top and bottom half of the value scale, which consisted of 12 values in Experiment 1, and 18 values in Experiments 2 and 3.

In every experiment, greater numbers of subjects ranking *equality* low reported dissatisfaction with their *equality* rankings, and greater numbers of subjects ranking *freedom* low reported dissatisfaction with their *freedom* rankings. In each experiment considered separately, and in all experiments combined, the differences in the expression of dissatisfaction between subjects ranking *equality* high and low and subjects ranking *freedom* high and low were uniformly significant, typically beyond the .001 level.

Experimental subgroups that had ranked both values high uniformly expressed the least dissatisfaction with their *equality* and *freedom* rankings; only about 10 percent of these subjects were dissatisfied. Subjects ranking *equality* high and *freedom* low more often expressed dissatisfaction with their *freedom* rankings, and subjects ranking *equality* low and *freedom* high more often expressed dissatisfaction with their *equality* rankings. Finally, approximately 50 percent of the subjects ranking both values low were dissatisfied with their rankings of both values.

From the standpoint of contemporary balance models, it may seem surprising to learn that subjects who had ranked both values low had uniformly expressed the most self-dissatisfaction with those rankings. Is there not as much consistency in caring little as in caring greatly for both of these values? We can understand this finding, however, if we assume that these subjects had just discovered, for perhaps the first time in their lives, that they had placed a low priority on *equality* and *freedom* notwithstanding the fact that they had, for the most part, been born, reared, and socialized within a democratic society and notwithstanding whatever conceptions they had built up of themselves as tolerant, just, fair, egalitarian, and so on.

Effects of Initial Value-Attitude Positions on Specific Self-dissatisfaction

Although there is no necessary logical connection between the two values *equality* and *freedom*, there is a logical relation between value for *equality* and attitude toward civil rights. It is therefore of some interest to see how much self-dissatisfaction was expressed with *equality* by persons scoring

TABLE 12.1   PERCENT OF EXPERIMENTAL SUBGROUPS VARYING INITIALLY ON EQUALITY AND FREEDOM EXPRESSING DISSATISFACTION WITH THEIR EQUALITY AND FREEDOM RANKINGS

	Experiment 1 Group E_1			Experiment 1 Group E_{12}			Experiment 2 (Madison)			Experiment 3 (Briggs)			All Experiments		
	(N)	Equality	Freedom	(N)	Equality	Freedom	(N)*	Equality	Freedom	(N)	Equality	Freedom	(N)	Equality	Freedom
							Percent Dissatisfied with:								
Equality high, freedom high	(55)	22	13	(61)	12	10	(55)	9	9	(37)	8	8	(208)	13	10
Equality high, freedom low	(4)	0	25	(8)	0	38	(6)	33	33	(4)	0	50	(22)	9	36
Equality low, freedom high	(52)	39	14	(78)	34	34	(26)	33	42	(36)	46	25	(192)	38	28
Equality low, freedom low	(24)	54	70	(31)	41	45	(10)	29	57	(22)	50	57	(87)	46	57

* One subject did not indicate whether he was satisfied or dissatisfied with his *equality* and *freedom* rankings.

high and low on *equality* and scoring pro- and anti-civil rights. (Measures of self-satisfaction with civil rights position were not obtained.) Table 12.2 shows the proportion of these four experimental subgroups who had reported dissatisfaction with their *equality* rankings in each experiment separately and in all experiments combined.

Half of the subjects who were low on *equality* yet pro-civil rights had expressed dissatisfaction with their *equality* rankings, which suggests that an awareness of logical inconsistency had been responsible for their self-dissatisfaction with *equality* rankings. But this interpretation loses its force somewhat when it is further noted that the next most dissatisfied subgroup is the one that had cared little for both *equality* and civil rights. Almost 30 percent of these subjects also reported dissatisfactions with their *equality* rankings, which suggests that something other than the logical relationship between *equality* and civil rights attitude had been responsible for the expressed dissatisfaction.

Effects of Initial Position on General Self-dissatisfaction and Hypocrisy

Supporting evidence about the emotional effects of awareness of initial value and attitude position comes from the subjects' reports about their general self-dissatisfaction and feelings of hypocrisy. Recall that each subject had responded to two questions at the end of the experiment: (1) "Right now, how satisfied do you feel about the way you have ranked the twelve (eighteen) values?"; (2) "Do you feel your responses were hypocritical?"

The mean ratings on general self-dissatisfaction (obtained in all three experiments) and felt hypocrisy (obtained only in Experiments 2 and 3) usually paralleled the findings on specific self-dissatisfaction. Subjects favoring *equality*, *freedom*, and civil rights typically reported the highest level of general satisfaction and the lowest degree of felt hypocrisy. On the other hand, subjects with antiegalitarian values and attitudes and subjects showing discrepancies between values and attitudes reported more general dissatisfaction and stronger feelings of hypocrisy. These findings are, however, only general trends; although consistent from experiment to experiment, they were usually not significant. Our data show that measures of specific self-dissatisfaction turned out consistently to be better predictors than measures of general self-dissatisfaction of long-term value change, as is indicated in the next two sections.

EFFECTS OF SPECIFIC SELF-DISSATISFACTION ON VALUE CHANGE

If feelings of specific self-dissatisfaction are indeed crucial to the initiation of change, then experimental subjects reporting dissatisfaction with their

TABLE 12.2   PERCENT OF EXPERIMENTAL SUBGROUPS VARYING INITIALLY ON EQUALITY AND CIVIL RIGHTS REPORTING THEMSELVES DISSATISFIED WITH THEIR EQUALITY RANKINGS

	Experiment 1 Group E_1*		Experiment 1 Group E_{12}		Experiment 2 (Madison)		Experiment 3 (Briggs)		All Experiments	
	(N)†	%	(N)	%	(N)	%	(N)	%	(N)	%
					Dissatisfied with Equality					
Equality high, pro-civil rights	(44)	25	(54)	9	(55)	11	(38)	8	(191)	13
Equality high, anti-civil rights	(15)	7	(13)	8	(6)	0	(4)	0	(38)	5
Equality low, pro-civil rights	(38)	56	(68)	51	(27)	33	(35)	50	(168)	50
Equality low, anti-civil rights	(38)	46	(35)	13	(10)	0	(22)	38	(105)	29

* These subjects were classified into the four subgroups on the basis of their pretest attitude toward blacks; others were classified on the basis of responses to the "sympathy toward civil rights demonstration" question.

† N's do not necessarily add up to the total N because some subjects failed to respond either to the "satisfied-dissatisfied" or to the civil rights question.

rankings of a particular value should exhibit more change on that value than subjects reporting satisfaction. These changes should be manifest not only for the target values *equality* and *freedom* but for all values. Whatever value positions subjects feel dissatisfied with should change in whichever direction is the more likely to reduce or eliminate such feelings. In the case of *equality* and *freedom*, the direction of change is predictable: These values should increase in importance as a result of the experimental treatment. The direction of change in the remaining values is not, however, predictable, because the experimental materials did not address themselves explicitly to these values. After comparing their own value rankings with those of others, the subjects merely reported which ones they felt "satisfied" and "dissatisfied" with. Therefore, all that can be hypothesized about the remaining values is that the absolute magnitude of change, without regard for direction, should be greater for subjects who were dissatisfied than for subjects who were satisfied with their value positions.

Effects of Self-dissatisfaction with Equality and Freedom

Table 12.3 shows the mean increases in importance placed on *equality* and *freedom* by the experimental subgroups expressing satisfaction and dissatisfaction with *equality* and *freedom* rankings in each experiment. Findings for all experiments and for all posttests are highly consistent. Self-reports of affective states of satisfaction and dissatisfaction that had been elicited at the end of the experimental session predicted the increases in *equality* and *freedom* rankings that were observed 3 weeks, 3 to 5 months, and 15 to 17 months afterward. (1) Subjects expressing satisfaction with their *equality* and *freedom* rankings changed the least on *equality* and *freedom* as compared with the other subgroups, (2) subjects satisfied with *equality* and dissatisfied with *freedom* usually changed more on *freedom*, and, conversely, (3) those dissatisfied with *equality* and satisfied with *freedom* usually changed more on *equality*. Finally (4) subjects who were dissatisfied with both of their value rankings markedly raised their rankings on both values. The increases are rather sizeable for the values that the subjects were dissatisfied with, are evident in all experiments for all posttests, and are more often than not statistically significant despite the small number of cases. In Experiment 3, for instance, subjects dissatisfied with *equality* and satisfied with *freedom* did not raise their *freedom* ranking significantly but raised their *equality* ranking a mean of 5.50 units 3 weeks after the experimental treatment. This level of increase persisted 3 to 5 months afterward, and was even greater 15 to 17 months afterward.

There is an important qualitative difference, however, between the findings for *equality* and *freedom* that should not be overlooked. Those who felt satisfied with their *freedom* rankings did not change their value for *freedom* significantly in any of the experiments, whereas those who felt dissatisfied did raise their *freedom* rankings markedly and often significant-

TABLE 12.3   MEAN CHANGES IN EQUALITY AND FREEDOM FOR
SUBJECTS SATISFIED AND DISSATISFIED WITH EQUALITY-FREEDOM
RANKINGS

		Satisfied E Satisfied F	Satisfied E Dissatisfied F	Dissatisfied E Satisfied F	Dissatisfied E Dissatisfied F
			$N =$		
Experiment 1:	3 wks	79	11	21	24
(Group E₁)	3 mos	51	11	15	16
Equality	3 wks	1.01†	1.18	2.29‡	2.42†
	3 mos	.71	2.55*	2.67*	2.06*
Freedom	3 wks	.25	2.55*	.57	1.88†
	3 mos	− .10	3.27†	− .20	1.06
			$N =$		
Experiment 1:	3 wks	108	17	24	29
(Group E₁₂)	3 mos	70	13	20	17
Equality	3 wks	1.07‡	1.59*	3.46‡	2.76‡
	3 mos	1.04†	1.77*	3.20†	2.47†
Freedom	3 wks	.44*	1.18	.08	1.90†
	3 mos	.09	2.00	− .75	2.24*
			$N =$		
Experiment 2:	3 wks	50	10	8	7
(Madison)	3 mos	25	8	5	4
	15 mos	28	7	6	7
Equality	3 wks	.66	2.00	2.50	4.14*
	3 mos	2.12†	5.63†	2.20	3.25
	15 mos	1.25*	5.86*	4.17†	4.29*
Freedom	3 wks	.38	3.70*	− .13	4.57†
	3 mos	.68	3.38	− .60	2.75
	15 mos	.50	2.43	−1.67	3.29
			$N =$		
Experiment 3:	3 wks	45	9	12	9
(Briggs)	3 mos	40	7	10	7
	15 mos	39	8	9	9
Equality	3 wks	1.31*	.33	5.50‡	6.00†
	3 mos	2.08†	5.43‡	5.50*	5.57†
	15 mos	1.41*	2.63	6.78†	3.89
Freedom	3 wks	1.31*	5.67*	− .50	4.78†
	3 mos	.75	5.43†	− .50	3.57
	15 mos	1.03	6.75†	1.78	3.11

* $p < .05.$
† $p < .01.$
‡ $p < .001.$
t test for correlated measures.

ly. In the case of *equality*, however, usually significant increases in ranking levels were obtained not only for those who were dissatisfied but also for those who were satisfied, suggesting perhaps that even subjects who had expressed satisfaction with their *equality* positions were not necessarily altogether satisfied with themselves.

In sum, the findings show that the experimental subjects had raised their rankings of the target values they felt dissatisfied with. But even those expressing satisfaction with their *equality* rankings had raised their *equality* rankings significantly, although these increases in rankings were not as large as those obtained for subjects expressing dissatisfaction.

Effects of Self-dissatisfaction with Other Values

Although our main theoretical focus is on the effects of specific self-dissatisfaction with the two target values, changes were also expected in all other values that subjects had become dissatisfied with following the experimental treatment. In Experiment 1, absolute change regardless of direction was computed for subjects who were "satisfied" and "dissatisfied" with their rankings of each of 12 values, including the two target values. In Experiments 2 and 3, absolute change was similarly computed for subjects satisfied and dissatisfied with their rankings of each of 18 values.

Table 12.4 shows the mean amount of absolute change in all values found for satisfied and dissatisfied subjects within groups E_1 and E_{12} in Experiment 1. The fifth and tenth columns of this table show whether the amounts of absolute change found for the satisfied and dissatisfied subjects are significantly different from one another. Table 12.5 shows the comparable findings for Experiments 2 and 3 combined, since the number of dissatisfied subjects obtained separately in these two experiments were too small to warrant separate reporting. (Not all experimental subjects indicated that they were satisfied or dissatisfied with every value ranking.)

Across all experiments, the incidence of expressed self-dissatisfaction with *equality* and *freedom* rankings was usually greater than that with the rankings of other values. Anywhere from about one-fourth to one-third of the experimental subjects had expressed dissatisfaction with their *equality* rankings, and the proportion expressing dissatisfaction with *freedom* rankings was usually not far behind. These findings confirm that the experimental treatment had succeeded in inducing greater self-dissatisfaction with these two particular values than with other values.

But a few other values, not mentioned in the experimental session, also elicited a relatively large proportion of dissatisfaction, even though this was not experimentally intended. Notice, for example, that a relatively high proportion of the subjects had expressed dissatisfaction with their rankings of *a world at peace* (all groups), *a sense of accomplishment*, *happiness*, *self-respect*, and *wisdom* (Experiments 2 and 3).

TABLE 12.4   EFFECTS OF SATISFACTION-DISSATISFACTION WITH ANY GIVEN VALUE ON ABSOLUTE CHANGE OF THAT VALUE EXPERIMENT 1

| | Experimental Group E_1 | | | | | Experimental Group E_{12} | | | | |
| | Satisfied* | | Dissatisfied | | | Satisfied | | Dissatisfied | | |
	N	Mean Change	N	Mean Change	p	N	Mean Change	N	Mean Change	p
A comfortable life										
3 weeks later	113	1.86	17	2.76	—	142	1.61	27	3.07	.01
3–5 months later	75	2.33	16	2.69	—	94	1.79	23	3.78	.001
A meaningful life										
3 weeks later	119	1.93	14	2.71	—	147	1.91	24	3.04	.02
3–5 months later	86	1.94	6	2.00	—	96	2.11	22	2.82	.025
A world at peace										
3 weeks later	98	2.43	35	3.03	—	133	2.00	35	2.43	—
3–5 months later	65	2.41	27	3.11	.025	92	2.25	25	3.76	.001
Equality										
3 weeks later	90	2.21	45	2.84	—	125	2.01	48	3.58	.001
3–5 months later	62	2.45	31	3.19	.002	83	2.34	36	3.64	.001
Freedom										
3 weeks later	100	1.54	31	3.23	.001	132	1.25	40	2.65	.001
3–5 months later	66	1.39	25	3.56	.001	90	1.66	29	3.28	.001
Maturity										
3 weeks later	114	2.26	18	2.61	—	148	2.41	24	2.96	—
3–5 months later	82	2.68	11	3.00	—	104	2.34	15	2.93	—
National security										
3 weeks later	118	2.06	13	2.62	—	142	1.87	26	2.58	—
3–5 months later	83	2.43	8	2.25	—	100	2.43	18	3.06	—

Respect for others										
3 weeks later	108	2.06	24	2.29	—	144	2.01	25	2.68	—
3–5 months later	75	1.92	18	2.28	—	97	2.28	20	2.75	—
Respect from others										
3 weeks later	115	2.01	16	2.19	—	144	1.77	26	2.04	—
3–5 months later	80	2.24	11	2.55	—	98	2.16	20	3.25	.001
Salvation										
3 weeks later	1'2	.97	19	2.05	.02	155	1.01	13	3.23	.001
3–5 months later	78	1.47	14	2.57	.025	108	1.31	9	3.89	.001
True friendship										
3 weeks later	116	2.45	15	1.80	—	142	2.31	28	2.61	—
3–5 months later	83	2.17	9	1.89	—	93	2.83	25	3.28	—
Wisdom										
3 weeks later	104	2.32	27	2.70	—	143	2.20	25	2.88	—
3–5 months later	72	2.76	19	2.47	—	98	2.47	19	2.32	—

* Not all subjects reported their feelings of satisfaction or dissatisfaction with all values, thus accounting for differences in number of cases.

TABLE 12.5   EFFECTS OF SATISFACTION-DISSATISFACTION WITH ANY GIVEN VALUE ON ABSOLUTE CHANGE OF THAT VALUE EXPERIMENTS 2 AND 3 COMBINED (MADISON AND BRIGGS)

| | Satisfied* | | Dissatisfied | | |
	N	Mean Change	N	Mean Change	p
A comfortable life					
3 weeks later	130	3.40	21	3.86	—
3–5 months later	94	3.49	11	5.73	.031
15–17 months later	100	3.77	13	5.08	—
An exciting life					
3 weeks later	122	3.29	29	2.93	—
3–5 months later	90	3.69	17	4.59	—
15–17 months later	92	3.91	22	5.27	—
A sense of accomplishment					
3 weeks later	116	3 72	36	3 61	—
3–5 months later	79	3.33	26	4.27	—
15–17 months later	85	3.29	29	4.07	—
A world at peace					
3 weeks later	127	2.68	25	2.76	—
3–5 months later	86	3.59	22	2.95	—
15–17 months later	88	3.90	23	3.70	—
A world of beauty					
3 weeks later	128	2.69	22	3.32	—
3–5 months later	92	2.58	15	4.20	.036
15–17 months later	97	3.05	16	3.44	—
Equality					
3 weeks later	116	2.56	36	5.22	.001
3–5 months later	83	3.58	25	5.96	.002
15–17 months later	85	3.12	30	5.77	.001
Freedom					
3 weeks later	116	2.22	36	4.86	.001
3–5 months later	82	2.54	26	4.54	.001
15–17 months later	85	2.72	30	5.20	.001
Family security					
3 weeks later	121	2.92	28	2.21	—
3–5 months later	84	3.10	22	3.27	—
15–17 months later	87	2.86	25	3.16	—
Happiness					
3 weeks later	122	3.24	30	4.07	—
3–5 months later	86	3.72	22	3.27	—
15–17 months later	91	3.89	24	3.62	—
Inner harmony					
3 weeks later	125	3.56	27	3.52	—
3–5 months later	89	3.67	19	4.11	—
15–17 months later	98	3.72	17	5.29	—
Mature love					
3 weeks later	131	2.15	21	3.48	.01
3–5 months later	96	2.71	12	5.17	.004
15–17 months later	100	2.79	15	4.87	.005

TABLE 12.5 (Continued)

	Satisfied*		Dissatisfied		
	N	Mean Change	N	Mean Change	p
National security					
3 weeks later	127	2.09	25	4.80	.001
3–5 months later	86	2.72	22	3.68	—
15–17 months later	92	2.67	23	4.78	.004
Pleasure					
3 weeks later	126	2.83	25	3.80	—
3–5 months later	94	2.86	14	3.71	—
15–17 months later	97	3.00	18	2.94	—
Salvation					
3 weeks later	123	1.68	29	3.34	.003
3–5 months later	92	1.83	16	3.50	.039
15–17 months later	93	2.41	22	4.23	.067
Self-respect					
3 weeks later	116	2.94	36	4.33	.01
3–5 months later	85	3.09	23	3.43	—
15–17 months later	91	3.34	24	4.58	.062
Social recognition					
3 weeks later	130	2.62	21	2.71	—
3–5 months later	94	2.63	13	2.38	—
15–17 months later	96	2.95	18	2.17	—
True friendship					
3 weeks later	128	3.08	24	2.62	—
3–5 months later	88	3.25	20	3.60	—
15–17 months later	95	3.86	20	3.40	—
Wisdom					
3 weeks later	118	2.80	34	3.56	—
3–5 months later	84	2.37	24	4.25	.001
15–17 months later	86	2.72	29	5.00	.001

* Not all subjects reported their feelings of satisfaction or dissatisfaction with all values, thus accounting for differences in number of cases.

The main finding shown in Tables 12.4 and 12.5, however, is that subjects reporting dissatisfaction with their rankings of any value typically showed greater long-term change in that value than satisfied subjects. If we compare the magnitude of absolute change exhibited by satisfied and dissatisfied subjects across all experiments, all values, and all posttests—102 comparisons in all—82 percent of all these comparisons show that those reporting dissatisfaction had exhibited the larger changes. Over a third of these 102 comparisons are statistically significant, and in every instance in which the difference is significant, it is the dissatisfied group that shows the larger change. It can therefore be concluded that an affective state of self-dissatisfaction with any value, for whatever reason it may have arisen, is likely to lead to a greater long-term change in that value than an affective state of self-satisfaction.

Table 12.4 (Experiment 1) shows another finding of theoretical interest, namely, that the self-dissatisfaction induced in group E_{12} by exposure to "Table 1" and "Table 2" led to more pervasive and more often significant changes in values than the exposure of group E_1 to only "Table 1." Even though the number of subjects dissatisfied with their rankings of each value in the two experimental conditions E_1 and E_{12} was about the same, E_{12} subjects who were dissatisfied with any given value usually changed more than E_1 subjects who were dissatisfied. These findings once again indicate that exposure of subjects to both tables had more pervasive experimental effects than their exposure to only "Table 1."

EFFECTS OF GENERAL SELF-DISSATISFACTION AND HYPOCRISY

Subjects reporting dissatisfaction with specific value rankings, particularly with *equality* rankings, reported more dissatisfaction in a general way with their value rankings and also reported feeling more hypocritical. Measures of specific self-dissatisfaction, feelings of general dissatisfaction, and hypocrisy were positively and significantly associated. We may therefore expect that greater value change would also be manifested among experimental subjects who reported general dissatisfaction and feelings of hypocrisy at the end of the experimental session.

Although the results showed a marked trend favoring these hypotheses, the findings were not altogether consistent and significant from experiment to experiment. Levels of *equality* but not *freedom* rankings increased consistently more for subjects who felt hypocritical and generally dissatisfied with themselves. Specific self-dissatisfaction was, however, a uniformly better predictor than general self-dissatisfaction and hypocrisy of the cognitive changes observed 3 weeks, 3 to 5 months, and 15 to 17 months after the experimental session. It may be concluded from these data, too extensive and complex to present here, that the primary instigator of change is not so much a global feeling of self-dissatisfaction or hypocrisy as a specific and focused feeling that identifies the cognitive components that require modification, one that indicates the direction of change demanded by society and self.

AFFECTIVE, COGNITIVE AND PERSONALITY VARIABLES THAT DID NOT AFFECT THE CHANGE PROCESS

We also investigated the role of a number of other affective, cognitive, and personality variables in the change process:

(1) *Strength of Commitment to One's Values.* Recall that after having

ranked the 18 terminal values at the beginning of the experimental session, the subjects were told: "Now we are interested in knowing how you feel about the way you ranked these 18 values in general." They then rated their value commitment on an 11-point scale, with 1 indicating "I care very much about the order in which I ranked these values" and 11 indicating "It does not make much difference which order I put them in." Assuming that contradictions implicating values would arouse stronger feelings of self-dissatisfaction among persons having strong value commitments, it was anticipated that experimental subjects having stronger value commitments would manifest more cognitive change than those having weaker ones.

(2) *Ego-involvement.* This variable was measured by ratings given on an 11-point scale in response to two questions asked at the end of the experiment: "Did you find it thought provoking?" and "Do you think this technique of teaching will lead you to do some more thinking about your own values?" Cognitive change should be greater for the more ego-involved subjects.

(3) *Perceived Validity of the Information Presented in "Table 1" and "Table 2."* Perceived validity was measured at the end of all three experiments by a "yes" or "no" response to the question: "In your opinion, do you think that the Michigan State findings I have described to you are scientifically valid?" Experimental subjects perceiving the data as scientifically valid should undergo more change than those perceiving the data as invalid.

(4) *Acceptance of the Interpretation Offered by the Experimenter.* In all experiments the experimenter had offered an interpretation of the data that had been displayed, namely, that Michigan State University students in general and those unsympathetic to civil rights demonstrations in particular care more for their own than for others' freedom. The extent to which the subject had agreed with this interpretation was measured by an 11-point rating scale, with 1 indicating "I agree strongly with this interpretation," 6 indicating "I'm not sure," and 11 indicating "I strongly disagree with this interpretation." Acceptance of the experimenter's interpretation should facilitate cognitive change, and rejection should hinder it.

(5) *Recall of "Table 1" and "Table 2" Data.* Accuracy of recall of data in "Table 1" and "Table 2" was measured in Experiment 1 during the first posttest, 3 weeks after the experimental treatment. On this occasion, group E_1 subjects were again shown "Table 1," and group E_{12} subjects were shown both tables, except for the fact that the composite averages were missing. They were asked to supply the omitted data from memory. Accuracy of recall of "Table 1" was measured for each subject by a correlation between his recalled and the actual rankings, and accuracy of recall of "Table 2" was measured by the total amount of discrepancy between recalled and actual rankings. Greater change in values and

attitudes should be found among experimental subjects who had better recall, on the assumption that memory mediates cognitive change.

(6) *Dogmatism.* This variable was measured by the 20-item Dogmatism Scale, Form E (Trohdahl and Powell, 1965). It had been administered along with other tests during the pretest session of Experiment 1. Dogmatic persons were expected to be more defensive or resistant to the experimental procedure.

(7) *Knowledge of the Purpose of the Experiment.* It is likely that informing subjects about the true purpose of the experiment would hinder or dissipate cognitive change. This hypothesis was tested only in Experiment 1. A few days after the first posttest, given 3 weeks after the experimental treatment, a mimeographed report was mailed to each experimental and control subject explaining the purpose of the experiment and containing pretest and posttest data. This report called attention to the value changes that had been obtained for experimental groups E_1 and E_{12} and for the control group. We assessed the effects of this debriefing 3 to 5 months after the experimental session, on the occasion of the second posttest.

Statistical analyses were carried out to ascertain the effects of the seven variables described above on value and attitude change. Not one of them was found to affect the change process. Moreover, no systematic relationships were found that would link any of these seven variables either with initial position on values or attitudes, or with self-dissatisfaction. Significant changes in values and attitudes were found about as often and to about the same extent among experimental subjects, regardless of variations in their value commitment, ego-involvement, perceived validity of the data, agreement with the experimenter's interpretation, accuracy of recall of "Table 1" and "Table 2," or level of dogmatism.

Moreover, the debriefing of the subjects in Experiment 1 after the first posttest did not affect the results. Significant value and attitude changes were even found among the debriefed experimental subjects on the second posttest, 3 to 5 months after the experimental treatment, as has already been reported in Chapter 10. These changes do not seem to be qualitatively different from those obtained for the experimental subjects in Experiments 2 and 3 who had not, of course, been informed about the purpose of the experiment.

A *post hoc* attempt to account for all these unexpected findings will be offered at the end of this chapter.

POST-EXPERIMENTAL INTERVIEWS
CONCERNING THE CHANGE
PROCESS

Upon termination of Experiments 2 and 3 we interviewed a sample of experimental and control subjects in the two residential colleges. The purpose of these interviews was to ascertain the subjects' perceptions of the purpose of the research, whether they were aware that their values, attitudes, and behavior had been influenced, and their reactions upon being told the purpose of the study. The interviews began with free-response questions of a general sort and became increasingly specific.

Interviews were conducted with 35 subjects in November 1969—about 22 months after the experimental session. These subjects had been selected to provide us with a cross section of the experimental and control subjects in the two residential colleges. From Experiment 2, 19 were selected, and from Experiment 3, 16; 19 were experimental and 16 were control subjects; 15 had joined NAACP and 20 had not. Moreover, the subjects were selected from among those who at the very least had participated in the pretest, the experimental treatment, and the third posttest given 15 to 17 months afterward. They were contacted by phone and virtually all of them agreed to be interviewed. All the interviews were completed within a three-day period in order to minimize communication among the subjects.

Interviews were conducted by two research assistants. The subjects were reminded of the various questionnaires they had filled out over the past year and a half and were given blank copies of the questionnaire materials to refresh their memories. "All that remains is Dr. Rokeach's final report back to you and your faculty and a number of conversations such as this . . . in order to gather some of your thoughts and reactions . . . There is diversity of opinion on the work of Dr. Rokeach. [Most particularly, resentment had been expressed concerning the many requests and follow-up reminders, and about filling out and returning the posttest questionnaires.] You may have strong feelings either way about your experience or you may be totally indifferent to the experience. Whatever your reactions, we are most interested in them." The subjects were then told that their replies would be held in the strictest confidence.

Perceived Purpose of the Study

Of the 35 interviewees, 31 ventured the opinion that the purpose of the study was (1) to compare the values of the students attending the two residential colleges; (2) to compare them with the values of students in the university at large; (3) to study the effects of a small, residential college atmosphere on student values; or (4) that they were unsure or did not know the purpose of the research.

The remaining four subjects, all experimental ones, replied that the purpose of the study was to find out whether the experimental session they had participated in would affect them in some way. One of these subjects further commented, "It had a hand in exposing racism in our society," and then ventured the opinion that the experimental treatment had made him more liberal. This comment notwithstanding, his final posttest *equality* ranking was 11, compared with a pretest ranking of 12. A second subject, whose *equality* ranking had risen from 8 to 4 and whose *freedom* ranking had fallen from 7 to 8, commented that even though her *equality* and *freedom* rankings were "not in conflict" she had discussed them with friends shortly after the experimental session and discovered inconsistencies in those around her, thus making her more aware of the importance of values and of the need to "bring values and opinions together."

A third subject replied in response to the question about the purpose of the experiment that the experimental treatment had had a considerable impact upon her behavior. She was unhappy about the inconsistencies that the experimental treatment had revealed within her. She felt she was "a hypocrite, pretending to be a liberal when in fact I was quite self-centered." To seek out new answers she had left the natural science-oriented Briggs College for the social science-oriented James Madison College "to directly confront the issues of civil and human rights." She responded to the NAACP solicitation by joining the association, campaigned afterwards for Charles Evers in Mississippi, and "spent the summer in New York ghettos working with teenage girls." She traced all these behaviors directly to the experimental session. Her pretest rankings of *equality* and *freedom* were 10 and 2; her final posttest rankings 15 to 17 months later were 2 and 3.

In response to the question about the perceived purpose of the study, a fourth subject replied that she felt the first NAACP solicitation was somehow connected with the research because of its timing; she had been solicited by NAACP shortly after she had filled out the second posttest questionnaire. This was "just a suspicion," however, which she did not discuss with other students. Nor did she hear others talk about it. She had joined NAACP despite her suspicion, and had a "bad reaction" because she had failed to hear from NAACP after she had joined. She remarked that the research project was "not relevant," and she did not think that she had changed as a result of the experimental treatment. She was right about her *equality* rankings but wrong about her *freedom* rankings; her *equality* ranking was 1 initially and 1 on the final posttest; her *freedom* ranking had, however, changed from 8 to 2.

This particular subject was the only one interviewed who spontaneously voiced a suspicion about a possible connection between the NAACP solicitation and the research project. When the remaining subjects were asked whether they were aware of the connection they uniformly replied that the thought had not occurred to them.

Discussing the Research Project with Others

Since all the subjects in Experiments 2 and 3 lived in two small residential colleges on the campus of Michigan State University, a question arises about the possibility of communication among them. To the question, "Did you discuss the research with others?" the great majority of the subjects responded in the affirmative, as shown in Table 12.6. Eighty-nine percent of the experimental subjects who were interviewed said they had discussed the research with others. But the finding for control subjects is

TABLE 12.6 PERCENT OF INTERVIEWEES DISCUSSING RESEARCH, REPORTING CHANGES IN ATTITUDES, VALUES, AND BEHAVIOR, AND REACTING FAVORABLY FOLLOWING FEEDBACK OF OWN PRETEST-POSTTEST RESULTS

	N	% Discussing Research with Others	% Reporting Attitude Change	% Reporting Value Change	% Reporting Behavior Change	% Reacting Favorably after Feedback
Experimental						
Control	19	89	21	53	21	79
Madison	16	88	0*	13†	0*	56*
Briggs	19	95	11	37	11	63
Joined NAACP	16	81	13	31	13	75
Did not join	15	93	13	33	20	80
	20	85	11	35	5	60

* p < .05.
† p < .01, significance of difference between proportions.

no different: 88 percent reported that they too had discussed the research.

These unusually high percentages suggest, first, that the pretest and posttest materials alone might have stimulated the control as well as the experimental subjects to discuss them with friends, roommates, or class-mates. Second, the findings suggest that communication among subjects cannot explain the extensive differences found between experimental and control groups.

These findings do not rule out the possibility, however, that the quality of such discussions had differed for experimental and control subjects. Closer analysis revealed, however, that the widespread discussions were of a procedural rather than a substantive nature. Approximately two-thirds of all the subjects reporting they had discussed the research with others further indicated that the discussions gave vent to various criticisms about the research project—the repeated posttests, the follow-up reminders by letter and phone to fill out and return the questionnaires, the invasion of privacy, the excessive demands on the student's time, the poor timing (conflict with exams), and the research being a waste of time.

Self-reports about Attitude, Value, and Behavioral Change

The subjects were then asked if they thought their (1) attitudes, (2) values, and (3) behavior had undergone change as a result of participation in the research. The proportion of affirmative answers to these questions is also shown in Table 12.6. Significantly greater numbers of experimental subjects responded affirmatively to all three questions. Especially note-worthy is the difference in response of experimental and control subjects to the question concerning value change: 10 out of the 19 experimental subjects who had been interviewed reported that they had undergone value change, whereas only 2 of the 16 control subjects reported such change.

When prodded further about the nature of the changes they had experienced, subjects who had reported attitude change identified civil rights and Vietnam as the issues toward which their attitude had changed, and the subjects reporting value change identified *equality* and *a world at peace*. It is interesting that no one mentioned *freedom*. Finally, none of the subjects reporting that their behavior had changed mentioned that they had joined NAACP. Instead, their responses included "active in civil rights work," "transfer from Briggs to Madison," "treatment of Negroes," and "discussion of the war."

Reactions Following Feedback of Pretest-Posttest Data

Prior to termination of the interview each subject was shown printouts concerning his own value and attitude positions at the time of the pretest and the third posttest:

I have here your answers to the public opinion questionnaire and your rankings of values. They show your opinions and values as a freshman and one year later, as a sophomore. I would like to show them to you and ask you if you have any comments on or reactions to how you changed or did not change.

It was anticipated that many experimental subjects would now protest having been unduly influenced or manipulated. To our surprise, not a single one of them reacted in this way. On the contrary, as shown in Table 12.6, significantly more of the experimental than the control subjects reacted in a generally favorable manner.

In sum, it would appear from the interviews that the great majority of the subjects had not accurately perceived the real purpose of the study or its connection with the NAACP solicitation. There was extensive discussion of the research by control as well as experimental subjects. Nonetheless, experimental subjects reported more often than control subjects that their values, attitudes, and behavior had changed, and they reacted more favorably than control subjects upon being shown their own pretest and posttest results.

OTHER EXPERIMENTAL INVESTIGATIONS OF THE CHANGE PROCESS

Many other questions can be raised about the psychological processes underlying the long-term cognitive and behavioral changes that have been reported here. A few such questions have been investigated in research studies carried out after the results of the present investigations became known. These studies are reported elsewhere and will therefore only be summarized here.

Inclusion versus Omission of Interpretation

Recall the experimenter's interpretation of "Table 1" and "Table 2," namely, that the data suggest that many subjects cared more for their own than for other people's freedom. McLellan (1973) investigated, among other things, the effects of inclusion versus omission of this interpretation. He found that this interpretation resulted in long-term value and attitude change whereas omission of this interpretation did not result in cognitive change.

Privacy versus Nonprivacy of Self-confrontation as a Determinant of Change

All the experiments that have been reported here were conducted under group conditions of anonymity and privacy. The experimental subjects were not acquainted with the experimenter, were not allowed to communicate with him or with others, and were not allowed to ask questions during the experiment.

What if, instead, the experimental subjects were in a face-to-face relationship with the experimenter, thus destroying the privacy afforded by the anonymous classroom condition? We may suppose that a person receiving feedback about possible contradictions within his belief system would become defensive under such a condition, thus inhibiting the change process. To determine whether this was the case, Rokeach and Cochrane (1972) repeated the basic experiment reported here, adding a second experimental condition of nonprivacy. The experimenter, in a one-to-one relationship with the subject, addressed him by name, sat next to him throughout the experimental session, and gave every indication that he was observing how the subject was responding to the value and attitude questionnaires.

Significant increases in *equality* and *freedom* were nonetheless found 8 to 9 weeks after this experimental treatment, and the increases were as great as those obtained under the usual condition of privacy. These findings suggest that it does not matter whether a subject is in an anonymous classroom condition or in a face-to-face relationship with a significant other.

Information about One's Own Values as a Determinant of Change

In the experiments reported here, the experimental subject first ranked his own values, and only then was he given comparable information about others. He was thus able to compare himself with others, and this comparison process presumably was crucial in leading many of the subjects to become aware of contradictions within their belief systems.

What if, instead, the experimental subject were not allowed to find out first about his own values and was exposed only to information about others? Rokeach and McLellan (1972) gave one experimental group information about others but not about themselves; that is, the experimental subjects were exposed to "Table 1" and "Table 2" without first being given the opportunity of finding out about their own values. Findings for this experimental group were compared with those obtained under the usual experimental condition, wherein the subjects first ranked their own values and then were shown "Table 1" and "Table 2." Significant changes in *equality* and *freedom* were obtained four weeks afterward in both experimental groups. Moreover, both experimental groups manifested greater behavioral change five months afterward when compared with a control group that had merely filled out the value scale but had not been exposed to "Table 1" or "Table 2."

These data suggest that a process of long-term cognitive and behavioral change can be initiated even in persons who are not first given an opportunity of finding out about their own values and who, instead, are merely exposed to information about others. The experimental subjects evidently compared the objective information they received about others with what they guessed, imagined, or knew subjectively about themselves. In this way many of these experimental subjects must have become conscious of contradictions within their own belief systems, even though they had been denied the opportunity of first finding out what their beliefs were.

Personality as a Determinant of Change

Already reported is the finding that individual differences in dogmatism did not affect long-term value or attitude change. Persons scoring either high or low in dogmatism were more or less equally affected by the experimental treatment. Cochrane and Kelly (1972) investigated the problem of individual differences more extensively. In two experiments which were basically the same as those described here, they obtained measures of a total of 19 personality variables for their experimental subjects: dogmatism, the F scale, neuroticism (Eysenck, 1962), social inhibition, and feelings of inadequacy and hyperaggressiveness (Janis and Field, 1959), plus 13 MMPI subscale measures.

In both studies, Cochrane and Kelly replicated the findings reported here. Experimental subjects manifested significant value change 5 to 8 weeks after the experimental treatment. However, not a single one of the 19 personality variables made any difference; high scorers and low scorers on each of these variables were affected equally. These personality variables, at least, do not seem to affect the change process.

Extensiveness of Behavioral Effects

The behavioral effects reported in Chapter 11 concerned both joining or not joining a civil rights organization and academic career choices. The question may be raised whether the behavioral effects following cognitive change can be extended to include more direct interpersonal interactions with others. Investigating this problem, Penner (1971) first repeated the basic experiment and found the usual significant value changes four weeks after the experimental treatment. Then, three months after the experimental treatment, Penner gave his white subjects the opportunity of interacting with a black confederate in a group laboratory situation. One measure of such interaction was the amount of eye contact with the black confederate. Penner found significantly more eye contact between experimental subjects and the black confederate than between control subjects and the black confederate. These findings suggest that the experimental treatment that had led to significant increases in *equality* also resulted in a more genuine interpersonal acceptance of persons of another race three months afterward.

Other Values as Experimental Targets

Finally, the question may be raised whether there might be something distinctive about the values of *equality* and *freedom* that might lead these particular values rather than all values to be especially vulnerable to long-term change. Can changes also be induced in other values, and, if so, what are the cognitive and behavioral consequences that might be expected to follow from such changes?

A World of Beauty. Employing experimental procedures similar to those described here, Hollen (1972) demonstrated a significant increase in the target value *a world of beauty* among college students a month after the experimental treatment. Hollen succeeded in altering this value merely by pointing out to the students that "young people and better-educated people tend to rank *a world of beauty* higher than the general public ranks it." Moreover, increase in value for *a world of beauty* was accompanied by changes in attitude toward various ecological issues, such as attitude toward highway beautification programs, the banning of nonreturnable bottles, and the banning of automobiles from cities. Thus, Hollen's findings suggest the possibility that enduring change can be effected in values and associated attitudes other than those that have been the main focus of attention in the present investigation.

Self-control. Through newspaper advertisements, 14 heavy cigarette smokers were recruited by Conroy, Katkin, and Barnette (1973) to participate in a "Smoking Cessation Clinic." They were exposed to a number of traditional techniques that were designed to induce them to quit smoking— a fear-inducing film and various lectures and instructions concerning habit formation and the monitoring of internal and external cues that precede or are associated with a craving for cigarettes. All subjects mailed in daily reports of their cigarette consumption.

Then, 7 of the 14 smokers were randomly selected to serve as subjects in a "5-minute" self-confrontation experiment, with the remaining smokers serving as controls. The experimental subjects first ranked the 18 instrumental values and were then shown "Table 1," which displayed the two instrumental values that, previous research had shown, distinguished cigarette smokers from cigarette quitters: Smokers ranked *broadminded* third and *self-disciplined* (self-controlled, restrained) eighth, whereas quitters ranked *broadminded* eighth and *self-disciplined* first. The experimenter interpreted these findings to mean that "people who have trouble quitting cigarettes are trying to be broadminded about a task that requires rigid self-discipline." They were then invited to compare their own value rankings with those displayed in "Table 1," and they then rated the extent to which they were satisfied or dissatisfied with what they found out about themselves during the course of the experiment. Finally, the experimental subjects were invited to alter the rankings of whichever values they chose.

Only the *self-disciplined* rankings increased as a result; the experimental subjects registered an immediate mean increase of 6.1 units in their rankings of *self-disciplined*. On a second posttest administered 17 to 19 days later, (1) the experimental subjects increased an average of 4.6 units

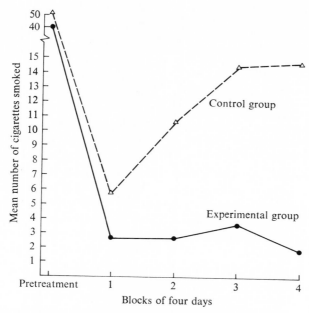

Figure 12.1   Mean number of cigarettes smoked during pretreatment day and for the four blocks of four days of treatment.

in their *self-disciplined* rankings, which was still significantly greater than the control subjects' mean increase of 1.71 units, and (2) increases in rankings of *self-disciplined* correlated .61 with self-dissatisfaction ratings. More crucial, however, are the data concerning changes in cigarette consumption during the course of the experiment. These data are reproduced in Figure 12.1 with the kind permission of the senior author, William J. Conroy of the Counseling Psychology Program at the State University of New York at Buffalo.

Figure 12.1 shows that the control and experimental subjects smoked about 50 and 40 cigarettes a day before the experimental treatment—not a significant pretest difference in cigarette consumption. During the first four-day block, both groups decreased sharply and to about the same extent in their cigarette consumption.

> Thereafter, the control group records a rapid increase in mean smoking rate for the second and third four-day blocks. This increase levels and stabilizes at a mean of 14.1 cigarettes for the fourth four-day block. The experimental group . . . shows no increase for the second block and only a slight increase for the third. What is of particular importance is the subsequent decline in the fourth block to a rate of 1.9 cigarettes per day which is lower than the rate of 2.6 recorded in the first block (p. 12).

A two-way analysis of variance revealed that cigarette consumption was significantly different for the four four-day blocks ($< .05$), and, moreover, that the interaction between the experimental treatment and the four-day blocks was also significant (< .05), suggesting that the treatment had produced experimental effects that increased over time.

Conroy, Katkin, and Barnette conclude their research report on a note of cautious optimism:

> The implications of this experiment . . . seem particularly relevant to smoking cessation research, psychotherapy, and to advertising techniques utilized in public health programs. That the design was limited in scope and that it utilized small numbers is obvious, but the findings offer solid support for more extensive investigations in the future, as well as a promise of better results in smoking cessation programs (p. 16).

Their findings are important for several reasons. First, they suggest that instrumental values as well as terminal values can be induced to undergo change as a result of the self-confrontation procedures described in this book. Second, the specific behavioral effects of value change that have been the overriding concern in the present research can be generalized to an entirely different realm of behavior—cigarette smoking. Third, if it is indeed the case that self-confrontation procedures can be employed to help cut down or quit smoking (four of the seven experimental subjects compared with two of the seven control subjects had quit smoking when the experiment was terminated), why not also to help people with other afflictions, such as obesity and drug addiction? Put another way, the findings of Conroy, Katkin, and Barnette as well as those reported here suggest that behavioral modification may be brought about in the personal as well as in the social arena by "value therapy." A great deal of additional research will, however, be required before it will be possible to assess the validity or the long-term effectiveness of value therapy.

All the studies reported in this section were designed to answer additional questions about the change process. In summary, the findings suggest that a process of directed change in values, attitudes, and behavior can be initiated by drawing a person's attention to data and interpretations that make him aware of contradictions within his own belief system. Such an awareness can be induced under conditions of nonprivacy or privacy, and regardless of whether the subject is first given feedback about his own values. Individual differences in personality—as measured by dogmatism, the F scale, neuroticism, social inhibition, feelings of inadequacy and hyperaggression, and the MMPI—did not affect the change process. Some of the behavioral effects of the experimental treatment are that not only did some subjects join a civil rights organization and make new academic career choices, but they also established rapport with persons to whom they had not been attracted before. Finally, other values besides *equality* and *freedom* have been shown to undergo long-term change as a result of experimental procedures designed to induce self-dissatisfaction, and these long-term value changes have also been shown to lead to related attitudinal and behavioral changes.

POST HOC EXPLANATION OF
UNEXPECTED FINDINGS

Many of the findings reported in this chapter were theoretically unexpected. How may we account for the fact that so many different variables did not inhibit or otherwise mediate the change process? At the least, they indicate that the long-term cognitive and behavioral effects are extremely robust. But this robustness must somehow be accounted for, and it is extremely unlikely that any single explanation will do for all such unexpected findings. The following speculations and observations are offered *post hoc* in the hope that they will stimulate further research about what conditions might facilitate or retard the change process:

Value Commitment. Hollen (1967) has shown that value commitment, as measured, is unrelated to value system reliability. Nor is there evidence as yet that value commitment validly measures what it is supposed to measure. Thus, the fact that value change was not found to be related to value commitment may indicate nothing more than that we do not as yet have a reliable and valid way of measuring value commitment.

Ego-involvement, Perceived Validity, and Agreement with Interpretation. Subjects reporting that they did not find the experimental material thought provoking, that they did not agree with the experimenter's interpretation, or that they did not perceive the data as scientifically valid may have been responding ego-defensively to the immediate experimental situation. These ego-defensive reactions may have been long dissipated when they took the posttests weeks and months later, thus possibly accounting for the fact that these variables did affect the experimental outcomes.

Recall of "Table 1" *and "Table* 2." The measures of recall used were measures of the accuracy of recall of all the data shown in "Table 1" and "Table 2." It is possible that the crucial issue is not so much the total accuracy of recall but the accuracy of recall of *equality* and *freedom* rankings. This issue merits far more detailed and systematic investigation than we have devoted to it in the present investigation. For it seems unlikely that memory does not mediate in any way the changes in values, attitudes, and behavior that were observed in our experiments.

Dogmatism, Authoritarianism and Other Personality Variables. Dogmatist as well as nondogmatist, authoritarian as well as antiauthoritarian, and people differing on other personality variables would all like to think of themselves as reasonably tolerant, democratic, competent, and moral human beings. When they are confronted with credible information about themselves that contradicts such self-conceptions, they are all equally capable of experiencing self-dissatisfaction. Because they all have the need to remove sources of self-dissatisfaction and to think well of themselves, they change their cognitions and behavior in order to bring them into closer alignment with self-conceptions, thus maintaining if not enhancing self-conceptions. If these admittedly *post hoc* speculations are valid, they would account for the findings that the many personality differences have no discernible effects. The question remains whether any other personality variable will be found to differentially affect the kinds of cognitive and behavioral changes that have been investigated here.

Knowledge about the True Purpose of the Experiment. If the crucial mechanism that initiates a process of change is the arousal of an affective state of self-dissatisfaction, then knowledge of the true purpose of the experiment is irrelevant. Any data that credibly inform a person about contradictions implicating his self-conceptions should arouse such feelings of self-dissatisfaction, regardless of awareness of the fact that the experiment was designed or intended to expose such contradictions. Consequently, experimental subjects who were informed about the true purpose of the research changed no less than those not so informed. There is no reason to think that the basic mechanism that initiates the change process, the arousal of an affective state of self-dissatisfaction, had been affected by the debriefing.

13
Some Alternative
Interpretations

The many experimental findings reported in Chapters 10, 11, and 12 indicate that genuine lasting changes in values, attitudes, and behavior had been effected as a result of a single experimental session. Before accepting such a radical interpretation, however, it is necessary to ask whether there are not alternative interpretations that can more simply account for all these findings.

A number of interpretations will be considered in this chapter. Before offering them, it might be helpful if we remind ourselves of the many experimental facts that any alternative interpretation will have to account for if it is to be considered compelling:

1. The significant differences between experimental and control groups concerning changes in the two target values, in remaining values, in attitudes, and in behavior
2. The larger experimental effects found in group E_{12} than in group E_1
3. The differential cognitive changes among experimental subgroups varying initially in the target values and related attitudes
4. The fact that attitude change came after value change, and the related observations of "backlash" and "sleeper" effects
5. The fact that the changes were long-term changes
6. The fact that cognitive changes occurred not only among subjects possessing discrepant values and attitudes but also among certain subgroups of subjects who were consistent in their values and attitudes
7. The fact that subjects varying in initial position on values and attitudes differed in their feelings of specific and general self-dissatisfaction

8. The fact that subjects dissatisfied with virtually any value changed more on that value than subjects satisfied with that value
9. The fact that experimental but not control subjects joining NAACP had raised their *equality* rankings significantly from pretest to posttest
10. The fact that lasting cognitive change occurred among experimental subjects regardless of (a) individual differences in personality, (b) whether or not they had been given the opportunity of finding out about their values beforehand, whether they (c) knew the true purpose of the experiment, (d) were committed to their values, (e) perceived the data as valid, (f) agreed with the experimenter's interpretation, (g) accurately recalled the data, or (h) became aware of contradictions within themselves under private or non-private conditions
11. Finally, long-term cognitive and behavioral changes have been found not only when *equality* and *freedom* but also when *a world of beauty* and *self-controlled* were the target values

METHODOLOGICAL CONSIDERATIONS

The best-known alternative interpretations of experimental findings in contemporary social psychology are those concerning the demand characteristics of the social psychological experiment (Orne, 1962), evaluation apprehension (Rosenberg, 1965), and experimenter bias (Rosenthal and Rosnow, 1969). All these provide alternative methodological interpretations of the data. If, singly or in combination, they could be demonstrated to be valid in the present context, they would provide arguments against interpreting the experimental findings as evidence of genuine long-term changes in values, attitudes, and behavior brought about by a single experimental session.

Each of these alternative interpretations could conceivably account for one or another of the experimental findings. But it seems highly unlikely that any of them will be able to account for all the findings cited above in a reasonable or compelling manner. The more extensive and systematic the experimental findings, the more they are removed in time from the experimental milieu, and the more unobtrusive the measurements, the less likely that they will yield to such alternative methodological interpretations as those mentioned above.

STATISTICAL CONSIDERATIONS

Another possibility that can less readily be dismissed is statistical rather than methodological in nature. It is possible to argue that the subjects in Experiments 1, 2, and 3 had not really been assigned randomly to experimental and control conditions. Recall that assignment to experimental and control conditions was made by classes or sections rather than by individuals. It is therefore possible that the comparisons between experimental and control groups were not altogether valid from a sampling or statistical inference standpoint. Such a manner of assignment requires that the section rather than the individual subject be treated as the unit of statistical comparison. Particular sections conducted by different instructors might have attracted different types of students, and it is therefore possible that the significant experimental findings were obtained from some of these non-randomly selected sections rather than from the experimental groups as a whole.

To determine whether the significant experimental findings could have unwittingly arisen from some nonrandom sampling bias, many additional analyses were undertaken with the intact experimental and control sections participating in Experiments 2 and 3 as the units of analysis. In Experiments 2 and 3, a total of 11 sections had been assigned to the experimental condition and a total of 8 sections had been assigned to the control condition. The data obtained for these intact groups are too voluminous to present and will instead only be summarized here: (1) Pretests data for experimental and control sections showed no significant differences in *equality, freedom*, or for the remaining values. (2) Not a single one of the 8 control sections exhibited significant value changes 3 weeks, 3 to 5 months, or 15 to 17 months later. In contrast, many such changes were found in the experimental sections considered separately. More specifically, 2, 5, and 6 of the 11 experimental sections exhibited significant *equality* changes 3 weeks, 3 to 5 months, and 15 to 17 months later. (3) A rank ordering of the magnitude of *equality* and *freedom* changes obtained for each of the 19 sections showed uniformly larger average increases for the experimental than for the control groups, with the findings for each of the three posttests statistically significant by the Mann-Whitney U test. (4) Finally, a rank ordering of the frequencies of behavioral response to the NAACP solicitations for the 19 experimental and control sections reveals a significant difference in the behavioral responses of experimental and control sections, as shown in Table 13.1. This table shows that anywhere from 4 to 50 percent of the subjects in each section had responded favorably to the NAACP solicitations. Notice, however, that nine of the 11 experimental sections had higher response rates to the NAACP solicitations than those obtained for any of the 8 control sections. The highest response rate to the NAACP solicitations that was obtained for any of the eight control sections was 20 percent. Nine out of the 11 experimental sections exceeded this response rate, a finding that is significant beyond the .005 level by the Mann-Whitney U test.

It is thus concluded that the differences reported in Chapters 10, 11, and 12 are differences that were generated by virtually all the experimental and control sections rather than by only a few of them. Biased sampling procedures arising from the employment of intact sections might but in

TABLE 13.1   PERCENT IN EACH EXPERIMENTAL AND CONTROL
SECTION RESPONDING FAVORABLY TO NAACP SOLICITATIONS
(EXPERIMENTS 2 AND 3 COMBINED)

Section	% Responding Favorably to NAACP Solicitations
E_1	50.0
E_2	35.7
E_3	31.3
E_4	30.8
E_5	30.0
E_6	28.6
E_7	23.5
E_8	21.7
E_9	21.7
C_1	20.0
C_2	17.6
C_3	15.8
C_4	10.0
C_5	9.5
E_{10}	8.7
C_6	8.7
C_7	8.3
E_{11}	7.7
C_8	4.0

fact do not account for the experimental findings, and statistical inferences drawn from data analyses of intact sections led to the same findings and conclusions as those emerging from data analyses based on individual subjects as the units of analysis.

SUBSTANTIVE CONSIDERATIONS

We next consider a number of substantive considerations which might possibly offer some viable alternative explanations of the experimental findings:

Charisma or Status of Experimenter as an Explanation of the Experimental Findings

Is it possible that the long-term experimental effects were a result of charisma or the status of the experimenter? This hypothesis does not seem to be a likely one in view of the fact that other experiments, carried out by other investigators, were also found to result in long-term cognitive and behavioral change. I served as experimenter in the three experiments that have been reported here. The experimenters in all other investigations were either a postdoctoral fellow in his mid-twenties (Rokeach and Cochrane,

1972; Cochrane and Kelly, 1972) or graduate students in psychology in their mid-twenties (Penner, 1971; Rokeach and McLellan, 1972; Hollen, 1972; McLellan, 1973; Conroy, Katkin, and Barnette, 1973).

Conformity as an Explanation of the Experimental Findings

Is it possible that the experimental effects were caused by conformity needs rather than by a need to eliminate or reduce self-dissatisfaction? If this explanation is valid, we would expect to find cognitive changes in the experimental groups in a direction that would bring them into a closer alignment with the values of Michigan State University students, as shown in "Table 1." The experimental findings, however, show just the opposite. As a result of the experimental treatment the experimental groups became less rather than more similar to their peers.

The Effects of Reactance

Brehm (1966) has shown that if a subject perceives a given situation as one in which his personal freedom is threatened he will behave in a manner that will restore it. To what extent can such reactance account for the experimental findings? A theory of reactance might well explain the "backlash" effects noted three weeks after the experimental treatment; that is, both control and experimental subjects had manifested consistently more negative attitudes toward blacks on this occasion. It seems unlikely, however, that a theory of reactance can account for most of the remaining experimental findings. The experimental subjects acted to remove internal contradictions and self-dissatisfactions rather than to restore their personal autonomy.

The Effects of Change in Social Climate

The college students who served as subjects may have been highly influenced by the experimental treatment because they had just entered a new social environment with new role expectations. The experimental treatment had merely induced changes that took the same direction as those sanctioned by the new environment, an environment sanctioning egalitarianism. Such a "social climate" explanation does not appear to account for the findings. For one thing, the values of college students in general are not particularly egalitarian—no more so than those of the adult white American population in general. More important, if a "social climate" interpretation were adequate, there would be significant changes toward egalitarianism in control as well as in experimental subjects; no such findings were obtained.

Social Pressure

Bem (1970) has suggested that the experimental findings are due to social pressure. He interprets the findings of Experiment 1 as follows: "The attitude and value changes that Rokeach observed in his study were in the 'socially desirable' direction, a result that the consistency hypothesis itself does not predict. This would seem to indicate that social pressure was operating rather strongly in these experiments, which leaves open the possibility that social pressure rather than inconsistency was responsible for *all* the changes" (p. 27). It is already clear that restoring consistency between cognitive elements is not the explanation, and several considerations suggest that social pressure is not the explanation either. First, it is extremely unlikely that social pressure could have produced the value and attitude changes observed 3 weeks, 3 to 5 months, and 15 to 17 months after the experimental treatment. Second, social pressure cannot account for the behavioral differences between experimental and control groups; joining NAACP, registering in ethnic core courses, and changing academic career choices can hardly be attributable to social pressure since these kinds of behavior were nonobtrusive, not perceived to be related to the experimental research program. Moreover, recall that the experimental subjects who felt dissatisfied with their rankings of *any* value usually changed more on that value than satisfied subjects changed. These pervasive differences between the dissatisfied and satisfied can hardly be attributable to social pressure, since at the most only two of the values could have been perceived by the experimental subjects as having been subjected to social pressure. Finally, the differences in cigarette consumption found by Conroy, Katkin, and Barnette (1973) can hardly be attributable to social pressure.

The Effects of Repeated Posttests

Finally, it is possible that the long-term changes in values, attitudes, and behavior were a function not only of the experimental treatment but also of the repeated posttests given to the experimental subjects. These posttests may have reactivated, reinstated, or possibly reinforced the self-dissatisfaction that had originally been induced by the experimental treatment, thus prolonging the experimental effects for many months following the experimental treatment. The behavioral differences between the experimental and control groups may also have been a consequence of the combined effects of the experimental treatment plus the repeated posttests.

Such an explanation obviously cannot account for all the experimental findings, especially those obtained on the first posttest. We can conclude at least that the experimental treatment alone led to the significant value changes that were evident from the results of the first posttest. In different experiments this first posttest had been administered anywhere from 3 to 5 weeks after the experimental treatment (Experiments 1, 2 and 3; Rokeach and McLellan, 1972; Cochrane and Kelly, 1972; Hollen, 1972) to 8 to 9 weeks afterward (Rokeach and Cochrane, 1972). The explanation concerning repeated posttests may, however, account for the temporally more remote effects that had been observed in results of later posttests. It is therefore impossible to conclude unequivocally that the cognitive and behavioral effects that had been observed 3 to 5 months, 15 to 17 months, and 21 months after the experimental treatment resulted from the experimental treatment alone. Such a conclusion suggests a need for further research designed to assess the long-term effects of the experimental treatment alone, uncontaminated by the possible effects of repeated post-tests.

After reviewing the various interpretations offered—methodological, statistical, and substantive—it seems safe to conclude that the most parsimonious explanation of the experimental findings is that the experimental treatment, with or without the reinforcing effects of the posttests, resulted in genuine and lasting changes in values, attitudes, and behavior. The psychological mechanism that initiated such changes was a conscious and specific feeling of self-dissatisfaction concerning contradictions implicating self-conceptions.

PART FIVE
Summary

14
Implications for the Behavioral Sciences and for Society

The conceptualizations and findings that have been reported in this work obviously have wide-ranging methodological, theoretical, practical, and ethical implications. I will try in this final chapter to identify and discuss those that appear to be the most important for the behavioral sciences and for society.

METHODOLOGICAL IMPLICATIONS

Our findings suggest that the instrument that has been developed to measure values is simple and economical and can be employed to describe the values of virtually all people who can read at a certain minimal level of proficiency. The methodological significance of the availability of such an instrument is that it is now possible to describe the values of virtually any individual or group in quantitative terms and to compare and contrast them with those of any other individual group. By using appropriate sampling procedures, it is also possible to make quantitative statements about the value priorities of a whole society and of various segments of society, thus providing a social indicator of the level of aspiration, adaptation, and degree of conflict within and between individuals and groups in a total society. By repeated measurement, it is methodologically feasible, too, to plot the course of change in various values over time.

A beginning has already been made in this direction. A first national survey of values was conducted in April 1968, and the results of this survey have been reported here and elsewhere (Rokeach, 1969a, 1969b, 1970a, 1970b; Rokeach and Parker, 1970; Rokeach, Miller, and Snyder, 1971;

Rokeach and Vidmar, 1973). A second national survey was conducted in spring 1971. Findings from both of these surveys as well as from future ones will be reported separately.

Our findings, which concern mainly American values, naturally generate questions about similarities to and differences from other cultural values. Cross-cultural studies of values have usually employed measuring instruments that are too complex, lengthy, or narrow in scope to provide valid information about representative national samples. Researchers have therefore contented themselves mainly with comparisons of highly literate college students in different countries. Assuming that the sets of 18 instrumental and 18 terminal values are reasonably universal and that problems of translation can be resolved, the availability of the Value Survey removes at least these methodological obstacles to the cross-national study of values. The fact that we have succeeded in obtaining meaningful data about the values of a representative sample of adult Americans encourages us to think that similar data can also be obtained for other national samples, providing us, we hope, with cross-cultural social indicators of value aspirations, value gaps, and value conflicts.

Another methodological implication derives from the fact that the Value Survey not only measures a person's own values but also the perceived values of others—other persons, groups, organizations, institutions, nations, and cultures. Corporate or organizational image can be conceptualized as a person's perception of the value system of a social organization. Feather (1970b, 1971, 1972a, 1972c) has compared the value systems of high school students with their perceptions of their educational institution's value system. At a more theoretical level, Feather (1971a) has identified a person's own values as an instance of *abstract structure* and those a person perceives others to have as an instance of *perceived structure*. Discrepancies between abstract and perceived cognitive structures can be resolved in various ways in order to achieve a better fit between person and environment. In research presently under way, subjects are being asked to rank not only their own values but also their perceived values of American society. Preliminary findings suggest that the greater the discrepancy between one's own and one's perception of societal values, the greater one's alienation. Similarly, a person's stereotypes of a cultural, racial, ethnic, or sexual (Horvath, 1972) group can be conceptualized as the values that he attributes to a particular group, and accuracy of stereotype can be conceptualized and measured as a discrepancy between perceived and actual value rankings.

Closely related to the measurement of the perceived values of others is the measurement of the perceived value consequences of certain "futures." Salancik (1971) asked subjects to judge the extent to which two potential future developments (a major shift in government spending from the military to urban planning and a major shift in equal opportunity employment for men and women) would contribute to the attainment of 18 terminal values. Salancik found that his subjects could reliably discriminate these two "futures" in terms of the values to which each of them would most contribute. Moreover, he found that these rankings of "futurist" values are related in certain predictable ways to the values of different income and racial groups. His findings therefore suggest that our approach to the measurement of values may prove to be useful in "futurist" research (Baier and Rescher, 1969). In a similar vein, Alvin Toffler has suggested that the forecasting of the impact of society on values may become a profession of the future (Toffler, 1969).

Yet another methodological implication is suggested by the findings obtained through content analysis. The value hierarchies extracted from the writings of Hitler, Lenin, Goldwater, and the socialists suggest that content analysis can reliably be employed to ascertain the terminal and instrumental value hierarchies contained within any political, historical, or literary document. Moreover, a content analysis of values can be used to resolve issues of disputed authorship (Rokeach, Homant, and Penner, 1970).

A final methodological implication concerns the measurement of self-dissatisfaction in the present work and will be most relevant to experimental research concerned with balance and consistency theories. Recall that self-dissatisfaction has been identified as the crucial variable that initiates a process of cognitive and behavioral change. The methodological import of this finding is that psychological states of imbalance or inconsistency need no longer be attributed to human subjects by outside observers on the basis of theoretical argument or speculation. Self-dissatisfaction can be measured routinely and can be brought under experimental control. Two dissonance type studies recently carried out at Michigan State University can be cited as illustrations. In a replication of Freedman's study (1965), TePaste (1969) found that subjects who reported they were satisfied with their performance in a choice situation more often preferred to expose themselves afterward to dissonant information, whereas dissatisfied subjects more often preferred consonant information. Opsinc (1970) independently manipulated self-satisfaction and the amount of effort expended on a task in order to compare their separate effects on task evaluation. He found that task evaluation was more clearly and significantly a function of self-satisfaction than of task effort: The satisfied group evaluated the task they had performed more favorably than the dissatisfied group, regardless of amount of effort expended.

THEORETICAL IMPLICATIONS

The theoretical implications of the present work concern many different issues: the conceptual distinctiveness of terminal and instrumental values, the conceptual place of values in all the behavioral sciences, the role that social institutions play in instilling and maintaining human values, the validity of conflicting theories of personality development and of Maslow's hierarchical theory of motivation. This work also has important implications for contemporary social psychological theories that are mainly concerned with attitudes, short-term change, persuasion, and consistency between cognitive elements. Finally, new theoretical questions are raised by the present work that only future research will be able to answer.

Terminal and Instrumental Values

Several lines of evidence confirm that terminal and instrumental values come from two different yet conceptually related universes of values. The reliabilities of terminal value systems are without exception found to be higher than those obtained for instrumental value systems: The disputed Federalist papers' instrumental but not terminal value systems established James Madison as their author (Rokeach, Homant, and Penner, 1970). Conversely, similarity of terminal but not instrumental value systems is an important determinant of harmonious interpersonal interaction (Shotland, 1968; Sikula, 1970). All these findings point to the conceptual distinctiveness of the two sets of values and suggest that terminal and instrumental values may play different roles in different areas of social life. Considerably more research is needed, however, to clarify further the relation between terminal and instrumental values and the various social conditions under which one or the other set will be the more important. Finally, a question may be raised about the possibility of inducing lasting change in instrumental values. There seems to be no compelling theoretical reason why instrumental values should not also be capable of being lastingly altered by procedures such as those that have been described here, and this seems to be supported by the work of Conroy, Katkin, and Barnette (1973) which has been described in Chapter 12.

Values and the Behavioral Sciences

The findings suggest that culture, society, and personality are the major antecedents of values and that attitudes and behavior are their major consequents. Virtually every comparison we have undertaken between groups differing in cultural, demographic, social class, or personality variables has uncovered distinctive value patterns. Similarly, distinctive value patterns have been found to underlie differences in virtually every attitudinal, behavioral, life style, interest, and occupational variable. Thus, values seem to be implicated either as dependent or independent variables at virtually all levels of social analysis—cultural, institutional, group, and individual. It is tempting to suggest, even at the risk of oversimplification, that the fields of anthropology and sociology are more concerned with values as dependent variables, and psychology is more concerned with values as independent variables. Whether or not others will agree with this view, value data such as those that we have reported seem to be relevant to all the behavioral sciences and to philosophy and religion as well.

Values and Social Institutions

Different social institutions can be conceptualized as specializing in the enhancement of different subsets of values. Our findings seem to be consistent with this hypothesis. The effects of Christian institutions are reflected mainly as variations in *salvation* and *forgiving*, and the effects of political institutions are reflected mainly as variations in *equality* and *freedom*. Similarly, the effects of educational, economic, and law enforcement institutions are reflected as variations in yet other subsets of values. Thus, a person's total value system may be an end result, at least in large part, of all the institutional forces or influences that have acted upon him. Further research is needed to identify more clearly the particular subset of values that each social institution focuses upon, the extent of overlap and competition among institutional values, the effectiveness of different social institutions and organizations as value-socializing agents, and the conditions under which institutional value change can be brought about.

Values and Personality Development

The classical psychoanalytic view of psychosexual development holds that personality is formed and stabilized by the end of the latency period of psychosexual development. If this were indeed the case, value development should parallel psychosexual development and one should end when the other ends. The data, however, show a continual development of values from early youth to old age, a finding that is more in accord with Erikson's (1950) than with Freud's view of personality development. Further research is now needed to describe more clearly the value systems that are characteristic of Erikson's eight identity stages and to determine the precise nature of the value changes that accompany change in stages of identity.

Maslow's Theory of Needs

Many of our findings are consistent with Maslow's hierarchical theory of human motivation (1954). If we assume that lower-order safety and security needs are reflected in a higher regard for values concerning material comfort, conventional forms of religion, and conformity, then our findings suggest that such lower-order needs are more important to the poor and the uneducated. In contrast, the affluent and educated typically regard values reflecting safety and security needs as relatively unimportant, not so much because they are not valued but because they are taken for granted. Taking such values for granted frees the affluent and educated to place greater emphasis on higher-order values, for instance, on love, competence, and self-actualization.

Implications for Psychological Theories of Change

Perhaps the most important theoretical implications of our work are those that are suggested by the extensive findings concerning long-term change in values, attitudes, and behavior and those concerning the mechanisms leading to such changes. They suggest that current knowledge about cognitive change, because it betrays an insensitivity to the values and the self-conceptions that functionally underlie attitudes and behavior, is limited knowledge—about short-term cognitive change, about persuasion rather than education, and about cognitive effects having negligible or even nonexistent behavioral effects. Our work suggests that such shortcomings can be overcome if a more central position is accorded in our social psychological theories to people's values and self-conceptions. Moreover, such a recentering should serve to integrate the presently compartmental-ized theories of personality change, cognitive change, and behavioral change that do not speak to each other into a more unified theory of psychological change.

The Nature of Consistency

That certain values and attitudes undergo lasting change even when they are altogether consistent with one another suggests that the crucial com-ponents that enter into psychologically inconsistent relations have not been properly identified. This is but another way of saying that the contemporary concept of consistency has been poorly understood. Our work suggests that psychological consistency concerns not any two relatable or related cognitions but two cognitions that are present in every human situation: self-conceptions and cognitions about performance. Such a reformulation of the nature of consistency, if accepted, would require a reinterpretation of all the findings and, consequently, a reassessment of the validity of all the hypotheses that have been generated by current consistency theories.

Direction of Change

All the long-term changes that have been demonstrated in this and in related work (Penner, 1971; Rokeach and Cochrane, 1972; Rokeach and McLellan, 1972; Cochrane and Kelly, 1971; McLellan, 1973; Hollen, 1972; Conroy, Katkin, and Barnette, 1973) have been toward an increase rather than a decrease in the importance of four values in particular— equality, freedom, a world of beauty, and self-controlled. One question that therefore arises is whether it would also be possible lastingly to alter such values in an opposite direction, so that they will become less important. Our theory ventures to suggest that value change, and attitude and beha-vioral change that might follow value change, may be unidirectional rather than bidirectional in nature. Such changes can be initiated only by inducing an affective state of self-dissatisfaction concerning contradictions with self-conceptions and are motivated by the desire at least to maintain and if possible to enhance conceptions of oneself as a moral and competent human being. It is easy to see how one's self-conceptions may be main-tained or enhanced by increasing one's regard for such values as equality, freedom, and a world of beauty or by decreasing one's regard for such values as *a comfortable life*, *national security*, and being *obedient*, but it is difficult to see how changes in the opposite direction would also serve such a purpose, at least in the same person. A person should undergo an increase or decrease in regard for any given value in only one direction—whichever direction will provide his self-conceptions with a certain mileage—and not in the other direction. In the final analysis, self-conceptions reflect social definitions of the self; self-conceptions will suffer or be maintained or enhanced within some social framework that defines how a person should behave and what he should strive for. The extent to which a person will think well of himself depends a great deal on the extent to which he thinks he satisfies the demands of certain social institutions, certain organizations or groups that he identifies with, and, in some instances, the demands of the total society.

It therefore seems unlikely on theoretical grounds that value change, and associated cognitive and behavioral changes, can be brought about arbitrarily in either direction. This is an issue that can be resolved, however, only by further research. But those who would contemplate doing such research confront grave ethical issues. These issues will be discussed in a later section of this chapter.

Implications for Inducing Personality Change

If lasting changes in values, attitudes, and behavior can be effected by self-confrontation, is it not also possible, using similar procedures, to effect lasting change in personality traits? The fact that persons varying in dogmatism, authoritarianism, and other personality traits had been equally affected by the experimental procedures suggests that even persons who are believed to be extremely resistant to change can be induced to change their basic outlooks and actions. It is perhaps necessary to emphasize that the variables that had been experimentally affected were values, attitudes, and behavior and not personality traits as ordinarily conceived. Nonetheless, the question arises whether personality variables per se could also be lastingly affected by arousing self-dissatisfaction over contradictions implicating self-conceptions on the one hand and knowledge about one's personality traits on the other.

Consider how we might proceed if we were to try to induce lasting changes in, say, authoritarianism, as measured by the F scale. We might start with the empirical fact that the correlation between authoritarianism and ethnocentrism is about .75 (Adorno, *et al.*, 1950, p. 263). Then, proceeding in a manner similar to that described in Chapter 9, experimental subjects could be asked to fill out the Ethnocentrism and F scales, taught how to score them and how to interpret their scores, and then exposed to, say, a simple 2×2 "Table 1" showing the previously obtained relation between high and low authoritarianism and high and low ethnocentrism. Some subjects, in comparing their own scores with those represented in the table, will discover that they had scored low or high on both variables, and others will discover that they had scored low on one and high on the other.

It may be conjectured that those discovering they had scored low on authoritarianism and ethnocentrism will remain satisfied with themselves upon learning of their performance. Many subjects in the latter three categories should, however, experience dismay or dissatisfaction upon learning of their test performance. Even authoritarians and bigots do not like to think of themselves as authoritarians and bigots (Allport and Kramer, 1946), and even authoritarians and bigots need to understand themselves and to think of themselves, in comparison with others, as decent and competent human beings.

Such considerations lead us to speculate that it should be possible to induce enduring change in any personality variable by self-confrontation procedures similar to those that we have employed. Any sort of information about oneself that is displeasing, whether it is information about one's values, attitudes, or behavior or about one's personality, should initiate some process of change in that variable, providing the information is credible and providing, of course, that the person has the ability to do something about it. Such conjectures about the possibility of changing personality variables invite further empirical research.

PRACTICAL IMPLICATIONS

A number of practical implications come to mind. That the Value Survey has been found to discriminate among so many different groups; that different values are central in different areas of social life; that values, attitudes, and behavior can undergo lasting change when people become aware of certain contradictions within themselves—all these have practical implications, especially for the fields of guidance and selection, education and therapy, and, of course, the world of politics.

The Value Survey can be used as a diagnostic tool to identify the needs, goals, aspirations, and conflicts within and between individuals and groups. At the individual level, it can, for instance, be used as a diagnostic tool in academic and vocational counselling and selection, or to chart the progress of psychotherapy, or to identify the political value orientations of electorates. At the group level, it can be employed as a social indicator to locate the sources of conflict and value gaps between such groups as students and teachers, young and old, establishment and antiestablishment, husbands and wives, police and policed, blacks and whites, superordinates and subordinates, and nation and nation.

Since value data are both intrinsically easy to understand and ego-involving for persons of various ages, educational levels, and occupations, they can be used to increase people's knowledge and understanding of themselves and others. The subjects in our studies and various student and adult audiences who have heard about the results of these studies have usually been curious about their own value positions and how their own positions compare with those of other reference persons and groups. These audiences are typically most curious about the similarities and differences between groups varying in culture, social class, race, age, sex, occupation, ethnic, religious, and political identification and about persons espousing different positions on the salient issues of our time.

Information about the values possessed by self and by others can be presented in various ways—orally, in written form, or by a combination of these two methods, as in the experiments reported in this book. Feedback of such information can also be programmed on a computer. In research now under way, the subject is asked to fill out the Value Survey and to communicate his value rankings via teletype to the computer. He then asks the computer to provide him with information about the values of certain reference groups he may be curious about, for example, men and women or the educated and the uneducated. The computer responds by printing out the subject's own values and those of various reference groups in which he had expressed an interest, and, moreover, it displays discrepancies between the subject's own and others' values. It is thus possible to envision the automated teaching of values about self and others via computers that are located in school buildings, museums, and expositions (Lee, 1968).

Teaching people about values is, however, intricately linked to changing values through an awareness of contradictions existing within their own belief systems. The experimental findings we have reported have concerned only a very small number of such contradictions, mainly between self-conceptions and a few preselected values, attitudes, and behavior. But the intricate network of functional connections that is conceived to exist among self-conceptions, terminal and instrumental values, attitudes, and behaviors makes it probable that virtually everyone has a number of contradictions within his total belief system. People in everyday life will remain chronically unaware of whatever contradicting beliefs they may have because most social circumstances will encourage camouflage and ego defense and few social circumstances will facilitate or force self-awareness. Data on the national sample collected in 1968, for instance, reveal that about 18 percent of adult Americans who had preferred George Wallace had nonetheless ranked *equality* in the upper third of the 18-value scale; about one out of seven adult Americans who had ranked *salvation* in the upper third had nonetheless ranked *forgiving* in the lower third; about one out of ten adult Americans who had ranked *independent* in the upper third had also ranked *obedient* there. The practical implication of such findings is that the potential for increased self-awareness and change in the values, attitudes, and behavior of Americans—indeed, of all human beings—would be very great if it were possible to bring contradictions such as these to their conscious attention.

The proposition that exposure to information can change values, attitudes, and behavior is certainly not new and is consistent with common sense. Yet, so formulated, the proposition has received little or no verification in research studies designed to test it. Thus, Lewin and Grabbe (1945) write:

> We know that lectures or other similarly abstract methods of transmitting knowledge are of little or no avail in changing his subsequent outlook and conduct. We might be tempted, therefore, to think that what is lacking in these methods is first-hand experience. The sad truth is that even first-hand experience will not necessarily produce the desired result (p. 56).

Two comments are in order about the above quotation. First, only first-hand experience of a specific kind should "produce the desired result," namely, a first-hand experience which produces an identifiable feeling of dissatisfaction with oneself. Second, the experimental findings we report here suggest that any information which produces such self-dissatisfaction, even if transmitted by a lecture, should "produce the desired result."

It is not necessary to assume, however, that value change can be induced only when target values are preselected by someone other than the subject. Recall that the experimental subjects who had expressed dissatisfaction with their rankings of virtually *any* value at the end of the experimental session had typically undergone more lasting change on that value than had those who had expressed satisfaction with their value rankings. Over and above the increases that had been experimentally induced by focusing the subject's attention on the two target values, many other value rankings had changed, either increasing or decreasing in importance depending upon the nature of the dissatisfaction the subjects had experienced with one value or another. These findings suggest that the real impetus for value change comes ultimately from the subject himself rather than from the experimenter and that change is a result of a process of inspecting and comparing one's own value rankings with those of others. Merely telling a person about his own values and giving him a free hand to compare them with those of significant others may be a sufficient condition for initiating value change.

Beyond the issue of strategies for the teaching and changing of values, there is a more general educational issue. We may assume that many students enroll in social science courses and especially in psychology courses because they are motivated by the desire to understand themselves and others better, in order to resolve conflicts, reduce anxiety, increase their ability to relate harmoniously with others, and, it is hoped, to apply such knowledge afterward in their daily lives. The textbooks they are assigned and the lectures they attend contain what must appear to the students to be countless reports of correlational and causal relationships among cultural, sociological, situational, personological, cognitive, and behavioral variables, as they have been demonstrated in empirical research with *others*. The students are expected to learn about such relationships on the assumption, no doubt, that such knowledge will increase their understanding not only of others but of themselves. But, curiously, great pains are usually taken to keep students in the dark about their own positions on the social and personal variables they are required to learn, and this may be tantamount to throwing away our best teaching tool—personal relevance—a teaching advantage the natural sciences do not possess. The way psychology typically is taught discourages students from making personal applications of empirical knowledge. Thus, they stand little chance of discovering, for instance, whether they are high, middle, or low on prejudice compared with others; or that they are authoritarian, dogmatic, rigid, Machiavellian, or aggressive; or achievement- or affiliation-oriented; externally or internally controlled; intolerant of ambiguity; or repressed, impulsive, extraverted, neurotic, or psychopathic.

Beyond the issue of self-knowledge about single variables there is the issue of self-knowledge about relationships between two or more variables. Relationships between psychological variables are always far from perfect, which means that there are always individuals who fall into the "wrong" cells. Because we do not give students in psychology courses (or in other social science courses) the opportunity of finding out about such relationships as they might exist within themselves, we pass up many valuable teaching and change-inducing opportunities—for example: making students aware that they are high in need achievement yet doing poorly in school; high in anti-Semitism yet low in authoritarianism; higher in anti-Semitism and authoritarianism than most others; high in altruism yet had not helped in a bystander experiment they had participated in; high in aesthetic interest yet had not attended an art exhibition or concert all year; high in need for independence yet had conformed in a Sherif-, Asch-, or Milgram-type experiment they had participated in; frequent churchgoers yet anti-black; or middle class yet alienated. All such personal knowledge is typically ruled out as not relevant to the conceptual understanding of relationships and generalizations derived from research with human subjects, perhaps on the assumption that such principles are to be learned and understood in the same way as the principle of gravity, the laws of logic, and the periodic tables are to be learned and understood.

Moving on to the matter of practical implications for psychotherapy, the aim of psychotherapy can be conceptualized, at least in part, as an attempt to bring about value change or value reeducation in a client or patient. Human conflicts, anxieties, addictive or compulsive behavior, and difficulties in interpersonal relations (Szasz, 1961) can all be assumed to leave traces in the client's or patient's value system (and also in the value systems of others with whom he interacts). If therapy is to be successful, it must surely be manifested as changes or rearrangements of value priorities and as changes in the degree of integration of the client's or patient's value system. Thus, our work is as relevant to the field of psychotherapy as it is to education: The two fields are equally concerned with increasing people's self-awareness and with value development, value change, value integration, and behavioral change. Value therapy is, after all, not all that different in aim from value education on the one hand and behavioral modification on the other.

It is, of course, impossible to ignore the political implications of our work. Recall that the experimental subjects had undergone lasting change in their rankings of the two values that have been found to be distinctively political, and that changes in rankings of these two political values had culminated in change in related political attitudes and behavior. The findings that political values represent basic ideological predispositions are significantly related to so many different kinds of attitudes and behaviors, can be experimentally altered, and can then lead to changes in associated attitudes and behavior all have obvious political implications. They suggest that changing political values may set in motion a general process of change in basic ideological predispositions, in attitudes toward the various political issues of the day, or in extent of political activism, culminating in preferences and ballots cast for political parties and candidates, and culminating, as Pepitone (1969) has suggested, in revolutionary behavior. Moreover, that such enduring value changes can be induced by a single experimental session takes on rather awesome and ominous political implications if the mass media is substituted for the classroom as the channel of communication and if the intended direction of change is to decrease rather than increase the importance of the two political values.

There are several other practical implications to which attention should briefly be drawn. Thus far, experimental attention has concentrated exclusively on the two distinctively political values as the target values (Rokeach, 1968a, 1968b, 1971; Penner, 1971; Rokeach and Cochrane, 1972; Rokeach and McLellan, 1972; Cochrane and Kelly, 1971; McLellan, 1973). Hollen (1972) and Conroy, Katkin, and Barnette (1973) have extended this work to a third and fourth value—*a world of beauty* and *self-control*—and have suggested, using procedures similar to those we employed, that experimental subjects will also undergo significant long-term increases in these values and that such increases will also lead to significant changes in related social attitudes or behaviors. Such findings have clear implications for issues concerning ecology on one hand and psychotherapy on the other.

In the same vein, educators might deem it desirable to select other values, for example, *a sense of accomplishment, capable,* or *intellectual,* as the target values to increase, on the hypothesis that increasing them might facilitate learning, creativeness, or self-actualization. Organized religion might wish to select other values, for instance, *salvation, forgiving,* and *loving,* as the values that deserve special attention, on the hypothesis that increasing them might increase a person's chances for an everlasting life or might lead him to become more truly compassionate. Other groups, such as the family, commercial institutions, Madison Avenue, the military, and law enforcement might each choose yet other values as targets for change, on the assumption that changing such other values will lead to changes in associated attitudes and behaviors.

ETHICAL IMPLICATIONS

How is it possible ethically to defend psychological research that is intended to bring about more or less permanent change in a person's values and associated attitudes and behavior without his fully informed consent? If we have indeed learned how to effect changes in values and associated attitudes and behavior, as the experiments we have reported suggest, is it ethically permissible to apply these research findings to meet practical ends, for instance, to bring about changes in political or religious values, attitudes, and behavior? If so, what kinds of change in the real world are ethically allowable? Who shall decide which values are ethically permissible targets for change, and who shall decide the ethically permissible directions of that change?

All such ethical issues seem to be reducible to two more fundamental questions: Is it ever permissible, in the scientific laboratory, in the classroom, or in the real world, to enduringly change other people without their fully informed consent? If so, what ethical criteria are to be employed as standards for deciding what is permissible and what is not?

In response to the first question, it may first be observed that every teacher who takes professional pride in his work would like to think that his teaching has affected the values, attitudes, and behavior of his students in some significant way. So long as he cannot prove that what he does in the classroom has in fact resulted in such change, his assertions that it has will go unnoticed and unchallenged. But as soon as he can demonstrate that his teaching methods have indeed resulted in enduring effects on his students, especially on their values, he risks the criticism that he is unethically manipulating them without their informed consent. We can expect criticism to be even more severe if the particular values the teacher has acted upon are considered to be the special prerogative of other social institutions, for instance, the family, the church, or political institutions.

Educational institutions have always been in the business of transmitting knowledge from one generation to the next and of shaping certain values in certain directions. They have also been in the business of producing new knowledge, including information about better teaching methods. Cognitively oriented psychologists like Jerome Bruner and antimentalist psychologists like B. F. Skinner have devoted much of their scientific attention to the development of new or better theories and methods for transmitting knowledge. But if we grant that educational insitutions shape values as well as produce new knowledge, then on both grounds research on better methods of shaping values deserves more of our research attention.

Educational institutions are, however, not the only institutions of society that are in the business of shaping values. As previously suggested, all social institutions can be thought to specialize in the shaping, enhancing, and changing of different subsets of values. For instance, the family, the church, and the military all see themselves as being legitimately concerned with the shaping of at least certain values, in directions that are congruent with the institution's values. Parents, ministers, and military men alike consider themselves competent to the extent that they succeed in doing so and, no less than the teacher, would like to think that their efforts had indeed significantly affected the values of those in their charge. Thus, in answer to the first question raised above, not only educational institutions but virtually every institution of society actually attempts to affect the values of those in its charge. Ethical issues concerning informed consent typically do not arise, except perhaps when one social institution encroaches upon or threatens the values of other institutions.

Turning now to the second question, what ethical criteria are to be employed in scientific research and in practical applications when deciding which values may be acted upon and when deciding the direction of change? In recent years, those engaged in research with human subjects have more or less universally accepted the proposition that ethical decisions concerning the welfare of human subjects should not be made solely by individual scientists. Research proposals by individual investigators involving the use of human subjects are increasingly subject to external review by committees selected from the wider academic community, to ensure that the welfare and rights of human subjects are protected and that the scientific gain that is anticipated clearly outweighs momentary inconvenience or harm to the subject. Ethical questions have been raised in such contexts not only about informed consent but also about invasion of privacy, the employment of deception, protection of confidentiality, physical and emotional harm to human subjects, the use of volunteers, and about debriefing and educational feedback.

It is appropriate to comment here on three major ethical criteria that have been especially pertinent in guiding our experimental work concerned with the issue of producing *lasting* cognitive and behavioral change. I had formulated them myself in collaboration with a university-wide ethics committee on human subjects, and there is no reason to think that these criteria would not apply to practical situations as well.

Selecting a particular value as the target value and changing its importance in the chosen direction is ethically permissible if, in the judgment of at least a majority of the reviewing committee, it is first, compatible with the basic assumptions of a democratic society and, even more important, in the interest of all humanity. On the basis of both of these criteria, research intended to induce decreases in such values as *freedom, equality, a world at peace*, or *a world of beauty* would not be ethically permissible. A third major criterion that had been formulated concerned the use of deception: False feedback about one's own or others' values, attitudes, and behavior is ethically indefensible.

As previously stated, perhaps the most frightening practical application of our work is to the political area. Is it ethically permissible to apply present theoretical and empirical knowledge to change the political values of the electorate in order to increase the chances of electing a Hitler? a George Wallace? a Richard Nixon? a Martin Luther King? a Kennedy? Is it ethically permissible to try to alter religious values in a direction that will make them more important? less important? If the ethical principles that guide our decisions about allowable practical applications are to be the same as those that guide our decisions about allowable scientific research, the same standards should apply: Is the practical application judged to be in the basic interests of a democratic society and, more important, of all humanity? Will it rely on feedback that tells the truth? If the answer to any one of these questions is a consensual no, then the practical application would be ethically indefensible, at least among those who would consider themselves bound to the same code of ethics that governs scientific research.

Since research and application intended to decrease the importance of such political values as *equality* and *freedom* are ethically indefensible, we can only speculate at this time on whether such decreases are actually possible. As previously stated, theoretical considerations suggest that the changes that can be experimentally induced in the ranking of such values by feedback of information about self and others are unidirectional rather than bidirectional in nature. Because of these theoretical considerations, I am unable to envision an experimental design, a set of instructions, and a set of data, truthful or not, that upon being fed back to two groups of comparable subjects would induce within them feelings of self-dissatisfaction over contradictions implicating their self-conceptions which would then be successfully alleviated in one group by lowering and in the other group by raising the importance that would be attached to the same value.

It must be confessed, however, that such speculations are at best uneasy ones. The issue of unidirectionality versus bidirectionality can be resolved only by further empirical research and not by theoretical argument.

Ethical considerations such as those discussed above clearly forbid such empirical research.

We are thus left with a paradox that neither the behavioral sciences nor society can allow to remain unresolved. We must find some other way out of this impasse—for science's sake, and even more, for society's sake.

A CONCLUDING PHILOSOPHICAL COMMENT

There are, finally, some philosophical implications to consider. This work on human values is clearly deterministic in outlook, aligning itself with

Skinner's arguments in *Beyond Freedom and Dignity* (1971) against "autonomous man" and for determinism. We have viewed self-conceptions and values as determined by environmental arrangements or contingencies of reinforcement that are cultural, social, and personal in origin, and these provide contingencies for reinforcing other mental states and behavior. But the matter of determinism, while still a philosophical issue, is rarely debated nowadays as a scientific issue. Social scientists of all theoretical persuasions, from Skinner at one extreme to Lewin, the symbolic interactionists, and Freud at the other, have long agreed that human behavior is determined by genetic endowment and by environmental circumstances.

Contrary to Skinner, however, I have argued that humans, determined though they all are, vary in how much they care about freedom, dignity, and other values; that they can indeed be said to possess values; that values determine behavior; and that value change leads to attitudinal and behavioral change. Even more extensively, I have argued throughout this work that many forms of behavior are determined by belief systems consisting of functionally interrelated self-conceptions, terminal and instrumental values, attitudes, cognitions about behavior, and cognitions about other people's cognitions and behavior. Moreover, man has been seen as one capable of feeling satisfied and dissatisfied with himself as he becomes aware of discrepancies that implicate self-conceptions, and such awareness and associated feelings have been seen as having cognitive and behavioral consequences. All such mentalistic formulations are anathema, of course, to those who would insist that contingencies of reinforcement "provide alternative formulations of so-called 'mental processes' " (Skinner, 1971, p. 149).

In the final analysis the validity of any "scientific analysis of behavior" hinges upon its ability to address itself to and account for the known empirical facts. In *Beyond Freedom and Dignity*, Skinner denies that man possesses values or, indeed, any mental state or feeling (conceded at most to be a by-product) and offers alternative explanations to account for behavior said to be determined by values, especially by the values of freedom and dignity. It is therefore fitting to consider, in concluding this work, the way a Skinner might proceed to account for the various kinds of empirical findings reported in this book.

These findings concern the stability of values and value systems; individual differences in value stability; age differences in values; value similarities and differences among groups varying in demographic, sociological, and psychological characteristics; and empirical relationships between values on the one hand and attitudes and behavior on the other. All these can readily be explained as verbal and nonverbal responses to differential contingencies of reinforcement provided by the external social environment.

More troublesome for a "scientific analysis of behavior," however, are the many experimental findings indicating lasting and remote cognitive and behavioral consequences following a single experimental treatment. The present formulation attempts to account for the various behavioral outcomes by proposing that they were consequences of objectively detectable mental reorganizations of belief systems that, in turn, were consequences of objectively detectable mental states of distress that, in turn, were consequences of mental awareness of certain contradictions that, in turn, were induced by an experimental situation providing contingencies of reinforcement massive enough *not* to require additional reinforcement.

We gain at best a faint understanding by explaining all such experimental effects as nothing more than verbal and nonverbal behavioral consequences of contingencies of reinforcement in no way mediated by mental processes. It is not readily apparent from Skinner's principles ("Behavior is shaped and maintained by its consequences" (p. 18) and "it is the contingencies which must be changed if . . . behavior is to be changed" (p. 147) which, if any, behaviors had been shaped or maintained by the experimental environment, what sorts of changes in contingencies, if any, had led to the verbal and nonverbal behavioral changes, and what sorts of consequences had shaped or maintained these behavioral changes. Nor is it apparent that the external environment of the subjects at the time of responding was responsible for the many behavioral differences observed within experimental groups or between experimental and control groups.

"Beliefs, preferences, perceptions, needs, purposes, and opinions," Skinner asserts, "are . . . said to change when we change minds. What is changed in each case is a probability of action" (Skinner, 1971, p. 93). Our findings do not become more understandable by asserting that the external environment changed a "probability of action," unless the external environment is conceded to be the environment that existed weeks and months before the observed effects and unless some effort is made to explain how the changed "probability of action" this external environment produced led to observable cognitive and behavioral changes weeks and months afterward. The findings become perhaps more understandable, however, when we assert that the external environment had induced changes in awareness, in feelings, and in mental states, that such changes persisted over time, and, in turn, induced behavioral changes. Admittedly, all this is mentalistic in formulation. Such a mentalistic formulation is, however, no less deterministic in outlook than an alternative deterministic formulation that denies mental states and feelings.

Considerations such as these suggest that what is needed is a more comprehensive and less dogmatic "scientific analysis of behavior" that addresses itself to and accounts for all the known facts, one that will go considerably beyond *Beyond Freedom and Dignity* in its philosophical conception of the nature of man and of human values and in its technological conception of the social controls required to bring about a surviving and sane social order.

References

Abelson, R. P., Aronson, E., McGuire, W. J., Newcomb, T. M., Rosenberg, M. J., & Tannenbaum, P. H. *Theories of cognitive consistency: A source book.* Chicago: Rand McNally, 1968.

Abelson, R. P., & Rosenberg, M. J. Symbolic psycho-logic: A model of attitudinal cognition. *Behavioral Science*, 1958, **3**, 1–13.

Adorno, T. W., Frenkel-Brunswik, E., Levinson, D. J., & Sanford, R. N. *The authoritarian personality.* New York: Harper, 1950.

Albert, E. M., & Kluckhohn, C. *A selected bibliography on values, ethics, and esthetics in the behavioral sciences and philosophy.* Glencoe, Ill.: Free Press, 1959.

Allen, R. O., & Spilka, B. Committed and consensual religion: A specification of religion-prejudice relationships. *Journal for the Scientific Study of Religion*, 1967, **6**, 191–206.

Allport, G. W. *The nature of prejudice.* Cambridge: Addison-Wesley, 1954.

Allport, G. W. *Pattern and growth in personality.* New York: Holt, Rinehart, & Winston, 1961.

Allport, G. W., & Kramer, B. M. Some roots of prejudice. *Journal of Psychology*, 1946, **22**, 9–39.

Allport, G. W., & Odbert, H. S. Trait-names: A psycho-lexical study. *Psychological Monographs*, 1936, **47** (Whole No. 211).

Allport, G. W., & Ross, J. M. Personal religious orientation and prejudice. *Journal of Personality and Social Psychology*, 1967, **5**, 432–443.

Allport, G. W., Vernon, P. E., & Lindzey, G. *A study of values.* Boston: Houghton Mifflin, 1960.

Anastasi, A. *Differential psychology: Individual and group differences in behavior.* New York: Macmillan, 1958.

Anderson, N. H. Likableness ratings of 555 personality-trait words. *Journal of Personality and Social Psychology*, 1968, **9**, 272–279.

Argyle, M., & Dean, J. Eye-contact, distance and affiliation. *Sociometry*, 1965, **28**, 289–304.

Argyris, C. The incompleteness of social-psychological theory. *American Psychologist*, 1969, **24**, 893–908.

341

Aronson, E. The theory of cognitive dissonance: A current perspective. In L. Berkowitz (Ed.), *Advances in experimental social psychology*. New York: Academic Press, 1969.

Atkinson, J. W. (Ed.) *Motives in fantasy, action and society: A method of assessment and study*. Princeton, N.J.: Van Nostrand, 1958.

Baier, K., & Rescher, N. (Eds.) *Values and the future*. New York: Free Press, 1969.

Bakan, D. The test of significance in psychological research. *Psychological Bulletin*, 1966, **66**, 423–437.

Ball-Rokeach, S. J. Values underlying attitude toward women's liberation. Unpublished paper, 1972.

Bandura, A. *Principles of behavior modification*. New York: Holt, Rinehart, & Winston, 1969.

Bauer, R. A. (Ed.) *Social indicators*. Cambridge: The M.I.T. Press, 1966.

Beech, R. P. Value systems, attitudes, and interpersonal attraction. Unpublished Ph.D. dissertation, Michigan State University Library, 1966.

Beech, R. P. Value systems in Calcutta: A study of four occupational groups. In R. P. Beech & M. J. Beech (Eds.), *Bengal: Change and continuity*. East Lansing, Mich.: Asian Studies Center, Michigan State University, undated.

Beech, R. P., & Schoeppe, A. A developmental study of value systems in adolescence. Paper presented at the meeting of the American Psychological Association, Miami Beach, Fla., 1970.

Bem, D. J. Self-perception: An alternative interpretation of cognitive dissonance phenomena. *Psychological Review*, 1967, **74**, 183–200.

Bem, D. J. *Beliefs, attitudes, and human affairs*. Belmont, Calif.: Brooks, Cole, 1970.

Bishop, G. F. Presidential preferences and values in 1968. Unpublished M.A. thesis, Michigan State University Library, 1969.

Blumenthal, M. D., Kahn, R. L., Andrews, F. M., & Head, K. B. *Justifying violence: Attitudes of American men*. Ann Arbor, Mich.: Institute for Social Research, 1972.

Bramel, D. Dissonance, expectation, and the self. In R. P. Abelson, *et al.* (Eds.), *Theories of cognitive consistency: A sourcebook*. Chicago: Rand McNally, 1968.

Brawer, F. B. *Values and the generation gap: Junior college freshmen and faculty*. ERIC Clearinghouse for Junior Colleges, Monograph Series, No. 11, Washington, D.C.: American Association of Junior Colleges (One Dupont Circle, N.W., 20036), 1971.

Brehm, J. W. *A theory of psychological reactance*. New York: Academic Press, 1966.

Brehm, J. W., & Cohen, A. R. *Explorations in cognitive dissonance*. New York: Wiley, 1962.

Bruner, J. S., & Postman, L. Perception, cognition, and behavior. *Journal of Personality*, 1949, **18**, 14–31.

Budner, S. Intolerance of ambiguity. *Journal of Personality*, 1962, **30**, 29–50.

Burton, A. (Ed.) *Encounter: The theory and practice of encounter groups*. San Francisco: Jossey-Bass, 1969.

Campbell, D. T. Social attitudes and other acquired behavioral dispositions. In S. Koch (Ed.), *Psychology: A study of a science*, Vol. 6. New York: McGraw-Hill, 1963.

Campbell, D. T., & Fiske, D. Convergent and discriminant validation by the multitrait-multimethod matrix. *Psychological Bulletin*, 1959, **56**, 81–105.

Campbell, D. T., & Stanley, J. C. *Experimental and quasi-experimental designs for research*. Chicago: Rand McNally, 1963.

Campbell, J. P., & Dunnette, M. D. Effectiveness of t-group experiences in managerial training and development. *Psychological Bulletin*, 1968, **70**, 73–104.

Carlson, E. R. Attitude change through modification of attitude structure. *Journal of Abnormal and Social Psychology*, 1956, **52**, 256–261.

Cattell, R. B. Psychological measurement: Normative, ipsative, interactive. *Psychological Review*, 1944, **51**, 292–303.

Caute, D. *The left in Europe*. New York: World University Library, 1966.

Christie, R. Eysenck's treatment of the personality of communists. *Psychological Bulletin*, 1956, **53**, 411–430. (a)

Christie, R. Some abuses of psychology. *Psychological Bulletin*, 1956, **53**, 439–451. (b)

Christie, R., & Merton, R. K. Procedure for the sociological study of the value climate of medical schools. *Journal of Medical Education*, 1958, **8**, 125–153.

Cochrane, R. The structure of value systems in male and female prisoners. *British Journal of Criminology*, 1971, **11**, 73–79.

Cochrane, R., & Kelly, K. Personality and the differential effectiveness of an experimental value change procedure. Unpublished paper, 1971.

Cochrane, R., & Rokeach, M. Rokeach's value survey: A methodological note. *Journal of Experimental Research in Personality*, 1970, **4**, 159–161.

Conroy, W. J., Katkin, E. S., & Barnette, W. L. Modification of smoking behavior by Rokeach's self-confrontation technique. Paper presented at the annual meetings of the Southeastern Psychological Association in New Orleans, April 7, 1973.

Cooley, C. H. *Two major works: Social organization & Human nature and the social order*. Glencoe, Ill.: Free Press, 1956.

Cronbach, L. J. Response sets and test validity. *Educational and Psychological Measurement*, 1946, **6**, 475–494.

Cronbach, L. J. Further evidence on response sets and test design. *Educational and Psychological Measurement*, 1950, **10**, 3–31.

Cronbach, L. J., & Furby, L. How should we measure "change"—or should we? *Psychological Bulletin*, 1970, **74**, 68–80.

Cronbach, L. J., & Meehl, P. E. Construct validity in psychological tests. *Psychological Bulletin*, 1955, **52**, 281–302.

Cross, H. J., Doost, R. M., & Tracy, J. J. A study of values among hippies. *Proceedings, 78th Annual Convention, American Psychological Association*, 1970, 449–450.

Crowne, D. P., & Marlowe, D. *The approval motive*. New York: Wiley, 1964.

de Tocqueville, A. The old regime and the French Revolution. In J. R. Gusfield (Ed.), *Protest, reform, and revolt*. New York: Wiley, 1970.

Deutsch, M., & Gerard, H. B. A study of normative and informational social influence upon individual judgment. *Journal of Abnormal and Social Psychology*, 1955, **51**, 629–636.

Duffy, E. A critical review of investigations employing the Allport-Vernon study of values and other tests of evaluative attitude. *Psychological Bulletin*, 1940, **37**, 597–612.

Dukes, W. F. Psychological studies of values. *Psychological Bulletin*, 1955, **52**, 24–50.

Eckhardt, W. War propaganda, welfare values, and political ideologies. *Journal of Conflict Resolution*, 1965, **9**, 345–358.

Eckhardt, W. Can this be the conscience of a convervative? *Journal of Human Relations*, 1967, **15**, 443–456.

Eckhardt, W. The values of fascism. *Journal of Social Issues*, 1968, **24**, 89–104.

Eckhardt, W. Communist values. *Journal of Human Relations*, 1970, **18**, 778–788.

Eckhardt, W. A cross-cultural test of Eysenck's theory of social attitudes. *Peace Research*, 1971, **3**, 7.

Edwards, J. D., & Ostrom, T. M. Value-bonded attitudes: Changes in attitude structure as a function of value bonding and type of communication discrepancy. *Proceedings, 77th Annual Convention, American Psychological Association*, 1969, 413–414.

Efran, J. S., & Broughton, A. Effect of expectancies for social approval on visual behavior. *Journal of Personality and Social Psychology*, 1966, **4**, 103–107.

Ellis, A. *Reason and emotion in psychotherapy.* New York: Lyle Stuart, 1962.

English, H. B., & English, A. C. *A comprehensive dictionary of psychological and psychoanalytic terms.* New York: Longmans, Green, 1958.

Erikson, E. H. *Childhood and society.* New York: Norton, 1950.

Exline, R. V., & Winters, L. C. Affective relations and mutual glances in dyads. In S. S. Tomkins & C. Izzard (Eds.), *Affect, cognition, and personality.* New York: Springer, 1965.

Eysenck, H. J. *The psychology of politics.* London: Routledge & Kegan Paul, 1954.

Eysenck, H. J. The psychology of politics: A reply. *Psychological Bulletin*, 1956, **53**, 177–182. (a)

Eysenck, H. J. The psychology of politics and the personality similarities between fascists and communists. *Psychological Bulletin*, 1956, **53**, 431–438. (b)

Eysenck, H. J. The effects of psychotherapy. In H. J. Eysenck (Ed.), *Handbook of abnormal psychology.* New York: Basic Books, 1961.

Eysenck, H. J. *Manual of Maudsley personality inventory.* San Diego: Educational and Industrial Training Service, 1962.

Feather, N. T. Educational choice and student attitudes in relation to terminal and instrumental values. *Australian Journal of Psychology*, 1970, **22**, 127–144. (a)

Feather, N. T. Value systems in state and church schools. *Australian Journal of Psychology*, 1970, **22**, 299–313. (b)

Feather, N. T. Organization and discrepancy in cognitive structures. *Psychological Review*, 1971, **78**, 355–379. (a)

Feather, N. T. Value differences in relation to ethnocentrism, intolerance of ambiguity, and dogmatism. *Personality*, 1971, **2**, 349–366. (b)

Feather, N. T. Similarity of value systems as a determinant of educational choice at university level. *Australian Journal of Psychology*, 1971, **23**, 201–211. (c)

Feather, N. T. Test-retest reliability of individual values and value systems. *Australian Psychologist*, 1971, **6**, 181–188. (d)

Feather, N. T. Value similarity and value systems in state and independent secondary schools. *Australian Journal of Psychology*, 1972, **24**, 305–315. (a)

Feather, N. T. Value similarity and school adjustment. *Australian Journal of Psychology*, 1972, **24**, 193–208. (b)

Feather, N. T. Value systems and education: The Flinders programme of value research. *Australian Journal of Education*, 1972, **16**, 136–149. (c)

Feather, N. T. Value change among university students. *Australian Journal of Psychology*, 1973, **25**, 57–70.

Festinger, L. A theory of social comparison processes. *Human Relations*, 1954, **7**, 117–140.

Festinger, L. *A theory of cognitive dissonance*. Evanston, Ill.: Row, Peterson, 1957.

Festinger, L. Behavioral support for opinion change. *Public Opinion Quarterly*, 1964, **28**, 404–417.

Fishbein, M. Beliefs, attitudes, and behavior. In S. Feldman (Ed.), *Cognitive consistency: Motivational antecedents and behavioral consequents*. New York: Academic Press, 1966.

Forbes, G. B., TeVault, R. K., & Gromoll, H. F. Willingness to help strangers as a function of liberal, conservative or Catholic church membership: A field study with the lost-letter technique. *Psychological Reports*, 1971, **28**, 947–949.

Freedman, J. L. Preference for dissonant information. *Journal of Personality and Social Psychology*, 1965, **2**, 287–289.

French, J. R. P., & Kahn, R. L. A programmatic approach to studying the industrial environment and mental health. *Journal of Social Issues*, 1962, **18**, 1–47.

Frenkel-Brunswik, E. Mechanisms of self-deception. *Journal of Social Psychology* (S.P.S.S.I. Bulletin), 1939, **10**, 409–420.

Freud, S. *Beyond the pleasure principle*. London: Hogarth Press, 1922.

Fromm, E. *Escape from freedom*. New York: Farrar & Rinehart, 1941.

Gans, H. J. Culture and class in the study of poverty: An approach to antipoverty research. In D. P. Moynihan (Ed.), *On understanding poverty*. New York: Basic Books, 1968.

Gilbert, G. M. Stereotype persistence and change among college students. *Journal of Abnormal and Social Psychology*, 1951, **46**, 245–254.

Glasser, W. *Reality therapy*. New York: Harper & Row, 1965.

Glock, C. Y., & Stark, R. *Religion and society in tension*. Chicago: Rand McNally, 1965.

Glock, C. Y., & Stark, R. *Christian beliefs and anti-Semitism*. New York: Harper & Row, 1966.

Goffman, E. *The presentation of self in everyday life*. Garden City, N.Y.: Doubleday, 1959.

Goranson, R. E. A review of recent literature on psychological effects of media portrayals of violence. In D. L. Lange, R. K. Baker, & S. J. Ball (Eds.), *Mass media and violence: A report to the National Commission on the Causes and Prevention of Violence*. Washington, D.C.: U.S. Government Printing Office, 1969.

Gorsuch, R. L. Rokeach's approach to value systems and social compassion. *Review of Religious Research*, 1970, **11**, 139–143.

Graham, W. K. A method for measuring the images of organizations. Paper presented at the meetings of the Western Psychological Association, Los Angeles, Calif., April, 1970.

Gross, B. M. *The state of the nation: Social systems accounting*. London: Tavistock, 1966.

Gross, B. M., & Springer, M. (Eds.) Political intelligence for America's future. *The Annals of the American Academy of Political and Social Science*, 1970, **388** (Whole issue).

Guilford, J. P. *Psychometric methods.* New York: McGraw-Hill, 1954.

Guttman, L. A general nonmetric technique for finding the smallest coordinate space for a configuration of points. *Psychometrika*, 1966, **33**, 469–506.

Hague, W. Value systems and vocational choice of the priesthood. Unpublished Ph.D. dissertation, University of Alberta Library, 1968.

Handy, R. *The measurement of values.* St. Louis, Mo.: Green, 1970.

Hanley, C., & Rokeach, M. Care and carelessness in psychology. *Psychological Bulletin*, 1956, **53**, 183–186.

Hartshorne, H., & May, M. A. *Studies in deceit.* New York: Macmillan, 1928.

Heider, F. *The psychology of interpersonal relations.* New York: Wiley, 1958.

Henle, M. On the relation between logic and thinking. *Psychological Review*, 1962, **69**, 366–378.

Hicks, L. E. Some properties of ipsative, normative, and forced-choice normative measures. *Psychological Bulletin*, 1970, **74**, 167–184.

Hilgard, E. R. Human motives and the concept of the self. *American Psychologist*, 1949, **4**, 374–382.

Hilliard, A. L. *The forms of value: The extension of a hedonistic axiology.* New York: Columbia University Press, 1950.

Hollen, C. C. The stability of values and value systems. Unpublished M.A. thesis, Michigan State University Library, 1967.

Hollen, C. C. Value change, perceived instrumentality, and attitude change. Unpublished Ph.D. dissertation, Michigan State University Library, 1972.

Homant, R. Semantic differential ratings and rank-ordering of values. *Educational and Psychological Measurement*, 1969, **29**, 885–889.

Homant, R. Values, attitudes, and perceived instrumentality. Unpublished Ph.D. dissertation, Michigan State University Library, 1970.

Homant, R., & Rokeach, M. Values for honesty and cheating behavior. *Personality*, 1970, **1**, 153–162.

Horvath, E. Some attributed and actual value differences between homosexual and heterosexual men and women. Unpublished M.A. thesis, University of Western Ontario Library, 1972.

Hovland, C. I., Janis, I. L., & Kelley, H. H. *Communication and persuasion: Psychological studies of opinion change.* New Haven: Yale University Press, 1953.

Hovland, C. I., et al. *The order of presentation in persuasion.* New Haven: Yale University Press, 1957.

Inglehart, R. The silent revolution in Europe: Intergenerational changes in post-industrial societies. *The American Political Science Review*, 1971, **65**, 991–1017.

Janis, I. L., & Field, P. B. Sex differences and personality factors related to persuasibility. In I. L. Janis et al., *Personality and persuasibility.* New Haven: Yale University Press, 1959.

Janis, I. L., & Gilmore, J. B. The influence of incentive conditions on the success of role playing in modifying attitudes. *Journal of Personality and Social Psychology*, 1965, **1**, 17–27.

Janis, I. L., & King, B. T. The influence of role-playing on opinion change. *Journal of Abnormal and Social Psychology*, 1954, **49**, 211–218.

Janis, I. L., & Mann, L. Effectiveness of emotional role playing in modifying smoking habits and attitudes. *Journal of Experimental Research in Personality*, 1965, **1**, 84–90.

Jones, E. E., & Davis, K. E. From acts to dispositions. In L. Berkowitz (Ed.), *Advances in experimental social psychology*, Vol. 2. New York: Academic Press, 1965.

Jones, E. E., & Gerard, H. B. *Foundations of social psychology*. New York: Wiley, 1967.

Jourard, S. M. *The transparent self*. New York: Van Nostrand, 1964.

Kaplan, A. *The conduct of inquiry: Methodology for behavioral science*. San Francisco: Chandler, 1964.

Katz, D. The functional approach to the study of attitudes. *Public Opinion Quarterly*, 1960, **24**, 163–204.

Katz, D., & Braly, K. W. Racial stereotypes of 100 college students. *Journal of Abnormal and Social Psychology*, 1933, **28**, 280–290.

Katz, D., & Stotland, E. A preliminary statement to a theory of attitude structure and change. In S. Koch (Ed.), *Psychology: A study of a science*. New York: McGraw-Hill, 1959.

Kelley, H. H. The two functions of reference groups. In G. E. Swanson, T. M. Newcomb, & E. L. Hartley (Eds.), *Readings in social psychology*. New York: Holt, 1952.

Kelley, H. H. Attribution theory in social psychology. In D. Levine (Ed.), *Nebraska symposium on motivation*. Lincoln, Neb.: University of Nebraska Press, 1967.

Kelly, K., Silverman, B. I., & Cochrane, R. Social desirability and the Rokeach value survey. *Journal of Experimental Research in Personality*, 1972, in press.

Kelman, H. C. Processes of opinion change. *Public Opinion Quarterly*, 1961, **25**, 57–78.

Kerlinger, F. N. Social attitudes and their criterial referents: A structural theory. *Psychological Review*, 1967, **74**, 110–122.

Kerlinger, F. N. A social attitude scale: Evidence on reliability and validity. *Psychological Reports*, 1970, **26**, 379–383.

Kerlinger, F. N. The structure and content of social attitude referents: A preliminary study. *Educational and Psychological Measurement*, 1972, **32**, 613–630.

Kiesler, C. A. *The psychology of commitment*. New York: Academic Press, 1971.

Kirkpatrick, C. Religion and humanitarianism: A study of institutional implications. *Psychological Monographs*, 1949, **63** (Whole No. 304).

Kluckhohn, C. Values and value orientations in the theory of action. In T. Parsons & E. A. Shils (Eds.), *Toward a general theory of action*. Cambridge: Harvard University Press, 1952.

Kluckhohn, R. & Strodtbeck, F. L. *Variations in value orientation*. Evanston, Ill.: Row, Peterson, 1961.

Kohlberg, L. The development of children's orientations toward a moral order. I. Sequences in the development of moral thought. *Vita Humana*, 1963, **6**, 11–33.

Kohlberg, L. Development of moral character and moral ideology. In H. Hoffman & L. Hoffman (Eds.), *Review of child development research*, Vol. 1. New York: Russell Sage Foundation, 1964.

Kohlberg, L. Moral judgment interview coding manual. Unpublished paper, 1969.

Kohler, W. *The place of value in a world of facts.* New York: Liveright, 1938.

Kohn, M. L. *Class and conformity: A study in values.* Homewood, Ill.: Dorsey, 1969.

Kuhn, M. H. Self attitudes by age and professional training. *Sociological Quarterly*, 1960, **1**, 39–55.

Latane, B. (Ed.) Studies in social comparison. *Journal of Experimental and Social Psychology*, 1966, Supplement 1 (Whole issue).

Lee, R. S. The future of the museum as a learning environment. Paper presented at the conference on computers and their potential applications in museums at Metropolitan Museum of Art, New York, April 15–17, 1968.

Lenski, G. *The religious factor.* Garden City, N.Y.: Doubleday, 1961.

Levin, J., & Spates, J. L. Hippie values: An analysis of the underground press. In B. Rosenberg & D. M. White (Eds.), *Mass culture revisited.* New York: Van Nostrand Reinhold, 1971.

Levinson, D. J. Conservatism and radicalism. In E. Sills (Ed.), *International encyclopedia of the social sciences.* New York: Macmillan, 1968.

Lewin, K. *Field theory in social science: Selected theoretical papers.* New York: Harper, 1951.

Lewin, K., & Grabbe, P. Conduct, knowledge, and acceptance of new values. *Journal of Social Issues*, 1945, **1**, 53–64.

Lewis, C. I. *An analysis of knowledge and valuation.* LaSalle, Ill.: Open Court, 1962.

Lewis, O. *La Vida: A Puerto Rican family in the culture of poverty—San Juan and New York.* New York: Random House, 1966.

Liebow, E. *Tally's corner: A study of Negro street-corner men.* Boston: Little, Brown, 1967.

Lingoes, J. C. An IBM 7090 program for Guttman-Lingoes smallest space analysis. *Behavioral Science*, 1966, **11**, 75–76.

Lipset, S. M. Democracy and working-class authoritarianism. *American Sociological Review*, 1959, **24**, 482–501.

Lipset, S. M. The value patterns of democracy: A case study in comparative analysis. *American Sociological Review*, 1963, **28**, 515–531.

Lipset, S. M. Why cops hate liberals—and vice versa. *Atlantic*, 1969, **223**, 76–83.

Lovejoy, A. O. Terminal and adjectival values. *Journal of Philosophy*, 1950, **47**, 593–608.

Mann, L. The effects of emotional role playing on desire to modify smoking habits. *Journal of Experimental Social Psychology*, 1967, **3**, 334–348.

Mann, L., & Janis, I. L. A follow-up study of the long-term effects of emotional role playing. *Journal of Personality and Social Psychology*, 1968, **8**, 339–342.

Mannheim, K. Conservative thought. In P. Kecskemeti (Ed.), *Essays on sociology and social psychology.* New York: Oxford University Press, 1953.

Maslow, A. H. *Motivation and personality.* New York: Harper, 1954.

Maslow, A. H. (Ed.) *New knowledge in human values.* New York: Harper, 1959.

Maslow, A. H. *Religions, values, and peak-experiences.* Columbus, Ohio: Ohio State University Press, 1964.

McClelland, D. C., Atkinson, J. W., Clark, R. A., & Lowell, E. L. *The achievement motive.* New York: Appleton-Century-Crofts, 1953.

McClelland, D. C., & Winter, D. G. *Motivating economic achievement.* New York: Free Press, 1969.

McClosky, H. Conservatism and personality. *American Political Science Review,* 1958, **52,** 27–45.

McDougal, W. *An introduction to social psychology.* Boston: John W. Luce, 1926.

McGuire, W. J. A syllogistic analysis of cognitive relationships. In M. J. Rosenberg, *et al.* (Eds.), *Attitude organization and change.* New Haven: Yale University Press, 1960.

McGuire, W. J. Inducing resistance to persuasion. In L. Berkowitz (Ed.), *Advances in experimental social psychology,* Vol. 1. New York: Academic Press, 1964.

McGuire, W. J. The nature of attitudes and attitude change. In G. Lindzey & E. Aronson (Eds.), *The handbook of social psychology,* Vol. 3. Reading, Mass.: Addison-Wesley, 1969.

McLaughlin, B. Values in behavioral science. *Journal of Religion and Health,* 1965, **4,** 258–279.

McLellan, D. D. Values, value systems, and the developmental structure of moral judgment. Unpublished M.A. thesis, Michigan State University Library, 1970.

McLellan, D. D. Level of moral development and feedback of information as determinants of value and attitude change. Unpublished Ph.D. dissertation, Michigan State University Library, 1973.

McQuitty, L. L., Banks, R. G., & Frary, J. M. Submatrices of interassociations for scoring interrelatedness within matrices as an index of psychological disturbance. *Multivariate Behavioral Research,* 1970, **5,** 479–488.

Mead, G. H. *Mind, self, and society: From the standpoint of a social behaviorist.* Chicago: University of Chicago Press, 1934.

Mehrabian, A. Significance of posture and position in the communication of attitude and status relationships. *Psychological Bulletin,* 1969, **71,** 359–372.

Miller, G. A. The magical number seven, plus-or-minus two: Some limits on our capacity for processing information. *Psychological Review,* 1956, **63,** 81–97.

Moreno, J. L. *Psychodrama.* New York: Beacon, 1946.

Morris, C. W. *Varieties of human value.* Chicago: University of Chicago Press, 1956.

Mosteller, F., & Wallace, D. *Inference and disputed authorship: The Federalist.* Reading, Mass.: Addison-Wesley, 1964.

Moynihan, D. P. Employment, income, and the ordeal of the Negro family. In T. Parsons and K. Clark (Eds.), *The American Negro.* Boston: Houghton Mifflin, 1966.

Moynihan, D. P. The Moynihan report and its critics. *Commentary,* 1967, **43,** 31–45.

Murphy, G., Murphy, L. B., & Newcomb, T. M. *Experimental social psychology.* New York: Harper, 1937.

Murray, H. A. *Explorations in personality: A clinical and experimental study of fifty men of college age.* New York: Oxford University Press, 1938.

Nel, E., Helmreich, R., & Aronson, E. Opinion change in the advocate as a function of the persuasibility of his audience: A clarification of the meaning of dissonance. *Journal of Personality and Social Psychology*, 1969, **12**, 117–124.

Newcomb, T. M. *Personality and social change.* New York: Dryden, 1943.

Newcomb, T. M. Individual systems of orientation. In S. Koch (Ed.), *Psychology: A study of a science*, Vol. 3. New York: McGraw-Hill, 1959.

Newcomb, T. M. *The acquaintance process.* New York: Holt, Rinehart, & Winston, 1961.

Newcomb, T. M., Koenig, K. E., Flacks, R., & Warwick, D. P. *Persistence and change: Bennington College and its students after twenty-five years.* New York: Wiley, 1967.

Newcomb, T. M., Turner, R. H., & Converse, P. E. *Social psychology.* New York: Holt, Rinehart, & Winston, 1965.

Opsinc, G. M. A reformulation of cognitive dissonance as it applies to the area of effort justification. Unpublished M.A. thesis, Michigan State University Library, 1970.

Orne, M. T. On the social psychology of the psychological experiment: With particular reference to demand characteristics and their implications. *American Psychologist*, 1962, **17**, 776–783.

Osgood, C. E., Suci, G. J., & Tannenbaum, P. H. *The measurement of meaning.* Urbana, Ill.: University of Illinois Press, 1957.

Osgood, C. E., & Tannenbaum, P. H. The principle of congruity in the prediction of attitude change. *Psychological Review*, 1955, **62**, 42–55.

Ostrom, T. M., & Brock, T. C. Cognitive bonding to central values and resistance to a communication advocating change in policy orientation. *Journal of Experimental Research in Personality*, 1969, **4**, 42–50.

Parker, S., & Kleiner, R. J. The culture of poverty: An adjustive dimension. *American Anthropologist*, 1970, **72**, 516–527.

Parrott, G. L., & Bloom, R. Peace marchers, the silent majority, and the John Birch Society: Psychological distinctions. Unpublished paper, 1971.

Peak, H. Attitude and motivation. In M. R. Jones (Ed.), *Nebraska symposium on motivation.* Lincoln, Neb.: University of Nebraska Press, 1955.

Penner, L. A. The functional relationship between values and interpersonal behavior. Unpublished Ph.D. dissertation, Michigan State University Library, 1969.

Penner, L. A. Interpersonal attraction toward a black person as a function of value importance. *Personality*, 1971, **2**, 175–187.

Penner, L. A., Homant, R., & Rokeach, M. Comparison of rank-order and paired-comparison methods for measuring value systems. *Perceptual and Motor Skills*, 1968, **27**, 417–418.

Pepitone, A. Values and revolution. In "The social psychology of justice, freedom, and responsibility" symposium, presented at the annual meetings of the American Psychological Association, Washington, D.C., September, 1969.

Perry, R. B. *Realms of value: A critique of human civilization.* Cambridge: Harvard University Press, 1954.

Piaget, J. *The moral judgment of the child.* New York: Free Press, 1965.

Pittel, S. M., & Mendelsohn, G. A. Measurement of moral values: A review and critique. *Psychological Bulletin*, 1966, **66**, 22–35.

Postman, L., Bruner, J. S., & McGinnies, E. Personal values as selective factors in perception. *Journal of Abnormal and Social Psychology*, 1948, **43**, 142–154.

Rainwater, L. The problem of lower class culture and poverty-war strategy. In D. P. Moynihan (Ed.), *On understanding poverty*. New York: Basic Books, 1968.

Rim, Y. Values and attitudes. *Personality*, 1970, **1**, 243–250.

Ring, K. Experimental social psychology: Some sober questions about some frivolous values. *Journal of Experimental Social Psychology*, 1967, **3**, 113–123.

Rogers, C. R. A theory of therapy, personality, and interpersonal relationships, as developed in the client-centered framework. In S. Koch (Ed.), *Psychology: A study of science*, Vol. 3. New York: McGraw-Hill, 1959.

Rokeach, M. *The open and closed mind*. New York: Basic Books, 1960.

Rokeach, M. *The three Christs of Ypsilanti*. New York: Knopf, 1964.

Rokeach, M. *Value survey*. Sunnyvale, Calif.: Halgren Tests (873 Persimmon Avenue, 94087), 1967.

Rokeach, M. A theory of organization and change within value-attitude systems. *Journal of Social Issues*, 1968, **24**, 13–33. (a)

Rokeach, M. *Beliefs, attitudes, and values*. San Francisco: Jossey-Bass, 1968. (b)

Rokeach, M. The nature of attitudes. In E. Sills (Ed.), *International encyclopedia of the social sciences*. New York: Macmillan, 1968. (c)

Rokeach, M. The role of values in public opinion research. *Public Opinion Quarterly*, 1968–69, **32**, 547–559.

Rokeach, M. Value systems in religion. *Review of Religious Research*, 1969, **11**, 3–23. (a)

Rokeach, M. Religious values and social compassion. *Review of Religious Research*, 1969, **11**, 24–38. (b)

Rokeach, M. Commentary on the commentaries. *Review of Religious Research*, 1970, **11**, 155–162. (a)

Rokeach, M. Faith, hope, and bigotry. *Psychology Today*, April 1970. (b)

Rokeach, M. Long-range experimental modification of values, attitudes, and behavior. *American Psychologist*, 1971, **26**, 453–459.

Rokeach, M., & Berman, E. Values and needs. Unpublished paper, 1971.

Rokeach, M., & Cochrane, R. Self-confrontation and confrontation with another as determinants of long-term value change. *Journal of Applied Social Psychology*, 1972, **2**, 283–292.

Rokeach, M., & Hanley, C. Eysenck's tender-mindedness dimension: A critique. *Psychological Bulletin*, 1956, **53**, 169–176.

Rokeach, M., Homant, R., & Penner, L. A. A value analysis of the disputed Federalist papers. *Journal of Personality and Social Psychology*, 1970, **16**, 245–250.

Rokeach, M., & Kleijunas, P. Behavior as a function of attitude-toward-object and attitude-toward-situation. *Journal of Personality and Social Psychology*, 1972, **22**, 194–201.

Rokeach, M., & McLellan, D. D. Feedback of information about the values and attitudes of self and others as determinants of long-term cognitive and behavioral change. *Journal of Applied Social Psychology*, 1972, **2**, 236–251.

Rokeach, M., Miller, M. G., & Snyder, J. A. The value gap between police and policed. *Journal of Social Issues*, 1971, **27**, 155–171.

Rokeach, M., & Parker, S. Values as social indicators of poverty and race relations in America. *The Annals of the American Academy of Political and Social Science*, 1970, **388**, 97–111.

Rokeach, M., & Vidmar, N. Testimony concerning possible jury bias in a Black Panther murder trial. *Journal of Applied Social Psychology*, 1973, **3**, 14–26.

Rosenberg, M. J. Cognitive structure and attitudinal affect. *Journal of Abnormal and Social Psychology*, 1956, **53**, 367–372.

Rosenberg, M. J. An analysis of affective-cognitive consistency. In M. J. Rosenberg *et al.* (Eds.), *Attitude organization and change*. New Haven: Yale University Press, 1960.

Rosenberg, M. J. When dissonance fails: On eliminating evaluation apprehension from attitude measurement. *Journal of Personality and Social Psychology*, 1965, **1**, 28–42.

Rosenthal, R. *Experimenter effects in behavioral research*. New York: Appleton-Century-Crofts, 1966.

Rosenthal, R., & Rosnow, R. L. (Eds.) *Artifact in behavioral research*. New York: Academic Press, 1969.

Rossiter, C. Conservatism. In E. Sills (Ed.), *International encyclopedia of the social sciences*. New York: Macmillan, 1968.

Rotter, J. *Social learning and clinical psychology*. New York: Prentice-Hall, 1954.

Salancik, G. R. Values and events of tomorrow. Unpublished paper, Institute of the Future, 1971.

Sanford, N. Whatever happened to action research? *Journal of Social Issues*, 1970, **26**, 3–23.

Scott, W. A. *Values and organizations*. Chicago: Rand McNally, 1965.

Secord, P. F., & Backman, W. An interpersonal approach to personality. In B. A. Maher (Ed.), *Progress in experimental personality research*, Vol. 2. New York: Academic Press, 1965.

Segal, D. R., & Hikel, G. K. The spatial distribution of the electoral market. Center for Research on Social Organization, University of Michigan, 1970, Paper #56.

Sherif, C. W., Sherif, M., & Nebergall, R. E. *Attitude and attitude change*. Philadelphia: Saunders, 1965.

Sherif, M., & Hovland, C. I. *Social judgement: Assimilation and contrast effects in communication and attitude change*. New Haven: Yale University Press, 1961.

Shotland, R. L. Client attrition during psychotherapy as it relates to the value structure of the patient and therapist. Unpublished M.A. thesis, Michigan State University Library, 1968.

Shotland, R. L., & Berger, W. G. Behavioral validation of several values from the Rokeach value scale as an index of honesty. *Journal of Applied Psychology*, 1970, **54**, 433–435.

Siegel, S. *Nonparametric statistics for the behavioral sciences*. New York: McGraw-Hill, 1956.

Sikula, A. F. A study of the values and value systems of college roommates in conflict and nonconflict situations, and an investigation to determine whether roommate conflict can be attributed to differing values and value systems. Unpublished Ph.D. dissertation, Michigan State University Library, 1970.

Skinner, B. F. *Beyond freedom and dignity*. New York: Knopf, 1971,

Smith, D. G. Liberalism. In E. Sills (Ed.), *International encyclopedia of the social sciences.* New York: Macmillan, 1968.

Smith, M. B. Personal values as determinants of a political attitude. *Journal of Psychology*, 1949, **28**, 477–486.

Smith, M. B. *Social psychology and human values.* Chicago: Aldine, 1969.

Smith, M. B., Bruner, J. S., & White, R. W. *Opinions and personality.* New York: Wiley, 1956.

Stark, R. Christian charity: A note on orthodoxy and personal philanthropy. Unpublished paper, 1971.

Szasz, T. S. *The myth of mental illness.* New York: Hoeber-Harper, 1961.

Taft, R., & Walker, K. F. Australia. In A. M. Rose (Ed.), *The institutions of advanced societies.* Minneapolis: University of Minnesota Press, 1958.

Tajfel, H. Experiments in a vacuum. In J. Israel & H. Tajfel (Eds.), *The context of social psychology: A critical assessment.* New York: Academic Press, 1972.

Tate, E. D., & Miller, G. R. Differences in value systems of persons with varying religious orientations. *Journal for the Scientific Study of Religion*, 1971, **10**, 357–365.

TePaste, S. Measurement of selective exposure to information. Unpublished paper, 1969.

Thibaut, J. W., & Strickland, L. H. Psychological set and social conformity. *Journal of Personality*, 1956, **25**, 115–129.

Thomas, W. I., & Znaniecki, F. *The Polish peasant in Europe and America*, Vol. 1. Boston: Badger, 1918–20.

Toffler, A. Value impact forecaster—a profession of the future. In K. Baier & N. Rescher (Eds.), *Values and the future.* New York: Free Press, 1969.

Tomkins, S. S. Left and right: A basic dimension of ideology and personality. In R. W. White (Ed.), *The study of lives.* New York: Atherton, 1963.

Troldahl, V. C., & Powell, F. A. A short-form dogmatism scale for use in field studies. *Social Forces*, 1965, **44**, 211–215.

U.S. Department of Health, Education and Welfare. *Toward a social report.* Washington, D.C.: U.S. Government Printing Office, 1969.

U.S. Department of Labor, Office of Policy Planning and Research. *The Negro family.* Washington, D.C.: U.S. Government Printing Office, 1965.

Ward, R. *The Australian legend.* Melbourne: Oxford University Press, 1958.

Watson, G. *Social psychology: Issues and insights.* Philadelphia: Lippincott, 1966.

Webb, E. J., Campbell, D. T., Schwartz, R. D., & Sechrest, L. *Unobtrusive measures: Nonreactive research in the social sciences.* Chicago: Rand McNally, 1966.

White, R. K. Hitler, Roosevelt, and the nature of war propaganda. *Journal of Abnormal and Social Psychology*, 1949, **44**, 157–174.

White, R. K. *Value analysis: Nature and use of the method.* Ann Arbor, Mich.: Society for the Psychological Study of Social Issues, 1951. (a)

White, R. K. *Value-analysis, the nature and use of the method.* Glen Gardner, N.J.: Libertarian Press, 1951. (b)

White, R. W. Motivation reconsidered: The concept of competence. *Psychological Review*, 1959, **66**, 297–333.

Wicker, A. W. Attitudes versus actions: The relationship of verbal and overt behavioral responses to attitude objects. *Journal of Social Issues*, 1969, **25**, 41–78.

Williams, R. M. Values. In E. Sills (Ed.), *Intenational encyclopedia of the social sciences.* New York: Macmillan, 1968.

Willis, C. T., & Goldberg, F. J. Some correlates of militancy and conservatism among black college students in the north and south. Paper presented at the annual convention of the American Psychological Association, Miami Beach, Fla., September, 1970.

Winer, B. J. *Statistical principles in experimental design.* New York: McGraw-Hill, 1962.

Woodruff, A. D. Personal values and the direction of behavior. *School Review,* 1942, **50,** 32–42.

Woodruff, A. D., & DiVesta, F. J. The relationship between values, concepts, and attitudes. *Educational and Psychological Measurement,* 1948, **8,** 645–659.

Wrightsman, L. S. Wallace supporters and adherence to "law and order." *Journal of Personality and Social Psychology,* 1969, **13,** 17–22.

APPENDIX A
The Rokeach Value Survey

FORM D

VALUE SURVEY

BIRTH DATE_____SEX: MALE_____FEMALE_____

CITY and STATE OF BIRTH_____

NAME (FILL IN ONLY IF REQUESTED)_____

DISTRIBUTED BY:
HALGREN TESTS
873 PERSIMMON AVE.
SUNNYVALE, CALIFORNIA 94087

INSTRUCTIONS

On the next page are 18 values listed in alphabetical order. Your task is to arrange them in order of their importance to YOU, as guiding principles in YOUR life. Each value is printed on a gummed label which can be easily peeled off and pasted in the boxes on the left-hand side of the page.

Study the list carefully and pick out the one value which is the most important for you. Peel it off and paste it in Box 1 on the left.

Then pick out the value which is second most important for you. Peel it off and paste it in Box 2. Then do the same for each of the remaining values. The value which is least important goes in Box 18.

Work slowly and think carefully. If you change your mind, feel free to change your answers. The labels peel off easily and can be moved from place to place. The end result should truly show how you really feel.

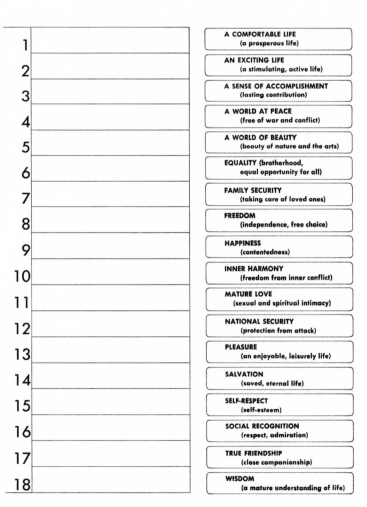

1	**A COMFORTABLE LIFE** (a prosperous life)
2	**AN EXCITING LIFE** (a stimulating, active life)
3	**A SENSE OF ACCOMPLISHMENT** (lasting contribution)
4	**A WORLD AT PEACE** (free of war and conflict)
5	**A WORLD OF BEAUTY** (beauty of nature and the arts)
6	**EQUALITY** (brotherhood, equal opportunity for all)
7	**FAMILY SECURITY** (taking care of loved ones)
8	**FREEDOM** (independence, free choice)
9	**HAPPINESS** (contentedness)
10	**INNER HARMONY** (freedom from inner conflict)
11	**MATURE LOVE** (sexual and spiritual intimacy)
12	**NATIONAL SECURITY** (protection from attack)
13	**PLEASURE** (an enjoyable, leisurely life)
14	**SALVATION** (saved, eternal life)
15	**SELF-RESPECT** (self-esteem)
16	**SOCIAL RECOGNITION** (respect, admiration)
17	**TRUE FRIENDSHIP** (close companionship)
18	**WISDOM** (a mature understanding of life)

WHEN YOU HAVE FINISHED, GO TO THE NEXT PAGE.

Below is another list of 18 values. Arrange them in order of importance, the same as before.

1	
2	
3	
4	
5	
6	
7	
8	
9	
10	
11	
12	
13	
14	
15	
16	
17	
18	

AMBITIOUS
(hard-working, aspiring)

BROADMINDED
(open-minded)

CAPABLE
(competent, effective)

CHEERFUL
(lighthearted, joyful)

CLEAN
(neat, tidy)

COURAGEOUS
(standing up for your beliefs)

FORGIVING
(willing to pardon others)

HELPFUL (working
for the welfare of others)

HONEST
(sincere, truthful)

IMAGINATIVE
(daring, creative)

INDEPENDENT
(self-reliant, self-sufficient)

INTELLECTUAL
(intelligent, reflective)

LOGICAL
(consistent, rational)

LOVING
(affectionate, tender)

OBEDIENT
(dutiful, respectful)

POLITE
(courteous, well-mannered)

RESPONSIBLE
(dependable, reliable)

SELF-CONTROLLED
(restrained, self-disciplined)

APPENDIX B
Frequency Distributions of
18 Terminal and 18 Instrumental
Values for National NORC
Sample Tested in 1968, by
Sex, Income, Education,
Race, Age, and Religion

SEX: FREQUENCY DISTRIBUTIONS

		1	2	3	4	5	6	7
A comfortable life	Male	79	49	35	30	31	53	44
	Female	52	38	33	37	37	35	39
An exciting life	Male	9	19	12	11	15	17	20
	Female	2	10	5	3	5	7	14
A sense of accomplishment	Male	19	43	43	43	42	54	48
	Female	20	19	35	36	42	53	41
A world at peace	Male	124	104	90	58	43	30	27
	Female	189	129	108	76	40	39	26
A world of beauty	Male	2	9	11	18	27	17	12
	Female	1	7	6	18	16	17	31
Equality	Male	16	41	57	50	40	36	48
	Female	16	48	65	58	55	45	55
Family security	Male	122	106	82	63	58	33	49
	Female	126	137	85	85	69	51	39
Freedom	Male	62	81	79	88	55	45	55
	Female	35	70	76	73	82	66	52
Happiness	Male	24	35	44	60	47	55	50
	Female	36	54	59	48	54	62	70
Inner harmony	Male	10	9	17	26	28	39	27
	Female	9	27	26	52	33	50	54
Mature love	Male	6	10	16	20	29	19	28
	Female	1	15	23	32	33	25	38
National security	Male	11	34	36	44	54	46	39
	Female	8	37	46	42	51	55	36
Pleasure	Male	1	5	9	5	13	13	20
	Female	1	0	5	4	11	9	16
Salvation	Male	114	34	29	30	24	20	24
	Female	191	33	35	35	29	29	24
Self-respect	Male	18	35	41	37	50	65	58
	Female	22	41	47	59	71	62	78
Social recognition	Male	2	3	4	8	17	18	23
	Female	0	2	0	2	11	13	17
True friendship	Male	9	17	24	35	33	55	49
	Female	1	13	31	52	52	61	61
Wisdom	Male	37	31	36	39	59	50	44
	Female	34	64	59	32	53	65	53
Ambitious	Male	118	76	56	39	39	40	27
	Female	82	65	49	51	57	34	41
Broadminded	Male	54	70	59	44	40	43	32
	Female	47	75	55	53	51	43	41
Capable	Male	10	45	51	48	35	37	44
	Female	13	25	48	45	34	41	40

8	9	10	11	12	13	14	15	16	17	18	N	MEDIAN
43	30	34	33	44	21	40	28	27	23	21	665	7.77
35	39	52	47	37	41	56	52	51	42	21	744	10.02
27	28	23	27	30	47	41	55	79	90	115	665	14.62
13	16	22	23	44	30	59	95	97	140	159	744	15.75
51	44	31	41	40	31	43	33	27	23	9	665	8.29
52	82	56	49	51	66	37	37	24	28	16	744	9.40
26	20	21	20	19	16	12	16	16	15	8	665	3.75
27	24	23	6	15	9	14	10	3	4	2	744	3.00
26	28	34	45	44	54	51	66	77	78	66	665	13.61
40	29	32	46	63	65	88	72	92	64	57	744	13.51
36	22	34	39	40	35	38	34	17	33	49	665	8.87
38	37	44	41	34	46	32	37	33	37	23	744	8.29
33	21	25	17	14	9	9	12	8	2	2	665	3.86
31	24	20	23	16	10	14	7	2	4	1	744	3.78
49	37	33	21	9	8	13	10	7	10	3	665	4.91
60	41	46	35	35	17	18	14	14	6	4	744	6.05
40	74	47	51	42	28	26	18	15	5	4	665	7.94
60	63	46	45	43	38	27	23	10	5	1	744	7.34
40	43	60	58	60	54	44	49	48	30	23	665	11.08
46	56	57	68	55	43	49	36	38	27	18	744	9.83
33	43	39	44	42	53	61	50	61	51	60	665	12.57
35	44	37	52	45	54	52	55	51	65	87	744	12.32
40	40	37	34	48	44	34	33	41	23	27	665	9.21
48	35	45	49	60	50	54	23	53	31	21	744	9.81
34	33	32	45	38	47	59	72	68	95	76	665	14.14
24	20	35	41	38	56	67	95	106	127	89	744	14.97
18	25	38	15	25	38	34	31	42	46	78	665	9.88
20	38	27	26	29	35	40	35	29	25	64	744	7.33
43	62	38	41	41	33	23	42	22	9	7	665	8.16
68	62	48	65	37	27	16	19	5	11	6	744	7.40
30	28	32	50	47	50	71	56	70	76	80	665	13.79
22	29	27	39	45	59	69	73	95	94	147	744	15.01
59	44	59	45	54	56	30	34	22	30	10	665	9.63
67	61	68	50	49	61	27	33	28	19	10	744	9.06
37	43	48	39	28	41	36	26	18	26	27	665	8.49
58	44	59	39	48	37	25	28	13	15	18	744	7.71
24	37	27	36	20	28	23	18	20	21	16	665	5.61
36	32	34	34	34	34	40	28	28	29	36	744	7.33
33	38	33	29	39	35	24	23	18	23	28	665	7.20
50	38	38	40	51	30	36	30	19	29	18	744	7.64
44	51	49	55	40	45	28	31	22	19	11	665	8.86
41	48	62	55	58	50	46	52	41	26	19	744	10.10

SEX: FREQUENCY DISTRIBUTIONS (*continued*)

		1	2	3	4	5	6	7
Cheerful	Male	14	22	26	50	34	30	23
	Female	18	41	34	42	31	51	60
Clean	Male	28	29	38	39	53	36	34
	Female	46	56	60	52	61	34	37
Courageous	Male	36	50	45	52	53	48	49
	Female	41	42	48	43	51	63	54
Forgiving	Male	33	49	44	38	48	47	43
	Female	51	61	75	60	71	58	61
Helpful	Male	21	34	44	54	48	40	42
	Female	23	40	49	65	44	51	61
Honest	Male	184	80	74	63	40	47	38
	Female	207	100	92	81	57	46	25
Imaginative	Male	4	11	12	19	20	14	29
	Female	2	5	3	11	8	11	8
Independent	Male	30	34	34	46	31	32	50
	Female	31	25	32	33	29	40	39
Intellectual	Male	10	16	22	16	23	30	25
	Female	17	17	14	21	26	24	33
Logical	Male	8	14	15	14	22	29	35
	Female	5	11	10	10	20	14	20
Loving	Male	21	23	15	31	46	37	33
	Female	65	54	48	36	51	40	38
Obedient	Male	5	13	10	17	21	28	20
	Female	4	15	14	15	17	39	35
Polite	Male	6	11	20	24	30	43	41
	Female	5	14	20	31	36	41	44
Responsible	Male	57	65	68	40	48	50	56
	Female	51	61	57	67	54	64	57
Self-controlled	Male	26	23	32	31	34	34	44
	Female	36	37	36	28	46	49	50

8	9	10	11	12	13	14	15	16	17	18	N	MEDIAN
43	46	49	39	45	40	60	46	35	31	32	665	10.41
54	44	47	46	41	46	54	49	45	23	18	744	9.43
43	35	37	42	34	42	37	29	43	31	35	665	9.43
41	47	43	36	37	36	39	32	35	23	29	744	8.13
37	37	42	37	34	37	28	16	31	19	14	665	7.49
54	35	43	49	53	33	27	40	32	20	16	744	8.06
42	32	34	33	50	42	43	33	23	19	12	665	8.23
40	46	38	45	36	26	25	16	16	7	12	744	6.43
58	45	41	32	41	38	29	33	23	19	23	665	8.35
68	48	52	54	43	31	39	30	22	17	7	744	8.07
26	36	24	19	10	5	7	5	1	4	2	665	3.43
30	41	14	16	12	9	4	6	2	1	1	744	3.21
20	21	35	29	39	45	44	58	57	85	123	665	14.28
16	20	31	30	25	34	46	67	91	137	199	744	16.10
31	25	29	51	43	40	38	45	39	26	41	665	10.17
45	51	36	51	48	56	56	51	56	39	26	744	10.72
29	38	31	36	47	35	50	69	62	61	65	665	12.77
27	33	43	28	51	53	61	64	85	96	51	744	13.22
27	17	36	35	35	45	47	53	73	79	81	665	13.51
27	29	35	34	36	55	56	68	85	101	128	744	14.65
46	29	39	31	37	40	62	48	41	65	21	665	10.90
34	42	37	41	52	34	38	43	30	37	24	744	8.64
29	28	25	41	37	58	43	68	77	72	73	665	13.51
26	34	43	42	48	69	54	63	62	67	97	744	13.08
42	42	55	53	48	30	48	43	57	39	33	665	10.85
53	49	67	56	50	52	57	44	57	42	26	744	10.71
43	56	23	24	29	24	23	14	17	19	9	665	6.58
58	63	43	31	30	36	15	22	10	19	6	744	6.82
48	52	56	43	37	36	31	33	26	33	46	665	9.65
44	44	38	56	39	60	51	39	29	31	31	744	9.55

INCOME: FREQUENCY DISTRIBUTIONS

		1	2	3	4	5	6	7
A comfortable life	< $2,000	22	9	7	7	7	11	9
	$2–3,999	32	11	10	9	12	16	17
	$4–5,999	23	11	13	14	13	16	11
	$6–7,999	22	13	12	10	18	17	18
	$8–9,999	9	13	11	8	9	10	9
	$10–15T	10	13	8	13	3	7	12
	$15,000+	3	9	1	2	1	6	2
An exciting life	< $2,000	2	5	1	0	1	1	3
	$2–3,999	1	9	4	2	4	2	7
	$4–5,999	2	3	0	3	5	7	4
	$6–7,999	0	2	3	1	2	5	7
	$8–9,999	3	0	2	1	3	4	2
	$10–15T	2	5	5	4	1	2	7
	$15,000+	1	2	1	3	2	2	3
A sense of accomplishment	< $2,000	4	2	9	7	3	5	10
	$2–3,999	4	9	12	12	9	18	9
	$4–5,999	6	6	10	12	13	15	11
	$6–7,999	2	9	12	8	13	19	19
	$8–9,999	4	11	11	13	11	13	14
	$10–15T	12	13	9	17	17	17	18
	$15,000+	6	6	9	7	12	13	4
A world at peace	< $2,000	40	27	15	18	5	6	5
	$2–3,999	63	33	41	19	7	12	10
	$4–5,999	46	41	31	20	17	10	3
	$6–7,999	58	36	34	30	11	11	9
	$8–9,999	33	31	19	14	17	7	7
	$10–15T	31	35	32	18	16	11	10
	$15,000+	15	16	17	8	6	7	4
A world of beauty	< $2,000	0	1	3	1	7	2	6
	$2–3,999	0	8	4	9	9	6	6
	$4–5,999	0	3	5	4	6	8	5
	$6–7,999	1	4	0	7	8	6	5
	$8–9,999	0	0	0	3	4	3	7
	$10–15T	1	0	4	8	4	7	4
	$15,000+	1	0	1	2	3	2	5
Equality	< $2,000	5	17	13	12	11	6	12
	$2–3,999	8	15	19	21	15	9	19
	$4–5,999	4	17	19	11	20	16	13
	$6–7,999	6	10	23	24	13	14	15
	$8–9,999	3	14	14	16	10	15	14
	$10–15T	3	11	17	11	17	11	10
	$15,000+	3	5	8	6	6	6	14
Family security	< $2,000	11	12	19	14	13	6	9
	$2–3,999	30	45	19	24	23	14	20
	$4–5,999	42	36	28	26	14	12	13
	$6–7,999	45	55	34	27	22	16	14
	$8–9,999	46	27	26	16	12	14	10
	$10–15T	43	41	19	22	22	13	14
	$15,000+	19	12	10	11	9	5	3

8	9	10	11	12	13	14	15	16	17	18	N	MEDIAN
7	9	10	4	6	3	10	7	4	4	3	139	7.22
13	16	20	17	10	15	11	10	9	4	7	239	8.46
9	13	11	8	15	9	13	9	12	11	6	217	8.33
23	10	16	18	17	12	16	9	6	9	3	249	8.13
5	9	11	6	6	6	15	18	11	15	7	178	10.05
11	8	10	18	16	10	18	12	19	10	10	208	11.00
3	3	4	4	5	5	10	10	11	11	5	95	13.40
4	2	5	6	9	9	10	14	21	18	28	139	15.32
4	10	13	5	14	14	9	25	21	41	54	239	15.36
6	6	4	8	10	14	14	21	18	39	53	217	15.58
8	11	8	14	13	9	22	22	35	46	41	249	15.39
5	5	7	6	9	7	16	22	24	24	38	178	15.36
7	5	4	5	11	15	15	23	32	34	31	208	15.20
5	4	3	4	7	6	6	10	16	13	7	95	14.25
9	12	9	10	11	12	12	4	9	8	3	139	10.44
16	23	10	18	16	20	18	12	17	9	7	239	10.25
22	23	10	17	12	17	12	14	4	9	4	217	9.09
18	27	22	19	19	18	11	17	5	5	6	249	9.41
12	14	13	8	7	9	9	10	10	7	2	178	8.50
16	17	18	7	12	14	10	2	3	4	2	208	7.56
7	4	3	7	7	3	2	1	2	1	1	95	6.08
4	0	3	2	4	2	2	1	2	2	1	139	2.67
12	7	7	3	8	6	5	1	4	1	0	239	3.07
8	7	7	4	9	3	2	6	1	2	0	217	3.19
8	8	10	3	6	7	5	4	1	6	2	249	3.40
6	7	5	7	4	1	5	7	3	4	1	178	3.93
12	9	6	7	1	2	5	5	2	3	3	208	3.83
1	4	4	0	1	3	0	2	4	1	2	95	3.47
5	7	7	5	12	11	19	12	20	12	9	139	13.63
11	9	15	22	17	19	17	27	24	16	20	239	12.68
6	11	11	15	17	17	23	21	24	21	20	217	13.52
13	6	8	20	17	18	21	27	34	32	22	249	14.05
10	4	11	8	17	19	15	18	19	22	18	178	13.70
11	11	9	6	13	21	28	18	27	19	17	208	13.68
5	6	4	9	9	7	7	7	11	8	8	95	12.57
6	5	7	4	5	4	9	12	5	4	2	139	6.96
14	7	13	12	14	11	18	10	13	10	11	239	8.46
10	5	6	14	12	14	15	6	9	14	12	217	8.35
14	12	15	15	8	20	8	20	9	10	13	249	8.96
10	8	10	11	10	7	6	8	4	9	9	178	7.80
5	15	18	10	14	14	7	8	8	15	14	208	9.72
12	4	3	7	-4	1	5	3	0	3	5	95	7.46
4	8	10	7	4	5	8	3	1	3	2	139	5.58
12	11	8	10	3	3	7	7	2	0	1	239	4.57
14	5	6	4	7	2	1	2	5	0	0	217	3.60
8	7	8	4	2	3	2	1	0	1	0	249	3.22
8	6	1	4	1	0	2	3	1	1	0	178	3.12
8	4	6	5	6	1	2	2	0	0	0	208	3.55
7	3	5	4	3	3	0	1	0	0	0	95	4.09

INCOME: FREQUENCY DISTRIBUTIONS (*continued*)

		1	2	3	4	5	6	7
Freedom	< $2,000	6	14	11	12	14	9	11
	$2–3,999	12	28	29	30	28	20	12
	$4–5,999	12	23	26	32	24	11	16
	$6–7,999	22	31	31	23	20	19	20
	$8–9,999	9	14	19	24	18	14	17
	$10–15T	16	16	17	28	18	24	20
	$15,000+	12	14	12	7	5	7	8
Happiness	< $2,000	8	7	8	15	8	11	10
	$2–3,999	8	14	17	18	15	23	15
	$4–5,999	9	18	18	15	18	16	22
	$6–7,999	8	15	17	24	23	30	17
	$8–9,999	9	16	13	9	15	14	12
	$10–15T	12	14	18	12	9	9	22
	$15,000+	1	3	4	7	6	7	11
Inner harmony	< $2,000	2	3	3	7	6	4	6
	$2–3,999	4	4	5	6	7	17	18
	$4–5,999	4	7	5	15	4	18	8
	$6–7,999	1	6	5	13	11	13	14
	$8–9,999	2	0	12	14	8	8	13
	$10–15T	3	8	6	9	15	16	14
	$15,000+	3	3	6	8	7	6	4
Mature love	< $2,000	1	1	3	9	2	2	4
	$2–3,999	0	4	4	4	9	3	12
	$4–5,999	0	6	8	9	9	6	9
	$6–7,999	2	3	8	10	12	9	14
	$8–9,999	2	7	5	9	9	8	13
	$10–15T	2	1	6	6	14	8	6
	$15,000+	0	0	4	2	4	3	4
National security	< $2,000	2	6	9	7	17	11	5
	$2–3,999	5	13	14	15	14	18	15
	$4–5,999	4	8	9	15	20	16	12
	$6–7,999	2	14	20	14	17	13	15
	$8–9,999	1	10	12	8	18	12	8
	$10–15T	3	10	11	15	6	21	11
	$15,000+	2	5	3	6	7	5	2
Pleasure	< $2,000	1	1	6	2	7	2	2
	$2–3,999	0	0	3	3	4	5	6
	$4–5,999	1	1	1	1	3	5	6
	$6–7,999	0	1	0	0	3	2	11
	$8–9,999	0	0	1	2	2	3	4
	$10–15T	0	2	2	1	2	2	5
	$15,000+	0	0	0	0	1	0	0
Salvation	< $2,000	24	10	10	5	6	14	7
	$2–3,999	56	9	15	16	6	10	10
	$4–5,999	43	8	10	11	7	5	10
	$6–7,999	57	17	10	7	11	8	7
	$8–9,999	44	6	7	9	8	2	4
	$10–15T	51	8	8	7	8	5	4
	$15,000+	17	1	1	5	4	2	2

8	9	10	11	12	13	14	15	16	17	18	N	MEDIAN
17	11	7	9	7	2	3	2	2	1	1	139	6.82
15	9	11	9	7	5	8	5	5	6	0	239	5.23
18	16	9	8	3	2	8	5	2	1	1	217	5.15
18	16	16	7	5	6	4	3	2	3	3	249	5.38
10	9	13	4	11	3	3	3	5	2	0	178	5.86
15	10	11	13	4	4	4	4	3	1	0	208	5.88
5	4	9	3	4	2	0	0	0	2	1	95	5.00
14	13	7	12	8	9	5	3	1	0	0	139	7.68
19	27	17	19	14	10	8	9	2	2	2	239	8.00
15	19	13	14	9	11	10	5	3	1	1	217	7.16
13	18	16	17	19	13	10	1	7	1	0	249	6.94
15	15	12	12	11	3	7	7	5	2	1	178	7.57
14	28	10	13	13	10	8	9	5	1	1	208	8.07
3	8	9	7	7	8	2	7	2	3	0	95	9.19
4	10	11	12	12	17	9	12	9	6	6	139	11.63
15	11	22	26	27	18	15	14	12	11	7	239	10.90
11	13	18	19	19	15	20	11	12	8	10	217	10.79
19	27	16	17	25	9	18	17	22	10	6	249	10.47
9	15	11	17	8	16	9	9	13	9	5	178	10.23
16	10	20	21	11	10	10	16	11	8	4	208	9.85
7	5	12	10	7	4	6	3	3	1	0	95	9.20
6	7	2	10	8	9	6	12	15	14	28	139	14.42
12	12	13	12	7	16	22	15	27	26	41	239	14.02
3	14	14	16	19	13	18	18	12	22	21	217	12.26
13	14	17	9	17	22	11	20	27	16	25	249	12.29
11	15	7	14	12	12	15	11	9	10	9	178	10.71
12	16	16	17	16	22	20	15	9	12	10	208	11.50
7	7	3	12	6	11	16	5	3	4	4	95	11.75
9	9	11	8	9	9	7	6	6	6	2	139	8.89
9	16	13	15	24	15	19	7	10	9	8	239	9.54
14	6	19	10	20	12	12	5	16	11	8	217	9.74
20	11	10	17	14	18	17	11	19	9	8	249	9.36
13	9	12	14	12	11	9	9	15	0	5	178	9.28
17	11	8	13	16	16	11	8	15	9	7	208	9.41
2	7	6	3	3	9	6	7	7	8	7	95	11.33
4	5	5	8	11	14	11	14	12	23	11	139	13.64
11	8	11	19	10	20	20	33	27	33	26	239	14.48
10	8	11	13	9	15	20	29	35	31	18	217	14.66
12	10	15	14	10	13	29	28	31	39	31	249	14.66
8	8	7	13	11	13	9	14	22	36	25	178	15.07
6	6	6	8	15	17	19	24	25	38	30	208	15.04
2	5	1	5	6	7	10	15	14	15	14	95	15.20
4	7	3	2	5	5	7	5	9	8	8	139	6.57
7	11	10	4	8	13	12	12	13	14	13	239	7.25
4	12	18	7	9	17	12	9	13	4	18	217	9.38
8	7	12	12	9	11	13	14	8	15	23	249	8.44
8	13	6	0	7	12	13	7	4	9	19	178	8.58
5	5	5	12	8	8	9	9	13	13	30	208	10.10
1	1	6	2	4	2	3	6	8	7	23	95	13.25

INCOME: FREQUENCY DISTRIBUTIONS (*continued*)

		1	2	3	4	5	6	7
Self-respect	< $2,000	4	6	6	9	13	9	18
	$2–3,999	5	13	17	20	32	19	19
	$4–5,999	7	15	14	9	14	24	24
	$6–7,999	9	10	12	19	25	19	18
	$8–9,999	1	11	12	10	12	21	17
	$10–15T	10	15	17	12	16	19	21
	$15,000+	2	5	4	11	4	6	12
Social recognition	< $2,000	0	0	1	3	2	4	6
	$2–3,999	1	3	0	3	10	5	11
	$4–5,999	0	0	1	1	5	1	8
	$6–7,999	0	0	0	1	3	7	3
	$8–9,999	1	0	0	0	2	4	2
	$10–15T	0	2	2	0	2	6	4
	$15,000+	0	0	0	1	3	2	3
True friendship	< $2,000	1	6	5	8	12	19	12
	$2–3,999	2	6	14	16	20	23	15
	$4–5,999	2	6	8	11	11	15	22
	$6–7,999	1	3	8	15	14	18	24
	$8–9,999	2	3	4	12	8	12	13
	$10–15T	1	2	9	12	11	17	11
	$15,000+	0	2	3	6	4	6	8
Wisdom	< $2,000	6	12	10	3	5	17	4
	$2–3,999	8	15	12	12	15	19	18
	$4–5,999	12	8	11	8	14	16	20
	$6–7,999	13	20	20	16	23	23	19
	$8–9,999	9	15	10	10	12	14	12
	$10–15T	8	12	18	13	27	13	15
	$15,000+	10	12	11	3	11	10	6
Ambitious	< $2,000	20	8	4	12	8	9	5
	$2–3,999	42	24	16	9	15	10	9
	$4–5,999	30	29	14	10	16	14	16
	$6–7,999	33	26	24	17	11	11	10
	$8–9,999	17	20	13	14	13	12	9
	$10–15T	30	21	18	12	20	9	14
	$15,000+	15	4	13	6	6	4	2
Broadminded	< $2,000	11	13	10	11	6	10	3
	$2–3,999	17	30	15	19	14	16	13
	$4–5,999	21	18	13	11	15	9	11
	$6–7,999	17	30	22	10	14	12	7
	$8–9,999	15	17	15	10	11	15	11
	$10–15T	13	17	21	23	18	13	15
	$15,000+	5	7	9	5	8	8	11
Capable	< $2,000	2	4	12	8	6	5	10
	$2–3,999	4	12	19	15	5	9	11
	$4–5,999	4	16	10	13	12	13	8
	$6–7,999	1	11	22	17	11	11	19
	$8–9,999	5	4	12	12	10	13	11
	$10–15T	3	11	14	18	14	17	12
	$15,000	1	8	5	7	7	5	8

8	9	10	11	12	13	14	15	16	17	18	N	MEDIAN
12	10	14	9	8	4	3	8	3	1	2	139	7.88
12	13	14	17	11	9	9	11	6	8	4	239	7.21
19	18	9	16	14	10	4	11	3	4	2	217	7.58
14	28	14	19	16	12	8	12	6	5	3	249	8.39
14	16	9	19	11	11	6	5	3	0	0	178	7.86
17	17	15	14	10	5	6	9	2	2	1	208	7.21
14	10	6	2	5	4	2	4	3	0	1	95	7.75
5	5	8	12	14	8	11	12	12	18	18	139	13.64
13	12	7	15	15	16	24	21	29	31	23	239	13.85
9	11	14	13	10	11	18	24	33	26	32	217	14.77
9	14	7	11	15	22	30	19	25	28	55	249	14.63
8	2	8	15	12	17	25	12	20	20	30	178	14.22
3	8	10	11	14	17	11	24	25	25	44	208	15.08
3	3	2	5	6	8	11	10	8	13	17	95	14.55
15	7	11	12	5	6	2	3	4	7	4	139	7.93
23	22	15	9	21	18	6	12	6	8	3	239	8.52
22	17	20	18	11	14	8	10	12	7	3	217	9.18
18	14	24	18	19	25	10	16	8	12	2	249	9.90
16	9	18	11	16	20	7	10	8	4	5	178	10.06
20	16	22	12	18	15	16	12	7	5	2	208	9.73
7	13	9	7	8	10	5	3	2	2	0	95	9.38
10	12	9	7	1	10	5	9	4	4	11	139	8.71
21	15	20	7	13	11	11	8	12	10	12	239	8.48
17	13	17	13	12	21	7	11	3	6	8	217	8.69
13	9	15	15	18	11	14	8	4	2	6	249	7.00
10	14	17	9	13	11	7	5	2	4	4	178	8.20
13	12	14	16	10	7	9	8	2	9	2	208	7.37
4	4	6	4	3	2	4	1	1	3	0	95	5.55
7	7	12	6	4	8	6	5	7	8	3	139	8.00
15	9	9	13	10	7	13	5	8	11	14	239	6.89
8	4	7	15	9	12	10	1	4	6	12	217	6.18
11	21	13	9	10	11	9	9	6	10	8	249	6.75
9	6	4	11	12	10	9	7	7	2	3	178	6.50
7	12	7	8	7	5	7	11	8	7	5	208	5.83
2	5	4	4	0	5	3	6	7	4	5	95	6.38
5	7	8	10	10	6	6	4	4	5	10	139	8.57
11	14	12	9	13	14	6	11	6	12	7	239	7.15
15	15	15	11	18	10	11	6	4	8	6	217	8.20
21	13	14	10	16	12	11	13	8	7	12	249	8.10
8	11	11	9	10	7	10	5	6	5	2	178	7.05
11	9	2	6	13	10	10	5	4	11	7	208	6.42
7	4	4	6	4	2	3	4	3	3	2	95	7.00
9	14	7	9	11	7	12	8	9	5	1	139	9.46
9	12	24	18	16	13	16	21	11	15	9	239	10.48
14	16	14	18	19	18	12	12	9	6	3	217	9.68
13	23	22	16	15	19	14	12	10	6	7	249	9.35
13	5	14	22	11	13	7	12	6	4	4	178	9.79
17	18	12	14	13	8	7	13	12	4	1	208	8.38
4	8	9	7	8	7	3	0	3	2	3	95	8.81

INCOME: FREQUENCY DISTRIBUTIONS (*continued*)

		1	2	3	4	5	6	7
Cheerful	< $2,000	5	9	7	11	11	8	9
	$2–3,999	8	17	10	19	16	13	18
	$4–5,999	4	12	13	16	9	10	9
	$6–7,999	1	12	6	17	9	13	16
	$8–9,999	7	4	6	6	9	11	8
	$10–15T	4	6	10	11	5	14	10
	$15,000+	0	0	2	5	2	4	6
Clean	< $2,000	12	10	16	8	17	7	8
	$2–3,999	24	12	18	18	19	16	15
	$4–5,999	15	10	14	16	21	17	8
	$6–7,999	10	15	20	23	13	9	18
	$8–9,999	7	13	10	15	13	9	8
	$10–15T	5	9	13	5	18	9	8
	$15,000+	0	4	1	1	3	1	1
Courageous	< $2,000	8	15	7	8	3	19	10
	$2–3,999	9	13	11	18	21	21	17
	$4–5,999	12	9	21	16	16	12	16
	$6–7,999	14	22	14	15	23	20	16
	$8–9,999	9	10	15	10	17	11	19
	$10–15T	17	12	11	14	10	15	17
	$15,000+	4	5	6	11	11	7	5
Forgiving	< $2,000	11	9	11	11	19	9	13
	$2–3,999	23	13	23	20	20	21	20
	$4–5,999	9	23	18	18	15	15	12
	$6–7,999	18	15	24	18	21	23	20
	$8–9,999	8	18	11	10	14	17	13
	$10–15T	5	20	13	14	18	13	16
	$15,000+	4	3	5	5	7	4	6
Helpful	< $2,000	7	13	14	12	13	6	7
	$2–3,999	8	17	17	20	17	21	23
	$4–5,999	4	13	19	19	12	14	1
	$6–7,999	8	9	15	23	17	8	2
	$8–9,999	1	13	10	18	10	8	1
	$10–15T	10	5	10	15	10	15	1
	$15,000+	3	2	2	8	4	10	9
Honest	< $2,000	32	23	18	15	12	8	6
	$2–3,999	47	35	33	25	14	21	13
	$4–5,999	62	29	19	28	21	9	6
	$6–7,999	76	31	33	19	11	25	9
	$8–9,999	59	22	17	14	14	10	7
	$10–15T	59	21	28	20	14	13	12
	$15,000+	29	12	13	9	5	4	6
Imaginative	< $2,000	0	0	0	3	0	3	3
	$2–3,999	0	2	4	2	3	1	6
	$4–5,999	2	1	1	4	2	3	4
	$6–7,999	1	2	1	3	4	4	3
	$8–9,999	0	1	2	4	5	6	6
	$10–15T	1	6	4	8	7	4	6
	$15,000+	1	3	2	6	7	2	7

8	9	10	11	12	13	14	15	16	17	18	N	MEDIAN
5	9	5	11	7	8	7	13	5	6	3	139	9.00
17	15	19	12	13	6	14	14	9	13	6	239	8.60
10	10	15	12	18	16	17	10	13	14	9	217	10.54
18	21	13	22	13	21	22	17	12	4	12	249	10.38
15	11	11	6	10	11	18	14	14	6	11	178	10.67
18	13	20	13	13	13	18	13	14	6	7	208	10.15
8	6	10	6	6	7	14	10	5	3	1	95	11.25
10	5	6	9	7	3	4	3	7	5	2	139	6.43
17	14	9	14	8	17	9	7	12	4	6	239	7.33
14	15	11	12	14	7	12	6	13	7	5	217	8.05
15	15	15	16	15	15	13	11	11	7	8	249	8.60
6	10	13	11	9	11	8	9	7	7	12	178	9.30
13	12	13	10	13	11	18	13	16	7	15	208	10.42
3	6	6	4	1	8	10	7	12	11	16	95	14.35
3	6	6	14	9	8	7	4	6	4	2	139	7.45
17	11	11	15	13	11	17	9	15	9	1	239	8.06
13	15	22	10	9	7	7	11	12	4	5	217	8.00
20	10	16	12	15	10	10	5	9	8	10	249	7.53
10	11	9	12	12	10	4	5	9	4	1	178	7.39
15	9	11	14	13	17	5	8	7	6	7	208	8.03
7	9	4	5	5	1	1	6	3	2	3	95	7.20
8	8	4	7	7	5	7	4	4	1	1	139	6.44
16	11	14	8	15	12	8	5	4	4	2	239	6.48
17	16	9	16	16	4	6	9	9	1	4	217	7.38
12	12	14	11	15	11	12	7	7	6	3	249	6.78
12	12	13	6	5	11	10	7	5	3	3	178	7.35
9	7	9	15	13	17	11	12	6	4	6	208	8.06
6	5	1	8	10	6	9	4	4	6	2	95	10.69
16	6	8	7	11	6	5	0	2	4	2	139	7.14
16	24	8	10	12	14	11	10	6	2	3	239	7.35
20	11	20	13	11	7	17	11	3	3	4	217	8.08
29	10	18	11	14	9	11	16	7	12	9	249	8.24
13	17	12	12	8	12	9	7	4	6	7	178	8.79
20	11	14	20	16	11	8	10	12	7	4	208	9.32
6	6	6	8	9	6	3	7	5	0	1	95	9.08
4	9	4	3	0	1	1	1	0	0	2	139	3.31
13	13	3	8	4	6	1	2	1	0	0	239	3.68
8	13	7	7	2	0	2	1	1	2	0	217	3.42
8	14	4	4	5	5	1	2	0	2	0	249	3.03
6	10	8	2	3	0	2	2	1	0	1	178	2.97
7	9	8	8	3	2	2	2	0	0	0	208	3.36
3	4	3	1	2	0	2	1	0	1	0	95	3.00
8	4	8	8	5	11	7	13	12	26	28	139	15.23
5	4	9	9	11	12	20	21	33	38	59	239	15.82
2	7	10	8	10	12	13	26	25	34	53	217	15.64
2	6	11	10	15	12	16	19	33	40	67	249	15.97
5	3	12	11	8	7	10	19	18	33	28	178	14.97
7	7	11	5	10	14	12	15	19	26	46	208	14.63
5	8	2	5	4	7	7	3	1	11	14	95	11.40

INCOME: FREQUENCY DISTRIBUTIONS (*continued*)

		1	2	3	4	5	6	
Independent	< $2,000	5	3	8	7	6	10	1
	$2–3,999	7	8	10	12	13	11	1
	$4–5,999	10	12	12	15	13	11	1
	$6–7,999	9	8	8	11	9	11	1
	$8–9,999	5	6	8	14	2	8	1
	$10–15T	11	14	7	9	10	8	
	$15,000+	8	6	8	7	4	7	
Intellectual	< $2,000	0	2	1	2	2	6	
	$2–3,999	4	4	5	4	6	4	1
	$4–5,999	4	5	7	4	8	13	
	$6–7,999	4	5	6	3	11	10	1
	$8–9,999	5	5	5	5	4	4	
	$10–15T	2	8	5	8	12	6	
	$15,000+	8	3	5	9	5	8	
Logical	< $2,000	1	1	2	2	2	1	
	$2–3,999	0	2	4	3	9	4	
	$4–5,999	2	1	4	1	5	5	
	$6–7,999	3	6	4	6	9	9	1
	$8–9,999	2	2	5	4	4	4	
	$10–15T	4	3	4	4	6	14	1
	$15,000+	1	8	1	2	5	6	
Loving	< $2,000	7	6	5	4	10	12	
	$2–3,999	12	12	5	15	18	10	
	$4–5,999	12	10	12	8	13	11	1
	$6–7,999	17	16	13	13	16	15	1
	$8–9,999	11	9	8	6	15	8	1
	$10–15T	18	13	12	10	11	10	
	$15,000+	5	9	5	3	6	6	
Obedient	< $2,000	3	3	6	5	2	8	1
	$2–3,999	0	9	8	9	10	15	1
	$4–5,999	1	1	2	5	6	13	
	$6–7,999	1	5	2	6	10	11	
	$8–9,999	1	4	2	2	3	6	
	$10–15T	0	6	2	2	2	7	
	$15,000+	0	0	1	0	3	3	
Polite	< $2,000	2	2	7	5	3	8	1
	$2–3,999	5	6	10	10	14	11	1
	$4–5,999	1	4	4	9	13	21	1
	$6–7,999	0	3	8	14	13	13	1
	$8–9,999	1	3	6	8	6	11	
	$10–15T	0	4	3	8	7	12	1
	$15,000+	1	1	1	1	2	2	
Responsible	< $2,000	9	9	7	8	16	3	
	$2–3,999	20	14	18	15	11	20	1
	$4–5,999	11	16	26	14	9	16	2
	$6–7,999	22	21	17	26	32	21	1
	$8–9,999	12	24	21	13	10	16	1
	$10–15T	20	24	20	18	13	20	2
	$15,000+	9	12	12	5	6	10	

8	9	10	11	12	13	14	15	16	17	18	N	MEDIAN
5	6	7	15	11	9	9	11	9	1	5	139	10.53
22	15	11	17	16	16	16	13	19	9	11	239	10.27
8	9	7	12	12	18	15	17	13	10	8	217	10.00
15	18	14	25	13	18	16	19	16	14	9	249	10.72
10	11	4	9	13	10	11	13	11	14	16	178	11.39
4	12	12	15	15	12	16	13	17	13	11	208	11.03
6	2	4	3	5	8	4	5	6	4	5	95	8.25
6	4	6	3	16	7	15	19	13	14	14	139	13.87
7	15	14	13	19	15	15	23	34	30	16	239	13.40
7	5	7	16	12	16	7	19	29	27	24	217	13.34
5	11	16	11	16	14	32	19	24	30	22	249	13.58
13	8	12	6	9	11	15	20	20	16	14	178	13.14
10	15	13	6	16	14	12	13	17	26	16	208	12.13
6	8	3	4	3	5	7	11	3	1	3	95	8.56
2	7	5	2	11	12	9	16	17	18	29	139	15.16
7	5	14	7	11	20	20	25	23	31	47	239	14.76
7	6	11	12	12	14	17	21	26	31	35	217	14.71
8	9	11	14	10	14	17	24	33	31	31	249	14.18
7	2	9	14	10	12	16	11	18	22	29	178	13.94
16	8	10	8	10	15	15	20	20	25	14	208	12.83
7	3	6	8	5	11	3	2	8	8	6	95	10.94
10	3	10	7	2	9	18	9	6	8	5	139	9.95
11	15	18	14	20	16	14	16	9	16	11	239	10.31
16	12	6	8	9	12	14	18	11	19	12	217	9.58
13	13	10	10	16	12	21	16	14	14	5	249	9.00
15	12	6	12	15	7	6	10	10	11	4	178	8.83
7	7	17	13	14	12	16	13	8	19	3	208	10.15
4	4	8	6	6	3	8	5	6	7	1	95	9.81
4	8	8	10	5	13	8	13	13	11	9	139	12.00
9	7	10	19	15	24	17	19	18	20	20	239	12.40
9	13	11	11	14	23	18	24	19	19	23	217	13.26
12	12	14	14	18	22	17	23	26	21	29	249	13.11
5	10	7	6	9	17	12	14	20	23	29	178	14.25
8	4	7	16	14	18	12	19	26	21	35	208	14.25
3	4	7	3	5	4	7	7	9	17	20	95	15.29
13	5	16	8	6	11	8	4	17	7	7	139	10.41
18	16	25	17	23	11	15	17	9	9	10	239	10.16
12	12	25	17	12	17	19	8	13	11	4	217	10.20
17	18	22	22	20	8	15	21	16	18	3	249	10.43
11	15	12	10	10	13	13	12	16	16	8	178	11.40
12	16	14	22	15	8	24	13	16	10	12	208	11.23
3	4	7	6	9	8	4	6	19	7	9	95	13.19
19	18	6	4	9	6	1	4	2	11	2	139	8.16
13	23	12	15	12	11	7	9	8	10	3	239	7.77
17	22	8	6	10	9	8	5	3	5	3	217	7.07
11	11	10	13	8	14	5	7	7	6	2	249	5.81
13	13	7	9	8	5	5	2	4	3	0	178	6.06
16	19	12	3	3	3	5	6	0	2	4	208	5.95
7	4	5	4	6	4	1	1	1	0	1	95	5.85

INCOME: FREQUENCY DISTRIBUTIONS (*continued*)

		1	2	3	4	5	6	7
Self-controlled	< $2,000	4	9	4	7	3	7	9
	$2–3,999	9	9	13	6	14	15	15
	$4–5,999	13	8	8	10	11	10	19
	$6–7,999	14	12	10	8	15	23	17
	$8–9,999	13	3	12	13	18	9	8
	$10–15T	6	8	13	9	13	9	12
	$15,000+	1	8	4	5	4	4	6

8	9	10	11	12	13	14	15	16	17	18	N	MEDIAN
5	13	13	6	8	9	9	8	6	5	14	139	10.15
16	16	17	21	8	14	20	12	14	6	14	239	9.88
20	16	12	13	10	15	12	12	11	10	7	217	9.09
19	12	12	19	15	22	7	9	10	13	12	249	9.04
7	11	14	10	16	11	13	9	2	3	6	178	9.05
11	20	16	12	7	18	10	9	6	14	15	208	9.69
8	5	6	7	7	3	6	10	0	8	3	95	9.92

EDUCATION: FREQUENCY DISTRIBUTIONS

		1	2	3	4	5	6	7
A comfortable life	0–4 YRS	16	5	7	1	3	9	3
	5–8 YRS	39	21	8	19	16	16	16
	SOME H S	35	21	20	13	19	21	22
	COMP H S	29	24	22	26	17	27	25
	SOMECOLL	7	13	7	4	10	6	10
	COMPCOLL	3	0	3	3	2	6	3
	GRADPROF	1	3	1	1	0	3	3
An exciting life	0–4 YRS	1	3	2	0	3	0	1
	5–8 YRS	2	11	3	2	3	5	7
	SOME H S	3	5	1	2	8	4	6
	COMP H S	2	5	7	5	3	6	9
	SOMECOLL	1	2	3	0	0	5	6
	COMPCOLL	1	2	0	0	2	2	3
	GRADPROF	1	1	1	5	1	2	2
A sense of accomplishment	0–4 YRS	1	1	3	4	4	3	4
	5–8 YRS	2	7	17	9	8	13	9
	SOME H S	6	8	19	13	12	23	23
	COMP H S	12	24	13	23	32	35	27
	SOMECOLL	3	11	12	15	16	16	17
	COMPCOLL	8	3	11	8	6	11	6
	GRADPROF	7	8	3	7	6	6	3
A world at peace	0–4 YRS	18	7	11	4	2	5	1
	5–8 YRS	74	48	36	32	14	6	14
	SOME H S	76	58	59	28	13	11	9
	COMP H S	91	70	45	43	38	27	16
	SOMECOLL	27	28	24	16	10	8	6
	COMPCOLL	13	15	11	7	2	8	3
	GRADPROF	14	6	11	3	4	3	4
A world of beauty	0–4 YRS	0	3	2	2	1	3	1
	5–8 YRS	0	7	3	8	17	10	9
	SOME H S	0	5	7	4	8	6	12
	COMP H S	2	1	2	9	8	10	6
	SOMECOLL	1	0	1	9	3	3	4
	COMPCOLL	0	0	1	1	0	2	6
	GRADPROF	0	0	1	3	6	0	5
Equality	0–4 YRS	1	4	4	6	1	3	6
	5–8 YRS	4	17	21	16	23	17	21
	SOME H S	8	18	23	29	25	20	18
	COMP H S	8	26	43	31	33	24	33
	SOMECOLL	4	12	22	11	6	11	13
	COMPCOLL	3	3	4	12	6	1	9
	GRADPROF	3	9	5	3	1	5	1
Family security	0–4 YRS	8	11	6	7	5	4	5
	5–8 YRS	29	41	35	24	26	13	19
	SOME H S	57	59	38	45	27	22	16
	COMP H S	90	83	52	34	41	24	31
	SOMECOLL	39	32	18	22	11	14	5
	COMPCOLL	17	14	13	8	9	5	5
	GRADPROF	8	3	2	8	7	2	6

8	9	10	11	12	13	14	15	16	17	18	N	MEDIAN
4	5	3	2	1	0	3	0	1	1	0	64	5.50
18	13	14	13	13	12	16	11	5	5	8	263	7.28
18	16	26	17	16	17	9	16	17	13	4	320	8.00
26	17	26	32	23	19	38	23	20	21	11	426	9.50
4	13	11	8	14	6	12	14	19	13	9	180	11.13
6	2	5	6	8	5	7	8	10	9	4	90	12.25
2	3	1	2	5	3	10	8	6	3	6	61	13.75
2	1	1	4	6	4	3	7	7	3	16	64	14.64
7	7	7	10	12	10	19	25	31	45	57	263	15.55
9	7	14	9	13	16	21	42	35	51	74	320	15.50
8	13	15	16	22	23	31	49	58	77	77	426	15.48
4	6	4	7	13	12	16	14	25	29	33	180	15.29
7	5	2	3	7	5	6	10	10	17	8	90	14.50
3	5	2	1	1	6	4	3	9	7	7	61	13.42
1	2	4	3	2	8	7	6	3	5	3	64	12.50
17	19	17	22	25	18	22	19	14	18	7	263	11.11
35	35	19	28	9	22	17	16	14	12	9	320	9.10
24	42	26	24	34	34	18	24	16	12	6	426	9.05
13	14	16	8	12	11	6	3	4	3	0	180	7.50
11	9	3	4	2	3	4	1	0	0	0	90	6.32
2	4	2	0	6	1	5	0	0	1	0	61	5.42
4	1	1	2	3	1	0	1	1	2	0	64	3.14
6	4	6	1	5	2	6	3	3	2	1	263	2.76
8	15	7	6	8	6	7	4	1	1	3	320	2.94
17	10	15	11	12	8	4	11	3	4	1	426	3.66
11	10	8	4	1	4	4	4	7	5	3	180	4.19
7	2	3	2	3	2	5	0	3	3	1	90	4.36
0	2	4	0	2	1	0	3	1	2	1	61	3.45
2	0	5	4	3	5	7	4	9	9	4	64	13.64
10	13	10	12	15	24	23	28	34	19	21	263	13.23
17	10	13	27	27	26	24	33	34	38	29	320	13.42
19	15	22	26	35	32	49	43	55	49	43	426	14.03
11	11	8	10	14	12	23	21	22	14	13	180	13.63
4	4	4	6	7	12	12	5	12	4	10	90	13.33
3	4	4	6	6	7	1	4	3	6	2	61	11.25
3	0	3	4	5	6	3	6	3	2	4	64	10.75
11	15	19	10	15	11	9	16	10	11	17	263	8.60
20	11	10	18	16	20	18	10	12	25	19	320	8.45
19	14	24	20	20	25	26	22	15	21	22	426	8.29
11	11	7	15	9	9	8	10	7	6	8	180	8.50
3	6	7	10	6	5	5	4	1	4	1	90	9.17
7	2	8	3	3	5	1	3	0	1	1	61	8.00
3	1	5	2	0	3	3	1	0	0	0	64	4.50
11	13	12	12	6	4	5	6	2	2	3	263	4.60
7	11	7	8	6	5	5	4	2	1	0	320	3.63
20	11	12	6	7	1	6	3	3	2	0	426	3.27
15	4	4	3	2	4	2	3	1	1	0	180	3.55
4	4	2	6	1	0	1	1	0	0	0	90	3.63
4	1	3	3	8	2	1	1	2	0	0	61	6.58

EDUCATION: FREQUENCY DISTRIBUTIONS (*continued*)

		1	*2*	*3*	*4*	*5*	*6*	*7*
Freedom	0–4 YRS	1	11	2	7	9	4	3
	5–8 YRS	12	28	28	29	22	20	18
	SOME H S	21	33	28	32	40	28	27
	COMP H S	29	42	63	51	38	33	34
	SOMECOLL	17	18	20	21	16	16	16
	COMPCOLL	13	11	7	13	5	5	7
	GRADPROF	4	8	6	8	7	5	2
Happiness	0–4 YRS	4	4	5	9	4	4	4
	5–8 YRS	12	18	16	23	21	28	19
	SOME H S	8	24	22	32	21	27	30
	COMP H S	23	29	41	19	38	37	40
	SOMECOLL	8	8	10	14	12	14	20
	COMPCOLL	3	4	5	5	2	4	4
	GRADPROF	2	2	4	4	2	2	3
Inner harmony	0–4 YRS	0	2	2	3	5	2	3
	5–8 YRS	5	5	5	11	12	13	12
	SOME H S	3	7	4	22	3	18	23
	COMP H S	5	7	15	29	17	32	21
	SOMECOLL	2	8	13	5	11	14	8
	COMPCOLL	2	5	2	6	9	5	7
	GRADPROF	2	2	2	2	4	4	7
Mature love	0–4 YRS	1	1	0	1	2	1	1
	5–8 YRS	2	1	5	9	4	9	16
	SOME H S	0	8	11	15	13	8	13
	COMP H S	2	7	11	14	13	15	21
	SOMECOLL	1	2	4	6	13	5	6
	COMPCOLL	1	4	4	4	9	3	5
	GRADPROF	0	2	4	3	6	2	4
National security	0–4 YRS	0	0	4	2	5	9	2
	5–8 YRS	5	10	19	15	21	19	16
	SOME H S	3	19	8	19	30	28	20
	COMP H S	6	24	27	27	33	30	23
	SOMECOLL	3	10	13	15	10	10	8
	COMPCOLL	0	6	7	5	6	2	4
	GRADPROF	1	2	4	2	0	2	2
Pleasure	0–4 YRS	0	1	5	2	3	0	6
	5–8 YRS	1	1	3	2	6	7	7
	SOME H S	1	1	1	2	5	8	8
	COMP H S	0	2	4	2	7	3	13
	SOMECOLL	0	0	1	1	2	1	1
	COMPCOLL	0	0	0	0	1	3	1
	GRADPROF	0	0	0	0	0	0	0
Salvation	0–4 YRS	9	7	3	2	2	3	4
	5–8 YRS	62	12	19	14	9	13	11
	SOME H S	75	15	20	13	9	12	14
	COMP H S	95	23	13	24	17	13	11
	SOMECOLL	39	6	6	7	7	4	5
	COMPCOLL	16	2	1	4	7	3	0
	GRADPROF	7	1	2	1	2	1	2

8	9	10	11	12	13	14	15	16	17	18	N	MEDIAN
12	5	1	3	2	1	0	1	1	1	0	64	6.00
26	19	13	11	9	3	12	2	3	6	2	263	6.13
24	12	21	10	9	7	9	8	7	3	1	320	5.71
23	27	24	16	14	8	7	7	4	4	2	426	5.24
13	5	11	9	5	6	1	2	3	1	0	180	5.38
4	5	7	4	4	0	1	2	1	0	1	90	4.70
5	5	1	3	1	0	1	1	2	1	1	61	5.14
6	6	4	4	4	4	0	1	1	0	0	64	7.00
14	37	2	21	16	12	9	8	4	2	1	263	7.21
30	26	20	19	24	14	12	3	5	1	2	320	7.37
34	36	30	26	16	17	21	9	6	3	1	426	7.15
10	17	19	13	13	8	3	7	2	2	0	180	7.90
3	8	9	10	8	5	7	6	5	2	0	90	10.28
3	7	8	3	4	6	1	7	2	0	1	61	9.69
3	10	3	4	3	5	7	2	1	3	6	64	10.17
9	12	32	22	30	18	19	18	16	13	11	263	11.20
17	19	22	31	30	24	28	22	24	17	6	320	11.21
33	33	26	37	32	27	22	32	30	15	13	426	10.31
18	11	18	15	11	9	8	8	11	6	4	180	9.50
3	8	8	8	6	10	2	3	3	2	1	90	9.25
3	6	8	9	2	4	5	0	1	0	0	61	9.25
3	6	3	5	2	4	5	6	8	6	9	64	13.90
8	14	17	20	11	18	17	15	22	29	46	263	13.36
13	18	13	13	23	21	24	27	32	29	39	320	13.07
22	28	26	36	29	36	35	35	28	34	34	426	12.12
13	13	8	12	10	14	19	14	15	14	11	180	12.20
5	5	5	6	5	7	8	5	6	4	4	90	10.50
4	3	4	4	7	6	5	3	1	0	3	61	10.13
2	4	4	4	8	3	4	5	4	4	0	64	10.50
19	16	19	18	22	13	12	11	15	8	5	263	8.97
24	21	17	17	22	21	17	9	24	11	10	320	8.93
28	20	26	19	31	34	29	14	31	8	16	426	9.25
6	8	10	11	18	14	13	9	9	6	7	180	10.20
3	4	5	6	6	6	6	6	4	9	5	90	11.00
6	2	1	6	1	3	7	2	7	8	5	61	13.00
1	4	4	2	2	6	5	6	7	6	4	64	12.83
16	9	13	16	19	28	22	27	27	39	20	263	13.66
15	11	12	24	20	16	31	44	40	40	41	320	14.61
18	21	28	23	20	28	30	45	63	67	52	426	14.81
4	4	6	15	9	16	22	25	13	35	25	180	14.82
1	1	3	2	4	6	10	15	11	17	15	90	15.37
2	3	0	4	2	3	6	4	12	18	7	61	16.04
1	1	2	2	7	3	5	3	5	3	2	64	9.50
9	12	15	6	4	16	16	12	10	10	13	263	6.73
5	24	14	12	10	13	17	12	19	13	23	320	7.90
6	18	16	12	25	21	22	22	18	24	36	426	8.56
4	6	8	7	4	12	10	7	11	10	27	180	10.25
1	1	7	1	2	6	2	6	5	7	19	90	12.50
1	1	3	1	2	2	2	4	3	4	22	61	15.13

EDUCATION: FREQUENCY DISTRIBUTIONS (*continued*)

		1	*2*	*3*	*4*	*5*	*6*	*7*
Self-respect	0–4 YRS	1	1	3	2	3	5	10
	5–8 YRS	3	12	15	15	24	26	20
	SOME H S	8	14	22	23	32	28	27
	COMP H S	13	28	24	30	35	25	47
	SOMECOLL	9	11	9	16	17	22	16
	COMPCOLL	5	6	8	5	5	13	11
	GRADPROF	1	4	7	4	5	8	5
Social recognition	0–4 YRS	1	0	0	1	1	0	1
	5–8 YRS	1	0	1	3	9	5	13
	SOME H S	0	1	2	1	7	4	10
	COMP H S	0	1	0	2	7	13	5
	SOMECOLL	0	1	1	1	4	3	8
	COMPCOLL	0	1	0	0	0	3	2
	GRADPROF	0	0	0	2	0	3	1
True friendship	0–4 YRS	1	1	2	9	9	5	4
	5–8 YRS	4	13	18	19	16	23	21
	SOME H S	4	5	14	14	17	28	20
	COMP H S	0	7	14	34	23	29	37
	SOMECOLL	1	1	3	6	8	15	14
	COMPCOLL	0	0	4	4	7	9	7
	GRADPROF	0	2	0	1	5	7	7
Wisdom	0–4 YRS	1	2	3	2	2	4	5
	5–8 YRS	6	11	11	13	12	20	15
	SOME H S	12	19	21	13	31	24	22
	COMP H S	19	23	30	23	26	43	27
	SOMECOLL	18	17	13	11	24	13	17
	COMPCOLL	5	14	9	5	12	5	7
	GRADPROF	10	8	8	4	5	6	4
Ambitious	0–4 YRS	11	7	5	2	7	6	0
	5–8 YRS	47	26	16	17	18	12	9
	SOME H S	51	30	23	28	20	15	17
	COMP H S	53	49	35	25	23	26	32
	SOMECOLL	27	14	14	7	13	8	5
	COMPCOLL	8	12	4	3	8	5	4
	GRADPROF	3	3	6	8	6	2	1
Broadminded	0–4 YRS	3	6	3	5	3	1	4
	5–8 YRS	22	30	18	16	12	18	8
	SOME H S	21	24	27	22	17	21	18
	COMP H S	30	46	33	31	37	28	20
	SOMECOLL	13	21	16	10	8	10	13
	COMPCOLL	7	8	10	10	8	3	6
	GRADPROF	4	9	7	3	6	4	4
Capable	0–4 YRS	0	3	10	2	2	2	5
	5–8 YRS	7	15	20	13	8	13	19
	SOME H S	3	21	16	16	15	19	12
	COMP H S	8	20	32	40	24	19	26
	SOMECOLL	3	7	8	10	14	14	11
	COMPCOLL	1	3	9	7	2	6	4
	GRADPROF	1	1	4	4	4	5	2

8	9	10	11	12	13	14	15	16	17	18	N	MEDIAN
3	9	3	7	3	1	4	4	3	0	2	64	8.94
22	18	21	22	12	12	5	22	7	4	3	263	8.25
26	21	29	25	20	10	12	9	5	5	4	320	7.73
33	47	15	34	25	21	15	16	8	9	1	426	7.83
12	17	8	11	12	6	3	7	0	2	2	180	6.88
9	9	6	1	3	4	0	1	3	0	1	90	6.77
5	3	4	5	2	5	0	2	1	0	0	61	6.80
5	3	7	3	6	4	2	5	7	11	7	64	13.50
12	12	7	18	13	27	31	20	39	29	23	263	13.84
7	19	12	21	29	24	37	34	30	38	44	320	14.12
16	14	20	27	24	33	42	32	46	49	95	426	14.78
8	5	9	9	9	12	10	17	22	25	36	180	15.09
3	2	3	4	6	6	9	9	13	11	18	90	15.17
1	1	1	7	4	3	9	11	7	7	4	61	14.33
7	2	5	5	4	2	1	1.	2	4	0	64	7.64
24	13	20	11	25	20	5	7	9	9	6	263	8.23
25	26	38	24	19	29	14	16	10	13	4	320	9.68
35	37	39	30	26	36	18	22	17	14	8	426	9.42
15	13	14	15	16	21	13	12	7	6	0	180	10.50
12	9	5	7	9	5	4	4	2	1	1	90	8.72
8	4	5	3	4	4	1	4	3	2	1	61	8.63
2	4	6	4	3	4	5	5	1	4	7	64	10.75
24	17	19	18	11	15	15	13	12	12	19	263	9.63
20	18	26	11	19	29	18	11	9	9	8	320	8.40
35	23	36	31	31	23	13	17	5	13	8	426	8.13
8	12	11	8	8	4	7	3	2	2	2	180	6.04
4	6	6	4	3	3	1	4	1	0	1	90	5.50
2	5	2	1	1	0	2	1	1	1	0	61	4.60
3	6	3	3	1	1	2	2	1	1	3	64	5.50
8	16	15	14	9	12	10	7	7	13	7	263	6.13
16	12	16	19	11	11	14	5	12	9	11	320	6.03
17	19	15	17	18	22	20	15	10	12	18	426	6.56
7	10	6	9	11	12	8	7	8	11	3	180	7.79
6	3	3	5	1	3	6	2	7	3	7	90	7.67
3	3	3	3	2	1	3	8	2	1	3	61	8.00
4	4	2	5	3	3	4	6	4	2	2	64	9.25
14	14	13	15	17	11	9	8	11	13	14	263	8.04
19	17	21	15	24	20	16	12	4	10	12	320	8.03
25	21	20	19	28	16	19	17	11	13	12	426	6.90
14	10	9	8	10	7	9	6	5	9	2	180	7.42
3	7	2	4	4	5	3	1	2	5	2	90	6.17
4	3	3	3	4	3	0	2	0	0	2	61	5.88
6	2	3	8	4	4	5	2	3	2	1	64	9.50
9	12	20	13	21	22	19	21	15	12	4	263	10.28
12	33	27	21	30	25	18	23	14	10	5	320	9.98
29	28	31	34	27	28	19	22	15	13	11	426	9.04
16	13	12	21	11	7	7	8	9	4	5	180	9.04
7	4	13	7	2	6	4	5	6	0	4	90	9.65
5	7	5	6	3	3	2	1	1	4	0	61	8.71

EDUCATION: FREQUENCY DISTRIBUTIONS (*continued*)

		1	*2*	*3*	*4*	*5*	*6*	*7*
Cheerful	0–4 YRS	5	2	4	5	5	8	2
	5–8 YRS	6	20	16	26	25	16	16
	SOME H S	12	23	12	18	16	15	20
	COMP H S	6	15	13	24	12	19	25
	SOMECOLL	3	2	11	11	4	13	9
	COMPCOLL	0	0	4	5	3	4	5
	GRADPROF	0	0	0	2	0	6	5
Clean	0–4 YRS	8	6	4	9	8	6	3
	5–8 YRS	21	18	26	23	29	13	14
	SOME H S	26	25	30	21	20	19	13
	COMP H S	16	28	27	25	40	21	23
	SOMECOLL	3	5	8	10	11	5	13
	COMPCOLL	0	3	2	3	4	4	3
	GRADPROF	0	0	0	0	2	2	2
Courageous	0–4 YRS	2	2	3	3	2	6	6
	5–8 YRS	13	16	14	20	24	21	18
	SOME H S	23	25	18	22	22	33	24
	COMP H S	25	21	31	28	26	24	27
	SOMECOLL	7	18	18	11	16	17	14
	COMPCOLL	4	5	3	5	7	7	11
	GRADPROF	3	5	6	5	5	3	3
Forgiving	0–4 YRS	4	4	6	6	6	4	7
	5–8 YRS	22	25	27	26	23	25	22
	SOME H S	19	29	32	20	22	24	27
	COMP H S	24	34	35	20	38	36	34
	SOMECOLL	9	12	10	15	15	8	8
	COMPCOLL	1	2	5	9	6	7	2
	GRADPROF	5	4	3	2	8	0	4
Helpful	0–4 YRS	4	2	3	7	5	4	2
	5–8 YRS	14	22	19	17	16	13	22
	SOME H S	9	15	34	34	32	20	26
	COMP H S	10	20	20	39	19	33	25
	SOMECOLL	3	6	10	11	11	10	10
	COMPCOLL	1	4	4	7	5	3	14
	GRADPROF	2	4	3	4	4	7	3
Honest	0–4 YRS	14	13	6	4	6	6	3
	5–8 YRS	64	28	38	31	18	21	11
	SOME H S	89	42	36	35	23	29	15
	COMP H S	128	54	49	44	32	21	12
	SOMECOLL	45	26	22	19	11	6	12
	COMPCOLL	33	13	6	4	5	6	4
	GRADPROF	16	4	9	6	2	3	6
Imaginative	0–4 YRS	0	1	1	0	0	0	1
	5–8 YRS	1	2	1	3	2	3	10
	SOME H S	1	1	1	3	2	3	5
	COMP H S	1	3	4	6	4	10	7
	SOMECOLL	1	3	5	7	10	3	5
	COMPCOLL	1	2	2	5	5	4	3
	GRADPROF	1	4	1	6	5	1	6

8	9	10	11	12	13	14	15	16	17	18	N	MEDIAN
5	3	4	5	1	1	4	5	1	3	1	64	7.70
11	18	14	14	14	12	21	10	8	9	7	263	8.09
26	21	13	20	19	21	22	25	19	12	6	320	9.36
34	28	43	29	27	29	32	25	25	18	22	426	10.36
10	12	10	8	11	12	17	14	14	8	11	180	11.13
6	5	5	5	12	4	9	12	6	2	3	90	11.75
4	3	6	4	2	7	9	4	7	2	0	61	11.75
4	3	2	1	5	1	2	0	1	1	0	64	5.13
15	12	12	14	12	12	13	10	10	4	5	263	6.61
18	27	15	18	15	13	13	12	16	12	7	320	7.83
29	28	29	22	25	19	27	20	19	10	18	426	8.64
11	8	14	15	7	13	9	11	14	10	13	180	10.63
3	4	5	5	2	10	8	5	9	7	13	90	13.20
3	0	3	2	5	8	4	3	9	10	8	61	14.38
2	2	2	6	3	5	5	3	6	6	0	64	10.83
22	10	17	17	16	15	19	9	7	3	2	263	7.75
22	11	20	21	18	15	8	11	13	8	6	320	7.21
27	29	25	24	34	23	14	17	28	13	10	426	8.64
9	7	8	11	11	5	4	7	3	7	7	180	6.71
8	8	6	5	4	3	2	5	4	2	1	90	7.88
1	5	6	2	1	4	3	3	2	0	4	61	8.00
4	4	5	2	4	4	2	0	2	0	0	64	6.79
16	11	10	11	13	11	11	3	4	2	1	263	5.84
24	21	18	17	19	3	18	8	9	7	3	320	7.02
21	22	21	31	30	25	18	13	8	6	10	426	7.26
7	15	12	6	13	12	9	12	9	6	2	180	8.90
4	4	4	6	5	10	5	10	3	4	3	90	10.67
6	0	2	4	2	3	5	3	4	1	5	61	8.25
5	10	4	5	1	3	4	1	2	2	0	64	8.50
36	16	14	19	11	13	9	11	8	2	1	263	7.74
25	17	24	11	14	14	9	13	5	9	9	320	7.12
33	30	29	26	33	22	31	22	16	9	9	426	8.97
18	10	15	11	12	11	8	11	8	8	7	180	9.57
6	4	2	10	9	4	4	3	2	4	4	90	8.75
3	6	5	4	3	2	3	2	4	2	0	61	8.58
2	4	3	0	1	0	0	1	0	0	1	64	3.33
9	17	7	10	2	1	1	3	0	1	1	263	3.55
11	10	5	7	5	4	3	2	1	2	1	320	3.31
18	26	11	10	9	5	1	3	2	1	0	426	3.13
9	10	6	5	3	3	3	0	0	0	0	180	3.36
3	6	4	0	0	1	3	1	0	1	0	90	2.42
4	4	2	2	2	0	0	1	0	0	0	61	3.75
2	0	4	2	4	6	2	9	7	11	14	64	15.50
5	7	8	6	12	16	15	27	31	50	64	263	15.94
9	7	21	13	12	13	19	38	38	63	71	320	15.82
3	13	17	21	16	28	32	39	49	61	112	426	15.68
8	4	10	9	11	9	10	7	13	20	45	180	14.00
5	5	5	6	6	6	6	1	6	14	8	90	11.83
4	5	1	2	3	1	5	4	3	3	6	61	9.00

EDUCATION: FREQUENCY DISTRIBUTIONS (*continued*)

		1	2	3	4	5	6	7
Independent	0–4 YRS	1	0	2	3	4	5	5
	5–8 YRS	4	9	10	15	12	12	20
	SOME H S	12	19	9	11	16	9	19
	COMP H S	22	13	25	28	17	23	27
	SOMECOLL	11	9	7	10	7	13	12
	COMPCOLL	4	6	9	8	2	7	3
	GRADPROF	7	3	4	4	2	3	3
Intellectual	0–4 YRS	0	0	0	0	1	0	1
	5–8 YRS	2	2	4	2	4	11	8
	SOME H S	1	4	9	8	8	9	11
	COMP H S	11	11	7	11	16	17	13
	SOMECOLL	8	11	10	9	7	10	12
	COMPCOLL	2	2	2	5	7	4	9
	GRADPROF	3	3	4	2	5	3	3
Logical	0–4 YRS	0	1	0	1	0	1	1
	5–8 YRS	0	3	5	0	9	2	5
	SOME H S	3	2	2	7	9	6	7
	COMP H S	4	5	5	8	11	13	23
	SOMECOLL	2	5	8	4	6	16	10
	COMPCOLL	2	4	3	1	5	4	4
	GRADPROF	2	5	2	3	2	1	5
Loving	0–4 YRS	3	5	2	4	4	3	8
	5–8 YRS	11	11	7	15	13	21	12
	SOME H S	13	18	16	11	27	14	20
	COMP H S	28	22	25	20	35	25	20
	SOMECOLL	16	10	6	11	12	6	6
	COMPCOLL	11	7	5	1	3	2	4
	GRADPROF	4	3	2	5	3	6	1
Obedient	0–4 YRS	3	3	1	2	2	2	6
	5–8 YRS	0	6	8	12	10	16	14
	SOME H S	2	5	8	8	6	20	16
	COMP H S	4	7	5	8	14	19	14
	SOMECOLL	0	5	0	1	3	7	2
	COMPCOLL	0	0	1	1	2	3	2
	GRADPROF	0	2	0	0	1	0	1
Polite	0–4 YRS	0	1	7	2	3	1	4
	5–8 YRS	4	7	7	7	18	20	17
	SOME H S	3	4	10	19	14	21	18
	COMP H S	3	10	11	19	18	30	31
	SOMECOLL	0	1	3	3	8	7	11
	COMPCOLL	1	1	2	1	5	5	2
	GRADPROF	0	1	0	4	0	0	2
Responsible	0–4 YRS	4	3	1	5	2	4	5
	5–8 YRS	16	19	13	13	14	12	23
	SOME H S	22	25	27	26	28	20	30
	COMP HS	35	45	45	32	32	40	35
	SOMECOLL	15	17	18	22	12	17	12
	COMPCOLL	8	10	13	6	9	12	5
	GRADPROF	7	7	8	2	5	9	3

8	9	10	11	12	13	14	15	16	17	18	N	MEDIAN
2	2	1	7	7	4	5	7	7	0	2	64	11.50
16	17	13	19	21	19	21	19	16	9	11	263	10.68
23	16	19	26	24	20	25	23	20	13	16	320	10.77
21	22	21	30	16	23	24	28	34	31	21	426	10.21
6	10	7	12	11	19	12	10	11	5	8	180	10.21
3	3	3	4	9	2	4	5	5	6	7	90	9.50
5	6	1	4	2	6	3	4	1	1	2	61	8.40
2	1	5	2	7	3	5	11	8	6	12	64	14.95
10	10	10	10	21	15	29	24	38	36	27	263	14.28
10	17	13	17	19	28	27	33	39	43	24	320	13.72
23	19	23	16	32	24	28	41	44	52	38	426	13.08
3	9	14	12	10	6	13	14	12	15	5	180	10.29
5	10	5	3	5	7	4	7	3	3	7	90	9.40
3	5	3	4	4	5	5	3	2	1	3	61	9.40
2	1	3	1	4	10	5	3	6	12	13	64	15.17
5	8	9	6	12	14	17	31	37	38	62	263	15.65
11	13	11	6	19	17	22	27	42	46	70	320	15.43
15	13	27	28	23	28	30	39	47	63	44	426	13.83
9	6	8	13	5	19	18	11	13	14	13	180	12.10
9	3	9	13	3	8	5	4	6	4	3	90	10.58
3	2	4	2	5	4	5	6	6	1	3	61	11.25
6	3	3	2	4	3	4	3	1	1	5	64	8.00
17	15	17	21	12	15	16	18	12	23	7	263	10.06
18	14	20	17	22	21	25	20	14	17	13	320	9.95
22	22	18	16	26	18	31	23	29	32	14	426	9.23
12	9	11	8	10	10	11	14	8	16	4	180	9.68
2	5	4	4	10	6	9	8	3	6	0	90	10.75
3	3	3	3	4	1	4	4	4	6	2	61	9.67
1	4	5	5	5	6	4	4	1	7	3	64	11.10
15	13	15	20	12	27	13	21	23	20	18	263	11.71
9	15	15	29	15	32	26	21	38	25	30	320	12.88
18	21	23	21	25	40	31	48	36	44	48	426	13.35
7	4	5	4	21	13	13	22	26	10	37	180	14.73
4	4	2	2	5	4	5	10	11	17	17	90	15.50
0	1	3	2	2	5	4	4	4	15	17	61	16.60
5	2	10	5	2	4	5	2	5	3	3	64	10.20
17	17	29	18	21	13	15	20	16	10	7	263	10.10
21	28	24	22	25	24	22	17	20	16	12	320	10.42
37	20	33	37	28	26	38	23	32	14	16	426	10.53
8	16	16	16	9	9	14	13	17	20	9	180	11.61
4	4	8	6	7	3	8	4	14	9	6	90	12.36
2	1	2	5	6	3	3	8	10	9	5	61	14.69
5	9	2	4	5	2	2	3	2	5	1	64	8.83
20	24	16	16	20	19	9	7	9	6	7	263	8.56
23	23	16	12	15	16	11	8	4	10	4	320	6.90
26	36	17	16	10	18	9	11	5	13	1	426	6.10
17	16	8	2	4	2	4	5	5	4	0	180	5.85
5	5	4	3	1	2	2	2	1	0	2	90	5.39
5	5	3	1	4	1	0	0	1	0	0	61	5.67

EDUCATION: FREQUENCY DISTRIBUTIONS (*continued*)

		1	2	3	4	5	6	7
Self-controlled	0–4 YRS	2	5	6	4	4	5	1
	5–8 YRS	9	4	14	7	8	14	15
	SOME H S	10	8	10	11	23	22	22
	COMP H S	18	23	24	18	28	22	32
	SOMECOLL	14	8	6	9	12	10	15
	COMPCOLL	6	8	6	9	4	4	5
	GRADPROF	3	3	2	1	1	6	4

8	9	10	11	12	13	14	15	16	17	18	N	MEDIAN
4	4	3	1	3	4	4	2	7	2	3	64	8.75
18	26	24	20	17	16	16	14	11	12	18	263	10.19
23	18	22	29	14	23	22	22	13	8	20	320	10.09
28	29	23	29	19	32	22	20	16	21	22	426	9.19
9	11	9	10	10	11	11	8	5	13	9	180	9.14
7	6	6	2	5	6	3	5	2	3	3	90	7.93
3	2	6	8	7	4	3	1	1	5	1	61	10.42

RACE: FREQUENCY DISTRIBUTIONS

		1	2	3	4	5	6	7
A comfortable life	White	94	69	62	57	49	73	7.
	Black	36	15	5	10	19	15	1(
An exciting life	White	11	25	13	10	16	20	2(
	Black	0	3	4	4	2	4	:
A sense of accomplishment	White	35	52	69	64	77	99	7(
	Black	3	10	8	13	7	8	1:
A world at peace	White	264	206	170	106	71	55	4'
	Black	46	27	28	27	12	13	(
A world of beauty	White	3	13	10	30	35	30	3.
	Black	0	3	7	5	8	3	:
Equality	White	17	59	83	88	74	70	8:
	Black	14	30	36	19	19	11	1(
Family security	White	222	214	145	125	111	70	7:
	Black	24	26	22	20	16	14	1:
Freedom	White	83	117	132	140	113	95	9(
	Black	14	32	22	21	23	14	1!
Happiness	White	54	81	89	94	87	90	9!
	Black	5	8	13	12	14	27	2(
Inner harmony	White	18	33	38	64	55	76	7!
	Black	1	3	5	14	6	12	1(
Mature love	White	6	22	35	45	56	41	5!
	Black	1	2	4	7	6	3	5
National security	White	18	67	78	79	88	89	6:
	Black	1	3	3	7	14	12	12
Pleasure	White	2	4	12	8	21	18	29
	Black	0	1	2	1	3	3	6
Salvation	White	273	57	55	55	51	37	37
	Black	31	10	8	10	2	12	10
Self-respect	White	29	68	75	83	99	110	113
	Black	10	8	11	13	21	15	23
Social recognition	White	2	2	4	6	24	28	33
	Black	0	2	0	3	4	2	7
True friendship	White	7	23	45	76	68	99	97
	Black	2	7	10	10	16	15	13
Wisdom	White	57	83	80	65	100	95	85
	Black	14	12	14	6	10	19	11
Ambitious	White	167	118	85	73	79	61	65
	Black	31	23	19	16	17	13	3
Broadminded	White	87	116	100	81	84	75	64
	Black	13	27	14	16	7	10	9
Capable	White	20	61	85	82	61	66	72
	Black	3	8	13	11	7	11	12

8	9	10	11	12	13	14	15	16	17	18	N	MEDIAN
61	53	66	71	76	55	84	77	72	63	40	1195	9.60
15	15	20	8	4	7	10	3	6	2	2	202	6.60
39	39	40	42	58	66	83	124	157	202	222	1195	15.37
1	4	5	8	15	11	16	25	18	26	51	202	15.26
94	102	74	76	77	78	67	55	39	44	17	1195	8.81
9	22	11	14	13	19	12	13	12	7	8	202	10.23
47	39	41	22	22	20	21	25	17	14	8	1195	3.25
6	4	2	4	10	4	5	1	1	4	2	202	3.50
57	45	59	77	97	111	120	111	139	121	102	1195	13.46
9	11	7	14	10	8	15	26	27	21	21	202	14.10
61	53	72	76	70	72	65	62	47	68	71	1195	9.58
13	5	6	4	3	8	5	7	3	2	1	202	4.61
43	37	34	32	26	15	17	16	9	4	2	1195	3.63
20	8	10	8	4	4	6	3	1	2	1	202	5.06
95	69	67	44	39	23	26	20	19	16	6	1195	5.63
12	7	11	12	5	2	5	4	2	0	1	202	5.02
79	122	78	79	69	57	47	34	22	10	5	1195	7.56
21	15	12	16	15	9	6	6	3	0	0	202	7.60
77	76	104	108	98	80	80	68	73	44	32	1195	10.36
9	23	11	17	16	13	12	17	12	13	8	202	10.91
62	77	62	87	77	83	94	82	92	93	122	1195	12.09
6	10	13	8	10	23	19	23	17	22	23	202	13.66
76	63	66	70	86	77	72	46	75	38	44	1195	9.13
10	11	16	13	21	17	16	8	19	16	3	202	11.42
46	45	52	72	65	89	108	148	144	191	141	1195	14.68
11	8	15	13	10	13	18	17	27	31	23	202	14.33
31	50	57	27	42	61	66	57	56	61	122	1195	8.53
7	13	8	13	12	10	8	9	15	7	17	202	9.35
93	109	75	87	65	56	31	55	21	15	11	1195	7.72
18	15	10	17	12	3	7	6	6	5	2	202	7.50
44	49	45	71	73	94	117	114	146	143	200	1195	14.55
8	7	14	16	19	15	22	15	19	24	25	202	13.68
112	93	111	83	87	98	49	52	42	37	16	1195	9.26
12	12	16	11	16	18	7	14	8	11	4	202	9.75
78	74	92	71	68	60	48	49	25	31	34	1195	7.92
15	12	15	6	7	18	13	5	6	9	10	202	8.50
51	58	48	61	46	53	52	42	44	45	47	1195	6.72
9	10	11	9	7	9	10	3	4	5	3	202	5.21
73	62	60	55	72	57	52	41	34	41	41	1195	7.35
10	13	11	13	17	7	8	9	3	11	4	202	8.00
77	82	93	94	83	84	60	65	48	37	25	1195	9.40
7	15	16	15	15	11	13	18	14	8	5	202	10.38

RACE: FREQUENCY DISTRIBUTIONS (*continued*)

		1	2	3	4	5	6	7
Cheerful	White	28	54	52	80	52	68	68
	Black	4	9	8	12	13	11	15
Clean	White	44	69	79	73	90	61	58
	Black	30	16	19	18	24	9	12
Courageous	White	65	71	79	86	88	93	90
	Black	11	19	13	9	16	18	12
Forgiving	White	74	96	105	86	105	85	87
	Black	10	14	13	11	14	20	17
Helpful	White	34	66	77	100	71	82	84
	Black	8	7	16	18	19	8	19
Honest	White	349	159	132	116	82	74	54
	Black	41	20	32	25	13	18	9
Imaginative	White	4	15	14	28	24	23	31
	Black	1	1	0	2	4	1	5
Independent	White	53	50	54	68	48	57	77
	Black	8	8	11	8	11	13	11
Intellectual	White	24	29	30	34	44	42	45
	Black	3	4	5	3	5	10	12
Logical	White	12	23	22	21	38	40	49
	Black	1	2	3	2	2	2	4
Loving	White	79	66	56	60	88	65	59
	Black	5	10	6	7	9	12	11
Obedient	White	3	22	18	26	29	57	38
	Black	6	6	6	6	8	10	16
Polite	White	6	20	33	44	56	71	69
	Black	5	5	6	10	10	13	14
Responsible	White	95	109	114	83	85	102	101
	Black	12	15	10	23	16	12	12
Self-controlled	White	51	51	60	54	71	72	84
	Black	10	8	8	5	7	11	9

8	9	10	11	12	13	14	15	16	17	18	N	MEDIAN
81	82	87	72	74	75	97	76	71	41	37	1195	9.87
16	7	8	11	12	10	16	18	9	10	13	202	10.25
73	66	74	72	67	73	68	56	63	50	59	1195	9.27
10	14	6	5	4	5	7	3	13	2	5	202	5.25
81	63	73	73	71	56	46	50	53	33	24	1195	7.81
9	9	12	12	15	12	8	6	9	6	6	202	7.83
64	68	58	67	75	61	53	43	30	21	17	1195	7.03
16	10	14	11	11	5	12	5	9	4	6	202	7.63
104	76	81	73	73	59	56	57	40	35	27	1195	8.30
22	17	12	12	8	10	12	6	4	1	3	202	7.77
45	62	35	30	17	12	10	11	3	1	3	1195	3.18
10	15	3	5	4	2	1	0	0	4	0	202	3.82
35	35	58	45	52	62	81	109	116	187	276	1195	15.33
1	6	8	13	10	17	8	16	30	35	44	202	15.77
64	66	52	83	78	80	84	83	83	57	58	1195	10.60
12	10	13	17	13	16	10	13	12	7	9	202	10.19
45	57	64	56	81	72	96	114	130	130	102	1195	13.15
11	12	9	8	17	14	13	19	17	26	14	202	12.64
48	38	63	59	60	86	88	94	136	152	166	1195	13.94
5	8	8	10	11	13	15	27	21	26	42	202	15.06
67	66	65	64	74	56	77	77	57	83	36	1195	9.37
11	5	11	8	15	16	22	12	14	19	9	202	11.90
48	49	57	69	74	112	83	110	119	128	153	1195	13.46
7	12	10	14	10	14	14	19	18	10	16	202	11.50
76	86	100	93	88	68	90	75	101	71	48	1195	10.89
18	5	21	15	10	14	15	12	11	10	8	202	10.21
88	98	54	46	51	48	30	29	22	29	11	1195	6.59
11	20	10	8	8	12	8	7	5	9	4	202	7.59
75	81	73	83	59	81	72	63	46	54	65	1195	9.48
17	14	19	16	15	15	10	9	9	9	11	202	10.13

AGE: FREQUENCY DISTRIBUTIONS

		1	2	3	4	5	6	7
A comfortable life	20–29	19	17	13	11	13	17	11
	30–39	15	13	16	13	13	19	16
	40–49	19	21	10	16	16	23	18
	50–59	16	19	9	12	12	9	17
	60–69	29	8	8	7	6	9	9
	70+	30	8	12	8	6	9	10
An exciting life	20–29	3	2	2	4	6	6	8
	30–39	2	5	4	1	5	11	9
	40–49	1	3	5	6	3	0	5
	50–59	1	4	3	3	2	3	6
	60–69	1	4	1	0	2	3	3
	70+	3	11	0	0	1	1	3
A sense of	20–29	5	14	12	14	13	13	17
accomplishment	30–39	13	9	15	19	20	25	18
	40–49	9	7	23	13	22	20	16
	50–59	3	14	7	18	13	23	18
	60–69	3	7	10	9	8	9	14
	70+	6	10	11	4	6	17	4
A world at peace	20–29	44	39	34	23	19	15	8
	30–39	53	43	33	27	21	15	13
	40–49	55	58	41	31	15	14	13
	50–59	59	40	35	22	16	14	5
	60–69	41	25	32	11	5	6	7
	70+	53	25	20	20	7	5	6
A world of beauty	20–29	1	1	5	12	2	5	9
	30–39	1	3	1	4	7	9	8
	40–49	1	1	4	5	11	9	8
	50–59	0	4	3	6	7	5	8
	60–69	0	3	3	4	6	4	7
	70+	0	4	1	4	10	2	2
Equality	20–29	6	17	29	16	18	15	15
	30–39	5	13	27	26	22	21	22
	40–49	4	18	21	28	19	15	18
	50–59	10	18	16	10	17	9	20
	60–69	5	5	12	12	5	9	15
	70+	2	15	16	13	11	11	13
Family security	20–29	54	38	24	26	25	15	13
	30–39	58	62	42	34	26	13	14
	40–49	56	62	28	35	21	19	9
	50–59	49	35	30	20	17	16	18
	60–69	17	27	16	20	19	9	9
	70+	12	18	24	12	16	11	21
Freedom	20–29	31	30	33	41	24	18	18
	30–39	29	30	34	27	31	24	22
	40–49	17	25	37	23	25	29	27
	50–59	12	27	19	29	20	16	20
	60–69	6	15	18	22	17	9	12
	70+	1	19	13	17	18	13	11

8	9	10	11	12	13	14	15	16	17	18	N	MEDIAN
14	10	9	15	13	12	21	16	15	15	10	251	9.56
17	12	22	16	19	17	23	15	27	17	7	297	10.16
13	16	20	16	13	10	14	21	11	10	11	278	8.69
17	12	18	10	16	10	15	12	11	13	8	236	9.08
7	8	8	15	11	7	7	3	7	6	4	159	8.00
10	10	6	6	8	6	13	13	7	3	2	167	7.55
10	8	9	10	14	11	20	19	33	42	44	251	15.16
12	11	8	13	20	22	23	33	22	46	50	297	14.58
7	9	10	10	12	18	21	28	43	46	51	278	15.52
6	9	6	9	14	12	14	29	36	34	45	236	15.40
2	4	6	5	7	5	13	25	17	29	32	159	15.44
3	3	5	3	5	7	9	15	21	27	50	167	16.19
22	31	16	12	18	13	16	11	10	12	2	251	9.00
20	26	17	15	23	21	19	15	11	6	5	297	8.87
20	23	20	19	19	21	11	13	9	8	5	278	8.89
16	25	10	17	14	15	9	15	7	4	8	236	8.74
12	9	11	12	5	12	10	7	6	11	4	159	9.33
9	9	11	15	12	14	11	9	8	10	1	167	10.18
9	8	8	1	11	5	5	11	7	3	1	251	3.87
14	18	14	9	6	7	8	4	1	6	5	297	4.22
5	7	14	6	4	4	2	3	2	2	2	278	3.13
8	7	3	3	2	4	4	6	2	5	1	236	3.04
9	2	2	4	4	1	4	1	4	1	0	159	2.92
8	1	3	3	5	3	2	0	3	2	1	167	2.78
5	9	12	12	19	20	25	25	32	26	31	251	14.04
20	13	15	19	19	22	39	23	38	28	28	297	13.69
13	11	12	19	24	18	20	30	31	32	29	278	13.65
15	10	10	15	20	20	16	25	31	24	17	236	13.25
6	5	5	12	9	13	28	13	14	16	11	159	13.59
6	6	11	12	15	24	10	19	21	14	6	167	12.94
19	10	21	8	13	15	10	11	7	10	11	251	8.00
19	15	13	27	10	13	14	15	5	19	11	297	8.16
10	12	14	15	11	19	18	12	12	10	22	278	9.00
9	12	15	14	14	14	8	12	7	15	16	236	9.25
7	4	6	9	17	8	7	12	8	8	10	159	10.42
9	5	8	7	8	10	13	9	10	5	2	167	7.78
15	4	10	6	6	3	6	4	1	1	0	251	3.87
12	8	5	10	3	2	2	4	2	0	0	297	3.18
14	5	7	3	8	2	3	3	1	1	1	278	3.25
11	8	11	10	3	5	1	2	0	0	0	236	3.70
7	11	5	2	2	3	5	2	3	0	2	159	4.48
4	9	6	8	6	3	6	4	3	4	0	167	5.64
8	6	13	14	5	4	2	4	1	2	1	251	4.27
27	17	16	9	7	3	6	5	8	0	2	297	5.42
16	20	11	9	12	7	6	6	3	3	2	278	5.91
19	13	19	10	8	4	3	3	8	5	1	236	6.19
12	8	11	4	5	4	10	2	0	3	1	159	5.67
26	12	9	9	7	3	2	3	1	3	0	167	6.73

AGE: FREQUENCY DISTRIBUTIONS (*continued*)

		1	2	3	4	5	6	7
Happiness	20–29	14	18	15	14	21	29	24
	30–39	18	25	28	24	15	18	21
	40–49	11	18	25	19	21	20	31
	50–59	6	11	18	21	18	18	17
	60–69	3	8	9	10	9	20	12
	70+	6	7	7	19	14	10	14
Inner harmony	20–29	5	7	9	11	12	15	13
	30–39	5	6	11	20	14	19	20
	40–49	2	3	7	17	11	22	19
	50–59	1	9	8	14	8	15	12
	60–69	3	4	4	11	8	9	7
	70+	3	5	3	5	8	8	9
Mature love	20–29	2	10	11	10	20	13	18
	30–39	3	8	12	13	17	13	15
	40–49	0	3	8	7	10	9	14
	50–59	1	2	2	8	8	6	11
	60–69	1	2	1	3	2	2	5
	70+	0	0	3	7	4	1	3
National security	20–29	1	12	13	13	16	17	18
	30–39	3	11	18	12	14	18	9
	40–49	2	9	16	19	25	15	16
	50–59	4	12	11	15	20	18	15
	60–69	6	13	7	17	18	11	8
	70+	3	12	16	9	11	19	8
Pleasure	20–29	0	2	1	2	1	5	5
	30–39	0	2	1	2	5	1	8
	40–49	1	0	0	1	3	3	7
	50–59	1	1	4	0	5	5	6
	60–69	0	0	2	1	4	4	3
	70+	0	0	6	3	5	3	6
Salvation	20–29	43	16	10	13	6	6	7
	30–39	66	14	9	12	11	6	12
	40–49	70	8	10	8	9	14	6
	50–59	53	10	19	10	13	10	9
	60–69	31	7	7	9	7	5	4
	70+	39	12	8	9	7	8	8
Self-respect	20–29	5	11	17	9	18	22	28
	30–39	11	18	14	30	28	30	37
	40–49	11	12	18	21	20	21	29
	50–59	6	12	20	11	25	22	11
	60–69	3	16	10	10	9	17	13
	70+	2	6	8	15	21	14	17
Social recognition	20–29	0	0	1	1	6	4	5
	30–39	0	0	0	1	2	10	12
	40–49	0	1	1	1	5	7	4
	50–59	2	2	1	0	7	3	4
	60–69	0	2	1	4	5	3	11
	70+	0	0	0	1	3	3	4

8	9	10	11	12	13	14	15	16	17	18	N	MEDIAN
22	22	14	14	13	9	8	8	3	2	1	251	7.10
16	25	19	19	20	19	12	8	8	1	1	297	7.48
18	23	20	18	12	12	12	11	6	1	0	278	7.31
16	27	15	19	20	8	10	5	3	3	1	236	8.06
15	13	9	13	11	9	6	7	3	2	0	159	8.07
11	27	13	12	8	7	5	2	2	1	2	167	8.09
10	16	16	25	16	19	16	15	24	11	11	251	10.96
27	21	17	22	18	20	22	15	17	12	11	297	9.82
15	29	29	22	25	16	15	17	15	10	4	278	9.98
14	12	19	25	21	16	22	13	10	13	4	236	10.74
12	10	18	11	11	13	6	14	10	3	5	159	10.14
7	10	17	19	21	11	12	9	9	6	5	167	10.95
12	20	18	15	20	16	14	19	10	13	10	251	10.03
17	25	19	22	21	27	20	25	19	15	6	297	10.80
15	17	5	24	17	25	31	17	24	25	27	278	12.90
16	13	15	10	11	24	19	20	20	20	30	236	13.13
3	8	11	14	9	10	10	12	15	18	33	159	14.35
5	3	8	11	6	5	17	10	23	22	39	167	15.52
14	15	15	9	18	21	11	14	18	8	18	251	9.93
12	15	20	18	24	24	23	17	28	17	14	297	11.42
27	6	17	22	20	18	23	6	16	12	9	278	9.74
17	15	12	15	13	18	13	6	19	10	3	236	8.90
9	8	8	9	18	5	7	6	3	5	1	159	7.44
8	15	9	10	15	6	10	5	7	2	2	167	8.19
16	12	10	25	11	11	23	26	33	44	24	251	14.56
7	12	13	13	13	16	25	39	35	62	43	297	15.28
14	9	14	17	16	22	24	26	44	40	37	278	14.81
6	6	10	11	18	19	25	29	27	30	33	236	14.53
8	8	8	7	11	11	14	21	19	23	15	159	14.39
6	6	12	10	6	22	13	22	13	21	13	167	13.43
7	16	14	10	6	14	13	11	16	10	33	251	9.61
3	8	13	10	16	16	11	17	13	18	42	297	10.08
12	15	15	6	10	12	15	17	12	16	23	278	8.63
10	5	11	5	8	12	12	11	9	8	21	236	6.83
2	14	5	4	5	11	8	6	16	6	12	159	9.04
4	4	7	4	8	7	14	3	5	12	8	167	6.56
18	28	12	22	14	18	11	7	5	5	1	251	8.36
16	15	20	21	20	8	7	9	5	5	3	297	6.97
20	28	15	18	18	13	7	12	7	5	3	278	7.85
23	25	11	22	12	8	6	9	6	4	3	236	7.98
17	13	12	9	5	5	6	11	2	0	1	159	7.59
12	12	14	11	9	7	1	13	2	1	2	167	7.54
9	8	13	20	14	19	27	23	25	30	46	251	14.44
14	11	10	17	22	20	24	29	37	30	58	297	14.69
10	10	11	14	24	22	30	28	28	41	41	278	14.47
3	14	11	15	14	19	32	22	26	30	31	236	14.22
6	6	8	13	7	13	9	8	26	18	19	159	13.56
10	8	6	8	10	15	17	18	21	20	23	167	14.41

AGE: FREQUENCY DISTRIBUTIONS (*continued*)

		1	2	3	4	5	6	7
True friendship	20–29	1	4	7	15	10	14	19
	30–39	1	5	7	16	17	24	19
	40–49	3	6	10	14	18	15	24
	50–59	1	5	11	19	13	25	23
	60–69	1	5	12	6	13	17	6
	70+	3	5	6	17	14	18	18
Wisdom	20–29	17	13	15	16	21	22	19
	30–39	14	30	25	16	29	21	22
	40–49	16	23	14	14	24	23	14
	50–59	11	11	20	18	15	19	16
	60–69	9	8	6	3	16	13	14
	70+	4	10	13	4	5	14	10
Ambitious	20–29	28	29	16	16	10	12	10
	30–39	35	22	33	22	22	17	20
	40–49	40	31	23	18	23	10	19
	50–59	29	24	21	10	18	17	14
	60–69	30	20	6	9	9	10	5
	70+	34	12	6	15	12	7	3
Broadminded	20–29	15	17	26	12	19	19	9
	30–39	22	23	24	20	17	15	15
	40–49	14	29	24	22	15	17	19
	50–59	19	26	17	22	17	20	13
	60–69	14	23	9	10	6	10	12
	70+	15	25	12	11	16	5	
Capable	20–29	4	11	10	12	10	16	20
	30–39	4	11	14	19	16	19	16
	40–49	7	15	16	22	13	19	16
	50–59	3	17	16	21	10	8	12
	60–69	3	5	20	11	7	9	11
	70+	2	10	22	7	12	6	8
Cheerful	20–29	7	5	13	12	13	11	11
	30–39	3	15	8	10	6	16	21
	40–49	2	10	12	22	12	19	17
	50–59	10	11	9	12	11	12	17
	60–69	4	6	4	21	14	7	11
	70+	5	15	12	14	9	14	
Clean	20–29	14	20	16	16	23	10	13
	30–39	10	16	12	14	22	13	18
	40–49	14	18	17	25	20	12	16
	50–59	14	16	19	14	10	16	9
	60–69	10	8	16	5	21	10	10
	70+	11	7	16	15	16	7	
Courageous	20–29	16	16	13	13	15	21	17
	30–39	12	21	23	25	23	22	2
	40–49	18	16	19	17	24	23	2
	50–59	18	18	16	14	20	17	1
	60–69	4	7	8	10	10	13	1
	70+	9	11	13	15	10	12	1

8	9	10	11	12	13	14	15	16	17	18	N	MEDIAN
29	14	23	17	20	27	14	15	9	9	4	251	10.04
25	25	28	26	23	23	12	20	15	6	5	297	9.84
23	20	27	18	21	23	14	20	9	8	5	278	9.72
19	14	22	15	18	16	10	5	6	11	3	236	8.64
16	19	12	7	13	16	3	4	3	5	1	159	8.68
13	11	11	11	8	11	3	2	5	10	1	167	7.69
12	14	18	16	20	14	9	12	2	8	3	251	7.71
19	20	28	11	13	17	7	4	6	9	6	297	7.11
26	18	17	22	12	16	12	8	5	8	6	278	7.92
11	9	18	11	10	12	17	12	8	7	11	236	8.23
9	9	14	9	9	13	6	5	3	5	8	159	8.67
16	16	11	8	10	6	9	11	6	4	10	167	8.97
14	13	12	15	16	19	10	7	5	8	11	251	7.82
11	12	14	11	10	8	21	10	12	11	6	297	6.35
12	14	11	13	9	9	10	14	10	7	9	278	5.90
7	12	10	13	9	12	9	8	10	6	7	236	6.44
8	10	4	9	7	6	4	3	4	6	9	159	6.05
7	6	6	9	3	6	9	4	6	12	10	167	6.14
15	16	11	12	18	14	18	9	7	12	2	251	8.07
19	16	11	18	19	13	12	14	14	13	12	297	8.16
17	14	16	16	18	13	9	9	2	12	12	278	7.45
10	10	8	11	14	13	8	8	4	9	7	236	6.35
11	12	11	5	6	5	7	6	6	1	5	159	7.13
11	7	12	4	12	7	5	6	4	3	7	167	6.40
14	11	17	23	18	17	13	19	13	12	11	251	10.52
26	26	25	24	18	21	12	19	14	8	5	297	9.40
17	24	25	19	19	18	13	12	14	4	5	278	9.08
12	16	18	19	14	17	17	17	9	6	4	236	9.67
9	10	12	12	15	12	7	4	5	4	3	159	8.95
6	9	14	11	9	10	10	12	7	10	2	167	9.61
18	11	16	14	16	17	30	19	16	12	10	251	11.11
25	21	22	17	23	16	26	20	20	10	18	297	10.59
14	18	16	19	16	22	21	19	18	10	11	278	10.31
20	21	20	13	13	13	18	16	8	6	6	236	9.26
13	6	11	9	8	8	9	9	7	10	2	159	8.46
4	12	9	12	10	9	10	10	8	6	3	167	8.96
17	16	11	13	10	8	14	13	13	11	13	251	8.29
15	18	17	21	17	20	19	12	20	12	21	297	10.12
15	16	15	14	13	12	18	8	20	11	14	278	8.63
15	16	19	12	11	15	11	11	12	9	7	236	8.81
9	8	8	10	9	9	9	9	3	3	2	159	7.45
11	6	9	7	11	12	4	7	10	7	6	167	8.09
10	19	18	16	21	9	9	13	12	6	7	251	8.74
17	14	19	12	21	21	7	12	13	6	4	297	7.40
23	14	13	11	15	15	13	9	11	9	8	278	7.59
17	11	16	20	12	9	6	7	10	7	5	236	7.62
13	9	9	13	10	9	6	9	7	6	2	159	8.56
10	4	10	13	8	6	12	5	8	5	3	167	7.55

AGE: FREQUENCY DISTRIBUTIONS (*continued*)

		1	*2*	*3*	*4*	*5*	*6*	
Forgiving	20–29	12	20	22	17	23	16	1
	30–39	16	19	20	21	22	20	2
	40–49	17	28	22	20	22	23	1
	50–59	14	19	20	15	18	16	1
	60–69	11	11	15	10	14	13	1
	70+	12	12	17	14	19	17	2
Helpful	20–29	5	10	19	20	15	13	1
	30–39	6	9	20	28	16	17	2
	40–49	5	13	14	30	19	22	2
	50–59	14	11	18	17	14	14	1
	60–69	7	12	12	10	15	7	
	70+	7	18	9	11	11	18	1
Honest	20–29	65	37	28	24	15	18	1
	30–39	102	41	25	27	20	22	
	40–49	82	23	38	25	25	7	1
	50–59	57	30	34	28	16	15	
	60–69	44	22	15	19	9	14	
	70+	37	23	22	20	11	15	1
Imaginative	20–29	1	8	1	8	6	5	
	30–39	3	4	6	9	10	5	
	40–49	2	2	4	3	5	2	
	50–59	0	1	3	5	5	4	
	60–69	0	0	1	2	1	4	
	70+	0	1	0	1	1	5	
Independent	20–29	13	11	12	19	8	11	1
	30–39	17	18	19	21	11	20	1
	40–49	13	11	16	6	12	12	1
	50–59	4	6	6	13	10	8	2
	60–69	7	8	6	10	7	10	
	70+	6	5	4	8	11	10	1
Intellectual	20–29	5	7	9	11	10	8	1
	30–39	4	14	6	6	14	13	1
	40–49	7	6	10	11	5	13	
	50–59	7	3	4	6	12	8	1
	60–69	2	1	4	2	3	3	
	70+	1	2	3	1	4	6	
Logical	20–29	3	5	6	3	8	10	1
	30–39	3	7	8	4	9	11	1
	40–49	2	6	4	6	4	10	1
	50–59	4	4	2	5	9	4	
	60–69	0	3	2	3	3	5	
	70+	0	0	3	3	8	2	
Loving	20–29	25	18	13	16	22	12	1
	30–39	20	23	20	10	24	16	1
	40–49	19	12	5	13	22	18	1
	50–59	11	13	13	13	12	15	1
	60–69	4	5	8	6	10	7	
	70+	5	4	3	9	6	8	1

8	9	10	11	12	13	14	15	16	17	18	N	MEDIAN
16	13	10	13	19	12	13	11	6	4	9	251	7.53
14	19	20	18	17	14	16	11	13	9	6	297	8.11
15	17	16	20	11	12	12	9	9	5	2	278	6.89
17	14	8	13	16	15	16	9	4	2	2	236	7.39
14	6	9	9	7	10	6	2	4	4	4	159	7.05
6	9	8	3	14	5	4	5	2	0	0	167	6.06
11	14	21	15	16	20	16	12	10	6	11	251	9.57
24	20	23	14	18	17	15	17	15	6	7	297	8.68
31	20	18	20	12	13	9	13	6	7	4	278	7.95
28	13	14	14	20	7	7	12	7	9	3	236	8.07
12	14	6	9	12	5	12	7	3	4	3	159	8.13
18	11	9	12	5	6	9	2	4	3	1	167	7.23
7	10	10	5	9	2	2	3	1	1	1	251	3.34
10	15	6	5	4	6	3	1	0	1	1	297	2.72
17	18	9	5	5	1	3	2	1	2	0	278	3.39
7	14	8	9	2	4	1	3	1	0	0	236	3.41
5	6	4	7	2	1	2	0	0	0	1	159	3.40
9	13	1	3	0	0	0	2	0	1	0	167	3.58
12	9	11	9	9	12	17	15	29	38	53	251	15.13
7	10	13	15	13	19	16	25	31	44	62	297	15.04
7	9	10	16	17	15	15	29	24	39	72	278	15.36
3	4	13	8	12	14	13	23	24	45	52	236	15.63
2	4	8	5	5	8	13	13	22	29	39	159	15.98
5	5	11	5	7	8	13	17	18	26	37	167	15.35
13	12	11	17	13	19	8	19	17	16	15	251	10.36
16	11	11	20	20	17	20	13	18	10	21	297	9.64
12	21	17	15	14	17	25	22	23	19	9	278	10.83
15	12	9	19	19	14	17	20	17	13	12	236	11.18
7	7	10	12	11	14	14	11	10	4	3	159	10.45
12	13	6	18	14	13	9	10	7	2	6	167	9.75
8	18	16	11	9	8	15	28	22	30	21	251	12.33
8	15	14	15	17	21	29	31	20	29	30	297	13.05
13	11	16	8	24	23	24	19	28	31	20	278	12.76
15	5	10	12	16	14	18	24	31	28	11	236	13.07
7	10	8	8	12	14	8	16	23	16	18	159	13.69
5	11	9	9	19	7	14	15	22	19	14	167	13.54
8	6	14	19	10	15	24	20	31	26	32	251	13.81
17	6	16	20	12	19	21	30	26	48	25	297	13.57
11	8	15	12	20	19	21	19	32	35	43	278	14.02
8	11	9	8	12	18	15	16	29	23	52	236	14.63
3	8	6	5	6	13	9	13	24	27	24	159	15.15
6	7	11	5	10	14	12	19	15	18	29	167	14.29
16	18	11	7	10	12	12	12	13	17	7	251	8.09
16	15	15	18	24	10	13	18	15	22	7	297	9.07
17	9	21	10	22	16	21	13	14	18	13	278	9.93
9	14	11	9	11	13	20	16	9	24	8	236	9.77
7	7	7	13	14	8	14	16	10	8	6	159	11.23
3	5	11	15	6	15	19	13	10	11	4	167	11.13

AGE: FREQUENCY DISTRIBUTIONS (*continued*)

		1	2	3	4	5	6	
Obedient	20–29	3	3	3	3	8	12	
	30–39	1	8	5	4	9	13	1
	40–49	1	6	5	6	7	12	1
	50–59	2	4	3	9	7	11	
	60–69	1	5	6	6	4	9	
	70+	1	1	2	4	3	10	
Polite	20–29	1	4	10	9	14	15	1
	30–39	3	7	7	16	10	14	1
	40–49	0	4	4	7	13	18	1
	50–59	4	2	6	10	11	17	1
	60–69	2	6	6	7	10	10	
	70+	1	2	7	3	6	9	
Responsible	20–29	22	21	24	28	19	28	2
	30–39	21	25	33	25	22	25	2
	40–49	24	33	29	18	23	21	2
	50–59	17	22	16	14	18	24	1
	60–69	7	12	14	11	10	8	1
	70+	17	11	9	8	7	6	1
Self-controlled	20–29	12	9	10	12	13	14	2
	30–39	15	14	14	16	24	19	2
	40–49	11	15	16	7	14	20	1
	50–59	9	9	13	8	18	10	1
	60–69	9	5	7	7	6	9	
	70+	4	8	7	8	5	10	1

8	9	10	11	12	13	14	15	16	17	18	N	MEDIAN
16	12	12	16	17	25	17	16	28	23	29	251	13.00
13	12	14	13	18	22	15	29	37	30	44	297	13.93
10	15	16	19	20	19	20	30	21	27	31	278	12.97
5	8	12	13	12	21	23	17	28	20	34	236	13.67
5	8	7	7	7	14	10	18	10	18	16	159	12.96
5	7	7	13	7	22	11	19	11	21	15	167	13.20
18	19	25	18	19	18	14	12	14	17	7	251	10.24
17	27	21	31	17	10	26	20	19	21	15	297	10.84
17	8	17	22	20	24	26	22	26	18	15	278	12.10
15	19	19	18	14	14	15	16	27	8	5	236	10.45
12	6	21	7	12	6	11	7	11	8	8	159	10.05
15	11	17	11	15	10	11	10	15	7	8	167	10.82
15	21	10	10	7	8	6	5	3	0	4	251	5.91
24	20	21	9	12	13	7	5	4	5	2	297	6.40
14	21	8	14	10	12	7	9	6	7	1	278	6.07
17	24	14	9	11	9	7	3	2	10	2	236	6.91
11	15	7	6	9	7	6	8	4	7	2	159	7.73
17	16	4	6	10	10	5	6	8	8	4	167	8.12
23	13	15	18	14	16	13	18	11	12	8	251	9.46
18	20	15	16	17	30	19	10	6	12	11	297	8.88
16	21	19	25	13	18	11	20	13	17	9	278	9.82
16	12	18	16	18	14	15	10	4	11	19	236	9.89
11	13	11	13	7	10	12	8	7	4	12	159	9.91
7	15	13	11	7	7	10	5	12	8	18	167	10.08

RELIGION: FREQUENCY DISTRIBUTIONS

		1	2	3	4	5	6	7
A comfortable life	Catholic	24	16	21	10	19	19	17
	Episcopalian	3	2	0	2	1	3	1
	Lutheran	11	6	7	7	4	9	8
	Presbyterian	2	2	5	2	6	7	5
	Congregational	6	3	2	1	2	2	4
	Methodist	21	16	9	9	12	8	15
	Baptist	40	19	13	21	18	20	1
	Jewish	2	4	3	0	0	2	
	None	3	6	0	1	0	5	4
An exciting life	Catholic	2	8	3	1	8	9	5
	Episcopalian	0	2	3	2	0	2	
	Lutheran	0	3	2	1	2	1	0
	Prebyterian	1	0	1	1	0	1	2
	Congregational	0	0	0	0	0	0	0
	Methodist	3	2	2	3	2	3	9
	Baptist	0	8	2	3	4	4	
	Jewish	1	1	2	0	1	1	0
	None	2	1	0	2	2	1	
A sense of accomplishment	Catholic	10	12	23	23	20	22	2
	Episcopalian	3	2	3	2	4	6	
	Lutheran	3	4	9	8	9	10	
	Presbyterian	1	8	3	5	6	4	
	Congregational	2	1	1	1	3	6	
	Methodist	8	7	8	13	6	14	
	Baptist	4	12	13	12	17	13	30
	Jewish	1	2	1	2	4	3	
	None	3	4	8	1	2	7	
A world at peace	Catholic	78	48	51	28	17	13	1
	Episcopalian	9	1	9	6	1	1	
	Lutheran	22	27	15	13	6	3	
	Presbyterian	23	11	7	8	5	0	
	Congregational	17	2	4	3	1	2	
	Methodist	55	40	17	14	9	10	1
	Baptist	61	56	50	39	22	23	1
	Jewish	6	5	7	1	0	2	
	None	7	6	4	2	1	1	
A world of beauty	Catholic	0	5	3	9	10	8	
	Episcopalian	0	0	0	0	1	1	
	Lutheran	0	2	0	3	2	4	
	Presbyterian	0	0	2	2	1	0	
	Congregational	0	0	0	2	1	1	
	Methodist	1	3	3	5	9	6	
	Baptist	0	4	4	7	9	6	
	Jewish	0	0	1	2	0	0	
	None	1	0	1	3	4	1	
Equality	Catholic	3	20	23	31	20	19	2
	Episcopalian	1	0	4	2	1	3	
	Lutheran	2	5	7	8	8	6	
	Presbyterian	1	3	4	7	6	5	

8	9	10	11	12	13	14	15	16	17	18	N	MEDIAN
11	17	17	18	21	15	19	16	26	23	13	322	9.91
3	2	4	1	1	0	3	3	3	5	2	39	10.13
2	4	6	7	4	6	7	8	5	6	6	113	9.13
3	1	3	3	7	1	8	6	7	4	4	76	11.17
2	1	1	5	2	1	3	2	1	0	1	39	7.38
15	11	13	9	10	6	13	11	9	6	6	199	8.13
24	21	23	18	14	17	25	15	11	8	4	324	8.25
2	1	2	1	3	2	1	2	1	1	0	28	8.50
4	1	3	3	3	0	4	1	5	1	1	45	8.38
16	5	11	16	12	16	25	30	46	49	60	322	15.30
2	0	0	1	3	2	3	4	4	4	6	39	14.00
2	4	5	3	7	3	9	16	17	22	16	113	15.41
1	4	1	0	7	7	1	8	13	15	13	76	15.73
1	0	2	2	3	5	3	3	5	6	9	39	15.60
5	9	8	7	15	9	15	20	22	31	34	199	14.88
5	11	11	12	15	16	20	38	37	50	81	324	15.66
0	0	0	0	0	2	1	3	6	7	3	28	15.83
3	5	2	3	2	4	3	4	3	2	4	45	11.33
26	29	26	12	21	22	15	15	8	10	4	322	8.53
0	2	0	3	7	1	0	1	1	2	0	39	6.42
9	8	6	10	11	3	3	4	4	4	3	113	8.44
2	7	2	6	4	7	5	1	6	2	2	76	9.07
4	4	1	3	2	3	0	1	1	1	0	39	7.63
19	21	15	13	10	18	11	15	4	6	4	199	9.33
12	31	20	27	18	25	28	27	14	16	5	324	10.40
2	2	0	4	3	0	1	0	1	0	0	28	7.00
3	2	0	1	0	1	5	2	1	0	2	45	6.14
14	5	9	7	12	8	3	7	5	2	3	322	3.19
1	2	4	0	0	0	1	0	1	0	1	39	3.58
4	1	5	2	3	1	2	2	1	1	0	113	3.00
3	3	2	1	2	1	2	2	2	1	0	76	3.07
0	2	1	0	2	1	2	0	1	1	0	39	2.63
12	4	7	2	5	2	6	3	1	2	0	199	2.76
7	12	6	3	3	8	6	8	1	6	2	324	3.40
1	2	0	0	0	0	0	0	1	1	0	28	2.93
4	4	0	4	1	1	2	1	3	2	1	45	7.63
16	11	9	27	19	28	38	29	36	26	41	322	13.74
2	5	2	0	3	3	6	1	6	5	1	39	13.33
8	4	8	6	8	6	12	9	4	18	14	113	13.54
3	6	4	5	6	7	8	10	6	8	7	76	13.63
3	1	4	1	3	3	2	5	4	6	1	39	13.00
6	8	16	14	17	21	16	18	25	12	16	199	12.90
14	11	15	19	18	29	31	31	46	37	35	324	14.08
0	1	3	1	3	0	4	3	4	5	0	28	14.00
5	1	2	1	5	4	4	5	3	3	0	45	11.80
12	16	22	15	17	22	13	19	13	22	12	322	9.13
3	1	0	8	1	4	0	1	0	2	4	39	10.56
7	3	7	5	9	9	14	5	3	7	3	113	10.29
7	2	4	9	2	2	4	5	3	0	7	76	8.50

RELIGION: FREQUENCY DISTRIBUTIONS (*continued*)

		1	2	3	4	5	6	7
	Congregational	0	5	3	3	1	2	3
	Methodist	8	17	19	16	8	10	14
	Baptist	11	20	36	21	25	14	21
	Jewish	1	2	3	2	4	1	2
	None	3	4	5	6	6	1	3
Family security	Catholic	69	67	35	39	26	14	22
	Episcopalian	11	9	2	1	6	1	1
	Lutheran	18	18	15	9	11	14	9
	Presbyterian	16	16	11	9	4	6	2
	Congregational	5	11	5	6	0	3	4
	Methodist	37	23	29	23	16	8	14
	Baptist	46	54	41	31	29	25	19
	Jewish	9	6	1	1	2	2	2
	None	4	4	4	3	6	4	4
Freedom	Catholic	28	33	31	29	34	28	29
	Episcopalian	2	5	5	2	4	5	3
	Lutheran	11	12	20	17	8	4	11
	Presbyterian	7	6	8	9	7	9	3
	Congregational	1	6	3	5	5	1	3
	Methodist	5	17	20	20	21	16	22
	Baptist	11	44	37	40	35	28	23
	Jewish	3	1	2	2	3	2	2
	None	11	4	4	7	3	3	3
Happiness	Catholic	16	26	21	31	19	30	28
	Episcopalian	1	1	1	4	4	5	6
	Lutheran	5	7	7	8	12	6	7
	Presbyterian	2	6	10	12	4	4	7
	Congregational	1	3	3	0	3	3	2
	Methodist	10	11	11	10	20	18	17
	Baptist	12	20	27	20	21	31	25
	Jewish	2	1	1	6	1	2	3
	None	1	5	4	2	0	1	4
Inner harmony	Catholic	6	7	15	16	10	24	23
	Episcopalian	0	2	0	1	5	1	5
	Lutheran	1	2	3	4	7	6	7
	Presbyterian	0	3	3	3	2	5	10
	Congregational	0	0	3	0	2	0	0
	Methodist	3	4	5	15	6	15	9
	Baptist	2	5	4	13	16	17	15
	Jewish	1	1	0	4	3	3	0
	None	0	1	4	4	1	3	1
Mature love	Catholic	4	4	10	14	11	8	13
	Episcopalian	0	1	0	0	0	2	2
	Lutheran	0	2	0	3	5	3	7
	Presbyterian	1	1	1	3	5	3	4
	Congregational	0	0	3	2	1	0	1
	Methodist	2	3	6	7	11	6	6
	Baptist	0	9	11	15	15	13	9
	Jewish	0	0	1	1	2	0	1
	None	0	2	1	1	2	1	6

8	9	10	11	12	13	14	15	16	17	18	N	MEDIAN
1	0	1	1	6	4	5	0	1	1	2	39	11.00
10	10	10	9	12	8	6	6	10	14	12	199	8.25
21	9	18	17	14	19	19	15	12	12	20	324	8.17
1	2	3	3	1	2	1	0	0	0	0	28	7.00
4	2	2	0	3	0	1	2	2	1	0	45	5.25
12	8	7	6	3	4	4	4	1	0	1	322	3.21
0	2	0	2	1	0	2	0	0	1	0	39	2.44
5	1	1	5	3	2	1	1	0	0	0	113	4.11
3	1	2	2	2	1	0	0	1	0	0	76	3.05
0	1	0	2	0	2	0	0	0	0	0	39	3.20
8	11	3	5	5	2	7	3	3	2	0	199	3.96
21	10	16	7	9	3	5	5	1	1	1	324	4.18
1	0	0	0	1	0	1	1	1	0	0	28	2.33
2	1	4	2	1	1	0	2	2	1	0	45	5.88
22	21	15	14	10	6	10	6	3	1	2	322	5.71
3	2	2	2	2	0	1	0	0	0	1	39	5.80
2	8	5	3	1	4	1	3	1	2	0	113	4.29
9	2	7	4	1	0	0	0	1	3	0	76	5.61
3	0	0	5	1	0	1	1	2	2	0	39	5.40
14	13	11	8	6	6	4	4	7	5	0	199	6.52
30	12	16	13	14	2	7	6	3	1	2	324	5.36
0	4	3	3	1	1	0	1	0	0	0	28	7.00
3	0	5	0	0	1	1	0	0	0	0	45	4.00
20	34	20	19	17	10	15	10	4	2	0	322	7.14
0	3	5	1	1	4	0	1	2	0	0	39	7.08
6	13	14	7	6	4	4	3	2	0	2	113	8.25
2	9	6	6	3	3	1	0	0	1	0	76	6.50
4	5	4	0	3	1	1	3	2	1	0	39	8.60
16	15	8	14	15	10	11	3	6	1	3	199	7.66
30	30	16	28	21	15	11	11	5	1	0	324	7.70
2	1	3	2	0	4	0	0	0	0	0	28	6.83
4	4	2	6	4	3	2	2	0	1	0	45	8.88
26	23	33	22	27	16	19	18	19	11	7	322	9.83
4	1	3	5	0	3	3	2	4	0	0	39	9.67
9	10	4	11	8	12	6	8	9	2	4	113	10.82
5	3	5	9	5	4	8	5	1	3	2	76	10.30
5	6	4	2	3	2	3	0	3	5	1	39	10.38
10	9	21	19	17	13	15	11	12	10	5	199	10.63
13	30	25	30	29	27	20	24	21	17	16	324	11.23
4	0	2	2	2	1	1	2	2	0	0	28	8.00
1	4	4	4	4	5	1	2	3	3	0	45	10.38
18	21	19	25	20	24	22	23	20	28	38	322	12.20
3	5	3	5	3	5	2	2	3	1	2	39	11.20
5	9	6	6	9	9	11	6	11	9	12	113	12.67
5	2	2	7	8	9	4	6	3	5	7	76	12.00
1	3	4	4	1	1	3	3	1	3	8	39	12.00
5	8	9	13	8	13	22	10	24	19	27	199	13.61
15	22	17	19	16	21	26	33	21	35	27	324	12.55
3	1	1	2	1	3	4	0	2	2	4	28	12.83
3	5	1	2	3	5	1	3	5	2	2	45	10.75

RELIGION: FREQUENCY DISTRIBUTIONS (*continued*)

		1	*2*	*3*	*4*	*5*	*6*	*7*
National security	Catholic	4	24	21	23	32	24	11
	Episcopalian	0	5	3	1	4	0	1
	Lutheran	2	5	8	10	10	7	6
	Presbyterian	2	4	4	2	4	8	4
	Congregational	0	3	2	6	2	0	5
	Methodist	4	11	13	9	10	17	16
	Baptist	3	11	18	17	24	28	15
	Jewish	1	1	1	4	1	1	1
	None	0	0	1	2	4	3	2
Pleasure	Catholic	1	2	4	2	0	7	12
	Episcopalian	0	0	0	0	1	0	0
	Lutheran	0	1	0	0	5	2	4
	Presbyterian	0	0	0	1	2	1	1
	Congregational	0	0	1	0	1	2	0
	Methodist	0	2	3	2	4	1	4
	Baptist	1	0	2	4	7	5	10
	Jewish	0	0	0	0	0	0	1
	None	0	0	3	0	1	1	0
Salvation	Catholic	47	5	13	12	16	9	10
	Episcopalian	4	2	1	2	1	1	2
	Lutheran	32	2	4	3	6	1	3
	Presbyterian	13	2	1	4	4	4	2
	Congregational	5	0	3	1	1	2	2
	Methodist	29	11	12	11	10	13	7
	Baptist	102	20	19	24	6	11	17
	Jewish	0	0	0	0	0	1	0
	None	2	0	0	2	0	0	0
Self-respect	Catholic	13	17	21	21	25	28	39
	Episcopalian	0	3	4	6	2	1	1
	Lutheran	2	4	7	6	5	13	9
	Presbyterian	1	5	7	3	5	5	6
	Congregational	0	2	0	3	5	6	2
	Methodist	5	11	16	11	21	17	13
	Baptist	13	19	13	21	31	30	44
	Jewish	0	2	1	1	1	2	3
	None	3	5	4	5	0	3	3
Social recognition	Catholic	0	3	1	2	4	15	10
	Episcopalian	0	0	1	0	2	2	0
	Lutheran	0	0	0	2	2	2	2
	Presbyterian	0	1	1	0	2	2	1
	Congregational	1	0	0	0	3	1	3
	Methodist	0	0	1	3	4	2	5
	Baptist	1	1	0	2	5	4	9
	Jewish	0	0	0	1	0	0	2
	None	0	0	0	0	2	0	1
True friendship	Catholic	1	8	12	17	24	23	18
	Episcopalian	0	0	2	3	0	3	3
	Lutheran	1	0	4	7	4	11	11
	Presbyterian	3	2	2	3	5	8	11

8	9	10	11	12	13	14	15	16	17	18	N	MEDIAN
22	21	20	24	21	16	20	12	15	5	7	322	8.50
8	0	1	1	4	5	1	1	0	3	1	39	8.19
12	6	2	6	8	7	5	6	6	2	5	113	8.21
3	8	5	3	6	4	4	1	7	4	3	76	9.38
1	2	3	3	2	3	1	1	3	0	2	39	8.75
14	13	11	16	12	9	16	7	8	7	6	199	8.92
17	13	19	16	30	29	20	10	32	14	8	324	10.34
3	0	1	1	1	3	1	3	2	3	0	28	10.50
0	4	3	2	6	2	1	3	5	3	4	45	11.75
11	10	12	18	16	21	32	40	37	56	41	322	14.83
3	1	0	0	2	2	5	8	5	6	6	39	15.19
5	7	5	4	3	7	8	12	20	19	11	113	14.96
4	2	3	5	3	4	10	11	8	12	9	76	14.68
1	1	1	3	1	1	2	10	4	6	5	39	15.05
9	7	10	10	13	20	8	27	26	34	19	199	14.74
15	12	19	23	21	21	26	29	43	48	38	324	14.35
1	3	0	1	3	3	6	5	2	1	2	28	13.83
2	2	3	4	2	5	9	4	2	6	1	45	13.40
11	17	18	10	20	26	18	21	20	19	30	322	10.80
0	1	1	0	4	1	4	0	3	4	8	39	13.00
4	5	13	3	4	6	9	4	5	2	7	113	8.80
3	4	2	2	0	8	7	5	5	7	3	76	10.00
3	3	2	1	0	2	4	2	1	1	6	39	9.33
5	9	8	8	10	9	7	15	10	7	18	199	8.67
9	14	11	12	7	11	13	10	16	9	13	324	4.38
0	1	0	0	1	1	1	1	2	3	17	28	17.68
0	1	1	0	3	2	4	2	2	7	19	45	17.00
24	28	17	27	18	12	12	12	2	4	2	322	7.42
1	5	6	5	1	1	0	3	0	0	0	39	8.80
7	15	10	13	4	4	2	5	4	2	1	113	8.73
8	9	6	3	6	6	1	3	1	1	0	76	8.25
3	3	3	3	4	1	0	0	2	1	1	39	8.00
17	19	12	11	11	8	3	11	7	4	2	199	7.82
25	24	21	21	22	13	6	9	4	5	3	324	7.30
5	3	2	3	1	1	1	2	0	0	0	28	8.30
2	2	1	4	1	4	3	3	2	0	0	45	7.33
12	14	9	21	24	28	27	30	42	33	47	322	14.17
1	0	0	1	2	4	7	5	5	4	5	39	14.43
5	3	5	6	7	7	8	9	17	14	24	113	15.33
1	1	5	3	2	7	6	7	10	8	19	76	15.36
1	3	1	1	5	3	3	5	5	4	0	39	12.67
4	7	6	15	12	19	24	20	13	25	39	199	14.40
12	17	15	23	22	25	35	25	35	41	52	324	14.24
2	2	1	2	4	2	2	2	2	4	2	28	12.50
1	1	4	2	4	1	3	6	5	10	5	45	15.08
32	24	31	20	21	28	14	17	13	16	3	322	9.56
2	6	5	1	3	3	0	4	2	1	1	39	9.60
12	7	6	11	9	13	4	7	2	1	3	113	9.43
10	3	9	7	5	4	0	1	2	1	0	76	7.90

RELIGION: FREQUENCY DISTRIBUTIONS (*continued*)

		1	2	3	4	5	6	7
	Congregational	0	2	1	3	3	5	0
	Methodist	0	7	10	17	13	21	14
	Baptist	2	7	11	20	19	20	27
	Jewish	0	0	0	0	3	3	2
	None	1	0	1	3	5	5	3
Wisdom	Catholic	16	17	14	14	27	22	19
	Episcopalian	5	4	1	5	2	2	2
	Lutheran	3	13	5	4	7	11	9
	Presbyterian	3	6	6	2	8	4	4
	Congregational	1	1	5	3	5	3	3
	Methodist	8	14	15	11	17	14	14
	Baptist	15	15	23	14	21	32	21
	Jewish	1	2	4	1	3	3	3
	None	4	3	1	1	6	5	3
Ambitious	Catholic	56	38	27	19	13	17	12
	Episcopalian	2	2	4	3	5	2	1
	Lutheran	19	10	6	11	6	8	9
	Presbyterian	7	11	8	5	3	2	6
	Congregational	5	3	2	2	2	3	3
	Methodist	26	22	14	14	16	7	12
	Baptist	43	29	26	25	35	19	8
	Jewish	3	5	1	1	1	2	1
	None	5	4	2	2	3	2	2
Broadminded	Catholic	29	35	21	20	15	15	16
	Episcopalian	2	6	2	4	3	2	1
	Lutheran	5	12	11	6	8	8	2
	Presbyterian	7	9	7	5	6	8	5
	Congregational	3	6	4	4	3	2	3
	Methodist	21	21	21	15	14	8	6
	Baptist	16	27	25	20	19	19	23
	Jewish	2	3	2	5	3	1	5
	None	5	6	6	4	4	4	1
Capable	Catholic	6	16	26	27	19	15	20
	Episcopalian	2	2	4	0	1	6	3
	Lutheran	0	2	9	9	3	8	11
	Presbyterian	0	3	8	3	6	8	8
	Congregational	1	3	3	4	0	1	0
	Methodist	6	14	15	13	8	11	11
	Baptist	4	15	14	19	13	17	14
	Jewish	2	2	3	1	4	1	2
	None	1	2	5	3	3	1	3
Cheerful	Catholic	3	18	14	25	15	18	23
	Episcopalian	1	0	2	2	1	1	3
	Lutheran	2	7	8	7	5	3	4
	Presbyterian	2	3	1	5	6	7	6
	Congregational	2	2	0	3	3	1	1
	Methodist	7	7	7	10	14	14	9
	Baptist	5	18	12	18	11	22	22
	Jewish	1	1	1	3	0	0	0
	None	2	0	2	4	1	2	5

8	9	10	11	12	13	14	15	16	17	18	N	MEDIAN
4	3	3	1	0	5	3	1	2	1	2	39	9.00
16	15	15	13	13	15	7	5	7	7	4	199	8.60
29	21	29	19	31	22	15	20	15	13	4	324	9.71
1	3	3	2	1	3	3	3	1	0	0	28	10.17
2	3	5	5	2	2	1	2	2	3	0	45	9.33
17	18	27	21	23	20	16	13	12	15	11	322	9.33
3	1	3	3	1	1	1	3	0	1	1	39	6.75
9	5	5	5	9	10	7	5	2	2	2	113	8.00
4	9	8	1	7	1	7	5	0	1	0	76	8.61
2	1	4	2	1	1	3	2	1	0	1	39	7.00
14	10	16	13	8	11	8	10	5	7	4	199	7.96
25	24	27	17	20	21	11	8	7	10	13	324	8.34
0	2	4	1	2	0	0	0	1	1	0	28	6.50
2	3	3	2	1	4	0	1	0	0	6	45	7.33
12	12	15	15	16	13	16	10	9	10	12	322	5.97
1	1	0	2	3	2	5	2	1	1	2	39	8.00
4	5	2	5	3	5	2	3	6	3	6	113	6.06
3	5	2	3	2	2	1	7	4	1	4	76	6.83
1	3	3	2	0	1	3	2	2	2	0	39	7.33
11	9	8	12	7	6	4	6	6	8	11	199	6.54
13	18	18	15	13	16	16	8	6	11	5	324	5.71
0	3	0	2	1	0	1	3	0	1	3	28	8.00
4	5	0	1	1	3	3	1	4	2	1	45	8.13
15	18	20	11	21	26	11	14	10	12	13	322	8.17
2	1	3	3	3	2	1	1	1	1	1	39	7.00
18	5	6	7	3	4	4	2	3	6	3	113	7.75
4	3	4	4	5	1	3	3	0	2	0	76	6.00
0	1	0	6	1	1	2	2	1	0	0	39	5.33
14	12	10	7	13	9	7	6	2	9	4	199	6.44
19	15	14	15	24	14	19	15	9	13	18	324	8.18
0	0	0	1	1	0	1	1	3	0	0	28	5.17
1	4	2	3	2	0	0	0	2	0	1	45	4.88
21	29	25	27	17	15	22	11	8	9	9	322	8.88
2	2	4	4	1	1	0	3	3	0	1	39	8.25
8	3	12	8	13	4	3	5	7	2	6	113	9.79
6	5	3	4	5	3	5	2	5	2	0	76	7.83
1	2	3	3	2	3	4	2	2	3	2	39	11.00
10	15	19	17	8	18	8	12	8	4	2	199	9.27
19	25	22	26	27	22	19	31	18	13	6	324	10.50
1	2	3	1	2	3	0	1	0	0	0	28	7.00
2	4	4	4	4	2	2	1	2	2	0	45	9.13
24	19	15	25	18	15	27	23	24	7	9	322	9.63
1	1	4	1	3	3	5	1	9	1	0	39	12.33
8	7	8	9	5	7	9	7	7	6	4	113	10.19
2	2	5	3	7	8	7	5	4	0	3	76	10.30
4	3	2	1	3	7	2	2	1	2	0	39	9.75
15	11	17	10	13	10	16	14	7	11	7	199	9.82
22	24	23	17	19	17	26	27	12	14	15	324	9.85
1	2	6	3	0	1	4	1	1	1	2	28	10.33
3	2	1	3	3	6	1	7	0	2	1	45	10.67

RELIGION: FREQUENCY DISTRIBUTIONS (*continued*)

		1	*2*	*3*	*4*	*5*	*6*	*7*
Clean	Catholic	11	15	29	16	28	13	17
	Episcopalian	2	2	1	2	1	3	1
	Lutheran	5	8	2	10	9	6	5
	Presbyterian	1	3	6	4	6	1	8
	Congregational	2	2	3	3	2	2	4
	Methodist	13	7	8	14	13	14	10
	Baptist	31	33	28	22	28	18	17
	Jewish	0	1	2	1	3	0	0
	None	0	2	1	3	3	1	1
Courageous	Catholic	24	19	20	21	20	30	18
	Episcopalian	1	2	2	1	4	5	3
	Lutheran	4	5	11	7	16	3	8
	Presbyterian	3	6	5	5	5	4	7
	Congregational	3	1	2	2	3	4	2
	Methodist	8	17	12	17	16	18	24
	Baptist	16	15	21	20	26	28	19
	Jewish	2	1	3	1	2	1	2
	None	2	6	2	5	0	4	1
Forgiving	Catholic	13	23	24	22	28	22	25
	Episcopalian	1	2	5	4	1	0	3
	Lutheran	5	17	15	5	7	12	12
	Presbyterian	7	3	6	5	5	7	2
	Congregational	2	4	4	3	4	4	4
	Methodist	11	13	20	14	18	18	12
	Baptist	25	23	24	26	36	25	21
	Jewish	0	1	1	0	0	4	0
	None	2	0	2	1	1	2	3
Helpful	Catholic	11	18	19	21	20	16	28
	Episcopalian	0	2	1	3	1	1	1
	Lutheran	5	5	4	7	4	12	10
	Presbyterian	3	5	5	6	5	5	4
	Congregational	1	1	5	2	4	4	2
	Methodist	5	13	13	18	17	13	13
	Baptist	8	17	22	37	22	21	25
	Jewish	1	2	1	3	1	1	2
	None	1	2	2	2	1	3	3
Honest	Catholic	86	43	30	28	18	31	15
	Episcopalian	16	1	3	5	5	2	3
	Lutheran	33	11	11	9	12	13	2
	Presbyterian	26	12	6	6	3	3	1
	Congregational	8	4	6	2	4	3	3
	Methodist	50	25	36	18	7	16	7
	Baptist	95	50	42	34	23	11	16
	Jewish	9	1	1	5	3	0	1
	None	10	3	5	6	5	4	3
Imaginative	Catholic	2	5	6	10	4	6	11
	Episcopalian	0	0	1	3	1	1	1
	Lutheran	0	0	1	1	1	0	2
	Presbyterian	0	2	1	0	2	1	1

8	9	10	11	12	13	14	15	16	17	18	N	MEDIAN
20	19	11	19	19	18	23	12	25	14	13	322	9.13
1	5	0	2	0	6	4	4	2	1	2	39	11.25
7	4	12	8	4	6	6	5	6	3	7	113	9.54
3	3	3	4	5	11	4	4	5	2	3	76	10.50
2	2	0	0	4	1	2	1	3	4	2	39	8.25
13	12	11	11	10	11	12	10	11	9	10	199	9.13
20	18	17	17	15	9	15	8	13	5	10	324	6.62
1	1	5	1	1	3	0	4	3	0	2	28	10.50
5	4	2	0	1	2	1	3	2	7	7	45	12.00
16	20	26	20	21	19	5	13	14	9	7	322	8.06
2	2	2	3	2	3	0	3	0	2	2	39	8.25
8	7	5	4	6	6	4	6	9	2	2	113	7.81
5	3	7	6	6	5	2	0	2	3	2	76	8.10
4	2	4	1	3	1	1	2	4	0	0	39	8.13
11	9	10	7	8	5	9	9	11	3	5	199	6.98
24	18	17	25	21	19	19	10	16	6	4	324	8.21
3	1	1	1	3	1	1	2	0	1	2	28	8.17
3	1	5	5	2	1	2	2	3	1	0	45	8.33
21	18	16	22	22	15	17	13	7	8	6	322	7.69
3	2	1	4	3	1	2	4	1	1	1	39	8.75
5	4	4	4	6	4	7	3	0	1	2	113	6.13
9	4	5	5	3	2	5	4	3	1	0	76	7.83
3	1	2	1	3	3	0	0	1	0	0	39	6.13
12	11	9	12	10	9	9	7	5	5	4	199	6.96
16	19	15	13	22	14	12	11	11	6	5	324	6.64
2	1	1	2	3	4	4	1	3	0	1	28	12.17
2	1	3	2	4	6	4	4	3	2	3	45	12.38
26	15	19	28	25	18	14	12	11	10	11	322	8.63
6	3	4	2	3	2	4	1	3	0	2	39	9.88
9	13	7	3	9	3	5	7	4	2	4	113	8.54
9	5	5	3	2	6	2	2	1	4	4	76	8.06
4	1	3	3	4	1	2	1	0	1	0	39	7.63
17	16	11	9	13	9	16	4	3	8	1	199	7.94
31	25	21	13	11	17	13	21	13	5	2	324	7.82
0	3	3	3	0	2	1	2	2	0	1	28	9.50
5	1	2	3	7	0	5	6	0	2	0	45	10.67
14	18	16	5	6	4	4	3	0	1	0	322	3.57
1	1	0	1	0	0	0	0	1	0	0	39	3.33
3	7	5	3	1	2	0	0	1	0	0	113	3.67
3	9	2	4	1	0	0	0	0	0	0	76	2.50
1	4	0	3	0	1	0	0	0	0	0	39	4.25
9	13	5	5	0	1	1	4	0	1	1	199	3.18
9	18	4	7	5	1	3	2	0	3	1	324	2.90
2	1	1	2	2	0	0	0	0	0	0	28	4.10
1	2	0	1	1	2	0	2	0	0	0	45	4.25
15	9	14	11	22	17	22	26	26	41	75	322	14.77
2	2	3	0	0	5	0	5	2	6	7	39	14.60
0	6	3	7	5	9	7	13	11	21	26	113	15.64
0	1	4	5	3	4	7	8	8	11	18	76	15.38

RELIGION: FREQUENCY DISTRIBUTIONS (*continued*)

		1	2	3	4	5	6	7
	Congregational	0	0	0	2	0	0	1
	Methodist	2	2	0	7	2	5	4
	Baptist	1	4	1	4	4	5	9
	Jewish	0	0	1	0	2	1	1
	None	0	1	2	1	8	3	2
Independent	Catholic	14	16	11	22	18	11	19
	Episcopalian	4	3	3	1	0	3	3
	Lutheran	9	4	3	5	5	6	6
	Presbyterian	2	2	7	1	6	4	6
	Congregational	2	0	0	4	2	3	3
	Methodist	5	6	7	10	6	14	19
	Baptist	6	15	21	18	10	16	19
	Jewish	5	2	1	2	3	2	1
	None	6	3	4	3	2	5	4
Intellectual	Catholic	6	9	14	12	14	17	10
	Episcopalian	1	0	2	1	2	1	5
	Lutheran	3	5	1	2	4	1	3
	Presbyterian	3	2	3	2	3	1	5
	Congregational	1	0	1	3	3	1	0
	Methodist	1	2	3	4	7	8	8
	Baptist	5	4	6	6	10	15	17
	Jewish	1	3	2	0	0	3	3
	None	2	3	0	3	1	0	2
Logical	Catholic	5	11	7	6	11	14	16
	Episcopalian	0	0	0	1	1	1	1
	Lutheran	1	0	2	2	5	9	5
	Presbyterian	2	3	1	3	0	2	3
	Congregational	0	2	0	0	0	0	1
	Methodist	1	0	3	1	8	4	7
	Baptist	1	2	5	5	8	4	11
	Jewish	0	1	2	1	2	2	3
	None	0	1	3	1	1	4	1
Loving	Catholic	20	14	17	11	22	19	13
	Episcopalian	3	2	3	2	3	0	1
	Lutheran	9	8	4	7	7	5	7
	Presbyterian	4	3	4	5	5	6	4
	Congregational	5	5	0	0	3	2	4
	Methodist	12	8	9	10	6	7	10
	Baptist	18	19	19	10	24	20	18
	Jewish	0	2	1	2	1	3	0
	None	0	5	1	3	4	0	3
Obedient	Catholic	1	6	5	11	10	14	15
	Episcopalian	0	1	0	0	0	2	1
	Lutheran	1	1	1	3	1	3	2
	Presbyterian	0	0	1	1	1	2	2
	Congregational	0	0	1	0	1	2	2
	Methodist	2	4	5	4	8	10	2
	Baptist	5	12	7	9	9	16	17
	Jewish	0	0	0	0	0	1	1
	None	0	0	1	0	1	1	0

8	9	10	11	12	13	14	15	16	17	18	N	MEDIAN
2	0	1	0	2	5	3	1	4	11	7	39	16.13
7	5	9	5	6	6	10	19	26	26	58	199	15.90
2	6	17	17	15	20	14	28	43	63	71	324	15.85
3	2	1	0	0	2	3	1	2	6	3	28	13.83
2	4	3	5	2	1	2	2	4	1	2	45	9.38
14	19	13	17	21	18	21	26	22	21	19	322	10.74
2	1	0	3	6	3	1	1	1	3	1	39	9.00
10	3	3	10	7	9	18	5	3	2	5	113	10.75
2	6	4	4	3	9	6	2	4	4	4	76	10.00
2	4	2	3	1	2	1	4	3	1	2	39	9.38
8	9	14	20	16	14	10	13	16	7	5	199	10.58
23	18	18	24	18	23	17	24	23	17	14	324	10.39
2	3	1	1	1	1	0	1	0	0	2	28	6.00
2	3	1	3	2	3	2	1	1	0	0	45	6.40
11	14	12	15	16	11	24	33	38	35	31	322	13.50
1	2	3	2	3	3	2	2	2	3	4	39	11.25
5	7	5	5	8	8	9	13	10	17	7	113	13.44
3	2	3	5	6	3	8	8	6	9	4	76	12.50
2	2	4	0	2	3	2	5	1	5	4	39	12.67
9	15	7	6	17	21	16	24	23	17	11	199	13.10
17	7	22	15	22	17	26	27	34	41	33	324	13.44
1	2	2	1	2	1	2	0	2	2	1	28	9.00
3	3	6	2	3	6	3	0	1	3	4	45	10.42
12	13	18	19	12	25	23	24	33	38	35	322	13.18
4	3	4	3	3	3	3	2	1	7	2	39	12.00
2	3	9	1	8	11	7	3	14	17	14	113	13.36
5	4	4	6	4	3	4	8	6	9	9	76	12.83
1	1	2	8	2	3	4	3	5	2	5	39	13.33
8	4	12	8	13	12	17	16	28	24	33	199	14.59
6	14	6	10	14	21	27	31	42	49	68	324	15.40
1	0	1	3	2	3	0	1	2	2	2	28	10.83
2	1	5	2	3	5	2	6	4	3	1	45	12.00
19	16	17	10	26	18	22	22	19	27	10	322	10.09
2	4	2	1	6	0	3	2	2	1	2	39	9.38
5	7	3	4	6	8	8	12	7	6	0	113	9.14
5	3	6	2	3	2	5	7	6	2	4	76	9.17
1	2	2	1	1	1	2	3	1	2	4	39	8.00
9	9	10	14	16	10	20	15	7	26	1	199	11.18
23	14	18	20	16	20	20	12	15	20	18	324	9.29
1	2	1	2	1	1	3	1	2	5	0	28	11.00
4	1	3	4	1	2	4	3	3	3	1	45	10.00
13	14	17	16	15	33	21	32	31	30	38	322	13.23
2	1	1	2	2	1	3	2	5	8	8	39	15.80
4	5	4	10	10	10	10	10	8	14	16	113	13.65
3	4	1	3	6	5	4	8	10	11	14	76	15.13
1	2	3	1	3	2	4	2	5	2	8	39	13.88
10	7	10	16	15	19	10	15	21	17	24	199	12.84
10	17	20	24	21	30	23	31	27	24	22	324	12.26
2	0	0	0	3	1	2	4	3	4	7	28	15.50
1	1	0	2	1	1	6	2	8	6	14	45	16.19

RELIGION: FREQUENCY DISTRIBUTIONS (*continued*)

		1	*2*	*3*	*4*	*5*	*6*	*7*
Polite	Catholic	1	4	7	12	20	19	16
	Episcopalian	0	0	2	4	3	1	3
	Lutheran	2	3	3	7	3	4	4
	Presbyterian	0	1	3	0	2	5	1
	Congregational	0	1	0	1	1	2	0
	Methodist	2	6	9	9	10	10	15
	Baptist	5	6	9	12	12	27	19
	Jewish	0	1	0	0	1	2	2
	None	0	0	1	1	2	1	4
Responsible	Catholic	23	24	29	24	31	23	24
	Episcopalian	1	9	3	2	4	4	3
	Lutheran	6	10	15	9	10	10	14
	Presbyterian	8	6	3	12	7	7	1
	Congregational	2	2	6	2	4	3	5
	Methodist	19	23	12	11	15	14	16
	Baptist	25	23	23	29	19	26	25
	Jewish	2	2	4	2	1	3	3
	None	5	4	4	1	3	3	4
Self-controlled	Catholic	11	8	16	15	16	22	24
	Episcopalian	3	5	1	1	3	4	2
	Lutheran	4	5	6	6	7	2	7
	Presbyterian	1	2	1	8	5	3	6
	Congregational	2	3	2	2	0	2	1
	Methodist	8	9	5	10	14	8	14
	Baptist	15	12	19	10	15	15	24
	Jewish	0	0	2	1	1	1	1
	None	4	3	2	2	2	4	3

8	9	10	11	12	13	14	15	16	17	18	N	MEDIAN
29	25	25	25	21	17	21	19	26	18	17	322	10.62
2	1	3	4	0	1	4	3	3	2	3	39	10.63
5	9	13	10	11	6	4	9	12	6	2	113	10.85
7	5	12	3	5	6	6	3	7	7	3	76	11.17
4	4	4	3	3	0	5	4	4	3	0	39	11.33
12	10	16	15	16	14	16	12	10	12	5	199	10.53
21	21	30	31	21	22	28	16	19	12	13	324	10.50
1	1	1	0	3	1	3	5	4	1	2	28	13.83
2	1	1	1	3	3	4	0	9	7	5	45	14.13
23	25	23	14	10	13	7	11	5	7	6	322	6.79
3	6	2	0	0	1	0	0	0	1	0	39	5.63
5	8	4	5	4	3	2	4	0	2	2	113	6.15
4	9	2	3	6	2	2	0	2	1	1	76	5.79
3	3	1	2	3	0	1	1	1	0	0	39	6.60
13	18	7	8	10	11	4	3	7	7	1	199	6.84
25	24	15	14	13	22	10	10	6	11	4	324	7.18
4	1	1	1	1	1	1	0	1	0	0	28	6.50
1	4	3	3	2	1	1	2	0	3	1	45	7.13
17	19	20	23	14	27	22	18	14	25	11	322	10.15
2	1	3	2	1	2	2	3	2	1	1	39	7.75
7	10	8	10	4	8	8	6	5	3	7	113	9.81
3	3	4	9	4	4	5	5	3	7	3	76	10.72
3	2	3	1	2	4	1	4	1	1	5	39	10.33
11	14	14	17	8	14	14	10	8	5	16	199	9.96
24	23	27	21	27	20	17	12	17	11	15	324	9.69
3	3	0	4	2	3	2	0	0	5	0	28	11.00
2	3	4	1	3	1	3	3	0	1	4	45	8.67

APPENDIX C
The Value Change Instrument

VALUE SURVEY — PART 1

Name _____ Sex: Male _____ Female _____

Birthdate _____ City and State of Birth _____

This is a scientific study of value systems. There are no right or wrong answers in this study. The best answer is your own personal opinion.

This questionnaire is intended not only to gather new scientific facts, but also as a teaching device. In return for your cooperation, we hope to provide you with some interesting insights into yourself.

Below is a list of 18 values in alphabetical order. We are interested in finding out the relative importance of these values to you.

Study the list carefully. Then place a 1 next to the value which is most important to *you*, place a 2 next to the value which is second most important, etc. The value which is least important should be ranked 18.

When you have completed ranking all the values, go back and check over your list. Feel free to make changes. Please take all the time you need to think about this, so that the end result truly represents *your* values.

_____ A COMFORTABLE LIFE (a prosperous life)
_____ AN EXCITING LIFE (a stimulating, active life)
_____ A SENSE OF ACCOMPLISHMENT (lasting contribution)
_____ A WORLD AT PEACE (free of war and conflict)
_____ A WORLD OF BEAUTY (beauty of nature and the arts)
_____ EQUALITY (brotherhood, equal opportunity for all)
_____ FAMILY SECURITY (taking care of loved ones)
_____ FREEDOM (independence, free choice)
_____ HAPPINESS (contentedness)
_____ INNER HARMONY (freedom from inner conflict)
_____ MATURE LOVE (sexual and spiritual intimacy)
_____ NATIONAL SECURITY (protection from attack)
_____ PLEASURE (an enjoyable, leisurely life)
_____ SALVATION (saved, eternal life)
_____ SELF-RESPECT (self-esteem)
_____ SOCIAL RECOGNITION (respect, admiration)
_____ TRUE FRIENDSHIP (close companionship)
_____ WISDOM (a mature understanding of life)

When you finish this page, go right on to the next page.

Now we are interested in knowing how you feel about the way you ranked these 18 values in general. Please circle one number on the following scale:

1	2	3	4	5	6	7	8	9	10	11

I care very
much about
the order in
which I ranked
these values.

It does not
make much
difference
which order
I put them in.

Below you will find the same 18 values listed again. This time, rank them in the order you think *MSU students on the average* would rank them.

_____ A COMFORTABLE LIFE (a prosperous life)
_____ AN EXCITING LIFE (a stimulating, active life)
_____ A SENSE OF ACCOMPLISHMENT (lasting contribution)
_____ A WORLD AT PEACE (free of war and conflict)
_____ A WORLD OF BEAUTY (beauty of nature and the arts)
_____ EQUALITY (brotherhood, equal opportunity for all)
_____ FAMILY SECURITY (taking care of loved ones)
_____ FREEDOM (independence, free choice)
_____ HAPPINESS (contentedness)
_____ INNER HARMONY (freedom from inner conflict)
_____ MATURE LOVE (sexual and spiritual intimacy)
_____ NATIONAL SECURITY (protection from attack)
_____ PLEASURE (an enjoyable, leisurely life)
_____ SALVATION (saved, eternal life)
_____ SELF-RESPECT (self-esteem)
_____ SOCIAL RECOGNITION (respect, admiration)
_____ TRUE FRIENDSHIP (close companionship)
_____ WISDOM (a mature understanding of life)

You have now completed Part 1 of the Value Survey.

When you finish this page, go right on to the next page.

VALUE SURVEY — PART 2

Please do not sign your name!

Now copy your answers from the value scale on Page 1 (your *own* value rankings) onto this page.

MY OWN VALUE SYSTEM

_____ A COMFORTABLE LIFE
_____ AN EXCITING LIFE
_____ A SENSE OF ACCOMPLISHMENT
_____ A WORLD AT PEACE
_____ A WORLD OF BEAUTY
_____ EQUALITY
_____ FAMILY SECURITY
_____ FREEDOM
_____ HAPPINESS
_____ INNER HARMONY
_____ MATURE LOVE
_____ NATIONAL SECURITY
_____ PLEASURE
_____ SALVATION
_____ SELF-RESPECT
_____ SOCIAL RECOGNITION
_____ TRUE FRIENDSHIP
_____ WISDOM

When you have finished this page:
1. *Hand in Part 1.*
2. Wait for further instructions. DO NOT GO ON TO THE NEXT PAGE.

Now, I would like to tell you some things we have already found out about the value systems of Michigan State students. I am sure that many of you would like to know what they are.

This same value system scale was filled out by 298 students in Psychology 151. The responses of these students were obtained and averaged together. The table below shows the results.

TABLE 1. RANK ORDER OF IMPORTANCE TO
298 MICHIGAN STATE STUDENTS

13	A COMFORTABLE LIFE
12	AN EXCITING LIFE
6	A SENSE OF ACCOMPLISHMENT
10	A WORLD AT PEACE
17	A WORLD OF BEAUTY
11	EQUALITY
9	FAMILY SECURITY
1	FREEDOM
2	HAPPINESS
8	INNER HARMONY
5	MATURE LOVE
16	NATIONAL SECURITY
18	PLEASURE
14	SALVATION
15	SOCIAL RECOGNITION
4	SELF-RESPECT
7	TRUE FRIENDSHIP
3	WISDOM

One of the most interesting findings shown in Table 1 is that the students, on the average, felt that *freedom* was very important—they ranked it 1; but they felt that *equality* was considerably less important—they ranked it 11. Apparently, Michigan State students value freedom far more highly than they value equality. This suggests that MSU students in general are much more interested in their own freedom than they are in freedom for other people.

Feel free to spend a few minutes comparing your own rankings on the preceding page with those of the 298 students, shown in Table 1. After doing that, please stop and wait for further instructions. DO NOT GO ON TO THE NEXT PAGE.

We have one other finding which we think is unusually interesting. In order to make this finding more meaningful and relevant to you personally, you should first answer honestly the following question on civil rights:

Are you sympathetic with the aims of the civil rights demonstrators?

_____ Yes, and I have personally participated in a civil rights demonstration.
_____ Yes, but I have not participated in a civil rights demonstration.
_____ No.

The 298 students who participated in the previous study of value systems were asked this same question. They were divided into three groups, according to how they responded. Table 2 shows the average rankings of Freedom and Equality for each of these three groups.

TABLE 2. AVERAGE RANKINGS OF FREEDOM AND EQUALITY BY MSU STUDENTS FOR AND AGAINST CIVIL RIGHTS

	Yes, and Have Participated	Yes, But Have Not Participated	No, Not Sympathetic to Civil Rights
FREEDOM	6	1	2
EQUALITY	5	11	17
DIFFERENCE	+1	−10	−15

Notice in Table 2 that:

1. Pro- and anti-civil rights students all value *freedom* relatively highly. Of 18 values all groups rank *freedom* among the top six.
2. Students who are *strongly for* civil rights value *equality* rather highly—they ranked it 5; but those *against* civil rights place a much *lower* value on equality—they ranked it 17 in importance. Those who are sympathetic but nonparticipants ranked equality 11.
3. The distance between freedom and equality is +1 for the strong civil rights group, −10 for the middle group, and −15 for the anti-civil rights group.

Apparently *both* freedom *and* equality are important to some people, while to others freedom is very important but equality is not.

This raises the question whether those who are *against* civil rights are really saying that they care a great deal about *their own* freedom but are indifferent to other people's freedom. Those who are *for* civil rights are perhaps really saying they not only want freedom for themselves, but for other people too. What do you think?

(Please circle one number)

1	2	3	4	5	6	7	8	9	10	11
I agree strongly with this interpretation.					I'm not sure.				I disagree strongly with this interpretation.	

Before you go on to the last part of this questionnaire, please spend a few minutes comparing your own rankings from the first page with these results. Then go on to the next page.

We would now be most interested to find out how you feel about the method we have used to teach you something about the value systems of Michigan State students.

Did you find it thought-provoking?

| ' | | | | | ' | | | | | ' |
| 1 | 2 | 3 | 4 | 5 | 6 | 7 | 8 | 9 | 10 | 11 |

Extremely   Extremely
thought-provoking   boring

Do you think this technique of teaching will lead you to do some more thinking about your own values?

| ' | | | | | ' | | | | | ' |
| 1 | 2 | 3 | 4 | 5 | 6 | 7 | 8 | 9 | 10 | 11 |

Yes, very   No, not
much   at all

Do you feel that your responses were somewhat hypocritical?

| ' | | | | | ' | | | | | ' |
| 1 | 2 | 3 | 4 | 5 | 6 | 7 | 8 | 9 | 10 | 11 |

Yes, very   No, not at all
hypocritical   hypocritical

Right now, how satisfied do you feel about the way you have ranked the eighteen values?

| ' | | | | | ' | | | | | ' |
| 1 | 2 | 3 | 4 | 5 | 6 | 7 | 8 | 9 | 10 | 11 |

Extremely   Extremely
satisfied   dissatisfied

GO ON TO THE NEXT PAGE.

Now look again for a moment at your own rankings on the first page. Which rankings do you now feel satisfied or dissatisfied with? (Please indicate whether you now feel satisfied or dissatisfied with each one, by a check mark or an X)

I am satisfied with my ranking of:	I am dissatisfied with my ranking of:	
_____	_____	A COMFORTABLE LIFE
_____	_____	AN EXCITING LIFE
_____	_____	A SENSE OF ACCOMPLISHMENT
_____	_____	A WORLD AT PEACE
_____	_____	A WORLD OF BEAUTY
_____	_____	EQUALITY
_____	_____	FAMILY SECURITY
_____	_____	FREEDOM
_____	_____	HAPPINESS
_____	_____	INNER HARMONY
_____	_____	MATURE LOVE
_____	_____	NATIONAL SECURITY
_____	_____	PLEASURE
_____	_____	SALVATION
_____	_____	SELF-RESPECT
_____	_____	SOCIAL RECOGNITION
_____	_____	TRUE FRIENDSHIP
_____	_____	WISDOM

In your own opinion, do you think that the Michigan State findings I have described to you are scientifically valid?

_____Yes _____No

In the space below, please explain why you answered the previous question the way you did.

Do you have any other comments you wish to make about this study? Please comment in the space below. Remember, everything in this questionnaire is absolutely confidential, and to be used *only* for scientific purposes.

Thank you for your cooperation.

Index

A comfortable life, 277
  age and developmental pattern for, 79
  change and, 252–257, 294, 296
  NORC findings for, 364, 368, 380, 392, 396, 406
  See also Terminal values
An exciting life:
  age and developmental pattern for, 79
  change and, 252-257, 294, 296
  NORC findings for, 364, 368, 380, 392, 396, 406
  See also Terminal values
A sense of accomplishment:
  age and developmental pattern for, 73
  change and, 252–256, 296
  NORC findings for, 364, 368, 380, 392, 396, 406
  See also Terminal values
A world at peace:
  age and developmental pattern for, 79–80
  change and, 252–256, 294, 296
  NORC findings for, 364, 368, 380, 392, 396, 406
  See also Terminal values
A world of beauty, 277
  age and developmental pattern for, 78
  change and, 252–256, 296, 308, 328–329
  NORC findings for, 364, 368, 380, 392, 396, 406
  See also Terminal values
Abelson, R. P., 148, 211, 222, 231
Academic artists, values of, 144–150
Academic pursuits, 139–140
Actors (student), 208
Actresses (student), 208
Adorno, T. W., 16, 102, 124, 166, 189, 190, 329
Age differences, 72-82
  NORC findings for, 396–405

Albert, E. M., 17
Allen, R. O., 16
Allport, G. W., 4, 7, 16, 18, 21, 22, 102, 111–114, 330
Ambitious, 277
  age and developmental pattern for, 79
  NORC findings for, 364, 372, 384, 392, 400, 412
  See also Instrumental values
American Civil Liberties Union, 244
Anderson, Judy, 247
Anderson, N. H., 29
Andrews, F. M., 118, 192
Argyle, M., 126
Argyris, C., 234
Aronson, E., 148, 211, 231
Atkinson, J. W., 48
Atlanta University, 102
Attitudes:
  changes of, 216–217, 229–231, 257–261, 303
  values and, 17–19, 95–121
  See also specific listings
Australia, cross-cultural value comparison to, 89–94
Authoritarianism, 116
  ethnocentricism and, 329–330
  value change and, 311–312

Baptists, 82
  NORC findings for, 406–419
Backlash effects, 257-260
Backman, W., 231
Baier, K., 325
Bakan, D., 144
Ball-Rokeach, Sandra J., x, 59
Bandura, A., 223
Banks, R. G., 37
Barnette, W. J., 308, 310, 317, 318, 326,